Across
the Great Divide

Across the Great Divide

THE BAND AND AMERICA

Barney Hoskyns

HYPERION

New York

For my son Jake—
'We've got work to do!'
And for Chris and Gail Bell

Library of Congress Cataloging-in-Publication Data
Hoskyns, Barney.
Across the Great Divide : the Band and America / Barney
Hoskyns.— 1st ed.
p. cm.
Discography:
Includes bibliographical references and index.
ISBN 1-56282-836-3
1. Band (Musical group) 2. Rock musicians—United
States— Biography. I. Title.
ML421.B32H7 1993
782.42166'092'2—dc20
[B] 93-17243 CIP
MN

FIRST EDITION

10 9 8 7 6 5 4 3 2 1

Contents

THE BAND'S AMERICA

British Columbia

C

VANCOUVER

Alberta

• CALGARY

A

Saskatchewan

N

Washington

Montana

North Dako

Oregon

Idaho

Wyoming

South Dak

SAN FRANCISCO

Nevada

Utah

Colorado

Nebrask

California

Kans

ZUMA • LOS ANGELES

Arizona

New Mexico

Ok

Texas

M E X I C O

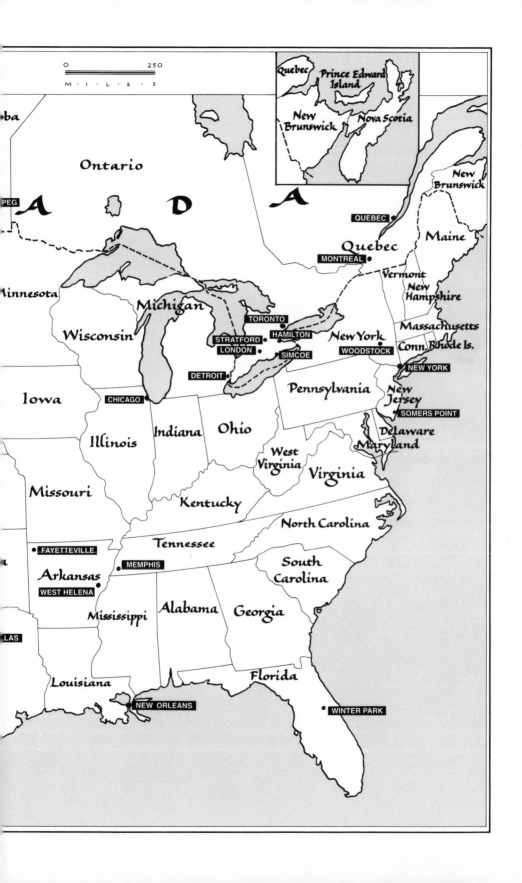

Prologue

You start off pure and then, as the wise guys say, you wise up, and the purity turns to ambition. If you're good and work hard, there's money and the kind of name and fame that make your life a story you're too busy or stoned to read.

Ron Horning, 'The Moving Shadow of Richard Manuel'

Richard Manuel's is the first voice you hear on the first Band album *Music From Big Pink* (1968). After a Robbie Robertson guitar intro that sounds as if it's being fed through Garth Hudson's Lowrey organ at its most distorted, his aching baritone launches into the first reproachful line of 'Tears Of Rage'. As it arches over 'arms', you can't help thinking of Ray Charles, the singer who more than any other shaped this unlikely white soul voice from Stratford, Ontario. And by the end of the first chorus you realize why, in an almost unspoken way, Manuel's fellow Band vocalists Levon Helm and Rick Danko always looked on him as the group's 'lead singer'.

Eighteen years after recording 'Tears Of Rage', a song he'd written with Bob Dylan at the Catskills house The Band knew and loved as 'Big Pink', Richard Manuel found himself at the end of his tether in a Florida motel room. Nothing had gone very right for him since The Last Waltz, The Band's official goodbye in 1976, and after a period of relative abstinence he'd begun drinking and drugging heavily again. Now, as The Band – reunited without its songwriter and guiding light Robertson – toured a circuit very different from the one they'd been used to a decade earlier,

1

Richard wondered whether it was really all worth it. A month shy of his forty-third birthday, he could see nothing ahead but these depressing one-nighters rehashing 'the old magic', and a continuing, fruitless struggle to moderate his intake of alcohol and cocaine. So what if the crowd at the Cheek-to-Cheek Lounge in Winter Park, Florida had lapped up his version of 'Georgia On My Mind'; he hadn't finished one of his *own* songs in years. Shortly after three o'clock on the morning of Tuesday, 4 March 1986, he tied one end of a plain black belt around his neck, looped the other end around the shower-curtain rod in the bathroom, and hanged himself.

The distance between 'Tears Of Rage' and Richard Manuel's lonely death at the Winter Park Quality Inn was the journey The Band travelled in their rise and fall as one of America's greatest rock groups. In the beginning they came out of nowhere, a different time and musical space. Their songs fashioned something magically new out of components that were musically old: old-time country and gospel, Preservation-Hall jazz, medicine-show vaudeville. They were bearded, behatted, anonymous, a bunch of hungry outlaws on the road. They had three outstanding singers but no stars. Each played several instruments and made all of them sound completely distinctive. *Time* called them 'The New Face of Country Rock' but they had as little to do with the Nudie-suited cowboys on the West Coast as they did with acid rock or The Velvet Underground. They claimed their name came *faute de mieux* but it was really born of a beguiling mixture of humility and arrogance. They were just 'the band' but they were also THE band; they knew exactly how special they were.

Things changed after the group came out of their Woodstock hibernation and faced the America they had reinvented in their songs. After years of working as 'a scrounge road group' behind Ronnie Hawkins and Bob Dylan, they found the stage an altogether different proposition once they were presenting their own fragile, intricate music on it. Although Robbie Robertson had flu on the eve of their 1969 debut at San Francisco's Winterland, the famous 1971 song 'Stage Fright' offered a more plausible explanation for his disastrous performance. Of all the groups at the Woodstock Festival that year, none was so ill-suited to the scale of the event as this quintet from Woodstock itself.

Drugs and alcohol were to take their toll not only on Richard Manuel but on Helm and Danko too. It was The Band's tragedy that, despite their resolve to stand apart from the deranged and dangerous world of rock'n'roll, they were ultimately sucked into it as deep as anyone else. By 1973 Robbie Robertson was tired enough of caretaking the group to depart Woodstock for good. The massively hyped Dylan/Band tour of 1974 kept the five of them together long enough to make their big send-off two years later one of the great events in rock history, but not long enough to produce the kind of music which had made them the darlings of *Rolling Stone* at the end of the '60s.

It was *Rolling Stone* writer Greil Marcus who guaranteed the group a place in rock history with his book *Mystery Train* (1975). Alongside Elvis Presley and Robert Johnson, Sly Stone and Randy Newman, The Band were discussed and celebrated by Marcus as an act with 'a magic feel for history', a group who'd come out of Canada and fallen in love with the American South of blues singers and minstrel shows. 'This is when we find out if there are still open spaces out there,' Marcus had been briefed by *Good Times* editor Marvin Garson before The Band's Winterland debut. Six years on, after the group had cut a version of Junior Parker's 'Mystery Train' which rivalled even Presley's, Marcus could write that 'their music gave us a sure sense that the country was richer than we had guessed'. If there was any band that could get to the heart of the mystery that pervaded rural life in America, then The Band was it. Nathaniel Hawthorne may have been right when he wrote of Americans that 'we have so much country that we have really no country at all', but The Band managed to create a sense of its adopted land that was at once precise and mythical. Mystery trains, highways lost and endless: coming out of trad, tedious, tight-knit Toronto, what could have been more enthralling to a shy dreamer and would-be mythologist like Jaime 'Robbie' Robertson?

The Band's story spans the entire course of American rock'n'roll from rhythm and blues to retro rockabilly. Through it all, their records have never dated. They sound as fresh and true as the day they were committed to tape – the most soulful, haunting music ever made about America.

Part One

NIGHTHAWKING
(1957–65)

1

Promised Lands

They call my home the land of snow . . .
'Acadian Driftwood'

It took Jaime 'Robbie' Robertson, born in Toronto in 1944, almost a decade of living in America to write a song about Canada. But when it came, it was a song full of yearning and homesickness, the saga of an Acadian family uprooted from its Nova Scotia home in 1759 and forced to sail down the Eastern seaboard till it reached the Gulf of Mexico. 'You know, Acadie, I am sick inside for my home', went the closing stanza of 'Acadian Driftwood', sung in a French translation by Marcel Lefebvre and François Cousineau.[1]

Sitting in his Malibu beach house in the summer of 1975, Robbie wrote his heart-rending song about a people with winter in their blood, a people for whom the swampy, evergreen bayous of Louisiana were as strange and uninviting as the landscapes of another planet. Listening to it, to the beleaguered and indignant voices of Richard Manuel and Rick Danko and Levon Helm, one realized that The Band had come full circle – that Robbie was writing about his homeland with the same empathy and compassion that had infused 'The Night They Drove Old Dixie Down' or 'King Harvest (Will Surely Come)'. Canada had finally become as distant and romantic to Robertson as the American South had seemed back in 1960.

'One of the things about growing up in Canada,' says Robbie Robertson today, 'is that you think: "Beyond that river, this lake, those mountains, is this place, and I can just imagine it." You grow up with a dream of discovering this place, not in terms of Columbus but in terms of your own imagination.' 'This place', of course, was America, and what Robbie is admitting is what every Canadian knows, secretly or otherwise: that his country is swamped, defined, and all but negated by the monstrous neighbour that lies over its four-thousand-mile border. ('Canada?' Al Capone is reputed to have said. 'I don't even know what *street* it's on.') It is impossible to grow up in Canada *without* dreaming of America: as *RPM* editor Walt Grealis once put it, 'America comes in clear and strong with a switch of a TV channel – why try and be different?'[2]

In some respects there are advantages to this. Just as coming from Canada gave Robbie 'a window to look through, so I didn't take things for granted', so newer Canadian bands find their very distance from America a challenge. 'I think it's precisely because we're outsiders that we're able to look at what makes the American imagination tick,' says Margo Timmins of Cowboy Junkies, a Toronto group whose songs reflect a preoccupation with the American South not unlike Robbie's. Another Torontonian who relishes his status as an 'outsider' is film director David Cronenberg, who remembers seeing Robbie play with Ronnie Hawkins in the city. 'The standard Canadian attitude to America is this,' he says. 'On the one hand we feel inferior, because our culture is so innocuous, and on the other we feel superior, because we have a kinder and gentler society.'[3]

For the teenage Robbie Robertson, a greasy-haired vagabond with a head full of the wild American sounds he picked up on distant midnight radio stations, Canada was just a blank canvas, a country that, in Elizabeth Smart's words, was 'waiting, unselfconscious as the unborn, for future history to be performed on it'. For him, as for all Canadians, there was no such thing as The Canadian Dream. As transplanted Torontonian Michael

Ignatieff observes, 'Paris, Texas stands as a metaphor for broken dreams; Paris, Saskatchewan just sounds ridiculous.' Years later Robbie could look back and pine for Canada's beautiful emptiness, just as Bob Dylan, born in Minnesota near the Canadian border, could gaze down from his Montreal hotel room during the Dylan/Band tour of 1974 and say: 'This is where I come from, this kind of setting – lakes and boats and bridges.' But in 1960 Robertson could only take his country for granted. He wanted out, and into the wild unknown that lay on the other side of Lake Ontario.[4]

In many respects, the Toronto Robbie grew up in was indistinguishable from an American city like nearby Buffalo; all it lacked, crucially, was the dimension of history. Where Quebec and Montreal hummed with old Anglo-French conflicts, Toronto was the same industrious, characterless city it had always been, the place Rupert Brooke in his *Letters from America* (1931) described as 'a clean-shaven, pink-faced, respectably dressed, fairly energetic, unintellectual, passably sociable, well-to-do, public-school-and-'varsity sort of city'. Even today, Toronto has a reputation as a place that, in one Montrealer's words, 'revels in its blandness'. 'Toronto was a great place to grow up,' smirks actor Keanu Reeves. 'You know, no graffiti or anything like that . . .' For the jingoistic Walt Grealis, Toronto wasn't Canadian at all. 'In Edmonton and Calgary, you find the real Canada,' he huffed. 'Toronto is just a second-class American city, with a ridiculous collection of hand-me-down people.' 'Thank God it's Monday,' people are rumoured to say in Toronto. Perhaps it was no coincidence that the unhappiest Canadians Stephen Brook interviewed for his book *Maple Leaf Rag* – or at least the most preoccupied with Canada's crippling inferiority complex – were all denizens of the country's financial capital.

Driving through downtown Toronto today, one sees a city dramatically changed from the city of Robbie's youth. Since the early '60s, when Robertson and his fellow Hawks were shaking it up behind Ronnie Hawkins on the city's main drag Yonge Street, Toronto has tripled in size, its population now knocking on three million. The architecture has changed correspondingly, boasting a skyscraping financial district as gleaming and marbled as that of any major American city, as well as such futuristic landmarks as the CN Tower, the Skydome, and the Eaton Center. The Toronto of the '90s is also a city of immigrants, of peoples who were only just beginning to trickle in when Robbie was a boy. Already the largest Italian city outside Italy itself, Toronto is now home to a significant number of Chinese and to the West Indian community which has produced Canada's first real rap stars, the excellent Dream Warriors.

In Robbie's youth there were few West Indians or African-Americans to be seen on Toronto's streets. The city, known familiarly as 'Hogtown', was still quintessentially Protestant, its skyline dominated by churches. Until the late '70s it was illegal to serve alcohol in a public place on the Sabbath, and discrimination against anyone who didn't fit the standard WASP profile was rife. Into this place – 'Toronto the Good', it called itself – Robbie was born to a Jewish gangster and a Mohawk Indian mother on 5 July 1944.

'The Six Nations meets the Six Tribes,' joked record producer Jimmy Iovine about Robbie Robertson's improbably exotic background. As a solo artist in the '80s and '90s Robbie has made much of his Amerindian identity – his status as a kind of 'half-breed' – but as a boy it was something, in his own words, 'better left unsaid'. His mother, born Rosemary Chrysler but known more familiarly as 'Dolly', was a beautiful girl who had grown up on the small Six Nations Reservation near Hagersville, just north of Lake Erie. In the early '40s she had come to live with her aunt in Toronto, which was where she met a beguiling 'sharpie' named Klagerman. Robbie never knew his father, who gambled for a living and ran with a fast crowd of mobsters: by the time he was old enough to ask Dolly questions, the man had been gunned down and killed in a shoot-out. The boy was shielded from the truth about him for some years, just as he was shielded from the fact that his uncle Nadie was doing a long stretch inside for one of the biggest diamond heists in Canadian history.

Robbie grew up an only child in Cabbagetown, a run-down inner-city enclave full of gabled, shabby-genteel boarding houses. Shortly after Klagerman's death, Dolly married the rather more respectable jeweller from whom Robbie takes his present surname. 'We weren't *poor* poor,' says Robbie, 'but we weren't middle-class.' Something of the flavour of Robbie's childhood can be sampled in 'Rags And Bones', another track on the 1975 *Northern Lights–Southern Cross* album that revisited Canada. The song drew on memories of Robbie's paternal great-grandfather, who had emigrated to Canada from Palestine in the early years of the century. 'He was a scholar,' recalled Robbie, 'and when he got here he was capable of nothing but reading and intellectualizing. He became a rag man, which was not an unusual thing at the time. He had a horse and wagon and he would go up and down the lanes singing this song "Rags, bones, and old used clothes". I never saw him doing it, but when I was a kid I would see the rag man, and it was a very frightening symbol to me.' In the song, the rag man and his chant provide the choruses that punctuate Robbie's portraits of the many characters he remembered from Cabbage-town: the shoeshine boy, the blind fiddler, a 'young Caruso' on a fire escape. 'My musical background was hearing those musical situations in the street,' said Robbie. 'The sound of the city.'

Robbie was exposed to less urban sounds when Dolly began taking him down to the Six Nations Reservation for the summer. Here his Mohawk relatives would gather round the camp-fire and sing Hank Williams or Lefty Frizzell songs to the accompaniment of guitars and mandolins. He felt awkward and inadequate around his cousins, whose relationship with their environment was very different from anything he had ever known. 'They had finely tuned senses,' he recalls. 'They could tell things just by listening to the ground, or they'd sniff the air and say when it was going to rain.' One of the great characters on the reservation was Robbie's great-grandfather, a venerable gent with a shock of white hair and a cane which he employed to hook his countless great-grandchildren to his side. The old man was the first of many storytellers in Robbie's life.

Back in the city, Robbie was itching to take guitar lessons. Being a hipper-than-average mom, Dolly tracked down a teacher who went by the unlikely name of 'Billy Blue'. Unfortunately, Mr Blue turned out to be a teacher of the Hawaiian guitar: when seven-year-old Robbie rolled up for his first lesson, he was greeted by a man in a hula shirt who proceeded to place a guitar on his new pupil's lap. 'The picture wasn't quite what I'd had in my mind,' Robbie later laughed. 'I had Hank Williams in mind and the music to "The Hawaiian War Chant" in front of me.' It proved to be Robbie's first and last guitar lesson, 'the full extent of my formal education'.

After a few years of strumming along to 'little cowboy songs' on a cheap acoustic guitar, Robbie caught the disease – the rockin' pneumonia, the boogie woogie flu – from which he would never quite recover. 'I was at the perfect age, puberty, when rock'n'roll hit me. It couldn't have been a more perfect sucker shot.' In the wee small hours when all good Canadian schoolboys should have been fast asleep, Robbie began tuning in to a radio station called WLAC Nashville. As he says himself, WLAC was 'a fluke of nature', its 50,000 watts beaming out in a band that stretched from Mexico to Canada. 'You could get it way up in Canada,' he says, 'but you couldn't get shit in Cleveland or Detroit.' What you actually got when you picked up WLAC was a trio of hepcat white disc jockeys – Gene Nobles, John R, and Hoss Allen – who played records for an audience of Southern blacks. 'It was called race music at the time,' John R (Richbourg) told the author shortly before his death in 1985. 'I would pick records up anywhere I could get them. I'd make a tour of Nashville and get anything I could lay my hands on – R&B, gospel, blues, you name it.'

What Richbourg and his colleagues initially failed to realize was just how many whites were tuning into the station as well. Dan Penn, composer of many of the great soul ballads that came out of Muscle Shoals, Alabama in the '60s, recalled huddling under the bedclothes on his parents' farm and cradling his ear to a little transistor radio. 'I'd turn that dial to WLAC, real low, and pretend to be asleep,' he remembered. 'I was listening to those strange old blues singers before I ever heard Elvis Presley.' Hundreds of miles north-east, things were no different for Robbie. 'I remember the night I first heard a Jimmy Reed record on WLAC,' he says. 'It came on, and I couldn't comprehend the instrumentation, couldn't tell if this was a harmonica, if that was a guitar, if the drums were regular drums or what.' From out of the night came this dark, raw, mysterious music, and Robbie's life was never the same again. WLAC was the gateway to his fantasy of the rural South, to a vision of America as potent, primeval, myth-infested.

Suddenly, the South exploded like a fireworks display over the North American continent. 'When rock'n'roll first came about,' Robbie says, 'I found it so heavy in my heart that I couldn't get around it, you know. And my whole schooling and everything I knew just took a back seat. I couldn't think of anything but Little Richard and Elvis.' Besides Alan Freed in Cleveland, there were disc jockeys even closer to home playing this Bacchanalian music. 'Probably my most influential teacher was George "Hound Dog" Lorenz, who had a show on a Buffalo radio station,' says Robbie. 'His show was the place to go if you wanted to get around listening to Pat Boone. When you heard the Hound playing Clyde

McPhatter and the Drifters' "Money Honey", you knew that was *real.*'

It was on Lorenz's show that Robbie heard records as diverse as Sanford Clark's rockabilly hit 'The Fool' and Little Willie John's swaggering jump-blues debut 'All Around The World'. Willie John in particular 'opened up a door to something for me', a searing emotional edge that Robbie never forgot throughout his years with The Band. It's Little Willie John that Robbie is 'laying in the back seat listening to' in his 1987 hit 'Somewhere Down The Crazy River', and Willie's anguished 'My Baby's In Love With Another Guy' that he asked Robert Palmer to cover for the soundtrack to Martin Scorsese's *The Color of Money*.

Even more significant for the pubescent Robbie Robertson was hearing the first great blues and rock'n'roll guitar players. Records like Link Wray's 'Rumble' and Dale Hawkins' 'Susie-Q' opened him up to the sheer power of the electric guitar. 'Link Wray had the rawest sound, just dirty and up to no good,' he says. 'Dirty to me also meant Bo Diddley and Hubert Sumlin, Howlin' Wolf's guitarist. They put me over the top. I had no choice but to play guitar.' Just as powerful was James Burton's febrile soloing on 'Susie-Q'. 'I wanted to be part of that *sound*,' says Robbie. 'At first I thought these guys like James Burton were really strong to be able to bend strings the way they did. It was only later that I found out they'd taken the heaviest string off, strung the other five down, and used a banjo string for the sixth!'

By the time Dale Hawkins was enjoying his Top 10 R&B hit in June 1957, Robbie Robertson was a good-looking teen rebel who spent much of his time combing the racks at a Toronto store called Records Unlimited. The store stocked rock'n'roll, blues, and gospel – in Robbie's words 'a combination of what you'd get from the rockabilly pipeline or mail-order stations like WLAC, and what came from across the lake in Buffalo or Detroit'. Occasionally, too, Robbie would get to see the likes of Bo Diddley or Carl Perkins in some dingy Toronto dance-hall. The more music he heard from below the Mason–Dixon line, the less interest he could muster in schoolwork or sports. Running away from home, he worked the 'swinger joint' in a local carnival. 'There was a ball on a chain and you swung it to knock down a bowling pin,' he recalled. 'Except you missed.' Many of the street-smarts Robbie picked up as a carny were to serve him well on the road. 'Robbie's got a heart of gold, but he's got some mischief in him as well,' says producer Daniel Lanois. 'He's a street kid from way back. He learned the ins and outs in scuzzy bars, and he's always got the point of view of that same young man.'

The turning point came when Robbie joined the first of several fledgling combos in his neighbourhood. The most important of these was Little Caesar and the Consuls, later described by Robbie as 'a New Orleans-wannabe band' whose forte was covering such Crescent City classics as Fats Domino's 'Blue Monday', Lloyd Price's 'Stagger Lee', and Huey 'Piano' Smith's 'Don't You Know Yockomo'. Robbie also led two little outfits of his own, the Rhythm Chords and Robbie and the Robots, the latter so named because band member Pete Traynor – later the founder of Canada's successful Traynor Amps company – had customized Robbie's Harmony guitar to the point where it had robot-like antennae sticking out of its body. Robbie also played in Pete's own group, the engagingly-named (and engagingly misspelt) Thumper and the Trambones.

By 1958, when he first saw a wild new band from the American South of his dreams, Robbie Robertson was sold body and soul to rock'n'roll.

Twenty miles down the road from the reservation where Robbie spent his summers stood the little town of Simcoe, and it was on a farm in the middle of the flat tobacco country around Simcoe that

Band bassist Rick Danko was born on 9 December 1943. The country music that Robbie heard his relatives playing on the reservation was the staple diet of the Danko family, who whooped it up on the farm jamboree-style most every weekend. 'We grew up with no TV or anything,' says Rick's younger brother Terry. 'Our entertainment was getting together at weekends, fourteen or fifteen musicians playing from Friday night through to Sunday.' A woodcutter from Manitoba, Rick's father Tom lived for music. Fortunately, his wife Leola felt the same way.

Rick himself, the third of four brothers, was quick to show his own musical aptitude. A feisty, knockabout urchin of a boy, he was banging away at various stringed instruments by the time he was five, and claims to have memorized many of the Hank Williams songs the family heard on WWVA, a country station in Wheeling, West Virginia that served as a 'hardcore' alternative to Nashville's Grand Ole Opry. 'Rick is like a damn musical sponge,' says Levon Helm. 'You can drop just one bit of music in there and boy, he'll soak it up and squeeze out a whole cupful.'

The music in this part of south-west Ontario had a peculiarly Appalachian bent, and for a good reason. In the Depression, many of the tobacco farmers from the Carolinas had moved up to the area because the land was so good for tobacco. Inevitably, the music came with it, as did an accent that can still be made out in farming families whose grandfathers and great-grandfathers migrated from the Carolinas. 'As a kid, you worked on their tobacco farms because there was nothing else to do,' says Terry Danko. 'You went to school with all the Southern kids and picked up on their traditions.' For Terry, this was why the music around Simcoe took on such a pronounced bluegrass and gospel character, as opposed to the Country and Western style exemplified in the songs of Canada's very own country superstar Hank Snow, or the Acadian style of music heard in Quebec. (In the summer, however, French Canadians would bring their music to the area when they came to pick tobacco: Daniel Lanois included a song about them – 'O Marie' – on his album *Acadie*.)[5]

Like Levon Helm's, Rick Danko's country roots were a vital ingredient in the sound of The Band, offsetting and complementing the bluesier leanings of Robbie Robertson and Richard Manuel. 'They come from hundreds of miles apart,' said Robbie in the '70s, 'but they are both considered the basic country influence in the band.' When Rick and Levon teamed up to play a series of two-man shows in the early '80s, their sets invariably featured two or three ballads ('Evangeline', 'Fifteen Years Ago', 'The Girl I Left Behind') sung in the 'high, lonesome' harmony style of duos like the Stanley Brothers. Mountain harmonies were something Rick learned from his mother and her stepsisters. 'Those Danko boys got weird ears,' says Ronnie Hawkins, who never ceased to be amazed at the harmonies Rick found for Hawks songs.

A typical Danko family weekend, or 'musicale', would follow a week of back-breaking work in the tobacco fields. A favourite assembly point was the farm on which the *Music From Big Pink* 'Next Of Kin' photograph was taken, home to Rick's great-grandpa and to his great-uncle Lee, whose home-made strawberry wine was later celebrated in the opening track on *Stage Fright*. Often there would be a guest appearance by Tom Danko's brother-in-law Spence Byers, a country disc jockey from Hamilton who wore a rhinestone suit and bragged shamelessly about Hank Williams' periodic visits to the station. The atmosphere, says Terry Danko, was one of 'permanent harvest time with home-made brew', and little Rick was not averse to the occasional nip of alcohol. At one such 'musicale', Rick made his debut performance with a four-string tenor banjo, warbling 'Red River Valley' in a tremulous but assured soprano. 'I was ready to go to Nashville when I was seven,' he laughs. 'But then I met some people from there, and it seemed like all the country people drank a lot, and you'd hear about people dying. That kinda changed my mind.'

At the age of ten, Rick began picking up the same 50,000 watt Nashville station that Robbie was hearing in Toronto. More than anything else it was the sound of the young Sam Cooke singing gospel with the Soul Stirrers that turned Rick on to black music. Playing little Saturday night shows with his eldest brother Junior, Rick was already exhibiting the kind of country-soul vocal style he would employ with The Band over a decade later. With Junior, Rick put together his first group, recruiting a teacher at the local high school to play drums. 'I used to rent the halls and my uncle Roly would put up posters as he delivered groceries', Rick recalled. 'People would come, and I would get to play country music and R&B.' Later the trio expanded the line-up to include an accordionist, a second guitarist, and a girl singer. There was never any shortage of bookings, what with the number of weddings being celebrated in the area. Often the band would be required to play polkas for the many transplanted central Europeans who'd settled around the nearby town of Delhi, and one hears the influence of this music in both the ghostly 'Last Waltz' theme and the delightful version of Anton Karas' *Third Man* theme on *Moondog Matinee*.

'There was nothing but tobacco for a hundred-mile radius around us in Simcoe,' says Terry Danko. 'Stratford, on the other hand, was a little more cosmopolitan. A little more English.'

Stratford, Ontario, which lies exactly half-way between Lake Erie and Lake Huron, not only took its name from William Shakespeare's birthplace but played host to an annual Shakespeare festival in a specially built theatre. Significantly larger than Simcoe, it was the town where Rick Danko's future Band colleague and carousing buddy Richard Manuel was born on 3 April 1944. The son of Pierre Manuel, a mechanic at Stratford's Chrysler plant, Richard grew up hearing country radio and singing in the choir at his local Baptist church. 'My brothers and I were all in the choir,' he later recalled. 'That's what turned me on to harmonies, and it's what made me very "chordy".'

When he was 8 years old, Manuel's parents encouraged him to take piano lessons. 'We had a family piano,' says his brother Don, 'but he didn't get along too well with the teacher.' Richard's own version of the story was that the teacher was a crusty old pedant who all but slammed the lid down on his pupil's fingers when he had the audacity to play a chord with a different voicing. 'It wasn't wrong,' Richard maintained. 'It was just that I put the E in a C chord on top instead of in the middle. But that was the end of my formal lessons, until Garth came along.' Actually, it wasn't quite the end of Richard's formal musical education. In 1959 he received a diploma in the Hawaiian guitar, no less, from the Ontario Conservatory of Music. A fellow musician remembers him practising 'Sleep Walk', Santo and Johnny's hit instrumental from that year, as well as a couple of bluesier pieces.

Like Robbie and Rick, Richard discovered blues (and rhythm and blues) after hitting WLAC one night on his AM dial. 'It was that era's underground radio,' Manuel was later to say of the station. On WLAC he first heard the mordant Chicago blues of Otis Rush, the sleepy bayou moan of Jimmy Reed, the gravelly, gospel-fired voices of Ray Charles and Bobby 'Blue' Bland. 'He'd listen to WLAC after midnight and send away for the records they advertised,' says John Till, later a member of Janis Joplin's Full Tilt Boogie Band. 'He'd come to school with his brand new albums. There was no blues around except for a few small circles, and he was the centre of one of them.' Till remembers the impact Charles and Bland had on Richard's own singing: 'He really respected them and tried to emulate them, even though his own voice was already starting to come through.' As for so many blue-eyed teenage soul-boys on both sides of the Mason–Dixon line, it was the radical fusion of blues and gospel in records like Charles' 'What'd I Say' and Bland's 'I'll Take Care Of You' that proved so catalytic to Richard. Soon he would come to know it as 'soul' music.

John Till played guitar in The Rebels, the Stratford band Richard joined with his oldest pal Jimmy Winkler in early 1959. With Winkler on drums, the line-up was completed by bassist Ken Kalmusky, then extended when the group's original vocalist Doug 'Bo' Rhodes rejoined. Learning of Duane Eddy's backing band, also called The Rebels, the quintet quickly changed their name to The Rockin' Revols. ('Revol' was 'Lover' spelt backwards!) They played a poppy brand of rock'n'roll, with Richard – by now nicknamed 'Beak', thanks to his aquiline nose – taking most of the lead vocals. Of the few Revols recordings that survive, 'Liebestraum' was a Jerry Lee Lewis-style boogie-woogie treatment of the famous Schubert piece; 'Promise Yourself' a charming, hard-driven little rocker with some wild drumming from Winkler (a.k.a. 'The Hammer'); and 'Eternal Love' a Bobby Vee-ish number with Manuel singing in an almost unrecognizably high tenor register.

'Richard would have the guys over in the living room making lots of noise,' says Don Manuel. 'But our parents were very tolerant, my mother especially. I think she figured it was a phase Richard would grow through, but he just kept getting deeper and deeper into it.' Once the Revols were playing regularly, usually at school dances in and around Stratford, there was no stopping Manuel. He was a man obsessed. 'Richard was just a stone rock'n'roll, rhythm and blues head,' says Robbie Robertson. He was also something of a budding hellraiser, prone to breaking out of his shy shell in bouts of drunken recklessness. Down in Ken Kalmusky's basement, which served as the Revols' HQ and principal rehearsal studio, Richard would court teenage girls and carouse all night to the sound of Ray Charles records. His parents were finding bottles stashed in his bedroom when he was 14. 'He was fairly introspective, even back then,' recalls

Garth Picot, a guitarist from Goderich, Ontario who replaced John Till in the Revols and stayed at the Manuels' house for nearly six months. 'I remember driving around all night with him and talking about the meaning of life. His philosophy was always: "Live tonight, coz tomorrow you might get hit by a truck"!'

Thirty miles south of Stratford across the tobacco fields was the even larger town of London. Appropriately enough, the river that ran through London, paralleling Interstate 401 almost the whole way to Detroit, was called the Thames.

Eric Garth Hudson, born several years earlier than his future Band cohorts on 2 August 1937, grew up in London, where his father was an entomologist and government farm inspector who'd conducted surveys on Dutch Elm and Japanese beetle disease. Garth himself had been destined to go into the agricultural field: the guidance counsellor at his high school told him that music 'should remain no more than a glorified hobby'. Yet Garth's own father played the flute, the cornet, and the saxophone, and his mother was an accomplished pianist.

Hudson was already playing accordion in a country band as a teenager, as well as developing a large repertoire of sepulchral hymns behind the organ in his uncle's funeral parlour. (One can detect this in the eerie Dylan basement song 'Sign On The Cross'.) 'We'd play some hymns from the higher church,' he says, 'but usually it was Baptist hymns like "What A Friend We Have In Jesus", "Softly And Tenderly Jesus Is Calling", or "Jesus Keep Me Near The Cross". The Anglican church has the best musical traditions of any church that I know of. It's the old voice leading that gives it the countermelodies and adds all those classical devices which are not right out there, but which add a little texture.' Garth's fascination with the organ began early, after he took apart an old reed pump organ belonging to his father and rebuilt it. 'All the little wooden parts were always breaking, and the reeds needed cleaning,' he recalls.

By the time Hudson had shelved the idea of agricultural college and begun studying music theory and harmony at the University of Western Ontario, he was a fully-fledged boffin, a highly eccentric character who looked not unlike the hero of David Lynch's *Eraserhead*.[6] Indeed, he was almost too eccentric for his teachers. 'I had a problem with classical notated music in that I was never able to memorize,' he admits. 'Oh, I did, but not to the extent that's necessary. I didn't like to practice too much. I found out that I could improvise, and to assist that I developed a method of ear training. I would memorize shapes and forms, and that's one of the things that happens: you begin to see form.' While he was exploring the outer limits of classical theory and improvisation, Garth was also falling in love with the R&B and rock'n'roll he heard on Alan Freed's Cleveland radio show. 'I remember Freed talking about the first Moondog ball they'd had, where there was almost a riot,' he says. 'So I knew someone over there was having more fun than I was!' In high school, after putting together a couple of vaudeville-style jazz groups, he'd taken the plunge and joined a little rockabilly band called the Melodines. 'I was the only guy in London who knew how to play rock'n'roll saxophone,' he laughs.

Things got more serious when Garth wound up in a group called the Silhouettes, who left London to work the lucrative club circuit around Windsor and Detroit. The Silhouettes mutated into the Capers, an all-purpose combo who played their own sets or backed touring stars as circumstances dictated. It was at a high school hop in 1959 that another London native, Paul Hutchins, got talking with the group. 'Garth was very professional, with a strange, dry sense of humour,' says Hutchins. 'He was kinda weird, but not weird weird. He played sax, piano, just about anything you care to mention, and he'd jump up and down while he played the accordion.' In due course, Hutchins became Paul London, the group's charismatic frontman, and helped make the group even more commercially viable.

Gigging around Detroit, and backing everyone from Bill Haley to Johnny Cash to the Everly Brothers, Paul London and the Capers eventually caught the attention of Arman Boladian, a local record promotion legend.[7] With Boladian's help, the Capers cut a cover of the Mello-Tones' 1957 hit 'Rosie Lee' at RCA-Victor's Toronto studio, following it up with 'Sugar Baby', cut in 1961 at the legendary Chess studio in Chicago. Garth arranged and played piano on both of these, overdubbing sax breaks in the style of his beloved Lee Allen. Neither release made a huge splash, though 'Sugar Baby', released on the Checkmate label, did reach #8 in Detroit.

'Tell your mama, tell your pa,' sang Ray Charles, 'Gonna send you back to Arkansas!' What picture, one wonders, did Robbie Robertson or Rick Danko or Richard Manuel or Garth Hudson have of 'Arkansas' as they listened to Ray Charles bawling out 'What'd I Say' on WLAC?

While Robbie dreamed of the South – of what James Agee called 'the whole memory of the South in its 6,000-mile parade, the trembling heat and the wide wild opening of the tragic land' – the fifth member of The Band was actually growing up there. 'If there's an opposite to being a Canadian,' says Robbie, 'where Levon's from would be the opposite!' Yet such was the beauty of rock'n'roll radio that Levon Helm was listening (on WLAC, no less) to the very same Southern music the others were picking up in Ontario. As he puts it himself, 'Mickey and Sylvia's "Love Is Strange" was just as popular in Toronto as it was in Memphis, so I can't take a whole lotta credit for Americanizing my Canadian partners.'

23

If you follow the Mississippi down from Memphis about sixty some-odd miles, you eventually come to an Arkansas town on its west bank called Helena. Follow Route 49 away from the river and you hit Marvell, a little town (pop. 1,200) where a redneck kid named Mark Levon Helm grew up in the '40s. 'It's the end of the line, boy,' Helm would joke. 'Only one way in and one way out!' Born on 26 May 1942, Levon grew up on the farm that belonged to his father Jasper 'Diamond' Helm. Diamond was like Tom Danko, slaving all week on his cotton fields only to let loose with a guitar at the weekend. Years later, after he'd been cast as Loretta Lynn's father in Michael Apted's *Coal Miner's Daughter*, Levon said it was like playing his own dad. Ted and Clara Webb, he swore, were the sharecropping image of Diamond and Nell 'Shuck' Helm. 'But it looks a lot rougher than it is,' he laughed. 'There is so much love and stuff inside a family that it makes up for a lot of other things that are missing.'

This is Levon Helm all over: Mr Downhome Apple Pie, painting the rosiest picture imaginable of life on the farm with his parents and his siblings Modena, Linda, and Wheeler. As with the Dankos, there were numerous uncles and cousins around Marvell, and most of them could play at least one instrument. Getting together with a bunch of fiddles and mandolins and a whole lot of moonshine whiskey was the focal point of family life in Phillips County. 'Where Levon grew up, they're ignorant mothers,' says Ronnie Hawkins. 'I mean, they're still in the Civil War there.' Living in the Civil War they might have been, but the music they played was a singularly bluesy kind of Country and Western. 'White music has always been very ricky-ticky, steppity-step, plunkety-plunk,' says Robbie Robertson. 'When it interchanged it became something else, which is what Levon's father sings like. He sings blues with a twang, with that different accent and a different bump on every place.'

Living in the Mississippi delta, it was hard not to mix it up.

Diamond Helm was an archetypal Arkansas 'good ol' boy', even serving as Marvell's deputy sheriff for some years, but much of the music he played at local country dances anticipated the hillbilly blues of Elvis Presley. Where a family living up in the mountains might have retained a certain musical 'purity', down in this neck of the woods it was pretty hard to escape the blues that came out of Helena, or out of the medicine shows which frequently passed through town with their quota of black songsters. Levon was already music-crazy by the age of four, when Diamond took him to see Bill Monroe and the Bluegrass Boys. It wasn't long before he was finding excuses to accompany his pa into Helena to hear the town's many blues singers.

'Helena was a little Chicago back in the '30s and '40s,' a lifelong resident of the town says in Robert Palmer's *Deep Blues*. There was cotton, railroads, even a Chrysler plant; more to the point, there was gambling, bootlegging, blues. Elm Street, the black strip that paralleled the whites-only Cherry Street, was dotted with little bars and joints. Robert Johnson played there, as did Howlin' Wolf. On the streets themselves, under the shade of the elm and sycamore trees, blues singers could be heard hollering at most hours of the day and night. From 1942 onwards, they could even be heard on Helena's very own radio station KFFA, founded by a white man called Sam Anderson. Mouthharp maestro Rice Miller, who called himself Sonny Boy Williamson despite the existence of the successful Chicago bluesman of the same name, rolled up at the station one day and suggested to Anderson that he be given a daily slot on the air. Anderson agreed, on the condition that Miller found a sponsor. He recommended approaching the Interstate Grocery Company, whose owner Max Moore wanted to advertise his King Biscuit Flour. Thus was born 'King Biscuit Time', a 15 minute show that went on the air every day from midday until 12.15 p.m.

Being a mere 250-watt station, KFFA had a range of little more than forty miles. But that was enough, in Robert Palmer's words, to make Miller and his guitarist sidekick Robert Jr Lockwood the delta's first media-made stars. Enough, too, to reach the ears of tow-headed little Levon Helm, whose 'main business' once he'd got into Helena with his dad was to 'run off to KFFA and watch Sonny Boy and the King Biscuit boys do their live broadcast'. The raw sound of Miller's harp, backed by Lockwood's electric guitar and sometimes by pianist 'Pinetop' Perkins and drummer James 'Peck' Curtis, set the little white boy on fire. Twenty years later he'd come back through Helena with his Canadian group the Hawks and track down the dying Sonny Boy Williamson for a drunken jam session.

The minstrel and medicine shows were another seminal experience for Levon. Troupes like F. S. Walcott's Rabbit Minstrels, who boasted a young Rufus Thomas in their ranks, opened up the illicit world of showbiz to Levon, and he loved it. 'In those kinds of shows, with horns and a full rhythm section,' he remembered, 'the drums always looked like the best seat in the house. The sound of cymbals and the snare drum popping in there just sounded like Saturday night and good times.' It was at the minstrel shows that Helm first saw the kind of animal walks and stage gymnastics that would become such an integral part of Ronnie Hawkins' act. In the words of Robbie Robertson, who based the song 'The W. S. Walcott Medicine Show' on Levon's reminiscences, 'when Elvis and Jerry Lee exposed this stuff to the rest of the world it was like some unknown beast the devil had sent, but to Southerners it was just the local entertainment.' Levon, of course, was canny enough to stick around after the other kids had gone to bed. 'That's when they'd have the "Midnight Ramble",' he recalled. 'The songs would get a little juicier and the jokes a lot racier, and the prettiest dancer would really get down and shake it a few times.'

Levon may have decided the drummer had 'the best seat in the house', a phrase he was to use for the title of his autobiography many years later, but his very first 'instrument' was a broom. 'I took a broom, held it sideways, and made believe it was a guitar,' he laughs. 'I'd take the broom out past the barn, down to the pump and around the watermelon patch, and pretend to play.' By the time he was eight years old the broom had become a real guitar, and Levon had all but mastered the harmonica into the bargain. With his sister Linda on washtub bass, he started playing local Lions' Clubs, Rotary Clubs, and 4-H Clubs around Arkansas and Mississippi. '4-H Clubs were the way a country kid got to travel around,' he says. County fairs and Miss Arkansas pageants provided further opportunities to test out their close harmony singing. For Levon, making music was 'the only way to get off that stinking tractor and out of that 105 degree heat'; otherwise, life consisted of little but cotton-picking from May through to September.

Once Levon was at Marvell High, Linda 'grew shy of that ol' washtub' and concerned herself with more feminine matters. Recruiting guitarist Thurlo Brown and bassist James Shottard, Levon formed a little band who became known, splendidly, as the Jungle Bush Beaters. Brown was the first guitar player Levon knew who could 'run up and down the neck and hit all those bar chords and augmented and diminished things,' while Shottard had himself a mean old doghouse bass with a pickup on it. 'We sorta jammed along,' recalls Levon. 'We'd do current hits of the day for dances. We didn't have any sorta tried-and-proven formula or anything, we just played.' Basing themselves on bands like those of Billy Lee Riley and Harold Jenkins – the Arkansas rockabilly man who became country singer Conway Twitty – the Beaters became a pretty tight little outfit. Tight enough, at any rate, for Levon to be thinking seriously of quitting Marvell High at the soonest possible juncture. Seeing Elvis Presley playing in nearby Marianna's high school gymnasium in 1955 only confirmed the direction in which he was headed. 'I really had rambling on my mind,' he says. 'I wanted to go. One of the prettiest sights in the world to me was a big ol' Cadillac rolling down the road with a doghouse bass tied to the top of it. That looked like the car I wanted to be in.'

Levon was in his last year at Marvell High when he got rat-assed drunk one night and sneaked into the Delta Supper Club in West Helena. Parked outside was a big ol' Cadillac. Parked *inside* was rompin' Ronnie Hawkins.

2

Endless Highway

What a wonderful thing it is to see an Ontario audience laugh . . . a sense of relief is felt all through the theatre, as though the straps and laces of a tight corset had been momentarily loosened.

Robertson Davies, *The Papers of Samuel Marchbanks*

On a wet Sunday night in the summer of 1991, the Mean Fiddler must be the closest thing to the Delta Supper Club north-west London has to offer. Admittedly, the joint ain't exactly cooking, what with the hot 'roots music' ticket tonight being the Texas Tornadoes show across town,[1] but the grizzly figure who takes Fiddler's stage shortly after 9.30 p.m. isn't exactly complaining. He and his band have just spent a week as a guest at the new Essex pile of his billionaire boyhood pal Don Tyson, chicken-farming tycoon of Arkansas, and the Fiddler gig is merely a last-minute one-nighter for the benefit of a few faithful old English rockers.

'This here's the one that took us from the hills and stills and put us on the pills,' Ronnie Hawkins growls the intro with which he's prefixed 'Forty Days' a thousand times. He's nursing a sonofabitch of a cold and he'd rather be anywhere than here, but he sure as hell isn't going let you see that. When you roll up to see Ronnie Hawkins and what is probably the hundredth edition of his Hawks, you get a decent show: precision rockabilly and R&B from the tightest bar band from anywhere between Vancouver and Nova Scotia. After 'Forty Days', it's 'Odessa', that lascivious toast to West Helena's prettiest prostitute, followed quickly by

29

'Wild Little Willie' and a medley of songs by 'the living Shakespeare of rock'n'roll', Mr Chuck Berry.

'I wanted to sound like Bobby "Blue" Bland,' announces Hawkins in his most effortlessly self-deprecating manner, 'but it came out sounding like Ernest Tubb and there wasn't nothin' I could do about it!' Like all his one-liners, it sounds great the first time you hear it, a mite stale thereafter. Staleness clearly doesn't bother Ronnie himself, since his 1991 show is only a slight variant on the one he was doing thirty years ago. Where once upon a time Richard 'Beak' Manuel would have taken over for a bit of sanctified R&B hollering, now Ronnie's daughter Leah, a sassy rock'n'roll vixen in leather pants, belts out a rousing version of Creedence Clearwater Revival's 'Proud Mary'. Or Miss Kimberley Richards, permed and Nashville-hygienic, gets a mini-showcase for her lifeless country songs. Later on, with Ronnie taking another long break from the stage, the kid at the piano will do a passable Jerry Lee Lewis pastiche and Ricky Danko's little brother Terry will duplicate the pounding bass riff of The Band's 'The Shape I'm In'.

Finally, Ronnie lurches back into the fray to close the set with a thunderous 'Bo Diddley'. Looking for all the world like some sweaty, Skid Row Kenny Rogers, he gives the chugging junglebilly classic everything he's got and returns to encore with his biggest '50s hit 'Mary Lou'. 'If I had to do one more song, I'd have to get Elvis Presley's doctor out here,' he guffaws. But the mighty 'Who Do You Love', Ronnie's signature tune and would-be autobiography, has to follow and bring the show to its climax. It's hardly as raw as it would have sounded at Toronto's Le Coq d'Or in 1963, but then it's not Jaime 'Robbie' Robertson cranking out Diddley's sten-gun guitar riff or Levon Helm laying down that primal voodoo beat.

Backstage in the Mean Fiddler's cramped dressing room, Ronnie Hawkins licks his wounds and signs vintage Roulette album covers for diehard rockabilly fans. He knows this has been just one more shitty job in the long anti-climax of his career as 'a legend in his spare time', but he's a gracious Big Daddy to the last, patiently answering the questions of two young Geordies in brothel creepers. A gruelling mini-tour through France and Germany up to Scandinavia looms on the horizon, but he'll put that out of his mind tonight. All that matters now is sleep.

Ronnie Hawkins, born two days after Elvis Presley on 10 January 1935, is the ultimate fantasy redneck: nothing less than *The Last of The Good Ol' Boys*, as he titled his very readable 1989 autobiography. Fantasy because in great part it's Ronnie's act, masking the truth that he's really a gentle old bear of a man who's managed to get by on tall tales for most of his life. 'He's a dangerous fighter, a disarming fool, a loyal friend,' says Kris Kristofferson. 'One minute he looks as deadly as the devil, the next he's smiling as innocent as an Arkansas farmboy'.

There *was* an Arkansas farm, as it happens. It was called Hawkins Holler, and it was almost two miles along a dirt road in the Ozark mountains near Huntsville. The Hawkins clan were hunters – 'hardy hillbillies', in the phrase of a lawyer who married Ronnie's great-aunt. (The area is still prime Klan country.) They were also, like the Helms three hundred miles away on the other side of the state, musicians with a fondness for fiddles and moonshine whiskey. One of Ronnie's uncles was Delmar 'Skipper' Hawkins, who'd made it as a country musician out in California and often came back to the Holler in a Cadillac. 'The thing for our family on Saturday nights,' says Delmar's son Dale, who hit the jackpot himself with the immortal 'Susie-Q', 'was going down to the little courthouse in St Paul, with everybody just getting together and playing.' Delmar's drinking soon forced Dale's mother to take her children down to Louisiana, where her own people lived, but not before young Ronnie had sized up the symbols of his uncle's success. 'I knew at five years old that that's what I wanted to do,' he says.

It wasn't long after saying goodbye to cousin Dale that Ronnie himself quit the Holler with his parents. Moving first to St Paul, they ended up in the much larger town of Fayetteville – pronounced 'Fateville' – where the hard-drinking Jasper Newton Hawkins opened a barbershop and his long-suffering wife Flora became a schoolteacher. 'Jasper was a drunk and a dangerous barber!' laughs Robbie Robertson. 'He nearly cut off somebody's ear one time.' It was in Jasper's barbershop that Ronnie Hawkins first heard the music that came to affect him so powerfully in the years to come. 'We had a shoeshine boy named Buddy Hayes in the shop, and Buddy had a little blues band,' recalls Ronnie. 'He'd rehearse in the back of the shop with a piano player called Little Joe.' What Buddy played was New Orleans-style jazz-blues, which didn't stop him turning the boss's son on to the more rural sounds of the Delta bluesmen who were recording at that time. Hanging around Hayes was a crash course in Southern black culture.

Just as it was for Levon Helm down in Marvell, a formative experience for young Ronnie Hawkins was the minstrel and medicine shows – like Colonel Tom Parker's 'country carnivals' – that regularly came through town. Here Ronnie first saw the camel and duck walks and the gravity-defying gymnastics that became such a focal point of his act, and of rock'n'roll in general. 'I started doing my camel walk about 1950,' says Ronnie. 'I'd seen those cats in the minstrel shows and I was a pretty good gymnast. I'd do backflips and splits, even though there wasn't always room on the stages we played.'

With guitarist Harold 'Pink' Pinkerton, Hawkins put his first band together that year at Fayetteville High. Playing 'l'il gutbucket honky-tonks' like Fayetteville's own Rockwood Club, this primitive, prototype version of the Hawks was already essaying a kind of redneck R & B style that drew heavily on the 'country boogie' sound of the '40s. 'Hot country', they'd call it when Elvis Presley revved up songs like Bill Monroe's 'Blue Moon Of Kentucky'; 'rockabilly', the media christened it. Hawkins even claims that in 1952 – the year Sam Phillips' Sun label made its debut – he cut 'the first rockabilly record', a version of the very same public domain traditional which became Bo Diddley's self-titled hit in 1955. Like all the other white Southern teenagers getting hip to the illicit pleasures of black rhythm, Ronnie abhorred what he called the 'who-shit-in-my-saddle-bag' country music he heard on stations like Fayetteville's appropriately-named KHOG. Only Hank Williams fired him up at all, and Hank had after all grown up with his very own Buddy Hayes, black guitarist 'Tee-Tot' Payne. One of Ronnie's earliest live appearances, fittingly, was at nearby Fort Smith, low on a bill headlined by Williams.

After a spell running liquor into the neighbouring states of Missouri and Oklahoma in a handsome Model A Roadster he'd acquired, Hawkins at his mother's behest entered the University of Arkansas as a physical education major. By 1954 he'd formed the second Hawks line-up, a wild bunch who tore it up at sorority and fraternity dances on campus and made several visits to Memphis to see the bright lights of Beale Street. 'In those days I never thought of L.A. or New York,' he says. 'I only thought of Memphis.' Clearly a big part of the city's appeal was that it had spawned Elvis, whom Ronnie recalls seeing in Beale Street's famous Lansky Brothers clothing store. Ronnie's greatest dream was to record at Sun, 'the chicken shack with the Cadillacs outside.'

In 1957, Hawkins dropped out of university and joined the army. Stationed at Fort Sill in Lawton, Oklahoma, he was propping up the bar one night at the Amvets Club when four black musicians took the stage and tore into the first of several storming R & B numbers. After watching pianist Rufus 'Big Meat' Markham do a riveting Little Richard routine, Ronnie felt emboldened to jump up onstage and sing with them. After three songs, it was clear they had a winning if unlikely combination in the making. 'One hayseed and four blacks,' Ronnie called them, and the sound they made was somewhere between blues and rockabilly – 'which was exactly what I wanted'. Calling themselves the Black Hawks after the Marvel Comics flying aces, they let rip a couple of times a week on a catholic selection of covers – 'Lawdy Miss Clawdy', 'Let The Good Times Roll', even Hank's 'You Win Again' – while Ronnie wowed the club with his lewd moves and double backflips.

Naturally, spearheading racial integration in this manner was not without its problems. 1957 was the year Eisenhower was forced to send paratroopers into Little Rock, Arkansas to prevent violent resistance to desegregation. 'Black most certainly wasn't beautiful in 1957,' says Hawkins. 'It was safe for mixed bands on army bases, but when we left the base we got into trouble.' The trouble wasn't helped by guitarist 'Pretty Boy' Leroy Moody, a lanky ladykiller whose appeal to white girls nearly got him lynched on several occasions. Ronnie still bears scars from the fights the Black Hawks incurred. Onstage it all seemed worth the aggravation, especially when sax man A. C. Reed joined the line-up. 'Ol' A. C. was pretty advanced, he could actually read and write music,' says Ronnie. 'I learned all I could from him.' In 1986, Hawkins spent several weeks dictating the Black Hawks story to Canadian film producer George Mendeluk. Had Michael Cimino's epic *Heaven's Gate* not been such a disaster, a movie based on those reminiscences might well have been Cimino's follow-up project.

Towards the end of 1957, Hawkins left the army and got a call from Rock'n'Roll Central: Sun Records, no less. Figuring that he might fit in well with the roster they'd built up since the departure of Elvis Presley, Sun wanted him to come to Memphis to audition. 'It was a long trip in them days, but I got all packed up and left that very day.' At the Union Avenue studio, Ronnie auditioned for Bill Justis and Jack Clement, cutting a bunch of demos that included 'Lawdy Miss Clawdy' and Hank Williams' 'Mansion On The Hill'. Sadly, the band Justis and 'Cowboy' Jack had lined up to play behind him fell apart, thanks to prima donna saxophonist Wee Willie Willis. However, guitarist Jimmy Ray 'Luke' Paulman, who'd gigged with Harold Jenkins, Roy Orbison, and Billy Lee Riley, was interested in pursuing something further with the newcomer. Ronnie couldn't face returning deal-less to Fayetteville, so he accompanied Paulman back to the guitarist's hometown, West Helena.

Work of any kind, let alone musical, was scarce in West Helena, but Hawkins managed to find a job working at the Rainbow Inn Motel for one Charlie Halbert. 'I had to get Jimmy Ray's guitar out of hock,' he grunts. 'Luke himself was too lazy to work.' Little did Ronnie know how much the motel's proprietor would help him in the weeks to come. It turned out that 'Uncle Charlie' was a keen supporter of local musicians – in Robbie Robertson's words 'a sort of patron of the rockabilly arts' – and had loaned money to most of them. Aside from giving Ronnie further work painting his *Delta Queen* ferry on the Mississippi, Halbert arranged free rehearsal time in the basement of the KFFA radio station, with the use of equipment belonging to the King Biscuit Boys. Recruiting Jimmy Ray's brother on stand-up bass and his cousin Willard 'Pop' Jones on piano, the Hawk finally had the makings of a band. All he needed now was a drummer.

Drummers being few and far between around West Helena, Ronnie and his fledgling Hawks began playing dates in the 'brass-knuckle bars' around eastern Arkansas without one. Ferrying their equipment about in a battered old Cadillac, Ronnie seemed to get by on sheer charisma. When Jimmy 'Lefty' Evans eventually took over on bass, the sound started to sizzle. Paulman was a fine rockabilly guitarist, and 'Pop' Jones, who hailed from the same Arkansas town as Harold Jenkins, was a crazed Jerry Lee Lewis disciple. 'I never heard anyone amplify a piano as loud as Pop,' says Hawkins. 'He was a big guy, with incredible thrust, and he could do all those Jerry Lee glissandos in his sleep.'

One night in West Helena's Delta Supper Club, 'Pop' noticed a kid in the audience he'd met before. Levon Helm was a skinny 16-year-old with a shock of blond hair who could already hold his own on most instruments. Towards the end of the band's set, Jones suggested to Ronnie that they let the kid grab a snare from backstage and sit in with them. Even on a single snare drum, Helm brought an extra snap and bite to the sound, leaning into the beat as he played. After the show was over, the band got talking to the wiry, grinning boy from Marvell.

'How backwoods he was!' laughs Ronnie Hawkins, looking back on those reckless, roustabout days. 'If it rained back then, Levon's house would be surrounded by water and he'd have to come in by boat. If it looked like it was gonna rain, we'd have to come get him before the weekend.' On the other hand, as Ronnie instinctively recognized, the Helm kid was no hillbilly bigot. 'He'd grown up with blacks, he had that music. He knew about Sonny Boy Williamson when Sonny Boy lived right there in Walnut Corners.' If anything, Levon was like a younger version of Hawkins himself, an Arkansas boy on fire with the madness of the medicine shows, a rockabilly renegade off the farm and raring to go. Like the many white musicians who would make up the studio bands in Memphis and Muscle Shoals, he was eschewing country for blues and R&B.

There was one minor obstacle to Levon's joining the band: he didn't actually possess a drum kit. 'I don't think he'd ever played a full kit in his life,' says Hawkins. Fortunately, there was always Uncle Charlie to turn to. 'You could pawn a guitar or a set of strings on a handshake with Charlie,' says Levon. 'He'd even pay for you to join the union!' With Halbert's help a makeshift kit was assembled, using a Biscuit Boys snare so old that Levon had to tighten its skin in an oven between sets. 'Right from the start, Levon played more drums with less licks than any drummer in the world,' remembers Ronnie. 'First job we ever played with him, he took a solo and it went over.' For Hawkins, as for the others, Levon was so darned musical he didn't even need to rehearse. 'Levon is a natural drummer, you'll never see him warming up for a gig,' says sometime Band producer John Simon, who once described Helm as a 'bayou folk drummer'. 'In *his* environment you just grew up with the music in you.'

While the Hawks waited for Levon to get out of high school, they honed their act to the point of perfection. 'I called us the Seldom Fed Quartet,' says Ronnie, who killed time in the arms of Odessa, 'a nice black gal in Helena who treated me so good I promised I'd write a song about her'. Ronnie wasn't the only one Odessa treated good, of course; when he was interviewed by *Rolling Stone* in August 1969, Hawkins was indiscreet enough to recall for the world the lady's verdict that 'Mr Levon has a strip of meat on him as big as a horse'.

One rainy morning in early 1958, Ronnie was in a drugstore back in Fayetteville when Harold Jenkins, already performing under the stage name Conway Twitty, sidled up to him. Jenkins told Ronnie he was just back from Canada, where there were rich pickings to be had from any American band playing Southern rock'n'roll music. 'He told me about this Canadian agent Harold Kudlets and said I should give him a call,' says Hawkins. 'The only thing I knew about Canada was pictures of the 1840 Gold Rush and dog-sleds from history books!' Like Ronnie, Jenkins had auditioned unsuccessfully for Sun with his band the Rockhousers, so they were in the same boat as far as the Memphis scene went. When Hawkins put the suggestion to the Seldom Fed Quartet, they were game for the adventure.

'You gotta watch them Canadians,' said Diamond Helm. 'They're just like Mexicans, they'll stick you fer a nickel.' Levon, who knew his dad had never been out of Phillips County in his life, took these words with a large pinch of salt. He saw that old doghouse bass tied to the top of the 1955 Chevvy Ronnie had borrowed, and promptly signed up for the ride.[2] Leaving behind Jimmy Evans, who'd fallen sick, the Hawks jumped aboard and headed north. Roy Orbison was standing outside the Sun studio on Union Avenue when the Chevvy came through Memphis. 'Ronnie leaned out the window and told me he was hitting the road,' Roy recalled. Orbison was later to regret recommending Young Jessie's 'Mary Lou' as a song Ronnie and the Hawks should cover. 'Before I knew it I was hearing him on the radio singing it,' he said. 'That hit before *I* ever did.'

Harold Kudlets was an agent based in Hamilton, Ontario who'd 'backed into the music business' in 1946 when he booked the Glen Miller Orchestra into a local roller rink. When he got a call in late 1957 asking whether he could book Twitty for some Canadian dates, he decided to take a risk with rock'n'roll. 'The scene up here was definitely more subdued than it was in America,' Kudlets says. 'It was all Dixieland and Jack Teagarden.' Much to his surprise, Twitty went over like hot cakes at every one of the venues he played: the Flamingo Lounge in Hamilton, the Brass Rail in London, the Brown Derby and Le Coq d'Or in Toronto. Starved for years of any live music with balls, the youth of Ontario gave the genuine American article an unequivocal thumbs-up.

It was while staying at Hamilton's Fisher Hotel, where he wrote his #1 hit 'It's Only Make Believe', that Twitty recommended Ronnie and the Hawks to Kudlets. Having seen Twitty's impact, Kudlets needed little persuading that another red-hot Arkansas rockabilly band – with the same tenuous Sun associations – could do well in Canada. He promptly booked the Hawks into Hamilton's Golden Rail Club for a week.

The trouble was, the Golden Rail had never seen anything like Ronnie Hawkins and the Hawks – or his Sun Records Quartet, as they shrewdly renamed themselves – when the Chevrolet pulled up outside the club one morning in the early spring of 1958. More to the point, they had never *heard* anything like them. 'When the bartenders overheard the band rehearsing for their opening night, they were so disgusted they all threatened to quit,' says Kudlets. 'The Golden Rail was not used to that kind of thing, they were used to duos, solo pianists, lounge bands. They figured they wouldn't be able to stand this crap for a whole week.' Hawkins himself figured the game was up when he overheard the club's owner telling Kudlets to 'get that bunch of redneck hillbillies outta here'. Without further ado he got on the phone and put out an SOS to a songwriter friend who lived locally, begging him to bring people down to the club to save their necks. Dallas Harms obliged him by organizing a posse of over sixty rock'n'roll fans, and the Hawks went over, says Kudlets, 'like gangbusters'. The crowds doubled every night right up to the weekend, and before they could make sense of anything the band had moved into a different league. At London's Brass Rail, they made $550 for a week's work; the following week it was $700 at the Le Coq d'Or in Toronto.

Ronnie Hawkins never looked back. 'I chiselled out a little circuit in Ontario,' he says. 'It was great not to have to travel so far, and we could stay in one place for a week or two weeks at a time. Finally, I got to where I stayed ten years in one club!' Happy to be a big fish in a small pond, Hawkins quickly adjusted to a cold northern world a universe away from the Mississippi delta and the Ozark mountains. Levon, too, was happy as a sandboy in his new environment. Diamond Helm wasn't so wrong when he described the Canadian climate as 'ten months of winter and two of bad sledding,' but the girls more than made up for it, and the Hawks had the pick of the crop. 'They were the kings of the entertainment business in Ontario,' says Harold Kudlets. 'They had the field all to themselves.'

It was the Le Coq d'Or – always *the* Le Coq d'Or – which proved to be the Hawks' most enduring home. Situated on the Yonge Street strip in the heart of downtown Toronto, where today it is an HMV record store, the Le Coq was the hippest club in town at a time when, as the classical pianist Glenn Gould wrote, 'you still had to drive to Buffalo for a *really* wild weekend.' Run by Gordon Josie, whose country combo Hank Gordon and the Melody Ramblers had at one time been the club's house band, the Le Coq was wising up to rock'n'roll and only too happy to pay Hawkins the $700 a week Harold Kudlets was demanding.

The investment quickly paid off. Scores of young rock'n'roll fans crowded out every Hawks show, spellbound by Ronnie's leering, wildcat persona. 'It was like the roaring twenties in Toronto,' says Hawkins. 'There were so many of those damn baby-boom kids coming along right after the war, and they wanted to get out and *do something*!' Beefed up by the return of 'Lefty' Evans, who was playing one of the new electric bass guitars built by Fender, the Hawks' sound was as raw and ribald as anything Toronto had ever witnessed. 'The music would just explode with dynamics,' one spruced-up teenager who caught these early shows would later recall. 'The solos would get really loud and Ronnie would come back in and sort of growl. He was like this Neanderthal animal lunging around with one arm hanging down. It was very fast, very violent, and very . . . primitive.'

The little hesitation at the end of that sentence is typical of Robbie Robertson, who was the spruced-up 14-year-old in question. What most struck Robertson was the kid behind the tiny drum kit, who didn't look any older than Robbie himself. 'You couldn't believe this kid was the drummer,' says Robbie, 'and yet he was terrific, terrific to look at and terrific to hear.' (Harold Kudlets recalls that Helm looked so young they had to put shades on him and hide him backstage between sets.) Watching Levon lay into his drums was the most liberating thing Robbie had ever seen, and when he learned that Helm had grown up within spitting distance of the Mississippi down in Arkansas it was as though every fantasy he had about the American South was somehow embodied right there in the flesh. 'He kind of represented the South to me,' says Robbie. 'And he didn't let down my fantasy of what this thing was.'

Yonge Street, named after the British Secretary of War in 1795, was Toronto's Broadway. Originally the trail by which settlers made their way north in the early nineteenth century, it was known as the world's longest street because it dissolved into a highway system running 1,200 miles through the magnificent bleakness of northern Ontario. The downtown blocks known as 'the Strip' were a tame version of 42nd Street, with hookers yelling at their johns in the street and neon lights flashing the attractions of striptease bars. The first live venue of any note, the Silver Rail, had opened in 1947, to be joined in rapid succession by the Upstairs, the Blue Note, the Famous Door, the Zanzibar, and the Bermuda. 'Civil libertarians find "the Strip" an irresistible cause,' Glenn Gould wrote sniffily in 1981; 'most of us simply find it an embarrassment.' At the time Gould was writing, the huge Eaton Centre was being built in hopes, as he noted, of 'revitalizing this rather seedy quarter'. When English writer Stephen Brook strolled down the Strip five years later, he saw little sign of such 'revitalization'. 'Hamburger hovels and other fast-food outlets fanned their revolting aromas into the street,' he wrote, 'while leather-jacketed youth ineffectually leered at passers-by in a politely unsavoury manner.' Things clearly hadn't changed much from the days when young Robbie Robertson and his fellow rebels-without-a-cause queued up outside the Le Coq d'Or.

For Levon, who admittedly had little experience of urban life, Toronto was 'the best place for live music outside of Memphis'.

'Canada couldn't have been better for me,' he has said. 'There were so many great characters along Yonge Street.' Pretty soon the greatest character of all was his own boss, an unofficial godfather holding court and trading on the strength of his Southern charm. 'Ronnie was always very clever,' says Gordon Josie, 'but he liked to portray the downhome country boy. He said he had to surround himself with talent to make himself look good. He sold himself on his personality, since he knew there wasn't enough quality in his voice to make it as a big recording star.' Perhaps this was why Hawkins was content to rule in a small kingdom: perhaps he knew in his heart that he would never have what a Presley or a Jerry Lee Lewis had, that demonic spark which set them apart from all the other rockabilly hoodlums.

It was at the Le Coq d'Or that Dan Bass, scouting for the small Toronto label Quality, first heard the Hawks. Impressed by the power of their live performance, and by the following they'd built up so rapidly, he proposed a recording session in a studio so primitive you could hear the car horns outside. In the late spring of 1958, Ronnie and the boys cut four tracks for Bass: Chuck Berry's 'Thirty Days', the Drifters' 'Ruby Baby', an insipid ballad called 'Love Me Like You Can', and a first stab at 'Hey Bo Diddley'. 'On "Bo Diddley",' says Ronnie, 'the tape stretched and it ended up sounding like the Chipmunks. They put it out anyway.' Indeed – released under the name the Ron Hawkins Quartet because Harold Kudlets advised against 'the Hawks' – 'Bo Diddley' became the top side of Quality X 8127, with 'Love Me Like You Can' on its flip.

Levon Helm had gotten off 'that stinking tractor' in no uncertain terms: life as an under-age Hawk was better than anything he could have imagined. 'I always aimed for the laughs,' he says. 'Everything from aggravatin' the desk clerk in a hotel to throwin' a cherry bomb in a car where someone was sleepin'.' As a drummer, he was improving with every show. He listened hard to the patterns and rolls Earl Palmer played on Little Richard's last big hits 'Keep A Knockin'' and 'Good Golly Miss Molly', and when Cannonball Adderley played the Blue Note, Levon was in the audience watching every move Adderley's drummer Louie Hayes made. 'I learned that the thing *not* to do is just get it down on the floor and stomp the hell out of it,' he told Max Weinberg. 'You're supposed to kind of dance the beat along.' 'Dancing the beat along': the expression summed up exactly what Levon Helm did with a drum kit.

1958 saw the Hawks cleaning up the Ontario circuit. Spending up to a month in each town, they played Toronto, Hamilton, London, Kitchener, Windsor, Oshawa, Kingston, even heading east over to Montreal and Quebec. 'The towns were a lot closer together than they were back home,' remembered Levon. 'It was less travelling time and more people.' By the following spring, Harold Kudlets – or *Colonel* Harold Kudlets, as Ronnie had renamed him – felt confident enough to book the band some American jobs. Hoping to attract some of the New York record companies, Kudlets called Joe Glazier's Associated Booking and got Ronnie a residency in Wildwood, a resort spot south of Atlantic City on the New Jersey seaboard. Within a couple of nights, purely on the strength of word-of-mouth, the Hawks were outselling the club's top pop attractions Frankie Laine and Teresa Brewer.

Of all the New York record companies at that time, the one which most attracted Hawkins was Atlantic, the rhythm and blues label started by two Turkish brothers at the end of the '40s. With the success of Bobby Darin, it looked as though Atlantic was starting to branch out from their black base. But it was Columbia, whose infamous A&R chief Mitch Miller detested rock'n'roll, which showed the most interest in the Hawks. Then, at the last minute, Harold Kudlets got word that Morris Levy of Roulette Records was sending a scout down to Wildwood.

'Moishe' Levy was a legend of the New York record industry. Born poor in the East Bronx, he owned several big clubs in midtown Manhattan and was the power behind Alan Freed's hugely successful shows at the Brooklyn Paramount. His real money came from publishing copyrights, 'pennies and nickels' that accumulated over the years into a vast fortune. In 1957, *Variety* had dubbed Levy the 'Octopus' of the music business, and it was hardly a secret that Levy had many silent partners in the underworld. Levy's first venture into vinyl was his acquisition of the clutch of labels – such as End, Gee, Gone, and Rama[3] – owned by compulsive gambler George Goldner. After Frankie Lymon and the Teenagers hit big on Gee in February 1956 with 'Why Do Fools Fall In Love?' (co-credited to Levy, naturally), Morris was firmly on the map as a label owner. A year later, he dipped into Southern waters for the first time with hits by Buddy Knox (the #1 'Party Doll') and Jimmy Bowen ('I'm Stickin' With You'). Issued back-to-back on the same single, they comprised the first release on Roulette, which would become Levy's flagship label for the ensuing decade. The label really hit the big time, though, when Jimmie Rodgers, a now-forgotten folk-pop singer from Washington state, had a #1 in August 1957 with 'Honeycomb', and promptly followed up with four more Top Ten smashes in a row.

Larry Bennett at Associated Booking urged Levy to give Ronnie Hawkins and the Hawks an audition, and Morris concurred. At 2 p.m. on 13 April 1959, Levy entered a Manhattan rehearsal room flanked by two very beefy bodyguards. He flipped. What he saw convinced him that he had something like the future of rock'n'roll, or at the very least an untamed redneck Dionysus, in his hands. Four hours later, the Hawks were recording the first of several sessions at Bell Studios, starting with their cheeky rewrite of Berry's 'Thirty Days'.

'Forty Days' was taken at a gallop, Levon's frantic drumming driving the other Hawks while Ronnie whooped and snarled across them like a rip-snorting Elvis from Hell. Hawkins may have arrived on the scene too late to make a proper mark as a rock'n'roll star, but 'Forty Days' was a splendid debut. Supervised by Roulette A&R man Joe Reisman, Ronnie and the Hawks cut most of their great early sides that month: 'Mary Lou', 'Odessa', 'Wild Little Willie', 'Ruby Baby', and 'One Of These Days'. 'Forty Days' almost made the Top 40 in May, but 'Mary Lou', the droll Young Jessie song recommended by Roy Orbison and later recorded by Steve Miller on his album *The Joker*, climbed all the way to #26. On the R&B chart, 'Mary Lou' was a Top 10 smash, fitting vindication of the fact that these Southern boys knew what they were doing with black music.

Morris Levy put all his guns behind Hawkins, taking him into his confidence and treating him like a son. 'I don't care what Morris was supposed to have done,' Ronnie says. 'He looked after me and he believed in me. I even lived with him in his million-dollar apartment on the Upper East Side. That was when showbiz was really rocking, with the pit orchestras and the chorus girls. He'd take us out to his clubs and invite all the chorus girls home for breakfast.' At the end of May, Ronnie and the Hawks were flown down to Miami Beach to support Count Basie, the biggest of several jazz acts on Roulette, at an all-night barbecue following the annual Disc Jockey's convention. The gig cost Levy $15,000, with 2,000 bottles of bourbon being provided and a large number of hookers being bussed in from Miami. 'BABES, BOOZE, AND BRIBES', cried the *Miami Herald* the next day, but Levy would survive the payola scandal that all but terminated the career of Alan Freed.

Morris' gangster cronies loved Hawkins: one of them gave him the affectionate soubriquet 'Country'. He was even by Levy's side when two hit men were dispatched to avenge the fatal stabbing in January of his brother Irving. Like so many others, Ronnie would have sworn that 'Moishe', with his endless donations to Jewish charities and random acts of generosity, was one of the good guys. In the words of Joe Smith, a Boston disc jockey who became a major player in the music industry, 'You never thought about the gangster thing with Moishe that much, it was always a joke . . .' Indeed, as Dorothy Wade and Justine Picardie wrote in their book *Music Man*, 'for thirty years there was simply no evidence that Levy was guilty of anything more than "knowing a lot of guys with funny names"'. By the end of the next decade, however, Hawkins would come to appreciate just what a ballbusting contract he had signed with Roulette. Wade and Picardie note that an emissary sent to collect royalties for him in the mid-'60s was offered two ways of leaving the office: through the front door, immediately, or through the window.[4]

New York was a crazy and scary enough place without having the mob involved in your career. 'I'd never seen people stepping over other bodies on sidewalks,' Ronnie recalls. 'I'd go down to 42nd Street and watch people go by. P. T. Barnum could have got his whole act there in five minutes.' Instinctively, Hawkins clung to some of his ornery Southern ways. 'I'll never forget the time I saw Ronnie in New York,' says Dale Hawkins, who was in town to play the famous Apollo Theater. 'Just a coupla country boys walking down Broadway, that was me and Ronnie. He would walk with one foot on the sidewalk and one off and say it was just like walking in the mountains. We had everybody looking at us like we was crazy, which we were at the time.'[5]

When 'Mary Lou' hit in September, Levy made sure Alan Freed gave them their fair share of appearances at the Brooklyn Paramount. Playing on bills with everyone from Bo Diddley to the Isley Brothers, the Hawks were rarely outclassed. 'The only person who could follow Ronnie Hawkins and the Hawks was Jackie Wilson,' says Robbie Robertson. 'Alan Freed *loved* Ronnie.' Nor was Freed the only one: Al Bruno, Dick Clark's musical director on *American Bandstand*, thought Hawkins the equal of both Jackie Wilson and James Brown. Levon still couldn't believe all this was happening. 'Every day for me was Sunday back in those days,' he smiles. 'I just liked travelling and playing. We seemed to be getting along all right. We'd even run in and out of New York every now and then and be on television. There was always something going on.'

The other Hawks were less sure, and more homesick. First to turn tail and head back to Arkansas was Jimmy Ray Paulman, who duly followed in the footsteps of James Burton and Roy Buchanan by becoming lead guitarist for Dale Hawkins. His replacement in the Hawks was Fred Carter Jr, another graduate of the *Louisiana Hayride* school of Telecaster-toting country-rock'n'roll guitarists that had spawned Burton and Buchanan. Buchanan himself came through Toronto in the late summer, and might have ended up as a Hawk if he hadn't been so fractious. 'For a while there,' says Ronnie, 'I was looking at having two lead guitars, using Roy alongside Fred.'

Another would-be Hawk guitarist was the greasy-looking Toronto delinquent who persisted in hanging around the band at the Le Coq d'Or. Robbie Robertson had turned fifteen that summer, and was more hopelessly smitten with Hawkins and Helm than ever. Happy to run around for them as a kind of unofficial 'go-fer' as long as he could be one of their crowd, he finally plucked up the courage to play Ronnie some of the songs he'd written. Two of them, 'Hey Boba Lou' and 'Someone Like You' – the first a Latin-tinged rocker, the second a limpid ballad in the style of Buddy Holly's 'Words Of Love' – impressed Hawkins enough for him to include them on his second Roulette album, cut in New York with Joe Reisman at the end of October.

But there was more to come. 'When I wrote those two songs,' says Robbie, 'Ronnie thought: "This guy can write, so maybe he can *hear* songs that would be good for me".' The next thing

Robbie knew, he was being flown to New York City as Ronnie's 'song consultant'. Among the legendary songwriters he met in Broadway's Brill Building that fall were Otis Blackwell, Titus Turner, Doc Pomus, Mort Shuman, Jerry Leiber, and Mike Stoller. These were men who'd written smash hits for *Elvis*, for chrissakes, and here was some jumped-up Canuck kid who didn't even shave passing judgement on their latest opuses. 'Did it strike them as odd, this fifteen-year-old kid?' laughs Robbie. 'God, probably! I sure tried to act like it wasn't! It was amazing that Ronnie put me in this position. Everyone around me was saying it was Dreamsville.'

The *Mr Dynamo* album, completed in early November and released in January 1960, marked Fred Carter's impressive recording debut as a Hawk. Alongside Robbie's songs (and versions of Carl Perkins' 'Honey Don't' and Fats Domino's 'Sick And Tired'), there were four tracks co-authored by Levon, by now virtually Ronnie's right-hand man. But the album wasn't a patch on the earlier *Ronnie Hawkins*, and fell very obviously into the limbo area between the demise of rockabilly and the dawn of teen-dream pop. Ronnie himself knew he'd missed his chance to become a major rock'n'roll star. 'All the Gene Vincents out there started looking a lot like Fabian,' he says. Morris Levy didn't agree, and was gutted when Hawkins decided to play safe and base himself up in Toronto. 'I wanted to bring Ronnie back to America,' he said. 'Elvis was in the army, Buddy Holly and Eddie Cochran were dead. There was a vacuum, and I knew there was only one guy who could fill it. Not Jerry Lee, not Roy Orbison, not any of the rockers of the time. Ronnie was the one. He moved better than Elvis, sang better than Elvis, looked better than Elvis. When Ronnie was up and bucking and singing, the girls used to scream and go crazy. But he went back to Canada right when he was on the verge of universal acclaim, and we never saw him again. Just vanished. I tried, but he wouldn't come home. Loved Canada, he said. It broke my heart.' Excessive claims, one might think: nobody will ever know if Hawkins made the right decision in pulling back from the limelight.

By the time *Mr Dynamo* was in the stores, 'Pop' Jones had followed Jimmy Ray Paulman home, having just undergone an operation to straighten out his crossed eyes. 'Straightening those eyes was the biggest mistake we ever made,' laughs Harold Kudlets. 'Pop started noticing girls!' Finding himself suddenly without a piano player for a show at London's Brass Rail in mid-December, Hawkins called Scott Cushnie, who at that very moment was staying at Dolly Robertson's house at Cabbagetown. Hitching to London in the freezing snow with Robbie, Cushnie told Ronnie that he wouldn't join without his buddy, an attempt at blackmail that quickly saw the pair headed back to Toronto.

Robbie never stopped trying to 'swindle' his way into the Hawks, even though his own band were now busy backing up acts like Johnny Rhythm and Billy Kent, the latter an Englishman billing himself as 'The Singing Milkman from Maidstone, Kent'! What Robbie really dreamed about was Fred Carter leaving the Hawks. He knew his chance was coming.

The Divide

We were out there for blood, and at that point everything in our lives changed.

Robbie Robertson

Ronnie Hawkins is lying on a sofa in his sprawling mansion on the edge of Ontario's Stoney Lake. He's just back from another run of club shows in and around Toronto and he's shattered. 'Ah cain't travel no more,' he moans to his wife Wanda. 'Jest standin' up there for two hours I'm wiped out.' Wanda points out that he might have more stamina if he cut down on all the eggs and hamburgers he devours, but he shrugs off the suggestion with a benign grunt. 'Mah system *requires* grease,' he says. The fact that a couple of heart attacks have finally put paid to the famous camel walks does not appear to perturb him.

The doorbell rings, and in walks one of the Hawk's oldest cronies, a man he claims was once the most notorious biker in all of Canada. Although Ronnie has never been in any serious trouble besides a couple of marijuana busts in the early '70s, he loves living on the fringes of danger and corruption. Most of all, he loves talking about the numerous scams he's got up his sleeve, the ones that are going to make him the fortune on which he'll retire. 'I got about 50,000 of them, one of 'em's gotta work,' he says. 'How to git your squarejohn farmers, them's your bread and butter.' But hold on a second, even these dastardly good ol' boys are not entirely devoid of environmental awareness. 'Stoney Lake's gittin' pretty fucked up,' muses Ronnie. 'Ah sure would like to do a benefit gig on my property. Lemme think now . . .'

To hang out with the Hawk is to realize what a sorry, shitty business rock'n'roll is and always has been, unless or until you're U2. Most of his talk is about money: wheeling and dealing, little-bitty property deals here and there. ('Ronnie's always cryin' broke,' the notorious biker whispers when the Hawk is out of the room.) Or it's about smut. 'That AIDS done stopped me jerkin' off,' he cackles. 'I don't know where mah left hand's been!'

Trying to imagine this great wreck of a man at the cutting edge of the Canadian music scene thirty years ago is not easy. Levon Helm has just asked him to guest on a cut for the new Band album called 'Never Too Old To Rock'n'Roll', but even Ronnie knows the song won't fool anybody. If he's never taken the soft Nashville option and 'gone country' – *'Somebody's* gotta stick to their guns!' he says defiantly – his greatest tragedy is that he's never been able to live up to the fearsome boasts of his greatest song, the mighty 'Who Do You Love'. And perhaps his second greatest tragedy is that he will chiefly be remembered for the ever-so-slightly fortuitous role he played in putting together the group which left him to become The Band. For all Bob Dylan's whimsical claims that 'he's my hero, the guru of rock'n'roll', it's what the Hawk *lost* that will ultimately put his name in the history books.

When Robbie Robertson finally got the call, he was ready, willing, and able. But the call came not from the Le Coq d'Or but from the Rockwood, a club Ronnie Hawkins had acquired down in Fayetteville, Arkansas. Nor was the call for a lead guitarist, since it was 'Lefty' Evans rather than Fred Carter Jr who was bailing out. Evans, it transpired, was yet another Southern boy who couldn't hack the Canadian climate. Playing with the Hawks around Arkansas in the early spring of 1960 merely served to remind him of what he missed when he was up in Ontario: mild winters, grits and biscuits, the smell of the leaves from the magnolia trees in the meadow . . .

Scott Cushnie, who'd eventually landed the Hawks job despite running up a huge hotel bill in Hawkins' name, managed to persuade Ronnie that Robbie was a proficient bass player, and urged him to bring the kid down to Fayetteville to fill Lefty's shoes. The Hawk wasn't convinced about Robbie's musicianship, but he was prepared to give him the benefit of the doubt. He knew Dolly Robertson, who sometimes came down to the Le Coq d'Or, and felt a semi-paternal responsibility for her son. Having heard the rumours about Robbie's late father, he figured the boy might be headed the same way if he wasn't pointed in another direction. Nor was he forgetting Robbie's potential as a songwriter.

The day Ronnie Hawkins told him to get on a train and head for Fayetteville was one Robbie Robertson was never to forget. 'I was born to do it, man,' he says. 'Born to pack my bag and be on my way down to the Mississippi river. I was music crazy, just a total fanatic, and I wanted to see all those places with those fantastic names. Chattanooga, Tennessee. Shreveport, Lu-zee-ana. Wow!' With Dolly's blessing, Robbie hocked his 1957 Fender Stratocaster and hit the road. The journey, unsurprisingly, was an almost religious experience. New York City was one thing, but this time he was headed for the source, the land his musical heroes had lived in and sung about. As he might have said with John Fogerty, who was fuelled by the same bayou fantasies a world away in northern California, 'rock'n'roll as I perceive it has always been of the South, and I never considered it being anywhere else'. The South was America's Other: when you came down from Canada, by train and Greyhound bus, it was as if you were descending into the country's unconscious. 'You come out of Missouri and rise up into the Ozarks, and it gets all twisty and turny,' recalled Robbie years later. 'It felt like this was a really dangerous ride, like the bus was going to flip over. I can remember thinking "Oh shit, don't tell me I'm going to die just when I'm about to reach the source . . ." '

But the bus made it into Fayetteville, where Ronnie and the Hawks were waiting to meet him. To Robbie's mortification, Ronnie and Levon howled with laughter on seeing the new recruit step off the bus. 'Robbie came down with his greasy hair and his strides, them pants where you had to take your socks off to get them on,' recalls the Hawk. 'He looked more Puerto Rican than Indian-Jewish.' 'I looked very city-ish, very punky,' admits Robbie. 'It was like I was some immigrant from Yugoslavia, wearing these winter clothes and a reversible coat.' This was the flipside of the cliché in which the country hayseed arrives in the big city: here was an urban rat suddenly washed up in the boondocks.

Once he'd got over his amusement, Hawkins lost no time in kitting Robbie out in more suitable Southern attire – and giving the kid a crash course in Southern *mores*. At the town's main furniture store, Robertson was introduced to a notorious local character named 'Killer' Tuck, choosing not to inquire too deeply as to the origins of the nickname. To Robbie, everything seemed magical: the smells, the street names, the expressions people used. If there was culture shock, it was a shock he had dreamed about for a long time. Besides, Levon quickly became his Dixie guide and mentor, a best friend-cum-big-brother. 'Levon saved my ass down there,' says Robbie. 'With Levon it was, here's the angle on this, the inside scoop . . . here's what you need to know.'

After a couple of days in Fayetteville, the Hawks and their new bass player hit the road to West Helena, coming down the mountains through Little Rock to the Mississippi delta country near Memphis. Slowly, the landscape became flatter and wetter, the air heavier. 'There'd been something refreshing in the Ozarks,' Robbie recalls, 'but you couldn't call this refreshing at all.'

53

Robertson had never seen cypress swamps or rice fields before, and he'd never seen black faces every which way he looked. There were eight black people to every white one round here, said Levon. Entering Phillips County, he felt as if he was on another planet.

West Helena was so far removed from anything Robbie had ever known that he could scarcely understand what people were saying. 'Even the white folks talked like blacks around here,' wrote Robert Palmer; 'a thick, rolling Afro-English that came out as heavy and sweet as molasses but could turn as acrid as turpentine if your accent or behaviour were strange.' At night you could hear voices and guitars coming through the humid air from the tar-paper shacks of sharecroppers. It made sense that Levon had grown up in this place, that he had as much black rhythm in him as he did bluegrass harmony. Down here, people almost seemed to walk in rhythm. 'This to me was the middle of the wagon of rock'n'roll,' says Robbie, 'and it was powerful medicine. The historic elements, the folklore, the lifestyle. Everything was more musically oriented, and I didn't know if it was coming from the people or just from the air.' At his first sight of the Mississippi river, running past Helena itself, Robbie's heart surged. 'If I'd grown up down there, I'd probably have said, "Well, this just looks a little muddy to me." But I thought, "My God! The mighty Mississippi! Right THERE!"'

While Fred Carter and Scott Cushnie broke Robbie in on the bass at Charlie Halbert's 'mansion on the hill', Ronnie and Levon flew to England to appear on the TV show *Boy Meets Girl*. 'I took Levon with me as mah musical director,' grins Hawkins. 'He couldn't read a newspaper, let alone music!' After performing the Hawks' 'Southern Love', backed by Joe Brown and the Bruvvers, the Arkansas boys returned to their hotel with some female company. 'I was in the adjoining suite when Levon had this pretty little angel in a double-pretzel hold,' says Ronnie. 'When we got home, he realized she'd given him crabs. Albino crabs they was, red-eyed little monsters eatin' his dick. Morris Levy put him with Frank Sinatra's doctor.'

The crabs zapped, Levon returned to West Helena, where he invited Robbie to come and stay with Diamond and Shuck. Robbie couldn't believe what he was seeing as they pulled up to the farmhouse, which was built on stilts to keep out the spring floods. If West Helena had been 'a town out of one of those great novels', a reservoir of rhythms and phrases and characters that would all surface in The Band's great songs years later, the Helm farm gave Robbie a taste of rural Southern community that was even more resonant. It wasn't just Levon's Uncle Pudge spooking him with stories of king snakes and water moccasins in the Big River. What really impressed Robbie was the way music – even rock'n'roll music – brought together relatives and family friends of all ages. 'You weren't just playing for a bunch of young people,' he later remembered. 'When you played, everybody would come, and they were able to appreciate the music as much as anyone else because they had no sophisticated background. They'd been hearing that music all their lives, it was no surprise to them at all, but it was really new to me. I was used to people their age scowling at it.'

Back in West Helena, Fred Carter Jr began making familiar noises: he wasn't sure he wanted to go back to Canada, he was thinking of heading over to Nashville, the usual bleatings. It was nothing definite, but Ronnie knew he had to start thinking ahead. His first thought was to find a new drummer in Toronto and switch Levon to guitar. 'Levon could play this nice Chuck Berry stuff,' says Scott Cushnie. 'He was a great rhythm player.' But good drummers were as thin on the ground in Canada as they were in West Helena, and it would be a great deal easier to find a new bassist. So he decided to start 'grooming' Robbie for the job instead. Fred, he thought, could take Robbie under his wing and pass on to him everything he knew about the *Louisiana Hayride* 'school' of guitar playing. The only trouble was that Robbie, in Carter's eyes, hadn't rightfully earned such tutelage. He was a Canadian whipper-snapper who hadn't paid his dues. Fred passed on a few tips, but no more than that. What he did do, much more importantly, was take Robbie up to Memphis, Mecca of a thousand schoolboy fantasies. 'I just thought, "I'm here, I made it",' says Robbie. 'I was a little kid realizing his dream at last.' Fred took him to the Sun studio, where Jerry Lee Lewis was cutting one of his less distinguished sides, and to the Beale Street store Home of the Blues, where Robbie blew all the money that Ronnie had advanced him on records by Howlin' Wolf, Muddy Waters, Little Walter, and Helena's own Sonny Boy Williamson.

It was the Howlin' Wolf albums *Howlin' Wolf* and *Moanin' In The Moonlight* that most seized Robertson's imagination. Listening to the Wolf's guitarists – first Willie Johnson on tracks like 'How Many More Years', then the great Hubert Sumlin on 'Wang Dang Doodle' – set him ablaze with blues fury. 'Robbie started with Diddley tunes and other rhythm things,' Scott Cushnie told Peter Goddard. 'He was great with rhythm and always went for the raunchiest, blackest riffs, like Hooker and Wolf.' In a spirit of zeal and obsession no less intense than that of the blues devotees over in drizzly England, he began practising the guitar for hours at a stretch, sometimes half the day. Like Eric Clapton and Peter Green, he felt that as a white kid from outside America he had twice as much to prove as any other blues guitarist.

Just as crucial an influence on Robbie's development as a guitarist was Roy Buchanan, the lone wolf from the Ozarks who'd taken over the lead-guitar slot in Dale Hawkins' band when James Burton left to join Ricky Nelson. It was Roy, son of a Pentecostal preacher and an ex-protégé of bandleader Johnny Otis, who'd played the blistering solo on Dale's 1957 Checker side 'My Babe'. 'Burton and Buchanan were mixing country music licks with this string-bending from blues,' says Robbie. 'It was a mishmash of white and black music that was basically happening in the South.' One of the principal tricks of the *Louisiana Hayride* school was to replace the two bottom strings of the Fender Telecaster with steel banjo strings, which made the guitar sound much bluesier. But where Burton and Fred Carter had restrained their raunchier impulses, Buchanan took rock'n'roll guitar playing to a savage extreme of emotional excitement, making his Telecaster 'cry' with searing harmonics.

Buchanan also happened to be one of the more mysterious and enigmatic characters Robbie had encountered. 'He was only three or four years older than me, but he'd been around quite a bit for his age,' Robbie remembers. 'He told me a lot of stories, *crazy* stories about how he was half-wolf and half-man. They were like the stories you heard about Robert Johnson selling his soul to the devil. We know these are just silly stories, but at the same time it's really fascinating American mythology. Like, we'd be sitting in a room playing together and I'd ask Buchanan how he'd figured out some lick and he'd say, "Well, I can't really tell you," clearly implying that he too had made some pact. Years later, it became obvious that he was playing a game with me.' With his goatee beard and transfixing eyes, Buchanan made an irresistible model for an impressionable young Canadian. 'When you've done what I've done,' Roy told Robbie, 'it means you're probably gonna die a violent death, and way before your time.' In the late summer of 1988, just weeks after Robbie had seen him play a show in Toronto, Buchanan was arrested for being drunk near his home in Reston, Virginia. That night he hanged himself in a police cell.[1]

Robbie's own playing gave rise to speculation that he'd entered into some diabolical pact. 'I was so obsessed that I was stealing everything in sight,' he laughs. 'From Fred Carter, Roy Buchanan, the Howlin' Wolf records. I came a long way in a short time, and people used to kid me, saying 'What is it with this guy, did he sell his soul?' Years later, I wrote 'Daniel And The Sacred Harp', and it was based on this whole mythology.' Crucially, he added a few of his own tricks to those he'd lifted from his peers: a unique type of vibrato developed in imitation of blues slide playing; a technique of maintaining rudimentary rhythm with a flatpick or fingerpick while playing lead; and the mandolin style of 'trilling' heard a decade later in the heartstopping solo on 'Unfaithful Servant' (*Rock Of Ages*). With Scott Cushnie's help, too, he'd started transposing some of Ray Charles' piano licks to the guitar, thus picking up 'that whole style of funky fourths and thirds that Ray Charles always played.' Even Robbie's harmonics were different from Buchanan's. 'I once asked Roy if he'd shown Robbie how to play harmonics,' says Jimmy Weider, Robbie's replacement in the 'reformed' Band of the mid-80s. 'He grinned and said he'd shown him the *wrong* way!' Robbie's harmonics, says Weider, were 'funkier, less squealing, and had a more cardboard tone': 'He muted the string with his right palm a lot, using only the tip of the pick, and that was a huge influence on Telecaster players in general.'

If Ronnie Hawkins was still toying with the idea of replacing Fred Carter with ol' werewolf Buchanan, Robbie was out to prove he was better than either of them. 'Ronnie wanted Roy,' he says, 'but he could also see that I was a comet at this point, that I had covered in two weeks what others cover in six months.' Hawkins claims cannily that his ploy all along had been to 'threaten Robbie into doing a good job'. If so, he'd succeeded. 'Roy had more tricks than I did,' admits Robbie, 'but I could play more excitingly at this point. I could scream like hundreds of birds.' By the time the two guitarists staged a 'showdown' in Grand Bend, Ontario that summer, it was clear that the shy street waif who'd run errands for the Hawks was a prodigious talent. 'He blew Roy right into next year,' says Ronnie.

Robbie Robertson has always maintained that his frenzied style of playing in those first years was purely the result of pressure. Whereas an Eric Clapton would take an Otis Rush or Buddy Guy lick and incorporate it meticulously into his own style, Robbie 'had to get to the point of invention *immediately*'. For him, the message of great players like Robert Johnson was: 'Become yourself as quick as you can'. Locked in his bedroom in Cabbagetown, he continued to hone his technique to a point of demented perfection. 'He practised day and night,' recalls Ronnie. 'He never had that guitar out of his hands hardly. And at his peak, when he was playing six or seven nights a week, he was the best guitar player I ever heard.'

Robbie at his peak paid his dues in the hottest Hawks line-up to date. Bringing in 'a real good Indian kid' called 'Rebel' Paine on bass, and replacing Scott Cushnie with Buffalo native Stan Szelest, Hawkins had himself a combo Torontians still recall with awe. Szelest, according to Ronnie, was 'probably the greatest pure rock'n'roll piano player alive': 'If he hadn't had a little drinking problem and a little personality problem, he'd have been Elvis' piano player.' The man was decidedly an oddball, a loner who stayed in the corner when he hung around at all. At the piano he cut the same possessed figure as Roy Buchanan did on the guitar, adopting curiously contorted postures as he played. 'Lon Chaney on helium,' Ronnie called him. Trading solos with Robbie, he electrified every club he played in.

Once again, it was the Le Coq d'Or which served as the Hawk's principal base. In Peter Goddard's words, Yonge Street on an early '60s Saturday night was 'a sort of Wild West movie with a James Brown soundtrack,' and the Hawks were at the centre of it. 'For the young musician there were no other options,' says David Clayton-Thomas, later the lead singer with Blood, Sweat and Tears. 'Yonge Street was the place you went and Ronnie's was the band you heard. They were gods to us, particularly Robbie.' Long before Eric Clapton ever hooked up with John Mayall's Bluesbreakers, Robbie was a guitar hero to a new breed of '60s rebel. 'I was the only one playing like this up north for a time,' he says, 'and I was absolutely a Soldier of Fortune on the guitar. My playing was like a premature ejaculation!' The word began to spread on 'this kid Ronnie's got on guitar', to the extent that when the Hawks were back in the South that fall he was greeted by the same kind of adulation. 'I remember in Tulsa, Oklahoma, there was this little Indian kid who just stood in the crowd and watched me, studying everything.' The kid turned out some years later to have been Jesse Ed Davis, L.A. sessionman extraordinaire. The only man who was less than enthused about Robbie was Alan Freed, then enmeshed in the payola scandal that was to ruin him. When the Hawks played the Brooklyn Paramount, Freed took one look at the boy and said: 'Ronnie, you wanna get me on a child labour rap, too?'

Hawkins seemed to have given up on his recording career, if the two albums released in 1960 were any indication of his goals. *The Folk Ballads Of Ronnie Hawkins* and *Ronnie Hawkins Sings Songs Of Hank Williams*, both recorded in Nashville without the Hawks, were desperate attempts by Roulette to find the Hawk a new market. Despite having the cream of Music City's session cats at his disposal, neither LP was remotely convincing. Whatever Morris Levy believed, Ronnie knew he was an entertainer before he was a 'recording artist'. That old rockabilly sound might not be making the charts any more, but it was sure as hell still pulling in the Saturday night crowds.

There was something else Hawkins was starting to recognize, in his customarily wily way. Being several years older than the members of his band, he could see the heart-throb 'po-ten-shul' of his young Hawks, particularly Levon and Robbie. Pretty soon he was going to have to depend on the sex appeal of his sidemen to pull in teenage girls, and hence teenage boys, to his shows. 'Under

Ronnie's tutelage,' admits Robbie, 'I became much better-looking overnight. I fell in love many times, one or two big times. Only the deal was *not* to fall in love, because if you were no longer on the prowl you weren't really doing your complete job.' Hawkins was delighted when Robbie became something of a dandy. 'I called Robbie "The Duke", 'cause when he got a little money he'd buy himself some suits,' Ronnie recalls. 'He played the uptown role, whereas Levon was always just Levon.'

The Hawk was less pleased when pretty boy Robbie began using his brain. With his bayou fantasies consolidated by his travels through Arkansas and its neighbouring states, the young guitarist started to explore the literature that had sustained – and in turn generated – so many Southern myths. As Greil Marcus wrote in *Mystery Train*, 'Robbie already had the beginnings of his idea that the land makes the music.' Suddenly, the guitar seemed to be taking a backseat to William Faulkner and Tennessee Williams, and Ronnie didn't care for it one bit. 'He didn't like this attitude and what it represented,' says Robbie. 'It had nothing to do with *the thing* – the music, the life. To him it was, first you're reading, God knows what you're going to be doing next. I remember one day, I really thought he'd fire me. I was reading this book *The Ways of Zen*, and he just wanted to puke!'

Like the little boy who ran away to join the circus – something all Ronnie's Hawks did in one way or another – Robertson was beginning to experience inevitable feelings of loss and regret, along with the exhilaration of freedom and rebellion. 'Life on the road got pretty hairy at times,' he admits, 'and it left a lot of frustration for normality in me. We'd play these schools in the South, and these kids would be going to their dances and everything and . . . it looked kind of silly, but they were my age, and I was missing this. I also felt an incredible vacuum in my life, just for school information you'd normally get, which is why I became a book junkie. Finally I was able to carry on a conversation that wasn't about Fats Domino.' Knocking on seventeen years of age, Robbie Robertson was starting to know the pain of the sacrifice that comes with life as a professional musician: when everyone else is partying, you're working; and when you're partying, everyone else is asleep.

There were other areas in which Robbie – together with Levon – was outgrowing his boss. Most crucially, Ronnie's young henchmen had begun to diverge from him in matters of musical direction. 'At first it was Ronnie and Levon and the bunch of us,' Robbie says. 'Then there was Ronnie, Levon, and me. Then it became more Levon and me. Eventually, the band started replacing guys. What it was, was that Levon and I were now on a mission – a mission to put together a bitch of a band. Ronnie was like the daddy of the group, the old guy, and we had to convince him.' What Robbie and Levon really wanted to do was to effect a radical change from rock'n'roll to rhythm and blues. Hornman Howard Johnson recalled The Band telling him about taking a boat trip to Cleveland to see a show. 'They were surprised to find themselves the only whites in the audience,' Johnson said. 'They came because they knew the music was good. They weren't slapping anyone on the back because black music was hip.' Ronnie loved black music as much as anyone, but he'd said it himself: 'I wanted to sound like Bobby "Blue" Band and it came out like Ernest Tubb.'

The first new recruit to the Hawks Mark 3 arrived in the spring of 1961. 17-year-old Ricky Danko had managed to get out of the tobacco fields around Simcoe, but only as far as the local butcher's shop. His dreams of country music superstardom in Nashville might have evaporated, but he was as determined as ever to make a living as a musician. With his brother Junior he continued to play little 'moondances' at venues like the Teenage Club, alternately screaming out Little Richard songs and crooning sweet ballads like Sam Cooke's 'You Send Me'.

Danko had seen Ronnie Hawkins and the Hawks the previous year and thrilled to their ferocious sound. When he learned that they were coming to play one of Pop Ivy's famous Sunday night shows in nearby Port Dover, his heart was set on landing the support slot for the date. What's more, he planned to include in his set most of the numbers he'd learned from the *Ronnie Hawkins* album. 'They ended up doing almost all the songs Ronnie was gonna do!' laughs Terry Danko. But Hawkins was magnanimous enough to overlook the Danko brothers' audacity, and he knew Ricky had something special: 'He looked good, had a white suit on, and he sung real different.'

That night, Danko joined the Hawks as a kind of apprentice rhythm guitarist. As his brother Terry observes, 'Ronnie had the ability to get rid of competition by hiring it,' a strategy Robbie summed up as 'picking out the best guy from the little support groups that opened for us and luring him into our web.' Usually this 'luring' took the form of Ronnie's most famous promise to prospective sidemen: 'Ah cain't pay you very much, but ah'll guarantee you more pussy than Frank Sinatra!' That sounded good to the ecstatic Rick, who drove back to his parents' house in a friend's Cadillac and announced: 'I've got to leave tonight! It's now or never!' Lost to rock'n'roll, he borrowed a coat and disappeared into the night.

At first, Levon and Robbie weren't so sure about the Danko kid, who drove them to distraction with his scratchy guitar riffs and raucous harmonies. On several occasions he was almost intimidated into quitting, but Hawkins always came to his rescue. 'Ronnie kinda smoothed him over a bit,' remembers Terry Danko, 'and he took him off guitar. He would always take you off your instrument and make you start on another. It definitely made you work a little harder. You'd work in the background, watching the original guitarist or bass player and learning from them.' The instrument Hawkins assigned to Danko was the bass, since 'Rebel'

Paine had been making restless signals and was in danger of jumping ship at any moment. Putting him on $50 a week with room and board while he practised, Ronnie felt confident that Rick would work out in time.

Another 'little support band' that attracted Hawkins' attention was Stratford's Rockin' Revols, 'as wild a bunch as you ever did see'. Playing on a bill with the Hawks at the Stratford Coliseum in the early summer of 1961, the Revols tore the house down when 17-year-old Richard Manuel opened their set with 'Georgia On My Mind', the song which had given Ray Charles a #1 hit the previous September. 'We were very nervous,' recalls Revols guitarist Garth Picot, 'but later we learned that *they* were a little nervous because of Richard.' It was hard to believe you were listening to a white kid when Manuel launched into the Hoagy Carmichael classic, so spine-tinglingly did he simulate every last pang of brother Ray's performance.

Knowing how difficult it was for Canadian bands to succeed in the country's minuscule pop market, Ronnie told the Rockin' Revols he wanted to help them. That summer, he offered them a short residency at his Rockwood Supper Club in Fayetteville, telling them he'd finance the trip and provide accommodation in the form of a mobile home he owned in the town. The Revols couldn't believe their luck, and set off on an adventure which proved more eventful than any of them could have foreseen. In Fayetteville, living on whiskey, they tore up Ronnie's trailer and wrecked one of his Cadillacs. Then, midway through their residency, they got a call asking them to come to Memphis to clear up an immigration problem. Setting off in the Hawk's other Cadillac after their final set that night, they finally pulled into Memphis at three o'clock in the morning.

'So we're driving around in the middle of the night in a 1959 white Cadillac,' remembered drummer Jimmy Winkler, 'and all of a sudden four cop cars surround us and cut us off, just like you see on TV. It's hands up on the roof and 'OK, boys, whose car is this? Where are you from? What are you doin' down here?', the whole works. And we're tellin' them the truth. Well, they find out that Ken Kalmusky and Garth Picot are only 16 years old, so they take them both off to Juvenile Detention. The rest of us are taken off to Memphis City Jail and thrown into different cells. One of us was with a guy being held on suspicion of murder!' Distinctly sobered up from the previous night, the Revols finally emerged from the jail at one o'clock the following afternoon.

Had the Hawks had their wits about them, they might have thought twice about trying to 'lure' Richard Manuel into the group. 'When I first met Richard, he was 17 and he was already a drunk,' says Robbie. Few people talked about 'the disease of alcoholism' in 1961, however: musicians drank a lot, and Richard 'Beak' Manuel drank a little more. It wasn't any big deal. The point, after all, was that he sang like nothing Canada had ever heard before, and played proficient piano into the bargain.

Hawkins has always claimed that the Rockin' Revols broke up just as Stan Szelest left the Hawks, but that is not the way the Revols themselves remember it. 'Beak got the call,' says Garth Picot, 'but he had a pact with his best buddy Jimmy Winkler that he wouldn't leave the band without him. They were gonna do it together, or not at all. So Richard refused Hawkins a number of times. In the end, he and Jimmy talked it out, and Jimmy said, "This is your chance, and you better take it." So he went, but he still felt badly about it.' After a tearful farewell, the Revols put Manuel on a plane at the tiny airport serving London. He was heading back to Arkansas.

It wasn't easy filling the void left by Stan Szelest, who'd gone back to Buffalo to study engineering at the University of New York. 'Richard wasn't a great piano player, but he had *the throat*,' says Ronnie. 'He could sing the black stuff way better'n I could.' Levon and Robbie were particularly taken with the possibilities that Manuel offered the Hawks, since 'the black stuff' was all they cared about now. 'Nearly all the singing influence is black,' Richard could still say in 1984. 'Primarily Ray Charles and Bobby Bland, but also bluesmen like Howlin' Wolf, Muddy Waters, Jimmy Reed.' Within weeks of joining the Hawks, Beak all but had his own spot in the show, an R&B/gospel eruption in the midst of Ronnie's old rock'n'roll chestnuts. Dominating it were the explosive recent hits of the great Bobby 'Blue' Bland: 'I Pity The Fool', 'Don't Cry No More', 'Turn On Your Love Light'.[2] As for his instrumental contribution, Manuel may not have been the piano player that Stan Szelest or Will 'Pop' Jones were, but the basic style of 'rhythm piano' he brought to the Hawks served them well. When Robbie (or, later, Garth Hudson) took solos, Richard was always there, underpinning them with a solid rhythmic groove.

With Beak on board, the Hawks soon acquired a reputation as a dissolute bunch of maniacs. 'I became a party star,' he later quipped. 'In fact, I became a party.' 'Crazy as a loon, he was,' says Ronnie. 'He just partied, chasin' the girls with Levon. He was drinking all along, but in those days he could hold it.' The girls were invariably in plentiful supply. 'Girls would drop their own boyfriends to go with you to a Hawks show,' remembers one fan. 'Then *you'd* get thrown out!' Hawkins himself held court at the Le Coq d'Or like some debauched Roman emperor, presiding over virtual orgies in the upstairs suite he used as an office-cum-apartment. 'Ahhhh, boy,' recalled Richard. 'Lots of "bring-out-the-wine-and-turn-up-the-music" parties, lots of people in one room just sweating . . . and the more parties Ronnie had, the more people would come to the club hoping to get invited upstairs.' To Robbie, the Hawk was a cheerleader, an almost Bacchic figure who pushed people to new depths of depravity. Others thought of the orgies as mini-circuses, with Ronnie directing them like a ringmaster. There was something of the Falstaff about him, too: as

Scott Cushnie put it, 'he embodied all of our wild youth on Yonge Street.'

Hawkins was certainly keeping his promise to Rick Danko. 'All Ricky had ever thought about up to that point was tobacco,' he says. 'He was going to marry this rich tobacco farmer's single daughter, and when I told him, Rick, she's fat, her ankles are this big around, he'd say "But she's gonna inherit the farm". Boy, was he green. So to show him there was another side of life, I sent him three of my girls.' If this makes the Hawk sound like some underworld tsar, it's because that wasn't so far from the truth. Harold Kudlets remembers the endless procession of nubile teen-agers through the Le Coq d'Or with anything but Ronnie's salacious glee. 'The boys were goggly-eyed,' he says. 'They'd never made so much money in their lives, and every night was party night. But after a while, the girls would turn up carrying babies, and the babies were the spitting image of Levon or Rick or Richard. To me, it was heartbreaking. You couldn't ask for a nicer bunch of guys, but they broke a lot of hearts.' One of the heartbroken girls was Cathy Smith, who later achieved a certain notoriety when she was charged with administering the heroin-and-cocaine 'snowball' that led to the death of comedian John Belushi. Starting her groupie career as Richard Manuel's 16-year-old girlfriend, she subsequently gave birth to a child known simply as 'the band baby', since its paternity was, to say the least, debatable. 'Cathy hung around the band all the time, and she got pregnant,' says Ronnie. 'She was terribly in love with Levon, but she ended up with Richard because he needed a lot of help and she liked mothering people. For a while there, she ended up being his nurse, just like she did with Belushi.'

Along with the wine and whiskey, of course, there were the inevitable drugs. Hawkins had never tried marijuana, and knew there were stiff penalties for possession in Canada. One afternoon he came into a dressing room at the Le Coq and found the Hawks sitting around listening to a Ray Charles album at 16 r.p.m. 'There was this real strange smell in the room, and they'd laid towels along the bottom of the door 'cause they didn't want me to know. From then on, I slapped fines on 'em for drugs, 'cause I said if *I* can catch you, you know damn well the Mounties'll catch you.' The little diet pills known as 'orange hearts' were more acceptable to Ronnie, especially on the long drives between shows. 'But I told 'em only the driver could take 'em, so they'd all fight like cats and dogs over who was gonna drive!' Mac Rebennack, then touring as a guitarist with Jerry ('Lights Out') Byrne, recalls seeing the Hawks' pink Cadillac tearing out of gas stations after shows in the South. 'That Levon was some Hot Rod-type driver!' he laughs.

Driving soon began to take up much of the Hawks' time. Once the band had cleaned up in the various 'bread-basket' towns in Canada, it would be time to hit that well-worn road down to Dixie, where, apart from the tried-and-tested circuit through Arkansas, Texas, and Oklahoma, there were now numerous fraternity and sorority dances to play in Alabama and Mississippi. Basing themselves at the Iris Motel in Fayetteville, or at Charlie Halbert's place in West Helena, they would spend a month at a time in the South. Along the way there were experiences that Levon, Robbie, Rick, and Richard would never forget. 'People think the chicken wire in *The Blues Brothers* was a joke, but it was mandatory in a lot of the places we played,' says Ronnie. 'We played some real tough joints, where the people didn't come to hear you, they came to mess with you. They'd flick cigarette butts, throw coins, steal your gear, and if you still kept on playing, well, they might just sit down and listen to you.'

One of the less salubrious venues the Hawks graced was the Skyliner Club, a joint in Dallas that came complete with bullet-riddled walls. 'It was a huge barn of a place with a vast dance floor,' recalls Robbie. 'On the first night we went down to

play, there were about three people in the place, a one-armed
go-go dancer and a couple of drunk waiters. And a fight broke
out!' So decrepit was the place that no one even bothered to lock
it up at night, forcing the band to encamp for the night to protect
their equipment. It later transpired that the Skyliner's proprietor
was none other than Lee Harvey Oswald's future assassin Jack
Ruby.

Equally unforgettable was the night Bo Diddley burst into
Robbie's hotel room singing 'I'm A Man' and telling the young
guitarist's terrified companion what he was going to do to her
body. Experiences like these formed Robbie Robertson's understanding of 'the road' for the next fifteen years. 'It was a rowdy
life, and fighting played a big part in it,' he says. 'Fighting and
woman-stealing. And you fall in, you just do what the custom is.
If they take off their shoes, you take off your shoes.' First in there
with the fists up, more often than not, was the Hawk himself. In
true redneck fashion, he seemed to be fearless, piling into scraps
with a heady abandon. Levon was usually just behind him, with
Rick and Richard bringing up the rear. Robbie himself usually
took a raincheck on these escapades. 'All the rest of us would be
down there fightin', kickin', clawin',' chuckles Ronnie, 'and
Robbie would be off somewhere wipin' his guitar strings!'

The truth is, Robbie was already tiring of the machismo of the
road: the drinking, the whoring, the brawling. He wanted to be
part of something more vital and meaningful than a travelling
alcoholic freakshow. 'I was feeling that I didn't want to get
involved in any more of these night charades,' he says. 'It was
like I was saying to the guys, "OK, just for you I'm going to take
this girl back to the hotel, so you'll think I'm one of the guys."
I was kind of growing away from the whole thing. What I
wanted was to up the ante.' Robbie knew there was enough
musical talent in the Hawks to push for something more special
than this relentless and occasionally life-threatening slog round the

roadhouses of Texas and Oklahoma. He knew Levon believed that too, Levon who 'had music coming out of his fingertips' and could holler a Muddy Waters song like a Mississippi field-hand. But Levon was lazy, or too apt to fall into good-ol'-boy mode with Ronnie.

In September 1961, Robbie made his recording debut when he travelled to New York with Ronnie and Levon for the first proper Hawks session in two years.[3] Assigned to supervise the recordings this time was black Roulette staffer Henry Glover, who'd not only produced Wynonie Harris and Little Willie John at King but written such classic songs as 'Annie Had A Baby' and 'Drown In My Own Tears'. Ronnie and Levon connected with Glover immediately, since he hailed originally from Hot Springs, Arkansas and lived for the same Southern 'soul food' they did. Bringing in sax legend King Curtis, along with backing singers Cissy Houston and the Warwicke sisters, Glover cut the Hawks on several songs that had a noticeably blacker tinge than anything on the *Mr Dynamo* album. The covers said it all: The Coasters' 'Searchin'', Jimmy Reed's 'You Know I Love You', Hank Ballard's 'Sexy Ways'. But the arrangements said even more, giving space as they did to biting Telecaster leads from Robbie. On his very first session, a loping blues called 'Come Love', the kid was already shooting from the hip, spitting out a sudden fill in the intro and providing a supremely confident solo after the second chorus. He was just as good on 'You Know I Love You', his stinging Steve Cropper-ish licks fusing with King Curtis' squalling tenor sax while Levon hammered out an ominous beat and the Warwickes wailed like banshees behind them. A measure of just how far he'd come was the fact that the bassist on these sessions was none other than his mentor Roy Buchanan, then briefly working as a New York sessionman.

It was at the tail end of this particular session that the Hawks went the whole way as blues contenders. When Ronnie knocked off for the night, Levon took over the vocal duties, growling out sassy renditions of Bobby Bland's 'Farther Up The Road' and Muddy Waters' 'She's Nineteen' that never saw the light until The Band emerged from Bob Dylan's shadow at the end of the decade. 'Nineteen years old,' Levon leered as Robbie crackled beside him, 'and she got ways just like a baby chile!' Rough as they were, the two tracks presaged the split – the great divide – that was now on the cards. Already the Hawks were tiring of Ronnie's slightly stilted showmanship, the cornball routines they all had to go through on stage. Roy Buchanan had said something which made them think. 'Ronnie was always teaching us that when you play you're having a great time,' says Robbie. 'It was "Now you move up here, now you move over there", show business. Then Roy came along and said, "Enough of this up-and-over bullshit, you can be just as effective just by pulling energy out of the music." And that shit started to embarrass me, all the leg kicks and stuff. I hated it.' They weren't to know it yet, but it was the dawn of the rock sensibility – the beginning of the end of 'Pop' as 'show-business'.

There was one final ingredient required before the Hawks could 'up the ante' convincingly. Garth Hudson was already a 'little legend' around the Ontario circuit, and the band had seen him play with both jazz bands and Paul London and the Capers. Back in Toronto that fall, they began paying serious attention to Garth, who in Robbie's words 'was just a kind of phenomenon to us'. 'There's no question in my mind that, at the time, Garth was far and away the most advanced musician in rock'n'roll,' says Robbie. 'He could just as easily have played with John Coltrane or the New York Symphony Orchestra as with us. He could listen to a song and tell us the chords as it went along. If we picked up something we wanted to cover, and we wanted to use the same harmony that they did in the horn section or the background, we could do it. It wasn't like a guessing game, like we'd miss something and use the excuse that we were doing our own thing. No. We wanted to understand exactly how the sound was made, what cluster of notes we were hearing, so that we could do it ourselves.' Garth, in turn, was hardly ignorant of the Hawks. 'Even when I worked back in Detroit,' he remembered, 'Ronnie was acclaimed as being the greatest rockabilly performer with the best band. Nobody could follow them, in terms of an organic unit that could get up there and shake it up.'

Robbie begged Hawkins to approach the keyboard boffin from London, and the Hawk gave in. There was a catch, however: feeling that he lacked the requisite 'pounding technique' of 'Pop' Jones and Stan Szelest, Hudson didn't actually want to join the band. Moreover, he had his ultra-middle-class family breathing down his neck, trying to get him out of the bars and into a more respectable – or more lucrative – musical career. 'Unfortunately,' he says dryly, 'in order to become acquainted with the idiom of rock'n'roll music it is necessary occasionally to play in a bar.' He was at least prepared to discuss the offer, and went up to Grand Bend on Lake Huron to talk to Robbie. Finally, a dual solution was reached. Garth would join the band as an organist, leaving Richard to supply 'rhythm piano', and he would be paid to give music lessons to the Hawks in order to satisfy his family. His first gig with the group was just before Christmas, 1961.

Temperamentally, Garth Hudson was – and always would be – an odd man out. 'At 24, he was exactly the same as at 50,' Robbie laughs. 'He talked reeeeeal slow, and he whored around a little less than everybody else. He was always inventing something, figuring something out.' But the extra dimension he brought to the group was astounding. The new piano/organ combination, common in the gospel field but virtually unheard-of in white rock'n'roll or even R&B, gave the Hawks' sound an unprecedented fullness. Nor was Garth simply padding out that sound: the beauty and zany intricacy of his playing was breath-taking. As Ralph J. Gleason later wrote, he was 'the first organ player since Fats Waller with a sense of humour.' 'Garth was different,' says Ronnie Hawkins. 'He heard all sorts of weird sounds in his head, and he played like the Phantom of the Opera. He wasn't a rock'n'roll person at all, but it fitted. Most organ players in those days would just play through everything, but Garth would lay back, hit licks, hit horn shots. He knew exactly what to put in and what to leave out.'

If Hawkins quickly saw the advantages in having a 'genius musician' on board who could work out arrangements in a matter of minutes, some of the others were a little nonplussed by Hudson. Garth certainly didn't accord with Levon's idea of a rock'n'roll musician: the guy never said anything, just grooved away at the back like some mad professor. Occasionally, too, Hudson touched nerves in his role as the band's 'teacher': Rick, for one, took mild umbrage at the suggestion that he practise his scales. Pretty soon, though, Levon and Rick came to see just what an asset the mad professor was. 'Once we had a musician of Garth's calibre in the band,' says Levon, 'we really started to sound like a professional act.'

The Hawks line-up that played behind Ronnie for the next two years was one of the hardest-working bands on any circuit in North America. Hawkins, knowing how stiff the competition was, drilled them like soldiers, and his troops were willing to go the distance. 'It was kinda like boot camp,' said Richard Manuel. 'We drove ourselves as near to perfection as we could get, to the point where we'd really thrill each other, where there was almost a clairvoyancy and we'd know before it happened if someone was gonna do something different.' Often the band would rehearse not just before shows but after them, starting at one o'clock in the morning and going on till four. People who thought of Ronnie strictly as a hard-drinking reveller were, as Peter Goddard noted, 'occasionally jolted into seeing another side of him which was altogether more professional.' It takes a year to get a unit good and tight,' Hawkins has said. 'At that time, when I was still dreaming of getting big, I knew we had to be better than anybody else.'

Robbie had finally got what he wanted: a band firmly committed to a vision of musical excellence, and one which was willing to dispense with the trappings of 'showbiz'. 'When I was about eighteen,' he told Tony Glover, 'we had been in it long enough, and we were playing hard, fast, and tight. We knew how wicked it was, because there was no dancing around.' When the Hawks played the Le Coq, or the nearby Concord Tavern, there were more kids squeezed into the place than ever. They came in their Cuban heels and Aquascutum raincoats, in their fedoras and mohair suits, and they came for the blood. (One of them was Neil Young, who'd moved to Toronto from Winnipeg with his band the Squires; Ronnie remembers him being ejected from the Le Coq because his hair was too long.) For John 'Ghetto' Gibbard, who took up the guitar after seeing the Hawks, Robbie was 'the Jimi Hendrix of his day'. But it wasn't just Robbie who was so electrifying. There was Garth doodling manically in the background, Richard rendering Sam Cooke's 'Bring It On Home To Me' like some possessed preacher. And there was a rhythm section so tight it could have stood comparison with the engine-houses at Chess or Atlantic. 'When you can work with someone the way Phil Upchurch and Al Duncan worked at Chess,' said Levon, 'then you really have the opportunity to listen to yourselves and critique each other.'

All of this can be heard in the session Ronnie and the Hawks cut in New York in the early spring of 1963. With Henry Glover at the controls once more, the band recorded the two sides that remain the best vinyl evidence of their heyday form. 'Bo Diddley' was the song Ronnie had been singing in various mutations for over a decade, but here it kicked and swaggered in a way that even Bo's original never did. With the Hawks yelping along behind him, Ronnie gave his strongest vocal performance in ages, and the band positively stormed through the track, Robbie slashing out a brutal rhythm pattern and Richard playing an infectious piano figure that Henry Glover had suggested. Even better was Diddley's 'Who Do You Love', the boast of a psychopathic outlaw delivered in Ronnie's most unsettling mock-Presley voice. The lyric was a catalogue of sinister details, all intercut with vicious stabs of guitar that expressed more than the Hawk ever could. It was no wonder that the protagonist's 'tombstone hand and graveyard mind' turned out to be the favourite jukebox selection of a Phoenix mass-murderer when 'Who Do You Love' was released on the flipside of 'Bo Diddley' in March.

The darkness and violence unleashed in 'Who Do You Love' may even have frightened the Hawks – Robbie later claimed it embodied the 'evilness' of life on the road – because when they returned to New York in May for another session it yielded only the inoffensive, Lee Dorsey-esque single 'High Blood Pressure', with its flipside 'There's A Screw Loose'. The latter was one of a spate of demented novelty instrumentals recorded in the early '60s, and notable principally for the gothic improvisations of Garth Hudson. A final session in the summer resulted in the raunchy 'Mojo Man', with a Coasters-style sax break from King Curtis, and in 'Arkansas', a delightfully droll vignette of Southern life written specially for Hawkins by Doc Pomus and Mort Shuman. Most of these tracks, along with those cut eighteen months earlier, eventually found their way on to *The Best Of Ronnie Hawkins* (1964), an odd title for a collection of brand new recordings. But by that time, Ronnie's Hawks had finally grown up and left home.

*

Everything had changed after the Hawk got hitched in March, 1962. It was Bill Avis, soon to become the Hawks' road manager, who'd brought the 21-year-old Wanda Nagurski down to the Concord Tavern the first time. A beautiful Ukrainian girl, Wanda couldn't resist Ronnie, even after seeing him at his lascivious worst. Hawkins, for his part, resisted marriage all the way to the altar, but in the end surprised even himself by wanting to settle down and raise a family on a piece of property he could call his own. His fondest dream was to return with his bride to the Arkansas farm on which he'd been making down payments for over two years.

The Hawks, in any case, were restless for change. When Levon and Robbie bought a Cadillac together, it seemed to symbolize their growing distance from Ronnie. Both of them knew that a kind of mutiny was on the cards. 'The band was becoming more and more knowledgeable about music,' says Robbie, 'and the old stuff we were doing was getting on our nerves. When the music got a little too far out for Ronnie's ear, and he couldn't tell when to come in singing, he'd tell us that nobody but Thelonious Monk could understand what we were playing.' Not even the temporary additions to the line-up of saxophonist Jerry Penfound and singer Bruce Bruno made enough difference to Ronnie's principal young gun-slingers. 'We still had this fire that we had to deal with,' says Robbie. 'Our curiosity factor was out of control.'

Two issues brought the increasingly tenuous relationship between the frontman and his band to a head. One was the increasing use of illegal substances, principally grass. 'Those boys were smoking more and more grass, and Ronnie was threatening them with fines,' recalls Wanda Hawkins. 'They didn't like that, but I'd always known Ronnie was an old-fashioned man.' The other was the female company they were keeping. If it was now acceptable for Ronnie himself to settle down with one good woman, it was still against the rules for any of the Hawks to get serious about girls. When Rick Danko committed the cardinal sin one evening of bringing a semi-steady girlfriend into the Concord Tavern, Hawkins fined him $50. For the Hawks, it was the last straw.

Harold Kudlets still remembers the morning, in the early summer of 1964, when he arrived at his office in Hamilton's Sheraton Hotel to find the Hawk-less Hawks waiting in the lobby. The band told him they were fed up with Ronnie, who was not only raking in most of the money from their labour but treating them like naughty schoolboys into the bargain. They said that they wanted to go out on their own, and would be content for the moment if the Colonel could get them what they'd been making with Hawkins. 'When they told me what they *had* been making, I was shocked,' says Kudlets, who still lives in Hamilton but is now retired from the music industry. 'I mean, Ronnie was the star of the show, but I guess he squeezed the lemon a little too dry.'⁴ Although a much less attractive proposition to clubowners without Ronnie, the band had no trouble finding work through Kudlets. The only question was one of nomenclature: what should they call themselves?

As the 'senior partner' in the band, Levon Helm quickly took over leadership of the Hawks, prompting them to bill themselves as either 'Levon and the Hawks' or 'The Levon Helm Sextet'. Despite being stuck behind his drum-kit, it was Levon who parleyed with their beer-drinking audiences, Levon who introduced the band and plugged forthcoming dates, even Levon who periodically took over the lead vocal spot from Richard. 'I had to do most of the driving,' says Levon. 'Other than that it was nothing serious. Different members would come forward in different situations, but it was always sort of a democratic group and we'd always share the money equally.' The material the Hawks played comprised many of the numbers they'd road-tested with Ronnie, filled out with newer covers (Barrett Strong's 'Money',

Ray Charles' 'You Don't Know Me') and long blues jams invariably dominated by Robbie and Garth.

If Ronnie was smarting from the blow of the Hawks' departure, he hid it well. 'They wanted to play heavier music than that barroom stuff,' he says, 'but I was interested in a job, I had to work. Whatever the clubowners said, that's what I had to do.' Such cold pragmatism seemed vindicated, moreover, when the radical white R&B brew of Levon and the Hawks turned out to be a little ahead of its time. Without Ronnie, they were just another Canadian band fighting to be taken seriously.

Part of the problem – and it was a problem that would always dog them to some degree – was that without a charismatic frontman they couldn't muster much of a 'show' for an audience. Canada, certainly, wasn't ready for that. Robbie Lane, whose Toronto band the Disciples became the mainstay of Ronnie's next line-up, recalls the shock of seeing the breakaway Hawks at the Friar's Tavern, a couple of blocks down Yonge Street from the Le Coq d'Or: 'We were playing with Ron at the Le Coq, but they were still our idols. So we went running down the street on our break to see them. They were still brilliant musicians, but something had happened to them – they were starting to play for themselves. Even though the place was packed, they were turning around onstage and looking at each other. And this was before they'd had any major record success, so they couldn't get away with it. They were completely ignoring the audience.' It was the first sign of the aloofness, a deliberate distance of the kind encouraged by Roy Buchanan, that would contribute so much to the 'mystique' of The Band in the years to come.

Along with the aloofness, however, came an even stronger unity within the band. Without the Hawk, they were no longer sidemen, but a gang sticking together through feast and famine. The circuits were the same – Ontario bars in the summer, greasy roadhouses in the mid-South through the spring and fall – but the competition was tougher. In the South, for example, there were now hundreds of white bands playing blues and R&B. Memphis, in particular, was a hotbed of honky soul, producing in the Mar-Keys the first white group ever to play the famous 'chitlin' circuit'. Performing, in Garth's words, for 'pimps, whores, rounders, and flakeouts', the Hawks were frequently reduced to stealing food from supermarkets, their outsize Canadian overcoats coming in very handy when the weather wasn't too hot. 'Some of it was great and some of it was scary and some of it was horrible,' says Robbie. 'But the point was, instead of throwing a knapsack over your back and getting out on the highway to learn about life, we were able to do it together. We were protected by one another, secured by one another.'

Behind the unity was the same granite conviction that the band was destined for greater things than eking out a living in bars. 'People never wanted to hear the songs you wrote,' says Robbie, 'but we always strongly objected to the hit parade. We thought of ourselves as beyond the things that were hits at the time.' Asked by Joshua Baer in 1982 when it had dawned on them that they were a cut above the numerous other bar-bands of the period, Robbie said simply: 'We all thought we were doing something special way back, early.' If they were, in Greil Marcus' phrase, 'a walking jukebox', it was a jukebox that did more than simply regurgitate the hits of the day. A decade later they would prove that when they recorded the superb 'oldies' collection *Moondog Matinee*, essentially a revisiting of their bar-room days as Levon and the Hawks. 'We just played joints, swinging and grooving the best we could,' says Levon. 'But after a while it got to be a drag. It was just reproduction, and when you do that you end up just being a house band. You either do that or you go home.'

Determined to break out of the circuit, the Hawks inked a one-off single deal with Toronto label Ware and hit the road to New York for a recording session. With Henry Glover at the helm, they cut two minor classics, 'Leave Me Alone' and 'Uh Uh Uh', both snarling blasts of street-punk energy that came from the same place as the Stones' 'Satisfaction' or the Animals' 'It's My Life'. 'Leave Me Alone' was especially powerful, with its thunderous beat and its early example of the vocal trading (here between Levon and Richard) that would become such a Band hallmark. The sound of the record was somewhere between American garage-band and Booker T. & the MGs, the Stax house band that had made such a big impression on the Hawks. 'We felt a real connection with those guys,' says Robbie. 'It seemed like there was no other band in the world who had fathomed that instead of doing a bunch of shit between the verses of a song, it was better to do nothing and just come back in. They kept things real tight, and that's what we tried to do.'

If the Hawks made a mistake with 'Leave Me Alone', it was in releasing it under the name The Canadian Squires. It was hard enough to attract attention *without* flaunting the fact that you were from Canada. With the exception of freak hits by the early Guess Who and Robbie's old band Little Caesar and the Consuls, Canadian bands were not taken seriously in either the States or Canada itself. As Ritchie Yorke noted in his 1971 history of Canadian rock *Axes, Chops, And Hot Licks*, the pro-American snobbery that had made life so easy for Ronnie Hawkins made it very tough for native talent. 'I guarantee a thousand different people – bookers, managers, radio station programmers, DJs – told me I could not push a Canadian group in Canada,' Ronnie told Yorke. 'They told me I was crazy to even think about it.'[5] Only after the launch of the Canadian trade magazine *RPM* in the very year 'Leave Me Alone' was released did things even begin to change. By the time Grealis' thorn-in-the-side tactics of championing Canadian bands had paid off with million-selling records by the Guess Who and others, the Hawks were long gone, together with Neil Young, Joni Mitchell, and half a dozen other future stars then hanging around the folk scene in the Yorkville section of Toronto.

'What's the use of growing your own tomatoes if you can buy them inexpensively at the nearest supermarket?' was how Ritchie Yorke posed the question on a hundred Canadian radio programmers' lips in the mid-'60s. This was the dilemma of the Hawks, who received almost no airplay with 'Leave Me Alone', or with the singles they cut – as Levon and the Hawks – for Atlantic subsidiary Atco in early 1965. After the raw blast of the first release, sides like 'The Stones I Throw', 'He Don't Love You', and 'Go Go, Liza Jane' sounded rather wet. 'Stones' at least had the merit of presaging the sound of The Band, with Garth's Lowrey organ swirling around Richard's vocal, but it was early days for Robbie as a songwriter, and his sub-folk rock lyric, set to an insipid if churchy melody, left a lot to be desired. As Greil Marcus noted, 'all of the reach, a bit of the sound, and none of the poetry of *Big Pink* and *The Band* are present on this song.' Richard was also in the vocal seat for the R&B-infused 'He Don't Love You', interjecting his best Ray Charles mannerisms at every turn, and for the first verse of the crudely recorded folk traditional 'Liza Jane'.

'Those records were just some people trying to sign us up,' says Robbie. 'We didn't know what was going on, and we didn't have any control over it. They just whipped us into the studio and we had to cut a few songs in an afternoon. We just kind of feebled our way through the thing and got the hell out of there. We didn't know that end of it at all, how you've got to be able to talk back a little if you're going to do what *you* want to do.' With the failure of the Atco singles, the despondent Hawks headed home once more to Toronto. 'We left with our tails dragging,' admits Rick.

Ronnie Hawkins recalls that each time the band returned to Yonge Street, they were a little more sloppily dressed. 'They looked like *Deliverance* crossed with the *The Grapes of Wrath*,' he laughs, 'and you couldn't play Canada like *that*.' Gordon Josie, the old Le Coq manager who was now booking at the Friar's Tavern, was certainly unprepared for the changes in Levon and the Hawks' dress sense, changes that would reach their full fruition on the cover of *Music From Big Pink*. He told them they had to wear tuxedos or else. This didn't especially bother the girls who still swarmed around the group at every show they played. One of them was Mary Martin, a Toronto native who'd worked in New York as a receptionist for Bob Dylan's manager Albert Grossman. 'We were truly groupies, though I hate to recognize that now,' she says of herself and her pal Toni Trow. 'But they were incredible, they talked to each other onstage musically. Then afterwards we'd talk to them about Bob Dylan and they'd talk to us about the Abyssinian Baptist Choir. They were heavily into gospel music.'

Another of the girls was Jane Kristiansen, a successful Danish-born model brought along to the Friar's by a girlfriend. 'I was famous and they weren't, but I was pretty naïve and sheltered,' she remembers. 'I met my girlfriend in the club, and all the young guys were suddenly around us. When everyone went up the street to see Muddy Waters, Richard was the only one sweet enough to notice I was having a problem getting into the place, because I was only nineteen.' Later that night, Jane watched Richard singing 'Georgia' and 'You Don't Know Me' at the Tavern. Later still, she became his wife.

When the band headed south with Bill Avis in the spring of '65, Jane went with them. She remembers accompanying the boys to a Junior Parker show in Oklahoma and realizing with a shock that they were the only white faces in the place. On the road, Richard told her stories of the band's days with Ronnie, ribald anecdotes which amused him but appalled her. A fragile, unworldly person, she was ill-equipped to deal with this strange new life she'd entered. In Arkansas, Levon's family were the soul of downhome hospitality, but she could barely understand a word they were saying.

While they were playing a brief residency at the old Delta Supper Club in West Helena, the Hawks ran into Levon's boyhood blues hero Sonny Boy Williamson, who'd surprised everyone by returning to Helena after his European tours with the Animals and the Yardbirds. According to blues scholar Paul Oliver, few people believed Williamson's story that he'd been touring European concert halls – and this despite the fact that the 70-year-old walked the streets of Helena in a bowler hat from London. 'Fact and fancy merged in the flow of his reminiscences real and imagined,' Oliver wrote by way of explanation, bringing to mind the hero of Peter Guralnick's novel *Nighthawk Blues*.[6]

'We were just hanging out and talking about music,' Robbie told Robert Palmer years later, 'and we thought about Sonny Boy. Somebody said "Maybe he's here," so we went down to the Holler – Levon knew where everything was – and found out that he was playing at the local café. And there he was, a big tall man in a bowler hat, white hair, white goatee, wearing this suit he'd had made in England that was grey on one side and black on the other. He looked kind of . . . fine.'

After Levon had introduced himself, Williamson and the Hawks adjourned to a friend's house to play some blues. A jug of corn liquor was produced, and a little kid beat time on a cardboard box. 'Sonny Boy was really beautiful,' says Robbie. 'He'd made some great records, but they were nowhere near as good as the music he could play in a little room.' Williamson, between blistering harmonica solos and regular slugs of hootch, told the Hawks they were a hell of a sight better than his English admirers, who were 'awful'. 'They want to play the blues so bad, and they play it so *bad*,' he groaned. 'They buy me everything, they treat me like God, but they can't play worth a shit.'

What the Hawks didn't know was that Sonny Boy Williamson had really come home to die, which was why he kept spitting blood into a tin can. That didn't stop him from discussing the

idea of hiring them as his backing band, but in his heart he knew
he'd never be going on the road again. Around sundown, the local
police came by and asked the band why they were hanging out in
'Niggertown'. Levon did his best local-good-ol'-boy act, explaining that his pa was the deputy sheriff in Marvell, but it only
seemed to make matters worse. 'You've got to realize,' Robbie
told Tony Glover, 'that this was near a place where they'd hung
thirteen blacks from a water tower only a few years before.' Before
they knew it, the Hawks were being run out of town. When Chris
Strachwitz of Arhoolie records visited Sonny Boy in early May, he
was working joints and doing the King Biscuit Show once again.
By the end of the month, his tuberculosis had killed him.

Blues brought the Hawks together not only with old legends
like Sonny Boy Williamson but with such like-minded white
hipsters as Mike Bloomfield and Paul Butterfield. The latter pair
took Levon and Robbie on a guided tour of the clubs on Chicago's
South Side, even inviting Robbie onstage to jam with them. A
more significant encounter was with John Hammond Jr, son of
the legendary Columbia Records A&R man who'd signed Billie
Holliday, Aretha Franklin, and Bob Dylan. Born in 1942, Hammond had tried to steer clear of his father, determined to make it
on his own. When Frank Driggs, compiler of the seminal Robert
Johnson albums *King Of The Delta Blues Singers Vols. 1 and 2*, gave
the kid a tape of ten Johnson songs, he sold him on acoustic
country blues for life. At art college, Hammond took up guitar
and harp, hanging out in Greenwich Village with his father's
protégé Dylan when that young Minnesotan strummer was still 'a
really open, friendly guy'.

Early shows took Hammond up to Toronto, where he began to
build a modest following amongst the folk music crowd. In 1964,
he was gigging at a club called the Purple Onion when fellow
American bluesman Stan Thomas dragged him over to the
Concord Tavern to see Levon and the Hawks. Hammond was

astonished by them. 'They were a *really* hot R&B band,' he remembers. 'Each of them had their own little showcase spots, doing Junior Parker and T-Bone Walker covers, and Robbie was the most intense, heavy-duty electric guitar player I have ever heard. I mean, this guy was so strong and hot. I don't care if you compare him to Buddy Guy or Otis Rush or whoever, that's irrelevant.' A firm friendship was struck up almost instantly, and Hammond would jam with the Hawks whenever he was in town. The New Yorker was a bit of an oddball by rock'n'roll standards, heavily into macrobiotic foods and yoga, but he knew his blues.

Hammond had already made two albums for Vanguard when he proposed that the Hawks back him on his third. As it happened, Harold Kudlets had just booked the band into various clubs on the east coast, including a long stint at Tony Mart's, a boardwalk joint on the New Jersey seaboard just south of Atlantic City. That meant the band would be available to record with Hammond in New York.

The band which played on *So Many Roads*, as the album came to be titled, was not quite the Hawks. Vanguard insisted that Hammond use bassist Jimmy Lewis, who'd played on his previous LP *Big City Blues*, and the piano player was none other than a visiting Mike Bloomfield, demoted from his primary instrument the guitar because of Robbie. Joining Robbie, Levon, and Garth in the line-up was Charlie Musselwhite, a skinny young harp wizard who'd come to New York with Bloomfield. 'I said we'd all get paid scale,' says Hammond, 'but Vanguard didn't like the look of my friends, so they only gave us one three-hour session.' If that is true, it only makes the session more remarkable, producing as it did some of Robbie's most exciting blues performances – what Greil Marcus described well as 'all rough edges, jagged bits of metal ripping through the spare rhythm section'. Marcus is cruel about Hammond's 'ludicrous blackface vocals', but compare the sub-Howlin' Wolf holler of the man's 'I Want You To Love Me' or 'Big Boss Man' to, say, the

Captain Beefheart of 'Sure'Nuff'n Yes, I Do' or the Tom Waits of '16 Shells From A Thirty-Ought Six' and you have to agree with him. Still, there were exciting moments: the brutal 'Gambling Blues', with John's and Robbie's guitars winding around Musselwhite's corruscating harp, and even a version of 'Who Do You Love,' which Hammond had started to include in his set.[7]

Hanging out with Hammond in New York was a welcome diversion from the grind of thrashing out covers in New Jersey. At Tony Mart's that summer, they would often have to start at noon, playing half-hour sets through the day till midnight. 'It was a place where two or three acts could play at any one time,' remembers Jane Manuel. 'Conway Twitty was there, and the Four Tops, all playing for college kids on vacation.' After running through 'Hi Heel Sneakers' or 'Walking The Dog' for the hundredth time, the Hawks felt not only jaded but severely homesick. 'We were separated from our families,' recalled Robbie, 'so we used to sit around in the sand and laugh about the funny things they did.'

Unbeknownst to the band, their Friar's Tavern friend Mary Martin had returned to New York to take up her old post with Albert Grossman. Anxious to do something for her compatriots, who she felt lacked the necessary vision to 'do something on their own', she was constantly dropping the band's name around her employers. When she managed to obtain a tape of unreleased Hawks tracks, she played it to Grossman's partner John Court, who sniffily told her that he and Albert were not interested in 'talent of that calibre'. Mary didn't give up, however. She took Danny Weiner, one of Grossman's scouts, down to Tony Mart's to see the band. She also knew that Bob Dylan was himself looking for an electric band to back him on live dates, and began mentioning the group to him whenever he came by the office. 'All I said to Dylan was just, "You *gotta* see these guys",' she says.

See these guys he did.

Part Two

HARVESTING
(1965–9)

1

A Scrounge Band for Judas

It used to go like that, and now it goes like this.
Bob Dylan introducing 'I Don't Believe You' in
Manchester, May 1966

Bob Dylan had *always* loved electric rock'n'roll. Far from emerging intact out of the American Midwest as some tousle-headed folk troubadour, he'd grown up as a leather-jacketed, motorcycling James Dean clone who worshipped the great rockabilly rebels. In January 1959 he saw Buddy Holly play a show in Duluth just days before the geeky Texan's plane-crash death, and in his High School yearbook that summer he wrote that his greatest ambition was 'to join the band of Little Richard'. He even got to play some Jerry Lee Lewis-style piano with a group of brothers who included the future Bobby Vee.

Throughout his protest-singing days in Greenwich Village, Dylan listened to rock'n'roll, later claiming that he'd merely taken advantage of the folk boom to further his career. 'I latched on when I got to New York,' he said, 'because I saw a huge audience was there. I knew I wasn't going to stay.' In November 1962, long before the Beatles hit America or 'folk-rock' dawned, he recorded the electric single 'Mixed-Up Confusion', a raucous little experiment that sounded like a garage-band take on Presley's vintage Sun sessions. The record sank without trace, but it didn't stop Dylan cutting four electric songs – subsequently not included on the album – for his *Freewheelin'* LP the following spring. 'If you put some background to this,' Dylan's Columbia producer Tom

Wilson had told Albert Grossman, 'you might have a white Ray Charles with a message.'

Dylan had already alienated the hardcore protest-song crowd with the revisionist 'subjectivity' of *Another Side Of Bob Dylan* when he began hearing electric sounds in his head again in the fall of 1964. With Tom Wilson's help, he put together a band for the sessions that resulted in *Bringing It All Back Home* in March 1965. The first taste of the revolution to come was the brilliant 'Subterranean Homesick Blues', which sounded like a beatnik Chuck Berry on speed. This was a new kind of surreal, sardonic street music that had very little to do with the Dylan of 'Masters Of War' or 'The Lonesome Death Of Hattie Carroll'.

On his last solo acoustic tour, the British jaunt documented in D. A. Pennebaker's film *Don't Look Back*, Dylan was already weary of the open-mouthed reverence accorded his more solemn classics of the protest 'genre'. He was sick of standing alone in the spotlight with his acoustic guitar, looking out over a sea of adoring students who treated him like the new Messiah. It was time to shrug off the mantle that had been draped over his slender shoulders. Significantly, two days after the tour ended, Dylan went into a London studio with John Mayall's Bluesbreakers – featuring Eric Clapton, no less – to cut some more electric music for the mind and body. Equally significantly, perhaps, the session degenerated into 'a drunken mess': Saint Bob was falling from grace and enjoying every moment of it.

It was up in Woodstock, the pretty Catskills town and artists' hideaway where he often stayed with Peter Yarrow of Peter, Paul and Mary, that Dylan wrote 'Like A Rolling Stone' that summer. The anthemic song, which eventually made #2 on the *Billboard* singles chart in August, confirmed what the electric side of *Bringing It All Back Home* had hinted: that Dylan had changed irrevocably. Yet it took one definitive event to fix that change in people's minds.

The Newport Festival in Rhode Island was America's premier folk music event, a gathering of the Great and the Good throughout the land to celebrate supposed musical purity and political righteousness. Albert Grossman had co-produced the first festival in 1959,[1] and Dylan himself had triumphed there in 1962. To inject some amplified rock'n'roll into this wholesome affair would be tantamount to sacrilege. 'To the folk community, rock and roll was greasers ... people who got drunk and boogied,' wrote Mike Bloomfield, who'd not only played on the just-released 'Rolling Stone' but was due to perform an electric set at Newport as part of the Butterfield Blues Band. 'Lightin' Hopkins had made electric records for twelve years, but he didn't bring his electric band from Texas. No sir, he came out at Newport like they'd just taken him out of the fields, like the tar baby.' To the Pete Seegers, noted Bloomfield, this was more romantic than rock'n'roll. 'They wanted Dylan to wear Iron Boy overalls and sing songs about Hattie Carroll.'

Dylan's decision not to comply with this romantic lie was somewhere between spontaneous and premeditated. The festival was already well under way on Saturday 24 July when he gathered together pianist Barry Goldberg and three members of the Butterfield band, telling them he wanted to recreate the sound of his imminent, virtually all-electric album *Highway 61 Revisited* onstage. Flying in organist Al Kooper to a join a line-up that comprised Bloomfield, Goldberg, Jerome Arnold (bass), and Sam Lay (drums), Dylan rehearsed the band all night at a mansion Albert Grossman had rented, plying them with copious amounts of the speed he was now using.

It did not augur well when, the next afternoon, Grossman got into a fight with Alan Lomax over the latter's patronizing introduction of the Butterfield band, another of his acts. Lomax, doyen of folk/blues collectors, did not approve of white boys playing blues, especially *electric* blues, and made that perfectly clear in the snide welcome he gave to the Chicago band at one of the festival's workshops. The rotund manager, known by some as 'The Bear' and by others as 'The Grey Cloud', was apoplectic with fury over the incident, attacking Lomax and knocking him to the ground. Meanwhile, Dylan stayed out of sight in his trailer, biding time in the company of his chief cronies Bobby Neuwirth and Victor Maimudes. At least a part of him knew the risk he was about to take.

The shock when Dylan took the stage, resplendent in skintight black jeans and an orange polka-dot shirt, was palpable. Immediately it was clear that he was no longer Newport's golden boy, that he was now a pop star in shades and mod Cuban heels. 'It was obvious that he was stoned,' recalled Liam Clancy of the Clancy Brothers. 'He was very Chaplinesque, bobbing around the stage.' As for the sound that came blaring out of the p.a. system when his band ripped into 'Maggie's Farm', few of the folk lovers in the audience had heard anything quite so deafening or abrasive. Watching the proceedings was Jonathan Taplin, a tall blond boy whom Grossman had appointed road manager for a jug band led by Harvard luminary Jim Kweskin. 'Bloomfield got real nervous,' Taplin recalled. 'Sammy and Jerome had never played anything but twelve-bar blues in their lives and were completely lost. Soon Mike was drowning out everybody, and it got so loud that the audience started to boo.' After a desultory version of 'Like A Rolling Stone' which made the song sound like a poor cousin to the Beatles' 'Twist And Shout', Dylan cued them into 'The Phantom Engineer' – the original title for 'It Takes A Lot To Laugh, It Takes A Train To Cry'. By the end of the number, which was again dominated by the frenzied, Robbie-esque soloing of Bloomfield, the booing was so loud that Dylan decided to terminate the set. 'Let's go, man, that's all,' he muttered as he unplugged his Strat.

Dylan managed to redeem himself by returning on his own to

play a mournful acoustic 'It's All Over Now, Baby Blue' – its pointed message missed by most of the audience – and a dutifully straightforward 'Mr Tambourine Man'. But the damage was done, and Dylan would never be the same in front of an audience again. 'There were a lot of old people there,' he later observed. 'Whole families had driven down from Vermont, lots of nurses and their parents and . . . well, they just came to hear some relaxing hoedowns, maybe an Indian polka or two. And just when everything's going alright, here I come on, and the whole place turns into a beer factory. There were a lot of people there who were very pleased I got booed.' Pete Seeger was outraged by Dylan's transgression, and a controversy raged in the folk magazine *Sing Out!* for months. 'Can there be no songs as violent as the age?' asked Jim Rooney in one of the few sympathetic pieces the magazine ran. 'Must a folk song always be of mountains, valleys, and love between my brother and sister all over this land?' Dylan gave his own answer in the caustic 'Positively Fourth Street'.

Far from discouraging Dylan in his new direction, the Newport 'scandal' served to convince him that he had made the right choice. There were others who supported him at this critical juncture in his journey. For Joe Boyd, production manager at Newport, Dylan's live electric debut was 'an object lesson in what was going on here – like, "You guys are all washed up".' In the new magazine *Crawdaddy!*, fellow singer Richard Fariña lauded 'the shift away from open-road-protest-flatpick style to more Nashville-Motown-Thameside, with the strong implication that some of us had been listening to AM radio.'[2] As *Crawdaddy!* founder Paul Williams wrote years later, pop was 'a huge new playground to create and communicate and be perverse in', and Dylan was damned if he was going to pull back from what the Beatles and the Stones had understood. He wasn't playing folk music any more, he wasn't even playing 'folk-rock'. He was playing urban rock'n'roll music, and he was a Pop Star. All he needed now was his own band.

Initially, Dylan had thought of borrowing the trio who backed L. A. singer Johnny Rivers and played on many West Coast sessions: drummer Mickey Jones, bassist Joe Osborn, and legendary guitarist James Burton. But Burton was contractually committed to the TV show *Shindig*, and Osborn didn't want to fly. Bob even attempted to lure Mike Bloomfield away from Paul Butterfield, but Bloomfield didn't want to play anything except blues. Finally, Mary Martin's persistence paid off. 'Mary was a rather persevering soul as she hurried around the office on her job,' Dylan later told *Rolling Stone* editor Jann Wenner. 'She knew all the bands and singers from Canada, and she kept pushing these guys the Hawks to me.'

Dylan's curiosity was further piqued when John Hammond Jr boasted to him about his pals the Hawks. One night he went down to see them jamming with Hammond in a Manhattan club. It was all he needed to know. If Robbie was a more restrained player than Mike Bloomfield, his riffs were more telling, and the band as a whole cooked in a way he'd never heard a white band do before. 'Dylan went to hear them with my son,' Hammond Sr recalled, 'and suddenly my son didn't have a band.'

Levon remembers how they were 'lolling in the sand' at Somers Point when the call came through from New York. It was a jubilant Mary Martin, asking if the Hawks would be interested in playing the Hollywood Bowl with Bob Dylan. 'Who else is on the bill?' Levon asked, knowing little about this Bob Dylan character besides the 'Rolling Stone' song he kept hearing on the radio. 'Nobody else,' Mary replied. His natural Southern scepticism alerted – together with a pig-headed refusal to be impressed by the damn *Hollywood Bowl* – Levon said he'd discuss it with 'the boys' and get back to her.

Robbie was rather more hip to Dylan than his cohorts. He knew the guy was big-time, and that this could be the break the Hawks needed. But he shared Levon's scepticism, and agreed that they shouldn't blow out the Tony Mart's gig just because a very tempting carrot was being dangled in front of their eyes. After lolling around in the sand a little longer, the band decided that Levon and Robbie should go into the city to meet with Dylan.

Grossman actually had two shows lined up for Dylan, the first being at the Forest Hills Tennis Stadium in Queen's on 28 August. Levon and Robbie weighed up their options as they drove the 150 miles north to New York City, and decided that the best compromise was to do the shows without the others, who could hold down the Tony Mart's gig on their own. That way they could check Dylan out and bring the others in if the situation felt good.

When they got into Manhattan, Dylan broke the ice by taking Robbie off to a midtown guitar shop. He asked Robbie to recommend some guitars, and they tried them out in the shop. Afterwards, they returned to Grossman's office on East 55th Street to play some songs. 'To be honest, *that* was the first time I ever really heard Bob Dylan,' says Robbie. 'Sitting on a couch playing with him singing in this room. And that was the first time I said to myself. "There's something to this, it kind of rambles a bit, but there is something about it." I was playing a little loud, and I could see from his attitude that he *wanted* it to be rough.'

Levon was less convinced. For him, Dylan's music had little or nothing to do with the R&B that the Hawks played. Nor could he make out where this pop-art, polka-dot Rimbaud was coming from – he sure wouldn't have lasted long around Marvell. 'Levon couldn't really buy into Dylan's thing,' says Jonathan Taplin, who saw several of the shows the Hawks were to play with Dylan. 'Even though he could see that it would be good money and big crowds, it wasn't his kind of music.' Robbie knew what Levon meant, of course: Dylan's background was poetry and hootenannies, whereas they were a blue-collar bar band steeped in blood, sweat, and beer. It was a clash of two worlds that just might not work out. The Byrds doing Bob's 'Mr Tambourine Man' was one thing, but the Hawks doing 'Like A Rolling Stone' would be something else again. 'In the very beginning, I didn't know if it was ever gonna be special,' admits Robbie. 'Just making electric folk music wasn't enough, it needed to be much more *violent* than that, and I didn't know whether he would ever get it. There was a lot of *strumming* going on in this music, and for us anyone who strummed just seemed to take the funkiness out of it. See, he didn't know anything about *music*. He was all folk songs, Big Bill Broonzy, and we were Jerry Lee Lewis.' Something, however, convinced Robbie that they would 'find the music' with Dylan.

With the line-up completed by Al Kooper and bassist Harvey Brooks, the band went into Carroll's Rehearsal Hall in Manhattan in the last week of August. Robbie found the rehearsals worryingly slapdash. 'We were playing so out of this world, we didn't even know what the fuck we were doing,' he told Larry Sloman. 'He didn't want to learn any of the songs, it was just play them.' Robbie said to Dylan, 'this isn't what it's about, going out there and fumbling through the tunes.' Levon, on the other hand, was almost converted by the looseness of Bob's approach. 'I liked walking on the edge,' he said. 'With Bob you could just about throw away the game plan for a show.' Both Brooks and Kooper responded well to Levon's musicianship. 'He breathes in his playing,' said Brooks. Kooper recalled in his book *Backstage Passes* that the drummer 'kept us together like an enormous iron metronome.'

If Dylan liked walking on the edge as much as Levon did, he didn't entirely dispense with a 'game plan' for Forest Hills, or for any of the performances that followed the Tennis Stadium show.

Knowing after Newport that there would have to be a measure of compromise in the electric assault on his audience, he and Albert decided that the show should be divided into two halves, the first featuring the solo acoustic Dylan, the second featuring the band.

Saturday 28 August was the last show of the summer at Forest Hills. A cold wind blew in from Long Island Sound and froze the 15,000 people who'd herded into the little stadium. It even chilled the band, who felt a 'frightening coldness' coming from the crowd after Dylan had finished an acoustic set that saw the debut of the epic 'Desolation Row'. 'I don't know what it'll be like out there,' Dylan told them during the intermission. 'It's gonna be *some* kind of carnival, and I want you all to know that upfront. So just go out there and keep playing no matter how weird it gets.' Robbie wasn't the only one to experience serious stage fright at that moment. 'We nearly shit our pants,' Harvey Brooks recalled later.

The band had barely kicked into 'Tombstone Blues', the second track from Dylan's imminent *Highway 61 Revisited* album, when the shouting commenced. For Al Kooper, they were booing 'because they'd read that they were supposed to', but that didn't make it any easier for Robbie or Levon, who'd never faced a crowd this big in their lives. 'Play folk music!' the crowd yelled. 'Where's Ringo?' snarled one wag. Finally, after 'Maggie's Farm', the charge of 'Traitor!' echoed around the stadium. Nor did it stop there: people hurled fruit at the stage, and Kooper was knocked off his seat. 'I thought we were gonna be playing some two-handed tag with a few people that night,' laughs Levon. 'They'd boo us, and I'd drop 'em a finger off the side for a little self-satisfaction.' Yet the more they shouted, the more defiant Dylan became; in the words of Harvey Brooks, 'he was playing as if he had a fucking army behind him'. After 'It Ain't Me, Babe', admittedly a song ill-suited to its new electric arrangement, a chant of 'Where's Dylan? We want Dylan!' started up. Instead of appeasing them, the object of their indignation instructed his band to keep playing the intro to 'Ballad Of A Thin Man' until the audience had shut up. The tactic worked. By the closing choruses of a furious 'Like A Rolling Stone', much of the crowd – which, after all, included as many new converts from the ranks of teenage Beatles fans as it did angry folkies – was singing along with the traitor.

Driving back into Manhattan after the show, Dylan was euphoric. At a party in Albert Grossman's huge Gramercy Park apartment, he hugged Brooks and Kooper, telling them it had been 'a real carnival and *fantastic*'. Many of the people around him agreed, however intimidating the experience had been. 'The sound was right, the programming intelligent, and the presentation persuasive', Dylan's biographer Robert Shelton was to write. What really excited Bob was the sure knowledge that he'd shaken off the trite label of 'folk rock'. 'Folk rock, I've never even said that word,' he told journalists Nora Ephron and Susan Edmiston that night, adding that his 'nose-thumbing' new music had 'a hard gutter sound' and 'a circussy atmosphere'.

Levon and Robbie were less convinced that they wanted to be part of the nose-thumbing circus, but they were committed to the Hollywood Bowl show on 3 September, and flew out to L. A. with Dylan two days before the performance. Ensconced at the Hollywood Sunset Hotel, the band quickly realized that people on the West Coast were less hostile to the changes Dylan had made than the East Coast folk establishment. Ewan MacColl might be huffing in *Sing Out!* that it was 'time for American folk revival writers . . . to decide whether their objective is to "improve" pop music or to extend the folk tradition', but in Hollywood people just wanted to join the party. Fêted by the hip and the glamorous, Dylan played a triumphant show before an audience that included not only the Byrds but a handful of famous movie stars, and even got to encore with 'Baby, Let Me Follow You Down'. Afterwards, agent Ben Shapiro threw a party for Dylan and 300 of Hollywood's coolest denizens. While Bob held court, Levon and Robbie wandered around in a culture-shocked daze. For a first trip to Tinseltown, this took some beating.

Dylan was so happy with his band that when they all got back to New York he was reluctant to break it up. 'After the two shows,' remembered Bill Avis, 'Dylan's people came back to me and wanted to know if Levon and Robbie were interested in joining Dylan's back-up band on a permanent basis. And of course it was "No way, you take Levon Helm and the Hawks as they are or you don't take 'em at all".' When Dylan weighed up Helm and Robertson against Brooks and Kooper, he realized there was no competition. Kooper, in any case, had had enough. The experiences of Newport and Forest Hills made the prospect of Dylan's fall tour singularly unappetizing.

With the Tony Mart's residency finally over, the Hawks had one last commitment to honour before they were free agents: a two-week stint at Toronto's Friar's Tavern. This meant that Dylan, whose American tour was due to begin in the last week of September, had to fly up to Toronto to rehearse with them. As *Variety* reported it:

> Secrecy was the word last week when folk composer and performer Bob Dylan jetted into Toronto by private plane to rehearse with Levon and the Hawks, a local rock'n'roll group that will back him on his current tour. In the city for two days, Dylan checked into a midtown motor hotel, said he wanted to work on his book *Tarantula*, and spent much of his evenings and early mornings at the Friar's Tavern, where the group was playing.

The trip, from 15 to 17 September, gave Dylan the chance not only to rehearse the Hawks for the electric half of his show – working with them after they'd finished their last set – but to get to know Rick, Richard, and Garth, whose background after all was not so different from his own in Hibbing, Minnesota. Dylan may have assumed the guise of a beatnik punk New Yorker, but under the wild bird's-nest of hair he sported he was as backwoods as they were.

Playing behind Dylan was a new and bizarre experience for a band used to ultra-tight discipline and arrangements. He could go anywhere with a song, and with no indication. For Robbie it meant that shows were 'like going out in your underwear', but the others were happy to 'wing it' with the unpredictable frontman. 'I'd watch where he was going all the time,' says Rick, 'and he really liked the fact that I could anticipate the way he broke metre.' If Levon found most of Dylan's songs pretentious and long-winded, he also found the guy's methods liberating. 'Bob's influence certainly helped us and encouraged us to play with a more personal style,' he concedes. 'By the time we came to do our own stuff, there were no longer any rules.' The biggest revelation for Dylan, of course, was Garth, whose extraordinary fills and interpolations bore out the trouble he had trying to play in the style of Al Kooper. 'The wonderful thing in working with Dylan was the imagery in his lyrics,' he said in 1983. 'I was allowed to play with these words. I didn't do it incessantly, I didn't try to catch the clouds or the moon or whatever it might be every time. But I would try and introduce some little thing at one point a third of the way through a song, which might have something to do with the words that were going by.' Nowhere was Hudson's playful genius more apparent than in the baroque squiggles he inserted into the great open spaces of 'Ballad Of A Thin Man'.

When *Time* called Dylan's linking up with Levon and the Hawks 'the most decisive moment in rock history', the magazine may have been overstating things a little, but it wasn't far off the mark. Before the electric tours of 1965 and 1966, 'rock' as such did not exist. There was pop, there was rock'n'roll, and there was R&B, but no one had ever fused all of these together with an avant-garde, anti-mainstream sensibility. Yes, Elvis had done something equally revolutionary a decade before, and yes, the Beatles and the Stones were on course for a similar fusion. But this was something different, and it took the collision of two fundamentally unlike phenomena for it to happen. More than just Big Bill meeting Jerry Lee, it was Rimbaud crashing into Ray Charles, the head connecting with the guts of rock'n'soul.

On the West Coast, Phil Spector pronounced that Dylan and the Hawks were 'absolutely it' – a breathtaking 'wall of sound' to rival his own – while Greil Marcus claims to this day that they were 'without exception or qualifications' the finest rock'n'roll band he has ever seen. 'If you weren't there, it will be difficult to convey the visual power of their performances', he wrote, adding that the sound the band produced was 'stately, extravagant, and visionary'. Dylan himself knew that 'something was happening', that this was the most potent and intoxicating sound imaginable within the framework of electric rock'n'roll. 'He had a feeling of a surge of power and volume,' says Robbie. 'He wasn't just flipping these songs out there, he was drilling them into the audience. He had never sensed that kind of power, so when it was there it just made him, you know, shoot for the heavens.'

Yet the booing went on. Almost everywhere Dylan went in the fall of '65, he encountered the same resistance to his changes, the same outrage at his 'selling out' to 'beat music'. 'Everyone was telling him to get rid of us,' recalled Robbie. 'They said we were sent from the devil and were putting this dirty, vulgar music on a pure folkloric tradition.' Bob had been their curly-haired bard, their conscience, and here he was jumping off their pedestal with gleeful contempt.

Things started well when Dylan and the Hawks flew down to Texas for two warm-up shows. There were few catcalls at Austin's

Municipal Auditorium on 23 September, or at Dallas' Southern Methodist University on the 25th. Both audiences may have included fans who knew the Hawks from their numerous slogs through the state; certainly it was gratifying to Levon to see that his fellow Southerners weren't so goddam uptight as those Yankee folk-fans up north. 'In the South it was just like any other Saturday night,' he said proudly, and praise from Levon Helm didn't come any higher than that.

Returning from Dallas, the Hawks accompanied Dylan up to Woodstock, New York, where he had bought a house that very summer. Here the band rehearsed for the tour proper, working on the *Highway 61* songs and older numbers like 'Maggie's Farm' and 'I Don't Believe You'. Also included in the repertoire were the brilliantly acid new single 'Positively Fourth Street', a *Highway 61* out-take called 'Can You Please Crawl Out Your Window?' – cut as a single with the Hawks three weeks later – and versions of Fats Domino's 'Please Don't Leave Me' and the Delmore Brothers' 'Blues Stay Away From Me'.

Like the Texas shows, the concert at New York's Carnegie Hall on Friday 1 October elicited little overt hostility. The acoustic half of the set was received rapturously, the electric half politely. As at Newport, 'Maggie's Farm' was the band's strident opening number, with 'I Don't Believe You' and the newly electrified 'Tambourine Man' following hot on its heels. 'Fourth Street' and 'Crawl Out Your Window' worked well together as a pair, though neither would be featured regularly over the ensuing weeks. Highlights were a majestically flowing 'Just Like Tom Thumb's Blues' and a withering 'Thin Man'.

Exploding behind Dylan in a dense swirl of guitar and keyboards, the Hawks threw themselves into his maelstrom of words. 'It was like thunder,' said Robbie, 'with this Elmer Gantry speaking, talking these words, singing them, preaching them. He was no longer doing his nasally folk thing, he was screaming his songs through the rafters.' Rick dipped and swayed as each line surged and unfurled, puffing out his cheeks before lending support to Dylan with one of those 'weird Danko harmonies'. Garth rocked back and forth behind his Lowrey organ, lost in the flights of his imagination. And when Robbie launched into a solo, it was generally with Dylan at his side, spurring him on, pushing him to new heights of ear-splitting intensity. 'Having this guy come in wailing between verses was like having a new toy to him,' Robbie said. (Dylan's oft-quoted remark that Robbie was 'the only mathematical guitar genius I've ever run into who does not offend my intestinal nervousness with his rearguard sound' was simply a more perverse way of saying the same thing.)

It wasn't hard to see that Dylan was enjoying himself. 'Playing is a kick for me now,' he said. 'It wasn't before, because I knew what I was doing then was just too empty. It was just dead ambassadors who would come and see me and clap and say "Oh, groovy, I would like to meet him and have a cocktail".' What Dylan was shooting for now was a music of frenzy and alienation, a sonic 'derangement of the senses' that would make it impossible for anyone ever to treat him – or patronize him – as a folk saviour again. The humanistic platitudes of the folk establishment no longer sufficed, as Dylan challenged everyone to see with the rhetorical question 'How does it feel to be on your own?' When dim-witted interviewers complained that they couldn't hear his 'message' through the proto-metal barrage of noise, he despaired. 'The word "message" strikes me as having a hernia-like sound,' he told Nat Hentoff in a famous *Playboy* interview. Onstage, the attitude was one of ice-cold disdain. Dylan dug the way Miles Davis turned his back on his audiences, adapting this terminal-cool stance to his own almost Brechtian purposes.

Not surprisingly, such antics went down less well when the tour took in the old folk strongholds on the East Coast. The October shows in cities like Worcester, Providence, Burlington, Boston, and Hartford were all disrupted by indignant shouts of 'Go back to England!' and 'Lose the band!' It seemed that the 'violence' Robbie had wanted to hear was doing more than merely alienating the old guard. 'There's something very dangerous, something very frightening about this whole thing now,' folkie Phil Ochs wrote somewhat histrionically in the October issue of *Broadside*. One of the things which particularly disturbed Ochs and others was Dylan's increasing use of drugs, primarily amphetamine. The boy seemed to be on a death trip.

For the Hawks, the 1965 tour became an increasingly vertiginous experience. 'The road' was one thing, but flying from city to city in a private Lockheed Lodestar plane, with a wired Dylan pushing himself to the brink of psychosis, was altogether more unreal. Frequently, Robbie would find himself sitting up with Bob till dawn in hotel rooms, running through endless half-formed songs.[3] Meanwhile the others – at least Richard, Rick, and Levon – indulged themselves in all the excesses at their disposal: weed, pills, girls. 'They were grabbin' hold of the old snuff-box a little too much,' says Ronnie Hawkins, who received occasional on-the-road reports from Rick and saw the band when the tour reached Toronto's Massey Hall on 14 November.

The Toronto show received what was by then a typical review of Dylan's 'sell out' show, with a gratuitous snub thrown in for the Hawks. 'Here,' wrote the *Star* reviewer, 'was a Bob Dylan who once was a purist, a folk-poet of America in direct line to Woody Guthrie, now electronically hooked up to a third-rate Yonge Street rock'n'roll band which he has now contracted. That great voice, a wonderfully clean poet's voice, is buried under the same Big Sound that draws all the Screamies to a Beatle orgy at Maple Leaf Gardens.' (A folk fan at Massey Hall had put it more succinctly: 'You're another Elvis!') Note the giveaway clues to the writer's puritanical hang-ups: 'purist', 'in direct line', 'clean', 'orgy'. The right thing was to be part of some unbroken bardic tradition. The wrong thing was noise, sex, teenagers – and being a Canadian rock'n'roll band. Yet the longer the 'scandal' persisted, the more Dylan refused to change or compromise. The Hawks kept waiting for the day when he'd walk into the dressing room and say 'Well, fellas, I guess this just isn't working out,' but it never came. 'He never caved in,' said Robbie, 'and that was truly amazing.'

The person who did 'cave in' was Levon, who by late November had had enough of the relentless flak. 'For the first time, I couldn't stick to my policy, which was to whistle while I worked,' he says. 'I just said to everybody I was going to take a pass when we finished the U.S. commitment, and that they should start to think of finding somebody to replace me.' Trusting that at some point the Hawks would reunite and 'do their own thing' again, but not ruling out the possibility that this was as far as he'd go with his Canadian pals, Levon bid farewell after a show at Washington D.C.'s Coliseum on 28 November and headed home to Arkansas. (Greil Marcus surmised in *Mystery Train* that Levon's departure was prompted by his pique at Dylan for stealing 'his' band. Levon denies this strongly, saying that the Hawks were *not* 'his' band.)

The others were hit hard by Levon's exit, but continued on with Dylan's speed-fuelled circus to L.A., where sessionman Bobby Gregg (who'd played on *Bringing It All Back Home* and *Highway 61 Revisited*) took over the drum stool. Gregg was a fast learner, and Dylan had time before the tour resumed to go into Hollywood's Sunset Sound studio to cut some of the songs he'd been writing along the way: the crackling 'I Wanna Be Your Lover', virtually a riposte to the Beatles' 'I Wanna Be Your Man'; a one-verse sketch for 'Temporary Like Achilles' called 'Medicine Sunday'; and best of all, 'Seems Like A Freeze-Out', an exquisite prototype for 'Visions Of Johanna'. Given the subsequent failure to produce any satisfying recorded material with the Hawks in 1966, this last must be taken as one of the group's finest moments with Dylan. Even without Levon at the centre of the sound, they managed to envelop Bob in a sound at once delicate and powerfully swirling, with Garth's organ meshing into Robbie's guitar and Richard's clavinet.

After a show in Seattle on 1 December, Dylan and band flew down to San Francisco in time to meet Beat veterans Allen Ginsberg, Lawrence Ferlinghetti, and Michael McClure for dinner in a Japanese restaurant. The Hawks weren't sure what to make of these characters, Rick and Richard sniggering behind their backs, Robbie feeling nervously inadequate in such elevated company. Jim Marshall's group photo of Dylan, Ginsberg, McClure, and Robertson taken the next day said it all: the three poets conferring together in a posey huddle, with Robbie standing awkwardly behind McClure, shut out of the conversation. In situations like these, the guitarist found himself suspended uneasily between the worlds of rock'n'roll and 'serious' art. As Dylan's new aide-de-camp – or at least a 'link man' between the star and his sidemen – Robbie was finally in a position to see the new possibilities Bob was opening up for rock'n'roll. Dylan may have exasperated him musically, but the guy was indisputably taking rock'n'roll into places it had never been before. And this was the proof, that these Beat poets were coming out of the woodwork to fête him in San Francisco.

It was Ginsberg and company who sat in on Dylan's 3 December press conference at KQED studios like merry pranksters and asked him absurd questions like: 'Can you ever envisage being hung like a thief?' This made it easier for Bob to tolerate the usual inane inquiries of local reporters. 'You can't tell where the booing's going to come up,' he said at one point. 'It comes up in the weirdest, strangest places, and when it comes it's quite a thing in itself. I figure there's a little "boo" in all of us.' Later, as a favour to Bill Graham, the tenacious San Francisco promoter who was present at the conference, Bob held up a poster for the very first Fillmore Auditorium show on 10 December.

The press conference was stage-managed by Ralph J. Gleason, the professorial *San Francisco Chronicle* columnist who two years later would co-found *Rolling Stone*. Gleason had started out as a jazz critic way back in the '30s, but he'd embraced rock'n'roll early on and was enthusiastically covering the nascent San Francisco scene springing up around Haight-Ashbury. Even this ageing hipster was not quite prepared for the changes he saw in Dylan. Indeed, he was disturbed by the power trip Dylan seemed to be on, surrounded as the singer was by an entourage of henchmen and hangers-on. Signifcantly, Dylan reminded him of Miles Davis, another 'little bantam rooster' who was 'seriously proud'. The only person Dylan really trusted, the veteran critic thought, was Robbie.

The two nights at Berkeley's Community Theater were triumphant. Once again Dylanites on the West Coast proved more receptive to change than their East Coast counterparts. 'Seems Like A Freeze-Out' was premiered during the acoustic half of the sets, while the electric half featured 'Long Distance Operator', a funky blues number that Richard Manuel would later make his own. If Lawrence Ferlinghetti, proprietor of the famous San Francisco bookstore City Lights, sat in the audience resenting the success of 'that stringy kid up there with his electric guitar', Allen Ginsberg and the 'fantastic assemblage' of Beats, Buddhists, and Hell's Angels he'd brought along were as spellbound by the show as the young Greil Marcus. Curiously, it wasn't Dylan who struck Marcus so much as Rick Danko. 'I couldn't take my eyes off him,' the writer later recalled. 'I'd come to see Dylan, but it was a real effort to pay attention. Rick's body translated his musical lines into physical motion.' For Marcus, the show marked the high point of Dylan's career, a 'riot of sounds and colours' whose 'rough, jerking marriage of blues and honky-tonk' was transformed by 'the fire and ice of Garth Hudson's organ and the young, brash clinches of Robbie Robertson's guitar.'

The West Coast tour continued on through December, taking in San Francisco, Long Beach, San Diego, San Jose, and finally L.A., where Dylan gave a terse audience to the press on the 16th. After shows in Pasadena and Santa Monica, Dylan and the Hawks – minus Bobby Gregg, who'd opted to resume the less stressful life of a sessionman – flew home. It was in New York that Christmas that Dylan embarked on a wild spree with his chief crony Bobby Neuwirth, then squiring Edie Sedgwick around town. (Edie had been the principal inspiration for 'Like A Rolling Stone'.) Hanging out on the fringes of the Warhol scene – and even sitting for a 'filmed portrait' at the Factory – was Bob's ultimate statement of 'impurity', and the whirl of fog, amphetamine, and pearls fuelled the narcotic reverie of the songs that would make up *Blonde On Blonde* the following year. As usual, the four Hawks fitted rather nervously into this scenario. 'Everywhere we went, things always seemed to have this edge to them,' said Robbie, unwittingly providing a neat description of the amphetamine lifestyle. Living it up at the Chelsea Hotel, they tagged along to parties but otherwise kept to themselves. Robbie educated himself further by reading screenplays he'd bought at the Gotham Book Mart. Years later, his days as a part-time film buff would pay off in his work with Martin Scorsese. They would also have a huge impact on his songwriting in general. 'I liked songs that I could see,' he says. 'Because of the constant touring, I couldn't get to the cinema very often, so my songs were like pining for the movies.'

It was Dylan's intention to cut tracks for his next album before setting off on tour again. On 21 January 1966, he went into New York's Columbia Studios with the Hawks and cut two versions of the haunting 'She's Your Lover Now' – one spine-chilling performance alone at the piano, the other a rougher, more cluttered take with the whole band. Paul Williams was later to write that 'if I had to choose a single performance to stand as evidence of Dylan's greatness as an artist, [the solo 'She's Your Lover Now'] would be the one' – nor was he the only Dylan fan mystified by the non-inclusion of the song on any official release. Recording resumed after the weekend on 24 and 25 January, when a modified line-up comprising Rick, Robbie, Al Kooper, and pianist Paul Griffin cut the majestic single 'One Of Us Must Know (Sooner Or Later)', together with a rough version of 'I'll Keep It With Mine'. (Bobby Gregg's successor on drums was one Sandy Konikoff, whom Robbie had lured away from his old boss Ronnie Hawkins.[4]) Why so little emerged from these sessions is not entirely clear. In one interview Dylan appeared to blame the Hawks for his failure to come up with sufficient material for an album, but Paul Williams later conjectured that 'the problem was not their musicianship but their familiarity,' adding that 'for the most part, Dylan has done his best studio work with musicians he didn't know very well'. The latter theory, of course, is all but borne out by the *Blonde On Blonde* sessions recorded a month later with a troupe of hardened Nashville sessionmen.

After rehearsing the live set with Konikoff in the last week of January, Dylan once again hit the road, commencing with three East Coast shows in early February. The acerbic 'Tell Me, Momma' had replaced 'Tombstone Blues' as the electric opener, while the sardonically bluesy 'Leopard-Skin Pill-Box Hat' – one of the songs that would make it on to *Blonde On Blonde* – was now rightly preferred to 'It Ain't Me Babe'. By 10 February, the Hawks were revisiting familiar terrain, playing the first of three Southern dates in Memphis. Thanks to a crucial basketball game in the city that night, the Ellis Auditorium Amphitheater was half-empty, but among the crowd were a bunch of wild Arkansas boys who'd driven up from West Helena and Little Rock to see their favourite roadhouse attraction serving as a 'scrounge band' for the scrawny kid Diamond Helm called 'Bob Dillard'. 'It was an unforgettable show,' wrote Robert Palmer, who'd played sax with bands along the same circuit the Hawks had trodden. 'After the unaccompanied first half, he brought out the band, who looked pretty much like they'd always looked, street casual, not too much hair, jeans, old sports jackets. The music was loud, intense, possessed – wrenching solos, Dylan miming throes of convulsion whenever Robbie tore into a solo, so that everyone but the Arkies thought *he* was soloing.'

After the 13 February show in Norfolk, Virginia, Dylan flew to Nashville for three deranged days and nights of recording with his country-music-schooled producer Bob Johnston. 'You've got more space in Nashville than you do in New York,' Dylan told an interviewer. 'If you want to make good records, people just sit around and wait all night till you're ready.' Conspicuous by their absence at the CBS Studios sessions were Rick Danko, Richard Manuel, and Garth Hudson. Robbie claims that 'to take everybody from where they were to Nashville was over-complicated', but it seems more likely that the inexplicable failure of 'Can You Please Crawl Out Your Window?' and 'One Of Us Must Know' on the singles charts had convinced Dylan he needed a different sound. Even Robbie took a backseat to guitarists Joe South and Wayne Moss, waiting till Dylan returned to the studio in early March to add his distinctively ratchety licks to the gritty blues of 'Obviously Five Believers'.

'*Blonde On Blonde* was very different from what we were doing out on the road,' says Robbie. 'This was a very controlled atmosphere. I remember the Nashville studio musicians playing a lot of card games. Dylan would finish a song, we'd cut the song, and they'd go back to their cards. They basically did their routine, and it sounded beautiful.' The paradox of Dylan fashioning this radical new rock style – his 'thin, wild mercury sound' – in the hokey capital of country music is perhaps less extraordinary when one takes into account the man's love of forcing incongruous elements together. In any case, musicians like the blind pianist

Hargus 'Pig' Robbins got to play the occasional country lick alongside the zanier arrangements of tracks like 'Rainy Day Women Nos. 12 & 35' and 'Most Likely You Go Your Way And I'll Go Mine'. The sessions are now legendary, of course. 'The amazing thing about cutting that album,' wrote Al Kooper, who was brought back in to supply his inimitable *Highway 61* Hammond sound, 'was the first-hand knowledge that we were making history.'

With five superb tracks in the can – including the epic 'Sad-Eyed Lady Of The Lowlands' – Dylan flew back to New York for further dates on the East Coast and two shows up in Canada. (Taking a break in Toronto, Dylan had his famous black and brown houndstooth suit made for him by a tailor friend of the dapper Robbie Robertson.) At a show on Long Island on 26 February, 'To Ramona' was replaced by '4th Time Around', Dylan's wry pastiche of Lennon's 'Norwegian Wood', while an old song called 'One Too Many Mornings' received the electric shock treatment in the second half. 'It was astonishing,' says Jonathan Taplin, who'd been recruited as a roadie for the show by Grossman aide Danny Weiner. 'They were louder than any band I'd ever heard, and Robbie was playing outrageous high-note blues guitar when nobody else was playing like that. The combination of what Bob was saying and the Hawks were playing was just amazing.'

In March, after a one-off date at Miami's Convention Hall, Dylan booked into Nashville's CBS Studios to finish recording *Blonde On Blonde*. Eight tracks were put down in two days and nights, including 'Obviously Five Believers', under the working title 'Black Dog Blues'. Dylan recovered from the madness of the final recording, 'Rainy Day Women', in time for shows in St Louis (11 March) and Lincoln, Nebraska, 'plumb dead centre in the Great Plains' (12 March), though not without the copious use of stimulants. Arriving in Denver at 3 a.m. on 13 March, he forced Robbie to stay awake in his hotel room while they worked on a concert version of 'Sad-Eyed Lady Of The Lowlands'. Robert Shelton, who was present, recalled the hapless guitarist looking 'grey with fatigue', while Dylan himself was later to admit that the pace of touring and recording was 'pretty straining'. 'I was more or less being pushed into it,' he said, with an obvious reference to his manager.

From Denver, Dylan went on to L.A., where he saw a rough cut of D. A. Pennebaker's film *Don't Look Back* and hung out with a frazzled Phil Spector, who'd just finished recording his misunderstood *magnum opus* 'River Deep, Mountain High'. It was Spector who'd seen the obvious parallels between the avalanche of noise Dylan and the Hawks were loosing on the world and his own Wagnerian 'wall of sound', making it easy for the two truculent geniuses to form a temporary mutual admiration society. Talking to Spector only further convinced Dylan that he'd chosen the right musical direction. With the Hawks backing him, his songs had become altogether more instinctive, even Bacchanalian. 'I used to have to go after a song, seek it out,' he told one journalist. 'Now, instead of going to *it*, I stay where I am and let everything disappear and the song rushes to me . . .' To Nat Hentoff, in the 'doctored' *Playboy* interview of March 1966, he said: 'The songs used to be about what I felt and saw, but nothing of my own rhythmic vomit ever entered into it. I used to think songs were supposed to be romantic, but vomit is not romantic.'

As the tour resumed once more in the Pacific north-west in late March, Dylan made it increasingly clear that he was bored by most of his solo acoustic numbers. He would sing the old folk chestnuts in a listless, disdainful voice, longing to plunge into the elemental, oceanic waves of 'Tom Thumb's Blues' or the transformed 'I Don't Believe You'. The only thing that ever aggravated him about the electric set was the sound problems that engineer Dick Alderson had to contend with along the way. 'Back then, the sound systems were not sophisticated like they are today,' he said in 1984. 'There were hardly any monitors at all, so you could never really hear yourself. I thought we did rather well for the equipment we had to use. We were in territory that nobody had ever been in. No one had played those kind of halls before.' Perhaps the worst sound yet was heard on the final show in March, at Vancouver's Pacific National Exhibition Agrodome.

The next leg of the tour, taking in Australia and Europe, promised to be at once the most exciting and the most gruelling of all. Dylan hadn't even finished mixing *Blonde On Blonde* in L.A. when he and the band were due to fly out to Honolulu for the first show. On 8 April, the *Honolulu Advertiser* reported that 'Bill Avis, manager of the Hawks, said the 24-year-old star of the show and the rest of the Hawks had skipped yesterday's flight from L.A. to do extra work on a long-playing album.' Avis, the genial Torontonian who'd road-managed the Hawks ever since their split from Ronnie, had flown on ahead to Hawaii with Dick Alderson.

When Dylan and the band did arrive, it was with yet another drummer in tow – this time Mickey Jones, the overweight Texan who'd played with Johnny Rivers and Trini Lopez. With his penchant for collecting Nazi regalia, Jones was decidedly eccentric, and his sensibility was as different from that of the Hawks as his ham-fisted drumming technique was from the rangy, loose-limbed style of Levon Helm. 'The Hawks' hearts were down in the swamps of Louisiana,' recalls D. A. Pennebaker. 'Mickey's wasn't, I'll tell you that. He'd gotten out of Texas as fast as he could, and he wanted the bright lights.' Australian journalist Edgar Waters was to write that Jones 'looked like an out-of-condition pug' and made Ringo Starr sound as subtle as 'an Indian tabla player'.

A long flight to Sydney followed the show at Honolulu's International Centre Arena on Saturday, 19 April. Among the journalists waiting for Dylan was the perceptive Craig McGregor, who'd already formed some impressions of the new Dylan from the *Playboy* interview. In the piece, Nat Hentoff had observed that Bob was now usually 'seen from afar at the epicentre of a protective coterie of tousle-topped young men dressed like him, and lissome, straight-haired young ladies who also seem to be dressed like him.' This image of Dylan as a power figure, surrounded by satellites like his bullying manager Albert Grossman, had already troubled Ralph J. Gleason in San Francisco, and it seemed to have more than a little basis in reality when McGregor was eventually summoned to Bob's hotel suite after the second Sydney Stadium show for an exclusive preview of *Blonde On Blonde*. To McGregor, the Hawks – like Grossman, Bobby Neuwirth, and Victor Maimudes – were indulging and mollycoddling Dylan as though he was a King Baby with absolute power over their lives. As Bob began, in his usual sadistic way, to play unnerving mind games with the young journalist, the others joined him in the ritual humiliation. 'Dylan's attitude to the press,' wrote his much-maligned biographer Bob Spitz, 'reflected the spirit of the whole Dylan camp, instilled originally by that great humanitarian Albert Grossman – namely, that all journalists were peckerheads.' When McGregor dared to say that 'Just Like A Woman' sounded 'sentimental', the 'pudgy bland façade' of Grossman's face betrayed 'real anger'. 'Bob has never written anything sentimental in his life!' the irate, pig-tailed manager shouted.

Dylan's cruelty was all part of his act in those heady days. Spinning out of control in a whirlwind of weed and speed, he was oblivious to innocent bystanders. Ironically, he was even turning the cruelty he'd learned from Albert Grossman on Grossman himself, who had come to represent a stifling father-figure to him. Meekly, obediently, the Hawks followed behind their leader, laughing at the right moments, hoovering up the surplus powders, hiding behind their Ray-Bans. Old friends back in America had already begun to suspect that the band – however anonymous they seemed behind Dylan – were getting sucked into the whole

Grossman/Dylan 'trip', or what Rick Danko aptly described as an atmosphere of 'professional paranoia'. John Hammond Jr, whose father had incurred Albert's resentment during Dylan's early years on the Columbia label, remembers his shock at realizing that Grossman had poisoned them against him. 'Albert didn't like me at all,' he says, 'and as soon as Robbie and the others got with Dylan, I fell out of touch with them. They had been the coolest guys – wide-open, full-throttle – but all of a sudden I was just a complete idiot to them. I really felt the loss.'

One Australian who was admitted into the Dylan entourage without having to suffer undue mental torture was poet Adrian Rawlins, Melbourne's very own Allen Ginsberg. Rawlins took Dylan and Robbie on a guided tour of Fitzroy, the city's slum area, then hung out with them till the tour moved on to Adelaide on 22 April. At Melbourne's Festival Hall, Dylan was so stoned he almost fell off the stage, which didn't prevent him from skinning up several more times with Rawlins and playing him a very slurred version of 'Sad-Eyed Lady Of The Lowlands'.

When they were less incapacitated by drugs, Bob and the band were considerably more productive. After the final Australian show at Perth's Capitol Theatre, marred by the booing that still accompanied the tour wherever it went, they had a couple of days to kill before flying to Europe. Rosemary Gerrette, a 20-year-old actress whom Dylan had picked up, later remembered an informal jam session in a hotel suite. 'It was amazing to see him work on a song,' she told Dylan's first biographer Anthony Scaduto. 'He would have the poetry of it worked out in his head, and he would say to Robbie: 'Listen, Robbie, just imagine this cat who is very Elizabethan, with garters and a long shepherd's horn, and he's coming over the hill in the morning with the sun rising behind him. That's the sound I want.' And then they would begin to play, and out of this would come some kind of rhythm, and then the music would take shape. They did this for hours and hours, Dylan setting a scene and everybody playing music to create the sound of that scene.' As the sound took shape, Garth noted down the chord changes, recording on paper what he would later record on tape in the basement of Big Pink.

The circus finally hit Europe on Wednesday, 27 April, touching down at 4 p.m. in Stockholm. The following night, despite extreme jet-lag all round, Dylan held court in his room at the Flamingo Hotel till seven in the morning. 'The last person to leave his room sees him take out his typewriter,' noted one of the reporters who'd been allowed to tag along after that afternoon's press conference. Dylan's mind was now full of plans for the film he wanted to make of the tour's European leg. That night, after a show at Stockholm's Konserthuset, D. A. Pennebaker arrived from New York with his assistants Howard and Jones Alk. 'Dylan had come to me and said, "I've helped you make *your* film. Now I want you to help me make *mine*," Pennebaker remembers. 'He said he wanted me to be the cameraman, but that it wasn't going to be *Don't Look Back 2*.'

The arrival of Pennebaker and the cameras signalled yet another change of gear on the tour. With the 'performance' now taking place offstage as well as on it, Dylan really went into overdrive. It quickly became clear to the director of the excellent *Don't Look Back* that the singer was scaling new heights of megalomania, and that he wanted to be taken seriously as a film-maker. 'I think he felt he was going to be Ingmar Bergman or something,' says Pennebaker. 'I didn't wanna get into a film contest with anyone, but there were problems I hadn't foreseen, because there was no one in charge. Dylan was supposed to be in charge, and in a way he was, but he was really *wild*, as wild as I've ever seen him. There were all-night sagas of traipsing around shooting bits of this and that, and none of it made any sense in *my* head. The assumption was that Dylan would somehow pull it off, but I could see it going a little bit like his book. He was out of his head and he was vamping, and I didn't know *what* to tell him. I mean, in a way, a bad film by Dylan might be the most fantastic film you ever saw. There was always that chance.'

One of the few amusing scenes in *Eat The Document*, the risible 'home movie' that Dylan eventually pieced together from the tour footage, was shot the day after Pennebaker's arrival, when Dylan and his entourage visited Kronberg Castle in Denmark. Against a backdrop of the castle, the model for Hamlet's Elsinore, Dylan attempted to procure the services of a blonde for Richard Manuel, offering to 'buy' the uncomprehending girl in question from her boyfriend. Watching the scene in *Eat The Document* – which opens with a shot of Richard snorting some speed – one sees with renewed shock just how much damage amphetamine had done to Dylan's body, though one also sees the wonderful spirit of mischief and revelry that existed between Bob and the Hawks. 'Swedish girls don't have any business sense,' quips Richard.

To Pennebaker, Dylan's insistence on putting together 'little scenes' – of the kind he and Howard Alk would later engineer for the disastrous *Renaldo And Clara* – was dismaying, for the simple reason that what was occurring *on* the stage seemed so revolutionary. Expending his energy on filming a scene at the Copenhagen docks, Bob was missing the point that the real action had taken place hours before at the city's KB Hallen. 'The sound of that band was extraordinary,' Pennebaker says, 'and what was most striking was that Dylan was obviously having the time of his life. He was hopping around like a cricket. That's why the booing was so ridiculous, because you only had to look at him to see that he'd made some enormous jump in his own head. But you couldn't film it by doing these goofy little scenes in rooms with nutty people. In a way, it was like they were saying, no, nothing went on onstage, whereas I felt that, unlike *Don't Look Back*, this film centred on the stage. He came to life in the middle of that stage.'

With Pennebaker and the Alks in tow, Dylan and the band flew
to London on 2 May. There was an intense air of anticipation and
controversy hanging over Dylan's British dates. Everyone from
the Beatles to the fan-in-the-street wanted to see the electric Dylan
and to know what all the fuss had been about in America and
Australia. Within hours of arriving, indeed, Dylan set off to meet
Paul McCartney, Brian Jones, and Keith Richard at one of Swinging London's innumerable new nightclubs, subsequently playing
McCartney the acetate of the imminent *Blonde On Blonde*. For the
Hawks, London was mind-blowing. Just a year before, they'd
been little more than a New Jersey bar band, and now here they
were in England, hob-nobbing with the Beatles and the Stones,
kings of the Great British Invasion of America.[5] 'The Hawks were
like foreign potentates,' says Pennebaker. 'People were coming to
them on their terms, so their provincialism didn't really set them
at a disadvantage. The way you know that what you're doing is
important is that people like the Beatles are coming to pay you a
sort of fealty. The Beatles were particularly interested to see what
kind of band Dylan would use. The idea of *working musicians* like
the Hawks really intrigued them, plus they'd all been so affected
by American music and had played so much of it. People wanted
to know what this meant, what it presaged: was this a new kind of
music coming in or what?' When Dylan told Keith Richard that
the Hawks were 'the greatest band in the world', the Stones'
guitarist looked wounded. 'What about us?' he asked. 'Oh, you
guys make the best philosophy,' Dylan replied. The Who's Keith
Moon was told the same thing, and asked a similar question. 'Well
now, you guys make the best history,' said Dylan.

Less impressed by Swinging London and its superstar denizens
– or at least less affected – was Garth Hudson, who preferred
pottering around looking at church organs to shopping sprees and
nightclubbing with Robbie, Rick, and Richard. 'It would have
been hard to throw Garth off balance in any social situation,' says

Pennebaker, who often went for long walks through the London streets with Hudson. 'He was just so firmly balanced, so *planted*. He didn't seem as irrational as most musicians are. He'd go whole days without speaking. We'd walk around and see places together, but not necessarily talk at all. I felt very close to him.' As for the rest of the band, Pennebaker got the distinct impression that Robbie had 'gone up a notch' after Levon's departure. 'It was hard to comprehend the pecking order, especially given that the leader of the group wasn't there any more. I sort of thought, oh, Dylan's copped the band and gotten rid of the leader as a political necessity.'

On 3 May, Dylan fielded the usual banalities from the press at the Mayfair Hotel. 'He treated the press like a faceless crowd of starving vultures, it was downright bad manners,' huffed Jonathan King, the Cambridge graduate who'd hit with 'Everyone's Gone To The Moon' the year before. A more amusing group of visitors were the teddy boys who dropped by the hotel to see the Hawks. Led by Ronnie Hawkins devotee Wild Willie Jeffrey, who later put together the Hawkins compilation *Arkansas Rockpile*, they wanted to know why Robbie and the boys had betrayed the rockabilly cause to play with this folk-rock pretender Dylan. 'They were a bunch of wild-looking characters who were into pure rock'n'roll,' Robbie remembers. 'They didn't like Bob's music at all, and they were giving me a whole story about giving up this Bob Dylan shit and getting back to the real meat of things.'

As it happened, Robbie had finally shaken off his reservations about Dylan's songs. True, there was still something more satisfying about the meticulous discipline of a Curtis Mayfield or a Smokey Robinson – or even about the practitioners of 'pure rock'n'roll' – but there was also a tremendous liberation in Dylan's 'disruption' of orthodox song form, and it had opened Robbie's eyes to the possibilities of songwriting. As he and Bob worked on songs in their hotel rooms night after night, he began thinking about his own songwriting again. 'Bob just made me think I could write these stories and not feel like every song I was writing was "Once upon a time . . .",' says Robbie. 'I'd have songs that I thought would only work if Jimmie Rodgers sang them, songs I'd be embarrassed to play to people. Bob broke down a barrier, and I wasn't embarrassed after that.'

D. A. Pennebaker recalled Dylan and Robbie running through over thirty songs one night, but the two of them were 'so far into what they were doing' that they had no time to write any of it down. Next day, Dylan tried to recall some of the ideas, but it was all in vain. Anyone who has abused amphetamine will know this syndrome well: you're racing at a hundred miles an hour, everything you do or say seems loaded with genius, but in the morning there's nothing to show for it. Pennebaker admits he was 'naïve' about the prodigious drug intake going on around him. 'I never knew what anybody was on,' he says. 'I wasn't interested in drugs, I was older and I didn't need them. I could only figure that it was really hard on you physically, and that somewhere along the line you were gonna pay a bill. Whatever was going on, everybody was racing at this *incredible* speed, and what happened was extraordinary. I ended up spending three or four days shooting what may have been a film about drugs, but it showed people at some incredible peak of their abilities.'

Dylan himself had moments of alarm at the tour's roller-coaster mayhem. 'We were going all the time, even when we weren't going,' he recalled. 'We were always doing something else, which is just as draining as performing. We were looking for Loch Ness monsters, staying up for four days running, and making all those 8 o'clock curtains besides.' In *Something Is Happening*, the unreleased 45-minute film Pennebaker himself made from his 1966 footage, there is a scene in which Dylan is being chauffeured through Hyde Park at dawn with John Lennon. It is obvious he has been awake for so long he is about to crash: even Lennon seems alarmed by his friend's condition. 'I wanna go home to baseball games and TV,' Dylan groans, anticipating the sentiments of 'When I Paint My Masterpiece'. Finally, he throws up in the back seat and crashes out.

The more strung-out he became, the more incandescent was the music. From the first date at Dublin's Adelphi on Thursday 5 May to the famous closing shows at London's Royal Albert Hall (26 and 27), the sound and spectacle of Dylan and the Hawks was more awesome – and more infuriating to small minds – than ever before. Only 'Just Like Tom Thumb's Blues' from the Liverpool show (14 May) and 'I Don't Believe You' from Belfast (6 May) have ever been released officially, but they are almost sufficient evidence of the splendour on display. 'Tom Thumb's Blues', released as the B-side of 'I Want You' later that summer, was especially powerful, a molten wave of skewered guitar and what Greil Marcus called the 'otherworldly tentacles' of Garth's organ fills. Underpinning everything was the grungy, lunging bass of Rick Danko and the cavernous, bottomless drums of Mickey Jones, with Richard's piano serving as a kind of adhesive in the middle. It was as if Dylan knew that the song summed up all the tour's dangerous glamour: when he sang about lacking the strength to take another shot, the harsh beauty of his voice was enough to make your flesh creep like a sick junkie's. 'The only reason those tapes exist is because we wanted to know, "Are we crazy?",' said Robbie. 'We'd go back to the hotel room, listen to a tape of the show and think, shit, that's not bad – why is everybody so upset? It did hurt a lot, because we played our hearts out, the best we could possibly play. But at the time people couldn't imagine it, they couldn't see it. So we just went blindly through with it.'

The other recorded evidence of the British tour, from the famous *In 1966 There Was* . . . bootleg, was inevitably of rougher quality, but no less exhilarating for that. Hailing mainly from the show at Manchester's Free Trade Hall on 17 May – not the Royal Albert Hall, as originally believed – the bootleg featured the electric set in its eight-song entirety, commencing with 'Tell Me, Momma' and climaxing in a furious, almost apocalyptic 'Like A Rolling Stone'. If one missed the more agile touch of a Levon Helm on the clumsy 'Baby, Let Me Follow You Down' – compare the version Dylan sang with The Band at The Last Waltz – on most of the other songs there was something not entirely inappropriate about Mickey Jones' oafish playing. Nor was the sight of Jones counting in the band, sticks held aloft as Rick, Bob, and Robbie faced him with their backs to the audience, easily forgotten. It was especially dramatic at Manchester, where one of the many betrayed fans dared to shout 'Judas' at Dylan from the audience. 'I don't believe you,' replied Dylan, 'you're a *liar*!' 'Quit talking Bob,' muttered Robbie, to which Dylan responded by turning to Mickey Jones and ordering him to 'play *fucking loud*!' Play fucking loud they did, leaving the audience reeling from the blows. Rick Sanders, a student working as a bodyguard at the show, recalled the state of shock he felt afterwards: 'Nobody ever made a more ominous sound than Dylan and the Hawks did that night. It was total menace, with no let-up. Song followed song, the terrible intense wall of sound pushing further and further to the limits of sanity. It was magnificent.'

Magnificent to Sanders, but not to the vast majority of Dylan fans. After the show at Bristol's Colston Hall on 10 May, a reviewer lamented the fact that Dylan had sacrificed lyric and melody to 'the god of big beat', his songs 'buried in a grave of guitars . . . and deafening drums'. Nick Kent, resident leather-trousered gonzo at *New Musical Express* in the '70s, recalled seeing the show at Cardiff's Capitol on 11 May, when the 'skeletal dandy' grappled with a 'mounting sprawl of derisive booing'. At Birmingham's Odeon the next night, Dylan was so fed up with the jeering and slow handclaps that he turned his back on the audience for much of the electric set, only bothering to announce 'Baby, Let Me Follow You Down' sneeringly 'as a *folk* song that mah grandaddy used to sing me'. At Leicester's De Montfort Hall on 15 May, loud shouts of 'Get them off!' greeted the appearance of the Hawks, while the Newcastle Odeon show on the 21st had one wag suggesting the band 'take some lessons from the Animals'!

Well might Erica Davies of Merthyr Tydfil have complained to *Melody Maker* that 'these people must have been walking around with their ears plugged, since Dylan's last two LPs and seven singles have all featured electric guitars.' It made no difference to his accusers, who clung obstinately to *their* Bob Dylan. 'There was one place in England where the people actually attacked the stage,' recalls Robbie. 'People had things like scissors in their hands, it was quite frightening. I mean, you were thinking in terms of instruments as weapons, that you were gonna have to knock somebody's head off. In one sense we were used to this, we'd been through much heavier things with Ronnie. But it had never been on such a large scale, with the private planes and the big hotels.'

If Howard Alk, with Dylan's prompting, made it his business to film the disaffected rabble pouring out of the shows – 'It were a bloody disgrace,' raged one Manchester fan; ''e wants shooting, 'e's a traitor!' – Don Pennebaker was still principally interested in the shows themselves. Frustrated that Dylan didn't feel the same way, but with some footage in the can, he left the tour on 11 May to attend a screening of *Don't Look Back* at the Cannes Film Festival. Once there, he decided he didn't want to show the film after all, and flew back to New York in a depression. But at home he took a look at the film he'd shot on Dylan's current tour, and discovered that that year's high-speed Eastman stock 'flared' in a most unusual way. 'I saw that it was amazing footage, really quite beautiful,' he says, 'so I figured it would probably be fantastic to shoot some concert footage with this film.'

Pennebaker caught up with the tour in time to shoot some remarkable film at the Glasgow Odeon on 19 May. With Robbie's complicity, and without Dylan's knowledge, he managed to sneak his way on to the Odeon stage itself. Tired of long-lens concert film that made concerts look like tapestries, he wanted to shoot Dylan's electric set with a wide-angle lens in the midst of the performance. When Dylan came out and saw Pennebaker onstage, he cracked up. The resulting film, shot from behind the band and virtually on top of them, was some of the most exciting live concert footage ever recorded. When Dylan moved to the piano for 'Ballad Of A Thin Man', Pennebaker all but clambered over the keys to shoot him. When Robbie took a solo, the camera picked up every look and gesture between him and Dylan. As Pennebaker had hoped, the giant orange spotlights trained on the stage flared dramatically, giving a decidedly 'psychedelic' aura to the film before that term even had any pop currency. Sadly, when Dylan and Howard Alk came to work on *Eat The Document*, they retained only six minutes of Pennebaker's live footage in the film.

As the tour drew to a close, Dylan became more wilfully provocative with each show. Determined to confound the expectations of people who looked to him for facile answers to global political problems, he began draping an enormous American flag behind the stage. Things reached a head during the show at Paris' Olympia Theatre on 24 May. In Godard's *Masculin Feminin* (1965), Jean-Pierre Léaud had called Dylan a 'Vietnik', but the singer was doing anything but toeing the leftist line this time around. After infuriating the audience during the acoustic half of the show, when he spent long periods of time tuning his guitar and saying things like 'Hasn't anyone got a newspaper to read?', he opened the electric half with the Stars and Stripes behind him and almost sparked off a riot. 'Bob Dylan Go Home!' shouted the *Paris-Jour* headline the next morning.

Amidst all the aggravation, there was some consolation for

Robbie. In Paris that week were two French-Canadian girls from Montreal, one of them a bright and attractive journalist called Dominique. 'The girls were very pissed off,' recalls Don Pennebaker, 'because the French are antagonistic towards French-Canadians, and no-one had bothered to tell them that. They'd thought they were coming back to the motherland.' Robbie instantly fell for Dominique, and asked her to come to London with him for the final shows.

The Royal Albert Hall shows on 26 and 27 May provided a fitting finale for the trauma of Dylan's 'apostasy'. As the Beatles gazed down from their box in admiration and told people to 'Leave him alone!', hardcore folkies yelled their usual objections. 'Folk music was just an interruption and was very useful,' responded Dylan from the stage, pouring gas on the flames. 'This is not English music you're listening to. You haven't actually heard American music before.' Fights broke out between pro and anti-electric factions, with Dylan appearing to take it in what Mick Farren called his 'wasted and somewhat stumbling stride'. 'Whenever a disturbance erupted in the audience,' Farren wrote, 'he either ignored it and carried on regardless, or he stared down from the stage with an enigmatic, almost Zen expression, as though he felt that everything was going according to plan.' In *Peace News*, Peter Willis argued that 'the total sound for those prepared to let themselves go with it was magnificent ... this was Wagnerian rock'n'roll', but many fans for whom the notion of 'letting yourself go' was a tall order walked out.

Finally it was all over. Dylan's anonymous henchmen had done their job, survived to tell the tale, and were on their way back to 'the land of Coca-Cola'. Just before they left, however, *Melody Maker* despatched a reporter to interview Robbie, already the spokesman for 'the band'. 'There is no name for the group,' Robbie told him. 'We've been playing together for a long time, working with different people, just for fun, and mainly in the South. Bob asked me to do a couple of jobs with him, and I did, just for the sake of science fiction. Then the other guys joined.' Had Dylan's music become watered-down R&B? Robbie was asked. 'It's not R&B and I certainly wouldn't call it folk-rock. It's street music. Everyone in this organization comes from the street.'

It was time to return to the land where the streets have no name.

2

Big Pink

We weren't looking for blood any more. We were just looking for music.

Robbie Robertson

The town of Woodstock, just two hours north of New York City in the Catskill mountains, has long been home to artists, writers, and composers escaping the stress and congestion of urban life. Nestling beneath the imposing ridge of Overlook Mountain, it had once been a hunting ground for Indians, who called it *Waghkunk*, 'a place near a mountain'. 'Down in the Woodstock-Bearsville area, there's a legend that the Indians wouldn't camp there for geomagnetic or spiritual reasons,' says Garth Hudson. The Indians preferred to live in rock shelters that still survive on Overlook's south-eastern slopes.

In the 1760s, Dutch settlers discovered the area's rich timber resources and the River Sawkill's potential for mills. A century later, the building of a resort hotel on the mountain led to the construction of proper roads and sidewalks in the town. Finally, in the summer of 1902, a group of artists led by Ralph Radcliffe Whitehead and his wife Emily Byrd arrived in Woodstock searching for a place to build an arts colony. Gazing down over the shimmering Woodstock Valley from his room at Mead's Hotel, Whitehead's friend Bolton Brown wrote: 'Like Balboa, I . . . first saw my South Sea. South indeed it was and wide and almost as blue as the sea, that extraordinarily beautiful view, amazing in extent.'

Looking down over Woodstock today from Byrdcliffe – a group of houses comprising the colony Whitehead founded the following year – the view is still extraordinarily beautiful. Thick with maple and pine trees, surrounded by lakes and the huge Ashokan reservoir, it is not hard to see why Woodstock so appealed to the numerous painters who poured into the area over the ensuing decades. 'Woodstock was work and relaxation and bohemian life,' said the painter Manuel Bromberg, who arrived in 1941. Other artists who settled in the town included George Bellows, Konrad Cramer, Charles Rosen, Milton Avery, Anton Refregier, and Philip Guston, the latter of whom moved down from Byrdcliffe to the rival Maverick colony in nearby West Hurley at the end of the '40s.[1] 'On the Maverick,' wrote Guston's daughter Musa Meyer in her 1991 memoir *Night Studio*, 'you stoked your own wood stove, pumped your own water, and padded to the outhouse in the moonlight.' The early '50s saw another influx of artists, from the Texan Fletcher Martin to the Japanese Yasuo Kuniyoshi. At other times, Woodstock has been home to Thomas Mann and Rabindranath Tagore; Aaron Copland and John Cage; Lee Marvin and Edward G. Robinson.

Bob Dylan had first visited Woodstock in 1963, staying in a summer cabin Peter Yarrow's mother owned on Broadview Road. He loved the town, and ended up writing most of the *Another Side Of Bob Dylan* and *Bringing It All Back Home* albums in a little room above the Café Espresso on Woodstock's main drag Tinker Street. 'The big word around here is privacy,' says Sally Grossman, Albert's widow. 'People come here to work. If you want manicured lawns and comfort, you go to Connecticut, but if you want to woodshed it you come here. We're in the woods, in the mountains, and it lends itself to fantasy. You have visions in your head.'

The visions in Dylan's head were certainly enough to bring him back to Woodstock after Albert and Sally Grossman acquired a large Bearsville estate from the artist John Striebel in 1964. At first using a cabin on the estate, Dylan a year later bought one of the 'Byrdcliffe' houses up on Camelot Road, an enormous cedarwood ranch built in 1910 by architect and stage director Ben Webster. Barely had he moved in, however, when the electric tour whisked him off around the world.

If the pastoral retreat of Woodstock was the last thing on Dylan's mind as he barnstormed the globe wreaking havoc with the expectations of his fans, it was the perfect sanctuary once the tour was over. After a brief holiday in Spain with Sara Lowndes, whom he'd married secretly the previous November, he came back to the Camelot Road house to recuperate before the roller-coaster ride started up again. Grossman had scheduled sixty more shows for Dylan and the Hawks, starting with major dates at the Yale Bowl and Shea Stadium in the first two weeks of August. Dylan wasn't altogether sure that he could take the pressure of another tour so soon, or even that he hadn't reached a major turning point in his life. Not only was he now married, but he had a stepdaughter and baby son in tow, with another child on the way. Clearly, these things didn't trouble Albert, who was determined to push Dylan up there with the Beatles in the superstar stakes. But that only riled Dylan the more. Sitting out under a full moon one night that July, he stared into the woods and decided something had to change.

The Hawks, meanwhile, were killing time in the summertime heat of New York City. Holed up at the Chelsea Hotel with such fellow guests as Arthur Miller and Gregory Corso, Robbie and Dominique spent time in the company of Warhol superstar Edie Sedgwick, who'd just signed to Albert Grossman's management stable. 'It was wonderful in a way,' says Robbie. 'Everybody talks like this was the period when we were all so fucked up, but we weren't so fucked up. It wasn't that we weren't *trying* to be, but we just weren't. The streets were so vivid and the parties were so much fun.' Robbie got another taste of the Warhol world – so diametrically opposed to everything The Band came to stand for – when Al Aronowitz took him to see a new band called the Velvet Underground. 'Some East Side hippies were having a ritual, the usual hippie bullshit,' says Aronowitz, who'd briefly managed the Velvets before their adoption by Warhol. 'Lou Reed had boasted that he was the fastest guitarist in the world, so Robbie wanted to check him out. He couldn't stand it and left after five minutes.'

When Robbie and Dominique decided to move into a little apartment in the village, Aronowitz and his wife gave them a set of dishes as a present. One of Dylan's earliest champions in the press, Aronowitz also spent time with the other Hawks, who visited him in his 'slum tenement' up on West 93rd Street. 'When I first met them,' he remembers, 'they'd tell me wild stories about touring down south, where they'd get young girls stoned on pills and fuck them.' Clearly their sex drive had not abated, since they were constantly pestering Aronowitz to find them female companions.

In the early morning of 29 July, the day before *Blonde On Blonde* first entered the U. S. album chart, Bob Dylan was riding his Triumph motorcycle along the Striebel Road when a sudden, panicky braking caused the back wheel to lock, throwing him over the handlebars. Fortunately, he'd been taking the bike in for repairs at a local garage, so Sara was driving behind him in a car. With his face badly cut and his neck possibly broken, she rushed him to nearby Middletown Hospital, from whence he emerged a week later in a neck brace.

Ever since that morning on Striebel Road, there has been heated conjecture as to just how serious Dylan's accident really was. While it's fairly clear that he did break several vertebrae in his neck, as well as suffer concussion and bruising, there were some very good reasons for exaggerating the damage. First and foremost, the accident got everyone off his back, not only Albert Grossman but the publishers Macmillan, who were waiting on Dylan's book *Tarantula*, and ABC Television, who had given him

$100,000 for his proposed film of the '66 tour. Second, it gave Dylan a chance to detox from the various substances he'd been abusing for so long. And third, it was a brilliant career move, not quite the terminal event James Dean's car crash had been but equally effective in building up mystique that even Albert couldn't argue with. As Mick Gold put it, 'what Dylan had really crashed into was the arrogance and tension his performances had come to represent – what Phil Ochs described as "LSD on stage" and Joan Baez called, "the ego bubble of superstardom"'. It was the beginning of seven and a half years of retreat and rethinking.

With rumours buzzing through the rock community – he was dead, or at least hideously disfigured – Dylan dropped out of view. 'What I've been doing mostly,' he said when a *Daily News* journalist finally tracked him down the following spring, 'is seeing only a few close friends, reading little about the outside world, pouring over books by people you never heard of, thinking about where I'm going and why I'm running and if I'm mixed up too much and what I'm knowing and what I'm giving and what I'm taking.' After lying in bed staring at the ceiling in the Camelot Road house for several weeks, he emerged a changed man, no longer the megalomaniac rooster in Carnaby Street pants and Cuban heels but an older and gentler man with new feelings of responsibility to his family. 'Up until then, I thought it was only a question of time until he died,' admitted Bernard Paturel, who'd owned the Café Espresso and now worked in various capacities for Dylan. 'But later, I never met such a dedicated family man.' Happy Traum, a folk singer who'd moved up to Woodstock from Greenwich Village, recalled that 'Dylan shut out the world of show business and all the Manhattan craziness and turned into such an ordinary guy that he was actually a little boring to be around.' Pictures of Dylan with his family taken by Daniel Kramer – which Grossman in his usual heavy-handed way tried to stop from being published – attest to his improved health and stability.

On 13 October, a fortnight after Allen Ginsberg came up to Woodstock bearing a trunkload of books for Dylan, Columbia Records announced that Dylan would be playing no more shows before March, 1967. This, of course, left the Hawks in a certain quandary. Stranded in New York with very little money and even less to do – the odd session for the likes of John Hammond notwithstanding – they thought seriously about heading back to Toronto. 'New York was expensive,' says Robbie, 'and we were just these road musicians with no road to go on. We were scrounging around trying to figure out a place to work on some music, and we really weren't sure what the next move was gonna be.'

The answer eventually arrived in the form of a call from Dylan, who suggested they come up to Woodstock to help him with his film for ABC. By this time, D. A. Pennebaker had dissociated himself from the film, which Dylan was working on with Howard Alk, a huge bear of a man who'd known Albert Grossman when they'd both been running folk clubs in Chicago. Alk had made several amateurish music documentaries of his own before working as a cameraman on *Don't Look Back*, and now Dylan wanted him to pull together the film that would come to be known as *Eat The Document*.[2] 'Howard's relationship with Dylan was very complicated,' recalls Pennebaker. 'Sometimes Dylan would be very friendly and sometimes he would abuse him horribly, and Howard had learned to just take that. At any rate, it was clear to me that Howard had gotten into something with Dylan, maybe based on *Tarantula*, of being oblique, of never being specific about anything. And they were determined to prove they could make a better film from our "outs" than I could. I was never sure what Dylan thought, but he certainly went to the most terrible, painful lengths not to be obvious.' Most heartbreaking for Pennebaker was the fact that Alk cut the original footage, leaving only the unseen 45-minute taster *Something Is Happening* as evidence of the film that might have been. 'I asked Howard not to cut it, because someday somebody would want to look at it,' he says. 'In a way, this was the inevitable sequel to *Don't Look Back*, because it's what happens if, you know, you don't look back.'

When Robbie first journeyed up to Woodstock in the late fall, he found Dylan not only fully recovered from his accident but surrounded by the trappings of domestic bliss. Toys were strewn along the corridors, cats and dogs roamed the four-acre grounds. Appropriately enough, given the history of the Byrdcliffe colony, Dylan had taken up painting. There was even a huge bible open on a reading stand. 'The house was a rambling American chateau of mahogany-stained shingles clinging to a mountain which had its head in the clouds,' wrote Al Aronowitz. 'It seemed as if God and man had joined in the conspiracy to help draw the veil of mystery and seclusion which had surrounded Dylan since his motorcycle accident.' Others, like photographer Elliott Landy and writer Mason Hoffenberg, thought the house more like a spooky museum or hotel than a home, especially with the dour sign Albert Grossman had erected outside the gates: 'If you have not telephoned, you are trespassing.'

Robbie knew even less about film-making than Dylan or Bobby Neuwirth, who was constantly popping in and out of the house, but he was happy to be there, watching Bob and Howard devise ever more eccentric methods of editing *Eat The Document*. At one point they broke down the footage into numbered sections – such as 'train clips' or 'angry fan clips' – and then attempted to 'orchestrate' these sections as though each number represented a note or a chord. When Rick and Richard followed Robbie up to Woodstock, they were even more nonplussed by the bizarre logic. But then, as Paul Williams had noted, the very title of the film indicated a desire to conceal and frustrate – to avoid making a documentary. 'The editors looked for conversations unheld, events untranspired,' Alk wrote mystifyingly in the programme notes which accompanied the film's first screening in February, 1971, when it was generously described as 'an anti-document . . . a challenge to all the preconceived notions we have of a star and his public image'.

Apart from the live footage of Dylan and the Hawks onstage, and fascinating snippets of Bob working on songs with Robbie in hotel rooms, there was very little that could have been said to 'challenge' in *Eat The Document*. The editing between performances, train journeys, and enraged fans was so incoherent that it looked haphazard, and the few real 'scenes' that survived in the film told the viewer little besides the fact that Dylan and the Hawks were partial to dark glasses, polo necks, and houndstooth jackets. 'I don't know how much Dylan actually did on *Eat The Document*,' says Pennebaker. ' I know Robbie kind got into it, too, but he didn't know anything about film either, so there was a lot of bullshit flying around.'

The bullshit notwithstanding, Dylan enjoyed having the Hawks in the house. 'By then,' says Robbie, 'the give-and-take in our relationship with Dylan was an everyday procedure, whether we were travelling round the world or just hanging out in someone's kitchen. All of a sudden, after the accident, he got this sense for once of not being all by himself in a situation.' After dispersing for the winter, the band 'kind of dribbled back up there one at a time'. In the early spring, on the suggestion of Albert Grossman, they moved to Woodstock permanently.

It was Rick who found the house known locally as 'Big Pink'. Hidden away at the end of a bumpy drive in the backwoods west of Saugerties, 2188 Stoll Road was an ugly but endearing edifice built over a garage, renting at $125 a month. It would have been hard to imagine a more peaceful spot for a rock'n'roll band 'getting it together in the country', as the cliché came to be known in that 'summer of love'. With a view of Overlook Mountain shimmering across the blue-green fields, it was the band's own sanctuary, a place where, in Robbie's words, they could 'hide out and shake off the years of wildness we'd spent on the road'.

Refugees from six years of sleazy hotels and rooming houses, the Hawks had finally arrived somewhere that they could call home. 'It couldn't have been a better place,' says Garth, who moved into Big Pink's upstairs living quarters with Rick and Richard. 'There was a lot of magic in Woodstock. Everywhere you went the legends were reflected in the names of places and streets – Warwarsing, Ohayo, Bearsville Flats.'

Leaving the others in their funky new bachelor pad, Robbie and Dominique moved into one of the cabins on Albert Grossman's estate a few miles west along Route 212. Within a few weeks, Big Pink had become a kind of clubhouse, and Robbie would drive over each day to mess around with musical ideas or play Canadian football. 'It was the first time since we'd been together that I'd had any time to sit down and gather it up in my mind and think about it at all.' Taking stock of what he'd learned working behind the Hawk and Dylan, Robbie was ready once again to change direction and 'up the ante'. Out of the conflict between his own fundamentally conservative musical instincts and Dylan's radical 'disruption' of rock'n'roll had come something new, something he would soon be able to call his own.

It is tempting to conjecture as to what would have become of the Hawks had they never crossed the path of Bob Dylan. Would they have plodded on as a bar band, tossing their pearls before beer-drinking swine in Texas honky-tonks, or would they have made the quantum leap to genuine creativity anyway? 'They might have remained a bar band, but I kinda doubt it,' says Jonathan Taplin. 'What happened with Bob changed things and made things happen faster – it gave them an inside line – but I think Robbie would eventually have gotten to where he got.' In any case, there was a two-way transaction going on here. If those endless nights with Dylan had, in Robbie's words, 'broken down a whole lot of the tradition of songwriting before my very eyes', by the same token Robbie and the Hawks had taught Dylan something about American music – about country, about rhythm and blues – that he hadn't properly appreciated before. It was Robbie who'd sat Dylan down with Percy Sledge's 'When A Man Loves A Woman' and the Impressions' *Keep On Pushing* album and told him: 'They're not *saying* anything much and this is killing me, whereas you're rambling on for an hour and you're losing me.' It was Robbie who talked to Dylan about *making records* rather than just 'bashing away in the studio'. 'We would talk about early rockabilly records and stuff like that,' Robbie remembers, 'and I was trying to get him to see that there was a vibe, a sound quality, to certain records, whether it was a Motown thing or a Sun records thing or a Phil Spector thing. Up to that point, Bob was saying "Who cares about that? I'm only interested in the lyrics".'

Just as the peace and seclusion of Woodstock was what Dylan needed after the globe-trotting psychosis of the 1966 world tour, so the discipline and sense of tradition in the Hawks' musicianship helped to calm him down after the frenzy of the live shows. It was as if the band had opened up a whole world of American music that he'd never tapped into before, and which was earthier, more rural than the hallucinatory sound of *Blonde On Blonde*, or even than the 'folk' songs he'd sung to the accompaniment of nothing more than an acoustic guitar and a wheezing harmonica. A big part of Robbie's beef with Dylan's songs was their verbal complexity, their dense subjectivity; now he was leading his mentor back to simplicity, to the concise Americana that as a Canadian he himself wanted to explore. 'I came in on a rock'n'roll train, blues and country music mixed together,' Robbie has said. 'That's what made rock'n'roll to me. You mix this and that and you get something and God knows what it is. It's just magical when you put it all together, and I wasn't getting that out of Dylan's music.' Having invented a kind of modernist 'hard rock', it was time to retreat to the backwaters of myth and tradition – to play some *music*.

*

'Dylan has been doing nothing, absolutely nothing,' Robbie told Michael Iachetta when the *Daily News* reporter attempted to get some dirt on the reclusive star in May. 'He's been looking at the gate around his house and training his dogs how to bite.' In fact, as Al Aronowitz knew, Dylan had for at least a month been driving over to Big Pink every day to play music with Robbie, Rick, Richard, and Garth. Once the idea of touring had 'faded away', Bob had suddenly begun firing out songs faster than he could type them. He himself told Iachetta that he'd been 'working on two musical sounds, one "staccato" and the other "resoundin'"', though he gave away no more than that.

Everything was kept very secret. Each day at one o'clock, Dylan and the band would assemble in the basement of Big Pink, get a little wasted, and make music. 'We were doing seven, eight, ten, sometimes fifteen songs a day,' recalled Garth. 'Some were old ballads and traditional songs, some were written by Bob, but others would be songs Bob made up as he went along. We'd play the melody, he'd sing a few words he'd written or else just mouth sounds or syllables. It was a pretty good way to write songs.' To a degree, Big Pink itself determined the nature of this homemade brew: playing too loud in the basement was aggravating to the ears, so the amplifiers were turned down low and the voices forsook the raucous screaming of the previous year's shows. 'We developed a style that balanced in the room,' recalls Robbie. 'Like, if you couldn't hear *this* guy, you were too loud. So it became a very musical atmosphere.'

Without the pressure of touring or studio recording hanging over them, the motley quintet had a ball with 'the little workshop situation' in the basement. Albert may have been pushing his reluctant superstar to write songs for other artists to cover, but Dylan was loving every minute of it, hamming up country songs like 'I Don't Hurt Anymore' or Luke the Drifter's doleful sermon 'Be Careful Of Stones That You Throw', trying his hand at the

Impressions' 'People Get Ready' and Elvis' 'I Forgot To Remember To Forget'. As Paul Williams wrote, it was as if Dylan was 'making faces' to entertain the Hawks. 'They were a kick to do,' Bob told Jann Wenner in 1969. 'Fact, I'd do it all again. You know, that's really the way to do a recording – in a peaceful, relaxed setting, in somebody's basement, with the windows open and a dog lying on the floor.'

Hamlet, the dog in question, was one Dylan had brought over from Camelot Road and entrusted to Rick Danko. The enormous black mutt was yet another feature of a backwoods lifestyle which saw them, in Rick's words, 'getting up in the morning instead of going to bed in the morning'. For Robbie, living in Woodstock was about having breakfast at the local diner and being greeted like 'a mechanic from down the road'. 'You feel like you're in the mountains because you *are* in the mountains,' he told Al Aronowitz. 'You get the feeling you can look down on New York City.' Garth, who like the others had begun sprouting the facial hair which would soon make them look like 19th-century out- laws, became a regular 'mountain man', an eccentric hillbilly with a large collection of guns and knives that surprised those who thought of him merely as a 'mad professor' playing Bach and Chopin all day. 'Garth was less of a hellraiser and more of a scholar,' says Libby Titus, who became Levon's girlfriend, 'but he was still very primitive. I'll never forget seeing him skin a deer that had been hit in the road.' 'We got to like this lifestyle,' Garth told Martin Scorsese in *The Last Waltz*. 'Chopping wood and hitting your thumb with a hammer, fixing the tape recorder or the screen door, wandering off into the woods with Hamlet . . . it was relaxed and low-key, which was something we hadn't enjoyed since we were children.' If Richard could still put away alarming amounts of liquor – there was unintended irony in one magazine's description of him as a man who 'likes to sip wine' – even he seemed to be getting off on healthier habits. 'We were shooting films up here, and then we were shooting vodka,' he told one journalist. 'Next thing you know, we took to shooting fresh air!' The influence of Woodstock's ambience was palpable in the songs they were playing. 'The feeling of the music wasn't as neurotic as it had been when I was living in the city,' said Robbie. 'It was the first time I'd ever really lived in the country and I liked it.'

As spring turned to summer, the basement songs came thick and fast. By turns lustily comic and mournfully beautiful, they seemed to have a healing warmth after the icy savagery of Dylan's 1966 music. Where the electric tours had been about alienation, the basement sessions were about community. As Greil Marcus put it, 'what was taking shape, as Dylan and the band fiddled with the tunes, was less a style than a spirit – a spirit that had to do with a delight in friendship.' A grab-bag cornucopia of mock-country ballads, sea shanties, surreal nonsense songs, and drawling blues jams, they sounded wonderfully loose and uninhibited, as if flowing from some wellspring of collective memory. There were zany, ribald 'comedy songs' like 'Million Dollar Bash', and 'Lo And Behold!'; plaintive ballads like 'I Shall Be Released' and 'Goin' To Acapulco'; and a whole slew of songs that fell somewhere in between and were eventually covered by acts like the Byrds and Peter, Paul and Mary – 'You Ain't Goin' Nowhere' and 'Too Much Of Nothing' being just two that were recorded by the end of August.

These were just some of the famous tracks that finally saw the licit light of day on Robbie's double-album compilation *The Basement Tapes* in 1975. As we now know, they represent only a fraction of the estimated 150 tracks recorded in one form or another by Dylan and the band between May and November 1967. Ever since the *Great White Wonder* bootleg first surfaced in California in the summer of 1969, basement tapes have continued to leak out from various shadowy sources, amounting to a mass of material that veers from the truly sublime to the absolutely ridiculous.[3] Given that the majority of the songs were never intended for public release, and were conceived merely as rough demos, it is hardly surprising that much of this music sounds like it was recorded in the Big Pink toilet rather than the basement. Yet however lamentable the sound quality, it isn't difficult to sort the wheat from the chaff. For every wacky fragment – 'See You Later, Allen Ginsberg', 'Every Time I Go To Town', 'Teenage Prayer' – there is a beguiling masterpiece like 'I'm Not There (1956)' or 'Sign On The Cross', the latter a wonderfully solemn gospel experiment sung in Dylan's most plangent voice. For every throwaway cover – Hank Williams' 'You Win Again', Elmore James' 'Down On Me', traditionals like 'Tiny Sparrow' and 'Joshua Gone Barbados' – there is something as genuinely inspired as the troubadour lament 'The French Girl' or the Dominic Behan ballad 'The Royal Canal'. (The range of the material was phenomenal, taking in everything from 'Wildwood Flower' and 'See That My Grave Is Kept Clean' to Johnny Cash's 'Folsom Prison Blues' and Ian and Sylvia's 'One Single River'.) Other highlights include the bizarre 'Give Me Another Bourbon Street, Please' – a kind of precursor to 'Rag Mama Rag' – and a hilariously over-the-top Mexican ballad called 'Louisa', replete with rattling tambourines and wolf-whistles that suggest a cowboy booze-up in a Sam Peckinpah bordello.[4]

On all of these and more, the Hawks – for the most part drummerless, though Robbie and Richard could both supply rudimentary rhythm when required – fleshed out Dylan's remarkable new grasp of American music as a vast repository of myths and fables. Fascinated as they themselves were by the America that psychedelic rock was rejecting, they had no hang-ups about playing country songs and old-time mountain ballads. If anything, there was a certain perverse pleasure in going against the grain with Dylan, who had paved the way for the new rock only to retreat from the carnival just as it was reaching its climax. Rick Danko's brother Terry claims Robbie called up their father to ask him whether the band 'should go psychedelic or country', but it's hard to believe the guitarist's tongue wasn't planted firmly in his cheek. Robbie instinctively knew that it was Flower Power and not the basement tapes that would date. For the rest of that 'summer of love', the band shut themselves off from the world of rock'n'roll, barely listening to the music of their contemporaries.

The Hawks were at their understated best on basement songs like 'Million Dollar Bash' and 'Open The Door, Homer', where choruses soared in sweet three-part harmony after Dylan's chattering, monologue-style verses. The rough rural voices of Rick Danko and Richard Manuel were seldom used to better effect than they were here, or on 'Goin' To Acapulco', 'Nothing Was Delivered', and Dylan's original basement versions of 'Tears Of Rage', 'This Wheel's On Fire', and 'I Shall Be Released'. Instrumentally, too, the Hawks were admirably unflashy. As if reacting against the overkill of his soloing on the '66 tour, Robbie instead emulated the kind of 'sweet little cries' that Curtis Mayfield had inserted discreetly between the lines of Impressions songs. Garth, too, provided only the subtlest textures on his increasingly souped-up Lowrey organ.

By August, when Dylan finally re-signed to Columbia Records,[5] Big Pink was a daily hive of activity. There was always a song being written somewhere in the house: if Rick and Bob were playing checkers, then Robbie and Richard were hammering out ideas on the piano; if Rick and Richard were throwing a ball around in the backyard, then Bob and Robbie were trading licks in the basement. The freewheeling system worked well, encouraging participation from all of them. 'The songs just kept coming, and we all felt there was something amazing going on,' says Robbie. 'Somebody would figure something out, we'd run down to the basement and record it, and a little later there'd be another one. I'd be up in the bedroom with the guitar, Bob would be at the typewriter, and somebody else would be in the corner working on something. It was definitely happening and it was really exhilarating.'

As with the 'automatic writing' of the Surrealists or the 'cut-ups' of William Burroughs, the random-input method at Big Pink could produce inconsequential ephemera or it could produce work of real anguish and ambiguity. 'Tears Of Rage' and 'This Wheel's On Fire' were just two of the songs which had their genesis in these sessions. Richard was fooling around on the piano one afternoon when Dylan raced down to the basement with the typed lyric of 'Tears' and asked if he had any music for it. 'I had a couple of movements that seemed to fit, so I just elaborated a little,' Richard recalled. 'I wasn't sure what the lyrics meant, but I couldn't run upstairs and say, "What's this mean, Bob?"' Rick Danko had a similar experience when Dylan gave him 'Wheel's'. 'At the time I was teaching myself to play the piano,' he remembered, 'and some music I'd written on the piano the day before just seemed to fit with Bob's lyrics. I worked on the phrasing and the melody, and then Bob and I wrote the chorus together.' Several songs underwent radical changes when they were re-recorded. After an initial attempt at 'Tears Of Rage', for example, the lyrics and phrasing were altered to fit a new rhythm.

The co-crediting of Manuel and Danko on 'Tears' and 'Wheel's' was symptomatic of the fact that the Hawks were beginning to find their own feet again. If they were still putatively 'Dylan's backing band', they also knew in the back of their minds that the time was coming when they would have to prove themselves as a separate entity. Dylan himself knew this, just as he knew that he was too much of a loner to be tied indefinitely to any one band. He could see and hear that the Hawks had something precious of their own which would only be stifled if they continued to hide behind him. Up to now, they'd only fooled around in the basement when Bob wasn't around, as if scared to take themselves too seriously. They'd get stoned, turn on the old reel-to-reel, and record everything from blues instrumentals to the inspired lunacy of 'Even If It's A Pig, Part Two', which began with Garth Hudson talking in his maddest Mad Professor guise, continued on through an instrumental version of 'Blue Moon', and ended up with an *a capella* rendition of 'The Banana Boat Song'. Occasionally, Richard would sit at the piano and fool around with half-written falsetto ballads like 'You Say That You Love Me' or 'Beautiful Thing', but they never seemed to go anywhere. Now it was time to find out if, after everything they'd been through, they really did have a voice of their own. 'We were up there just living,' says Robbie. 'There was nothing that we had to do, no obligations. But Bob had been wanting us to record for a long time, and our fun was beginning to run out. We needed to take care of business a little.'

The first thing they had to do was persuade Levon Helm to return to the fold. That crucial Southern ingredient had been missing for almost a year, and Levon wasn't someone you could replace. In order to lure him up to Woodstock, however, they were going to have to dangle some pretty attractive bait in front of his nose. As it happened, Albert Grossman was already busy stirring up interest in the band. Flying to L. A. with the intention of signing them to Warner Brothers, Albert discovered that the company's MD Mo Ostin was out of town, and so went instead to see Stanley Gortikov at Capitol. Founded by songwriter Johnny Mercer in 1942, Capitol had made its mark with Sinatra, Nat 'King' Cole, and Peggy Lee in the '50s, but had really come into its own with the Beatles and the Beach Boys – plus a country division strong on Bakersfield artists like Merle Haggard and Buck Owens – a decade later. Now the label, based on the West Coast as it was, was moving in on the post-Monterey Festival rock sound, snapping up groups that Albert himself had been interested in: the Steve Miller Band and the Quicksilver Messenger Service, whose 1969 live album *Happy Trails* would be dominated by an epic version of the Hawks' 'Who Do You Love'.[6] Gortikov leapt at the chance to sign 'Dylan's backing band', who had instructed Albert to sign them under the name 'The Crackers' – a derogatory term for poor white Southern trash that went completely over Gortikov's head. Although the contract would ultimately depend on some recorded evidence of the Crackers' greatness, the meeting with Capitol was enough for Rick to call Levon down in Arkansas and tell him they were getting ready to record. 'I called him and said we'd be getting a couple of hundred thousand dollars we wanted to share,' Danko remembered. 'He said "I'll be on the next plane!"'

Despite being a diehard razorback Confederate, Levon instantly fell for Woodstock's Yankee charms when he arrived in late October. 'The people here are like the people down in the Ozark mountains,' he said. 'They're just as country in that good kind of solid citizen way as they are back home. You won't hear any horror stories here, like the Sheriff stringing somebody up on the village green. Anyone who lives here is blessed.' The long-delayed reunion of the five Hawks seemed to spark them all into renewed activity. As he had always been, Levon was once again the musical life and soul of the party, leading impromptu jam sessions in which he'd grab his mandolin and sing Louis Jordan's 'Caldonia' or an old-time song his father had written:

> Little birds are singing all around me
> On every bush and vine.
> My pleasures would be double
> If I could call you mine.

When Levon sunk roots in Woodstock, noted Robert Palmer, 'they were no longer the Hawks, a band; they were The Band'. 'We'd always wanted our own life, so to speak,' the drummer says. 'I never wanted to be Dylan's drummer, or anybody else's. We were The Band for several people, and it worked out well, but now it was time to be The Band for ourselves.'

The songs that Robbie and Richard wrote that fall – both independently and together – all but announced the birth of The Band. From 'Katie's Been Gone', first of a succession of superb songs written and sung by Richard, to the frazzled New Orleans funk of Robbie's 'Yazoo Street Scandal', bawled by Levon in his best redneck-wildcat yelp, here was the hard proof of something grittily distinctive. The group's scope was breathtaking: under one umbrella there was room for the pure hillbilly harmonizing of the chain-gang traditional 'Ain't No More Cane (On The Brazos)', the rollicking bar-room R&B of Richard's 'Orange Juice Blues', and the bawdy swagger of Dylan's 'Don't Ya Tell Henry'. But perhaps most intriguing of all were those songs that only The Band could ever have performed, songs whose quirky changes and arrangements made them impossible to categorize: 'Bessie Smith', a Danko-Robertson ballad about the blues empress transformed by Garth into something as magically evocative as an old silent movie, or Robbie's unreleased 'Ferdinand The Impostor', a surreal yarn sung by Rick in a quizzical voice pitched midway between Richard's melancholy and Levon's redneck glee. ('Benny the barber looked at me, passed out tickets cautiously,' went the second verse, 'To see the burning of the soup, down at Lucy's chicken coop'!) Here, intact, was The Band's world: fantastic but precise, peopled by freaks and drifters, a lost America coming to life in the voices and the playing of five men who, as Robbie said, were themselves 'unique characters you could read about in a book'. 'I didn't want to write Bob Dylan poems,' Robbie said. 'Not because I didn't like them, just because it wasn't my job. I always felt I had to connect the songs with this world that was true to The Band's music.'

Shortly after Levon had moved up to Woodstock, the band met the man who was to play a key role in the recording of their first three albums. John Simon had started out producing novelty records at Columbia, eventually giving the label a smash hit with The Cyrkle's 'Red Rubber Ball' in 1966. After he'd produced the first Blood, Sweat and Tears album, the group's leader Al Kooper told him he would make more money working freelance. 'I bumped into Albert Grossman on the street,' Simon remembers. 'He said "You scratch my back and I'll scratch yours," which actually meant "You scratch my back and *I'll* scratch my back."' At the Monterey Pop Festival in July, Simon hooked up with Peter Yarrow, who asked him to help produce a soundtrack for *You Are What You Eat*, an appalling 'rockumentary' rightly condemned by Pauline Kael as 'the kind of movie about youth one might expect Spiro Agnew or George Wallace to make'. By late October, he was in Woodstock, working on the film with none other than Howard Alk. 'On the night of Howard's birthday, we were editing *You Are What You Eat* when this eerie noise came from outside the house,' says Simon. 'We opened a window and there were these guys dressed up in crazy costumes and playing crazy instruments. It was the band, serenading Howard.' In fact, it had already occurred to Alk that Simon might hit it off with the Hawks, or the Crackers, or whatever they were going to call themselves. Having heard a John Simon-produced album by the band's fellow countryman Marshall McLuhan (*The Medium Is The Massage*), Alk figured John was on roughly the same wavelength as the geniuses behind 'Even If It's A Pig, Part Two'.

Simon was so struck by the curious-looking quintet that he immediately press-ganged them into work on the *You Are What You Eat* soundtrack. Earlier in the year, Bob Dylan had met the eccentric Tiny Tim and invited him up to Woodstock. The freakish falsetto singer, yet to break through on Rowan and Martin's *Laugh-In* with the unforgettable 'Tiptoe Thru' The Tulips', was now being let loose by Simon on pop classics like the Ronettes' 'Be My Baby' and Sonny and Cher's 'I Got You, Babe', with predictably hysterical results. All he required was a band, which was how the Hawks found themselves playing behind one last frontman – the strangest yet – before breaking out on their own.

Through the late fall and winter of 1967, with John Simon's help, 'The Crackers' (or 'The Honkies', as they equally mischievously dubbed themselves) demo'd tracks for Capitol. Along with the eight songs that later appeared on *The Basement Tapes* – despite not being recorded in the basement at all – these included 'Ferdinand The Impostor', 'You Say That You Love Me', 'Little Birdies', and 'I Want To Be A Single Girl Again', the last sung rather improbably by Levon Helm. Already the group's versatility was in evidence, with instruments traded back and forth between them. On 'Don't Ya Tell Henry', Levon played mandolin while Richard took over on drums; on 'Ain't No More Cane', it was Rick playing the mandolin, with Levon switching to bass. Garth played the funky piano part on the Dylan song 'Long Distance Operator' while Richard alternately sang and blew harp. The chemistry that had served the Hawks so well through their years on the road was fizzing again. 'It was just like a soup that worked out great,' Robbie told Ruth Albert Spencer in 1985. 'What I really liked about The Band was that everybody made up their own little element of it and it all added up. Everybody contributed something, it wasn't like there were two guys doing everything and the other guys were along for the ride. It really was a unit, and the way we delegated the musical responsibilities seemed really natural.'

A further sign that Dylan and his 'backing band' were now firmly set on different courses was the *John Wesley Harding* album Bob recorded in Nashville in November. Although it shared the rural, downhome quality of the basement tapes he'd recorded with the Hawks, the record was an altogether more sparse and austere affair, and for the most part – shot through with biblical references as it was – devoid of the humour and revelry of the songs he'd written that summer. Ironically, it was Robbie who could inadvertently have taken credit for the severely stripped-down sound. When Dylan returned from Nashville, having cut only basic tracks with bassist Charlie McCoy and drummer Kenny Buttrey, he asked Robbie and Garth to overdub guitar and organ. But Robbie thought the tracks worked as they were – 'it was the right kind of unique after *Blonde On Blonde*,' he said – and urged Bob to leave them alone. The result was a record that distilled many of the themes of the more serious basement songs – guilt and retribution, faith and responsibility, the search for salvation – while starkly setting itself apart from the prevailing sonic overkill of Anglo-American rock. If it ended on an upbeat country note that anticipated the light pleasantries of *Nashville Skyline*, *John Wesley Harding* was in the main a sombre but oddly compelling statement from a man the world still hoped would emerge as some kind of spokesman for youth. (The world would wait in vain: when Happy Traum and John Cohen pressed him for a statement on Vietnam the following June, Dylan seemed 'unconcerned with anything outside Woodstock' and preferred to talk about a local stonemason than about politics.)

That Dylan hadn't completely abandoned the spirit of the basement became clear when he asked the band to back him at a Carnegie Hall tribute to the recently deceased Woody Guthrie on 20 January 1968. In contrast to the mood of *John Wesley Harding*, which on the eve of its release was perplexing everyone from Albert Grossman to Columbia's Clive Davis, the three songs he played that night with 'The Crackers' were like an explosion of lusty energy in the midst of the wholesome right-on-ness displayed by Dylan's old folk chums (Odetta, Pete Seeger, Judy Collins and company). Kicking off with 'I Ain't Got No Home' – not to be confused with the Clarence 'Frogman' Henry song The Band covered on *Moondog Matinee* – the band played with no holds barred, lifting Dylan in the verses and howling along with him when the instruments dropped away for the chorus. 'Dear Mrs

Roosevelt' was slower, but wonderfully redolent of lazy basement afternoons; again Rick, Levon, and Richard wailed along in coarse three-part harmony on the choruses. Rounding off Dylan's thirteen-minute mini-jamboree, which as his first public appearance in over eighteen months had all but upstaged the rest of the performers, was a rip-roaring 'Grand Coulee Dam'. Much to the annoyance of folk's elder statesmen, a handful of girls in the audience actually had the temerity to *dance* to this song. 'Everybody else was on a different plane musically,' says Robbie. 'But we just played what we were doing at the time. I can't help but think Woody Guthrie would have approved. I mean, if a song is going to live it must live in its contemporary surrounding.'[7]

Working as stage manager at the Guthrie show was Jonathan Taplin, the lanky college kid who'd helped out at Newport and was currently road-managing Judy Collins. 'I knew the band had been working on songs with Dylan, but it was all incredibly mysterious,' he says. 'Nobody really knew what was going on up there. Big Pink had been kept *very* secret, no one knew where it was.' After the show, at a party in Robert Ryan's Dakota Building apartment on Central Park West, Taplin got talking with Robbie, who told him a little about the band's activities and plans. Knowing Robbie was a guitar freak, Taplin mentioned a new guitar-cum-pedal steel instrument which was about to come on the market, and earned an invitation to Woodstock and demonstrate it. A year later he would be road-managing The Band.

Shortly after the Guthrie concert, the band finally went into A&R Studios in New York to begin work on their first album. The studio on the seventh floor was an enormous barn-shaped room which had been used for several of the 'live dance-party records' popular in the mid-'60s, so its acoustics couldn't have been better for the songs – both old and new – that the group was planning to record. If the technology was intimidating after the primitive set-up at Big Pink, John Simon and engineer Shelly Yakus quickly made it user-friendly. 'John understood the recording console, he understood tape machines,' says Robbie. 'We'd hardly been around this kind of stuff, and he brought it close to home. He asked us how we wanted the record to sound, and we told him: "Just like it did in the basement".' Simon also helped the band appreciate the importance of arrangements and dynamics within songs: recording was a very different business to performing live, since you had to hold the listener without any visual distraction. 'First came the song,' says Simon. 'Then we saw what we could find in the bass and drums that was interesting, trying always to ensure that the parts were different for each section of the song. Finally, the other instruments fell in around the different grooves.'

Simon would be the first to admit that he learned as much from the band as they did from him. 'They taught me an awful lot,' he says. 'Taught me to write songs not at the piano but from vocal melodies in my head. I got very infatuated with them, I thought it was just the best music I'd ever heard. They were true originals, they didn't listen to the music of the day.' What particularly struck Simon was the sheer affection and empathy between the five of them – something he'd never seen in a rock'n'roll band before. 'They were absolutely like brothers, all of them. I can't recall a single real argument during those sessions.' It was as if there was something organic and innately democratic within the group, so that the songs appeared almost to arrange themselves. 'We'd be working on a tune,' said Levon, 'and the song would dictate who'd sing it and who'd play the supporting roles. Luckily, nobody had such a big head that you couldn't get a tub over it. If we couldn't get a song right, we'd just take the last cut we had of it, put it over to the side, and go on to something else.'

Seasoned sidemen that they were, the band consistently refrained from overplaying. Thinking always as a unit, they seldom trod on each other's toes or felt any need to show off. What counted was the total sound of the song, not disruptive bursts of individual glory. 'There's only a certain amount of room in a song,' said Levon. 'Some things just won't fit. But we're not there to do what we want to do. We're there to do what we're supposed to do. You either get the song to breathe or you don't, and that's the only way to get the song to play *you*.' Robbie was especially concerned to downplay the guitar heroics, rejecting the fuzzboxes and wah-wah gadgets that were becoming ubiquitous in rock. His gauge was still the playing of Curtis Mayfield, once described by Chicago soul man Billy Butler as 'very liquidy, almost fluid'. 'Robbie is among the two or three most *selfless* guitarists in the business,' said Bill Graham. 'And the best, bar none, of any of the guitar players who play with a singer, in unison with the vocals.'

The same selflessness applied to the band's vocal arrangements: 'One voice for all/Echoing around the hall', Richard Manuel sang Musketeer-style on 'We Can Talk'. On that song, above all, the group showed their obvious fascination with the rough-hewn, overlapping voices of gospel music. 'I didn't want screaming vocals,' said Robbie after the album was finished. 'I wanted sensitive vocals where you could hear the breathing and the voices coming in. Everybody in records is working on getting all the voices together until they neutralize themselves. I like voices coming in one at a time, in a chain reaction kind of thing like the Staple Singers did.' The Staples were a particular favourite with the band, who studied the group's classic Vee Jay recordings to understand the way Pop Staples and his daughters 'sang to each other'. Musicologist Dave Emblidge noted how The Band's harmonies frequently contained a deliberate 'space', achieved by combining a highly pitched voice – often Richard's falsetto – with a much lower alto or bass. The resulting texture, 'stark and "incomplete"', was redolent of early gospel recordings. 'It was like a country wail or moan,' says John Simon. 'The Four Tops was a city kind of blend, very slick and sweet. This was more of a wail from the heart or gut.'

The *Big Pink* sessions started at seven in the evening and went on through the night till exhaustion set in. With Levon set up behind barriers in the middle of the room, Rick and Robbie sat next to their amps on chairs and Richard stayed behind the grand piano in the corner. On the other side of the room, Garth put a couple of speakers inside a sound booth so that he could distort his organ sound. By this time, he'd made all sorts of modifications to his Lowrey Festival, an organ almost no other rock bands were using at the time. The sounds and textures he was creating, especially with the pitch-bending facility the Lowrey gave him, were so much more sensual than anything the countless Hammond organ players of the time were producing. 'It always helped having Garth playing beside you,' says Levon. 'He kind of bounced the ball back and forth with you.' Garth was still the band member everybody turned to when there was a query about a chord or a harmony. He rarely said much, but his playing spoke volumes. 'People said Garth lived in his own little world, but it was a big world,' says John Simon. 'And he was less a mad professor than a very dedicated pedant, a great respecter of musical tradition.'

Garth certainly dominated at least one of the five tracks recorded at A&R Studios. Robbie's 'Chest Fever' was easily the most aggressive song on *Big Pink*, and the mighty organ sound, with its intro parodying Bach's famous Toccata and Fugue in D minor, was chiefly responsible. The track was really just one glorious groove, with a lyric that made little sense, but as such it worked. 'It's kind of a hard love song,' Robbie told Robert Palmer, 'but it's a reversal on that old rock and roll thing where they're always telling the girl, you know, "he's a rebel, he'll never be any good". This time it's the other way around.' The best moment in the song was a hilarious middle eight section in which all five Band

Above: Big Pink, still pink in 1991.

Below: Back to country roots in Woodstock, 1968. *(Elliott Landy/Redferns)*

Above: Recording *The Band* in the poolhouse on Sunset Plaza Drive, Los Angeles, February 1969. *(Elliott Landy/Redferns)*

Below: The classic second album, which included 'The Night They Drove Old Dixie Down', 'Rag Mama Rag' and 'Up On Cripple Creek'. *(Courtesy EMI)*

Above: The Band's debut performance, San Francisco, April 1969. A combination of flu and chronic stage fright forced Robbie to call a halt to the set after just seven numbers. *(Elliott Landy/ Redferns)*

Below: Levon and Robbie at the Woodstock Festival, 17 August 1969. Sandwiched between Ten Years After and Johnny Winter, The Band felt (in Robbie's words) like 'a bunch of preacher boys' amidst of 'a ripped army of mud people'. *(Elliott Landy/ Redferns)*

Above: Rick and Robbie back Dylan at the Isle of Wight Festival, 31 August 1969. To the crowd's great displeasure, Dylan played for little over an hour. *(LFI)*

Below: Albert Grossman, The Band's manager, in uncharacteristically cheery mood at the Isle of Wight. *(Barry Plummer)*

Above: Back in America, the group made the cover of *Time* magazine in January 1970. *(Courtesy Bill Millar)*

Below: Posing for the press at London's Inn on the Park hotel, May 1971. *(LFI)*

Above: Albert Grossman's Bearsville Studio, where *Cahoots* (1971) and *Moondog Matinee* (1973) were recorded.

Below: The wraparound poster which accompanied *Moondog Matinee*, featuring an evocative painting by Toronto artist Edward Kasper.

members, joined by John Simon on baritone sax, wheezed along on various horns like some decrepit Salvation Army band.

The horns on *Music From Big Pink* were recorded on the third of the four tracks available, with vocals and all other instruments cut live on tracks 1 and 2. Something of the flavour of the A&R sessions can be sampled on a tape of the band working on 'We Can Talk'. What is remarkable is how few mistakes are made on any of the full takes, despite continual minor variations in the performances of each player. John Simon occasionally stops a take or interjects a remark – 'Garth, do you keep turning the volume up or am I imagining it?' he asks before Take 10 – but otherwise he lets the band finish each take in order to get the feel of the whole song. The web of interplay within the group is astonishing, the voices combining to form a kind of three-headed beast while the churchy piano and organ fit together like hand and glove. Listening to the playbacks in the control room afterwards, Richard heard 'a whole vocal thing I wasn't even aware we had before': 'I remember thinking "I really like this stuff"', he later said, 'and I don't have anything to compare it to.' The song stands as one of The Band's masterworks, a breathless call-and-response yelp of sanctified joy. 'I don't know where that gospel thing came from,' Richard claimed. 'I just got up one morning and found it on the piano.' Self-deprecating as he later was about his talents as a lyricist, 'We Can Talk' was as good in its humorously cryptic way as anything Robbie ever wrote.

Of the other *Big Pink* songs cut during the A&R sessions, 'Tears Of Rage' and 'This Wheel's On Fire' had of course been written and recorded with Bob in the basement. Using the basement tape originals as guides, John Simon helped transform both of them into songs that belonged definitively to The Band. Dylan's 'Tears' was just as mournfully reproachful in its admonition of a rebellious daughter by her father, but the band turned it into something not simply dirge-like but positively *dragging*, a great groan of woe such as Shakespeare's King Lear uttered when he finally understood that he was alone in the world. Over Garth's funereal organ, Robbie's anguished guitar, and Levon's ominous toms, Richard gave the performance of his life, singing Dylan's words with a heartbreaking reverence. At the end of the chorus, on which Rick sang a strangulated harmony, Garth and John blew two bars of sleepy soprano-and-baritone sax that served as a kind of lamentation. Happy Traum was to compare it to 'She's Leaving Home', but as the opening track on *Big Pink* – a decision that Robbie fought for against considerable opposition – 'Tears Of Rage' was more radical even than that. No one hearing the album for the first time, whilst simultaneously inspecting the photograph of the group with their families on the gatefold sleeve, could easily forget the shock of a rock'n'roll band appearing to side with tradition against revolution.[8]

'This Wheel's On Fire' was more overblown, sacrificing the quasi-religious portentousness of Dylan's vocal for something rather less certain of itself – in terms used by Robert Palmer in his sleeve-notes to The Band's *Anthology*, 'a piece of rock'n'roll burnout bravado' rather than 'a spiritual declaration'. Sung by Danko and taken much faster than the Julie Driscoll and Brian Auger version which would make the British Top 10 in April, the arrangement felt laboured and unconvincing. Only the array of peculiar keyboard sounds – one of them produced by a telegraph key that Garth hooked up to a cheap keyboard called a Roxochord – stopped one deducing cynically that the song had been included merely because it had Bob Dylan's name on it.

Curiously enough, given that it remains probably The Band's most famous song – covered by everyone from Aretha Franklin to the Temptations and the Supremes – 'The Weight' was recorded only as an afterthought for *Big Pink*. '"The Weight" was, like, "OK, this doesn't have a very complicated chord progression, it's just kind of traditional, so we'll cut that when we get stuck for a

song,"' recalled Robbie. 'And then we cut it and thought, "Gee, it's
kind of effective when you hear it back at you like that."' On
'The Weight', Southern rock met the Old Testament by way of
the basement tapes. Inspired by the films of the Spanish director
Luis Buñuel, Robbie penned a laid-back country-gospel parable
about 'the impossibility of sainthood', the story of a poor *schmuck*
who does a friend a favour that only leads to people asking further
favours. 'One thing leads to another,' says Robbie, 'and all of a
sudden it's like "Holy shit, what has this turned into?"' Over
Robbie's acoustic guitar and Garth's old-time upright piano, the
three voices once again wailed alongside each other, Levon growling the first three verses in his best Virgil Caine accent, Rick
taking the fourth, the pair of them sharing the fifth, and Richard
helping out on the choruses. (In The Band's staple three-part
harmony, Richard's falsetto sat on top, Rick was in the middle,
and Levon lay on the bottom.)

Like 'Ferdinand The Impostor', 'The Weight' was stuffed with
enough characters for a short story by William Faulkner or Carson
McCullers: apart from the Fanny off whom the protagonist was
repeatedly being asked to 'take the load', there was Carmen, Miss
Moses, Luke, Anna Lee, Crazy Chester, and even a dog called
Jack. As with 'Ferdinand', too, it was hard to determine what the
hell was going on in the song. But once again, words and music
had combined to create a place – a surreal version of Nazareth,
Pennsylvania – that felt vividly real in the telling and singing. As
Dave Marsh wrote, 'the words are bizarre but the meaning that
the singers bring to them has an everyday concreteness, and that's
the contradiction that the music fights to resolve.'

The 'sense of place' in 'The Weight', and on *Big Pink* as a
whole, was one that would continue to haunt Robbie Robertson
for years to come. 'In my mind,' he said in 1987, 'there's this
mythical place in America where *the storyteller* lives. And he tells
stories based on this place and on people who've passed through

it. I've never been there, but we all know it's there.' Clearly it was a place that haunted many of *Big Pink*'s listeners, too, critics and fans alike who longed to believe in the mysterious, pre-industrial America of folk stories and blues songs. As Greil Marcus later wrote of Robertson, 'perhaps because he comes from outside, the storyteller can see the country whole, just as those who have always lived there can see it only in pieces.'

Capitol Records were so pleased with the five tracks which emerged from the A&R sessions that they asked the band to come out to L.A. to finish the album at the company's own 8-track studio in the famous Capitol Tower. Bringing in engineer Rex Updegraft, whom John Simon remembered as 'a very cool gentleman' bearing a striking resemblance to Gregory Peck, they spent almost a month in Hollywood, not only recording the six songs that made up the rest of *Big Pink* but also cutting four additional tracks at the Gold Star studio on Santa Monica Boulevard.

The Capitol sessions saw the recording of two of Richard Manuel's loveliest songs, 'In A Station' and 'Lonesome Suzie'. Partly inspired by the beauty of Woodstock's Overlook Mountain, 'Station' was an enchanting ballad arranged and sung in a supremely distinctive style. The singing was wistful, the dreamy sound made up of plinky toytown keyboards and a pining pedal-steel-style guitar. 'I always liked that line "I could taste your hair",' said Richard, who claimed he thought of 'In A Station' as his 'George Harrison-type song'. Perhaps if he'd thought of himself a little less as a George Harrison figure – 'I can write music very easily, but when it comes to words I cringe,' he said just before his death – we'd have had more songs like this and 'Lonesome Suzie', a portrait of a small-town spinster that inadvertently said so much about Manuel's own loneliness. Pointing forward to 'Whispering Pines', and even to his anguished reading of Bobby Bland's 'Share Your Love With Me', 'Suzie' was classic Manuel: sung in his richest falsetto voice, supported by delicate guitar and organ fills, the track dripped with longing and despair, with the tender sympathy only a fellow lonelyheart could possibly muster. Richard wrote the song as 'a hit record', but he couldn't have known how chillingly naked his performance would sound.

It was Richard's falsetto, too, which closed out *Big Pink* with the 'benediction' of Dylan's 'I Shall Be Released'. A song that now seems to mark a transitional point between the basement tapes and *John Wesley Harding*, 'Released' was the yearning testament of a prisoner, a man who, if not in an actual prison cell, was in some religious sense incarcerated and dreaming of freedom. (In time, the song would come to speak metaphorically for Manuel's own release from what rock folk love to call 'the demons'.) Taking its cue from Dylan's unreleased basement tape of the song – though in pronounced contrast to the almost jaunty version Bob would record for his 1971 album *Greatest Hits Vol. 2* – the band's 'I Shall Be Released' could almost be a theme song for Amnesty International. Richard sang it like a prayer, bathed in the ambient sound of a Roxochord Garth played through a wah-wah, and the others joined him on the hushed, devotional choruses. Robbie played his old Stella acoustic through one of Garth's 'little black boxes', and John Simon had the idea of getting Levon to brush his fingers through the snares of his drum. The total effect was akin to a hymn of faith, which was why it was later the obvious choice for the all-star, pre-Live Aid-style finale at The Last Waltz.

You couldn't exactly have called 'I Shall Be Released' a 'cover version'. 'Long Black Veil', on the other hand, was very obviously a cover. An 'instant murder ballad' penned by writers Marijohn Wilkin and Danny Dill, the song had been a hit for several artists, notably the Texan country singer Lefty Frizzell. 'I thought it was a great song,' said Robbie. 'It was in the tradition that I wanted to begin writing in.' Robbie also claimed that they covered the song 'to get across the point that we don't feel we're the only song-writers around'. The trouble was, the sombre tale – about a man hanged because he couldn't use the alibi that he was 'in bed with his best friend's wife' – was too literal, too studied by half. Sung by Rick to the accompaniment of Richard's Wurlitzer electric piano, 'Long Black Veil' *sounded* like something cooked up by a couple of Nashville hacks – not like the haunting Carter Family-style ballad Robbie obviously wanted it to be.

Another track on *Big Pink* that carried less impact than 'Tears Of Rage' or 'In A Station' was 'To Kingdom Come', a song Robbie virtually wrote in the Capitol studio. Despite its engaging lyric, very much in the apocalyptic Southern mode of Dylan's less ribald basement songs, it was let down by the only lead vocal Robbie was to record until 'Knockin' Lost John' in 1976. Mark Wiliams in the 1983 *History of Rock* series argued that in this song the 'lost soul' of the preceding track 'Tears Of Rage' has given up on life and longs for death to relieve him of his grief. But the music, punchy and defiant after 'Tears Of Rage', hardly suggests that kind of resignation.

A more successful Robertson composition was 'Caledonia Mission', a song which John Simon remembers 'just popping up – like "Remember that one? Let's pull that up and fill the album out with it."' A wryly oblique song of longing for a missionary in the non-existent town of Modock, Arkansas, it exactly fits the description Ronnie Hawkins was to use for *Big Pink* as a whole: 'funky country'. Rick sings the verses in a typically bumpkin-sincere voice, with purring falsetto support from Richard, then lets rip on a chorus Steely Dan might have written had they hailed from somewhere below the Mason–Dixon line.

During the one week that the Capitol studio was unavailable, the band went into Gold Star, where Phil Spector had cut his classic Crystals and Ronettes sides. Here they recorded four blues songs, including Big Bill Broonzy's 'Key To The Highway', remembered by Robbie as 'a kind of obnoxious throwback' to his guitar-hero days with Hawkins and Dylan. None of the tracks was ever used, but then neither were 'Little Birdies', 'Ferdinand The Impostor', or even 'Yazoo Street Scandal', which was listed on the promotional *Big Pink* sleeves sent out to disc jockeys in the late summer.

With the album finally in the can and ready to be mixed, it was time for the band to head back to Woodstock and prepare for their encounter with the America that awaited them. It was also time to find a proper name.

3

Caviar and Harveyburgers

Crossing the great divide, The Band left community in their wake.

Greil Marcus

The Woodstock to which the band returned in the spring of 1968 was not quite the backwater retreat it had been a year before; not for nothing did *Village Voice* columnist Richard Goldstein call the town 'the great green hope for the urban blues'. The very fact that Bob Dylan had chosen it as his personal hideaway ensured that it would not remain a hideaway for long. 'Those were the years,' wrote Musa Meyer, 'when Tinker Street came to resemble a bucolic extension of St Mark's Place and Tompkins Square East . . . when the sleepy little town of Woodstock exploded from the modest artists' colony it still was in the '50s to become the booming summer resort it is now, crowded with gift shops and boutiques.'

Sadly, it was time to move out of Big Pink: the house may have been 'Big' but it was too small to accommodate four band members and their sometime female companions. While Rick and Levon found a house to share out on Wittenberg Road near the Grossman estate, the others moved into a place off Ohayo Mountain Road, just south of Tinker Street. The geographical dispersion had little effect on the group's unity, since they saw each other virtually every day. Often the meetings would take place at Albert's house, where life revolved around the kitchen and its huge stock of gourmet delicacies.

The band's relationship with their manager was growing under the shadow of another relationship that had gone badly wrong –

160

the one between Grossman and Dylan. Ever since the motorcycle accident, Dylan had decided he wanted nothing more to do with Albert, who'd overworked and possibly cheated him for several years. At least two songs on *John Wesley Harding*, 'Dear Landlord' and 'The Ballad Of Frankie Lee And Judas Priest', were veiled attacks on Grossman, and at the Woody Guthrie concert the two had barely spoken to one another.

Finding themselves caught in the crossfire, the band – and Robbie in particular – trod carefully. 'Robbie was one of the most gracious, charming, and diplomatic of all the musicians I've ever known,' Al Aronowitz wrote. 'He straddled the fence with tact and style to remain a buddy of both Albert and Bob without recriminations from either.' To Robbie, Grossman was even more of a mentor than Dylan had been: at Albert's funeral in 1986, he went so far as to describe the man as his 'teacher'. 'Robbie always liked Albert,' says Jonathan Taplin. 'They lived right next door to each other and shared certain intellectual interests. There wasn't that much closeness between Albert and the others. They were kinda country guys in a lot of ways, and quite self-contained.'[1] When the legendary West Coast promoter Bill Graham came up to Woodstock, he was struck by 'the very simple and respectful relationship' the group had with their manager, an impression borne out by Libby Titus' feeling that they were 'almost like his children'. 'Albert really wanted the best for them,' she recalls. 'He wanted to educate them, to take them to Paris and teach them about *filet mignon* and *sauce bernaise*.'

Grossman was not an easy man to like. One viewing of Pennebaker's *Don't Look Back* is all it takes to demonstrate what a mercenary and humourless ogre he was. 'You could see that Albert was capable of almost anything, because he hardly ever changed in appearance,' remarked pianist Nick Gravenites before Albert's death. 'He *is* a little sinister . . . to the point where you can *see* him being sinister!' It was Albert who'd nurtured the megalomaniac power-tripper in Dylan, Albert who was breeding the same standoffishness in Robbie. 'You could have spent the entire evening with all three of them and they wouldn't say a word,' recalls Artie Traum. 'You'd end up thinking, "What's going on? Have I done something wrong?"'

Having lost Dylan's trust, Albert was now concentrating on the band, whose music he genuinely loved, and on his other artists. The New York *Daily News* accused Grossman of wrapping Janis Joplin in a 'Garboesque' image, but Joplin herself would have defended the strategy as part of her manager's attempts to protect her privacy. 'Albert taught us something about protection that we didn't even know was necessary,' says Robbie. 'You can protect a lot of things, I guess. Your sanity, your privacy ... whatever's hanging out the most.' The truth is, Albert was ultimately less interested in 'protecting' his artists than in building up impregnable fortresses of mystique around them. It was a strategy that had worked with Mary Travers of Peter, Paul and Mary – 'Albert's edict was that Mary should not speak,' remembered Peter Yarrow – and it was one which was working for his newer acts. 'Albert takes a lot of the rap for turning his artists into arrogant poseurs,' says Al Aronowitz. John Hammond Jr for one could have testified to that.

Albert knew there was already an aura of mystery and conjecture around the band. It was simply a question of capitalizing on it, finding the right name and the right image for the release of the album. Capitol, home to a number of Southern artists (Joe South, Bobbie Gentry, and others), had now woken up to the full connotations of the name 'The Crackers'; nor did they care much for 'The Honkies'. By the late spring, Albert and the band had decided to take the mystique factor to the limit and release *Music From Big Pink* without a name on it at all. If the spine of the sleeve said 'The Band' – 'just so they can file it in the stores,' said Levon – the LP label simply listed the names of the five members.

Indeed, when 'The Weight' was released as a single in September, many reviewers listed the five names as the name of 'the band'. 'This is even worse than Dave Dee, Dozy, Beaky, Mick and Tich,' complained one British writer.

Both Albert and Ronnie knew it was now vital for the group to distance itself from Dylan without losing the value of the connection. Dylan himself had offered to play and sing backing vocals on *Big Pink*, but understood completely when Robbie declined. Instead, he donated the *faux naif* album cover, significantly featuring not five but six musicians, together with an elephant and an apple tree. 'A very warm, neighbourly gift,' said Robbie, who described the painting as 'a panorama of the rock'n'roll scene'. 'We saw there could no longer be any advantage to either one of us in playing together,' Robbie added. 'We were starting to arouse attention, and all we could do was get in his way. I mean, he has a thing to do, he doesn't need a co-star. And we didn't need a star. The band doesn't have any stars. You know, stars are something that have always been in the sky, and we just never felt the need to bring them down here.'

It was this sense of anonymity which had to be communicated on the cover of the album, not just in Dylan's playful painting but in the photograph of the group. 'After we'd recorded the album,' says Robbie, 'we thought about the cover and everybody was saying, "Oh, you should use this photographer, he's the best in the country". But it just seemed like we were gonna come out with some kind of cutesy picture, and we didn't want that.' Everyone agreed that they wanted a far rougher image for the band. 'People were telling us about the best photographer, so I asked who was the *worst* photographer in New York! Someone said, "There's this guy, the staff photographer for *Rat* magazine, I don't know if he's the worst, but he works for this magazine which is unquestionably the worst." So I said, "Well, let's try him out."'

*

Elliott Landy was a New Yorker who, in his own words, 'had flipped out on a combination of strong grass and high-quality sound'. He'd started taking pictures at anti-war marches and rock concerts, giving them to the New York underground press free and helping with layouts. Along with one or two other snappers, he'd managed to sneak a camera into the Woody Guthrie concert, only to be bundled unceremoniously out of Carnegie Hall by a couple of Grossman stooges for his troubles. This, surprisingly, did not deter him from presenting Albert with some shots of Janis Joplin which he'd taken at the Anderson Theater. 'Albert was scary,' says Landy, 'but to his credit he overlooked our little contretemps when he saw my photographs.'

Landy went to meet the band while they were mixing *Big Pink* at A&R Studios just before Easter. 'I did everything wrong that I could have done to get the Band shoot,' he laughs. 'I had a bad relationship with Albert, I brought only performance shots when Robbie was only interested in outdoor stuff . . . but it all worked out.' The following weekend, Elliott drove up to Woodstock and hung out with the group. He immediately felt comfortable with them. 'I felt fairly early on that they were not just another rock'n'roll band,' he says. 'They were unusually wise about life, and there wasn't one of them that I felt was in any sense lesser than the others, in terms of the ability to comprehend the essence of every situation they found themselves in.' The chemistry within the group struck Landy in the same way that it had struck John Simon. 'They were like brothers. Robbie was the organizer. Levon was a little angrier than he is now, he didn't like being photographed at all. Rick acted the country cousin, but that was a Mark Twain character he used in order to say things without being condescending. He and Levon genuinely liked people, regardless of how strange they were or how redneck, how liberal, how bright, how dumb.'

John Simon would have agreed with Landy's observation that

Robbie was already 'the organizer' of the group. 'He was the smartest of the bunch,' says the producer. 'He had his agenda figured out way in advance, and he wasn't going to be held back.' But if Robbie was starting to outgrow the others intellectually – and to take himself increasingly seriously – it wasn't something that affected his relationship with them. 'He wouldn't be talking about Buñuel in front of Rick and Levon anyway,' says Simon. 'You've got to remember that he was a *fantastic* rock'n'roll guitar player, and if sometimes the others joked with him about his lyrics, they *always* respected him as a musician.'

It was certainly Robbie whose vision determined the nature of *Big Pink*'s cover. Keen to make a visual statement that would set them apart from the incendiary, post-Flower Power mood of 1968, he hit on the idea of Landy's photographing the band together with their families up in Ontario. 'We were rebelling against the rebellion,' he says. 'If everybody else was going east, then we were going west. It wasn't like we even discussed it, there was this kind of ingrained thing from us all along. It was an instinct to separate ourselves from the pack.' For Robbie, the spectacle of Jim Morrison extolling the Oedipal desires and patricide of 'The End' was not shocking but merely faddish. Nor was he prepared to jump on any anti-American bandwagon. 'I never ran around with flags on my car or anything, but I did think that America had given me the opportunity to do something I was very appreciative of.' Like so many immigrants, this outsider was far more reactionary than the angry sons and daughters of the establishment of the time. In a year when the time was right for violent revolution, The Band were about to release the oddly plaintive, explicitly conservative 'Tears Of Rage'.

After flying to Toronto with John Simon, Landy was driven down to Simcoe, where the group had assembled with their relatives on the Danko chicken farm. For Landy, the experience was bizarre. 'The whole idea of the picture was totally unusual to me,' he says, 'because despite having a lot of relatives my whole issue at the time was to separate from my family.' None the less, the portrait – entitled 'Next Of Kin' as it was on the *Big Pink* cover – had its desired effect. Surrounded by a veritable mob of Dankos, Manuels, and Hudsons, with a separate photo of Diamond and Nell Helm up in the left hand corner, the five band members stood serenely in front of a red barn, spring bursting into life around them. Right at the front of the gathering were Tom and Leola Danko with six of their grandchildren. The sense of serenity on the cover was completed by a little picture of Big Pink itself, captioned by Robbie's girlfriend Dominique: 'A pink house seated in the sun of Overlook Mountain in West Saugerties, New York. Big Pink bore this music and these songs along its way. It's the first witness of this album that's been thought and composed right there inside its walls.'

It took considerably longer to get the famous photo of the band standing against the backdrop of the Catskill mountains. Two shoots produced a lot of nice compositions, but no definitive image. The group briefly considered using a shot Landy had taken of them on a bench, with their backs turned to the camera. 'We thought about going with that shot, because they wanted to be anonymous,' recalls Landy. 'Dylan had influenced them in that respect – a lot of their thinking about going public with their music had come from him. They were always coming from a place of integrity about music. Music was music, it wasn't personalities doing songs, so the idea was to keep the egos out of it.' In the end, the inspiration came from a book of nineteenth-century photographs of the American West: fuzzy, haunting portraits of miners and prospectors holding stiff poses and shy expressions. 'They liked that style,' says Landy. 'I told them that in those days film was very slow and that people had to stand very still: you were posed, you took a deep breath, and you didn't move. Also, when a photographer came you got dressed up for the occasion.

So we put these elements together. I gave it about a quarter-second exposure, which is why it's a little bit blurry. Just to give it that old look, they wore hats, which they loved anyway.'

When he finally found the right place at the right time of day, Landy created a time-warped portrait of the band which fixed them in an actual time-warp, since this is how most people think of The Band if they 'imagine' them at all. The composition seemed effortless: just the five of them in hats, waistcoats, and bootlace ties, Levon with his thumbs in his pockets, Garth with a water-divining stick, Robbie ever so slightly set apart from them at one end. To anyone who didn't know, they could as easily have been five desperadoes on the loose during the Gold Rush. As Greil Marcus observed the following year, 'they might be an accident of the frontier, a group of happy, weathered outcasts who fell to-gether in Tombstone, Arizona and decided to give it all up and play music'. The dissimulation was so effective that after *Big Pink*'s release a producer from Apple Films, Joe Massat, saw the picture and asked the band to play an outlaw gang in a western called *Zachariah*. (Recalled Robbie, 'it was about a bunch of bandits who go into town, rob a bank, then go back into the hills and pull out some electric guitars!') On another occasion, the slightly rabbinical-looking guitarist was stopped for speeding while en route to New York. 'The state trooper just looked at me and said, "We'll let you off this time, rabbi, but please be careful in future"!'[2]

Landy's picture also had the effect of cementing the idea of the group *as a band*, all of them looking sufficiently alike in appearance and height for there to be no real distinction between them. 'Collectively,' said Levon, 'five people can add up to more than five. That's what helped us: we'd been back-to-back for a long time, we were birds of a feather. We all had a common appreciation of music, art, and nature, and our chemistry had been tried and tested under fire.' This was partly what made it so easy for writers like Marcus to see in The Band a kind of microcosmic community, a potent model of the early American pioneer settlements. 'I thought of the band as a little workshop,' said Robbie. 'This guy fixes the furniture, this guy takes care of the glass, this one does the plumbing. Everyone has his own little job.' For Marcus, too, their very 'brotherliness' accorded neatly with Leslie Fiedler's ideas about male bonding and escape from matriarchy in *Love And Death In The American Novel*. There were no Haight-Ashbury-style love-ins or tie-dyed earth mothers in *this* neck of the woods.

When *Music From Big Pink* was finally released in early August, 1968, the band kept their heads down and let the rumours of Dylan's involvement in the record do the talking: Bob was playing piano on it, people said, and could even be made out at the back of the 'Next Of Kin' picture if you looked carefully. There was so much word-of-mouth hype about the album that actual promotion by the group seemed unnecessary. As Robbie told Susan Lydon: 'It was summertime, and hot, and there wasn't much to do. So we just sat around Woodstock some more. We didn't expect the hullabaloo, and I guess we weren't ready to come out in public yet. Actually, we had thought about it some: if we put out this record and it does do really well, it might be nice not to jump on the bandwagon and shout, "It was us, it was us!". We thought it would be better to go somewhere like Jamaica and watch it all happen from there, rather than jump right out and milk ourselves dry.' Again it was Albert who encouraged the band to keep their distance from the media. 'With Albert,' says Rick, 'you could always pick and choose. And if you weren't sure, you stayed home.'

Capitol Records, not surprisingly, were unhappy about the Grossman strategy, mystique or no mystique. Without consulting the band, they planned an inane 'Big Pink Think Campaign', featuring a contest to name Dylan's cover painting and a competition entry blank that read: 'If I could be a Big Pink anything, I'd be a Big Pink ——' Prizes included a pink Yamaha motorcycle, pink panda bears, and bottles of pink lemonade. When Albert got wind of the campaign, Robbie flew straight out to L.A. and asked Capitol 'very strongly just to leave us alone'. The whole debacle was only too clearly symptomatic of the band's uneasy relationship with the pop industry.

Capitol couldn't have complained about the reviews *Big Pink* elicited. 'The band dips into the well of tradition and comes up with bucketsfull of clear, cool, country soul that washes the ears with a sound never heard before,' wrote Al Aronowitz in *Life*. 'Traditionalists may not like it because it's too original. Pop faddists won't like it because it's too traditional. It is the kind of album which will have to open its own door to a new category.' In *Sing Out!*, of all places, Happy Traum called the album 'the most funky, most heartfelt, and most original record to come out in some time'. In *Rolling Stone*, part-time scribe Al Kooper described the music as 'that good old intangible, can't-put-your-finger-on-it "White Soul", not so much a white cat imitating a spade, but something else that reaches you on a non-Negro level like church music or country music or Jewish music or Dylan'. This sense of the band creating their own kind of 'country soul' sound was precisely what appealed to Elvis Costello when he first heard *Big Pink*. 'I always thought The Band were the most convincing white band doing music based on deep soul,' he says. 'They kind of invented their own version of it, almost by accident or out of the limitations and quirks of the instrumentalists' styles. I always suspected white singers who tried too hard to sound like soul singers, but The Band never did that. Rick Danko, in particular, had a unique style, it was kind of nasal and it had a little bit of what I now realize is country in it, but at the same time it was just so unusual to me, such a lovely and relaxed sound.'

Al Kooper claimed he could hear all kinds of influences in *Big Pink*: the Beach Boys, the Coasters, Hank Williams, and the Swan Silvertones being just a few of them. The band might have argued with some of the names, but they would probably have agreed with Greil Marcus' verdict that their music was 'an unpredictable resolution of a common inheritance'. 'It was like adding up these pieces together,' says Robbie, 'so that you actually hear the humour of Little Willie John's "All Around The World", and you hear these voices doing Staple Singers stuff, and a high singer like Smokey Robinson, but with these kind of Hank Williams-influenced lyrics.' In late 1969, after the release of *The Band*, Robbie would tell *Time*'s William Bender that 'your roots are really everything that's ever impressed you, whether that's a bridge from a Little Milton song, an impressive horn line by Cannonball Adderley, or a singing harmony that J. E. Mainer and His Mountaineers did years ago.'

Of all the qualities manifested on *Music From Big Pink*, it seems to have been the pronounced rural leaning that most impressed – and surprised – its first listeners. 'I was so shocked,' recalls Ronnie Hawkins, who was expecting the band's first album to sound like 'Howlin' Wolf on benzedrine'. 'I mean, they were a rhythm and blues act, they didn't *like* country music. When Robbie brought me the tape I said, Goddamn, that's country as hell, but it's *funky* country, I like it. I could hear Levon in there all right. Robbie got most of the credit but Levon was the funk in the music.' Even Rick's brother Terry was amazed that they had 'gone country': 'I still thought of them as one of the best R&B bands around,' he says.

Of course, the band hadn't 'gone country' as such, as Paul Nelson made clear in a sceptical *Hullabaloo* piece about 'the new country rock' in November. 'The Tin Pan Alley hypesters always go at things backwards,' Nelson noted. '"Hmmm", they say, "Dylan's *John Wesley Harding*, the band's *Big Pink*, the Byrds' *Sweetheart Of The Rodeo* are selling like hot cakes, and they sound like country music. So country rock is going to be the next big thing." But it doesn't work that way – their music would be moving well if Antarctican rock were the next big thing and no one had heard of country music.' None the less, the country factor was there, and it was part of what made the three albums Nelson mentioned so influential. Coming when they did, after the dizzying psychedelia and acid jams of 1967, they seemed to signal a retreat from drugs and sonic overkill – a 'pastoralism' of the kind Leo Marx described in his 1967 book *The Machine In The Garden*. Marx, however, distinguished between writers for whom 'the pastoral instinct' reflected only a Freudian sense of 'the need for freedom' and those – from Thoreau and Melville to Frost and Hemingway – who had embraced the violence and loneliness of nature. As musicologist Dave Emblidge argued, The Band's music may have appealed to many people because of its 'country flavour', but their pastoralism was rarely idealized, and focused as much on the pain and darkness of rural life as on 'the salving beauties of nature'.

Idealized or not, it was the gutty, downhome flavour of *Big Pink*'s brew that so impressed the band's fellow musicians on both sides of the Atlantic. The album may not have been a huge commercial success, never rising above #30 on the *Billboard* album chart, but it had a huge impact on the leading lights of the British rock scene: George Harrison, Mick Jagger, Pete Townshend, and particularly Cream's Eric Clapton. 'I got hold of a bootleg tape of *Big Pink* at the end of the last Cream tour,' Clapton recalled, 'and I used to put it on as soon as I checked into my hotel room, do the gig and be utterly miserable, then rush back and put the tape on and go to sleep fairly contented until I woke up the next morning and remembered who I was and what I was doing. It was *that* potent!' For Clapton, the album showed up the hollow virtuosity that Cream were peddling; it made him long to return to something simpler, more sincere. 'The album wasn't publicly exposed in the same way as it was to musicians,' he remembered, and it had a shocking effect on more people than you can actually ever realize. The sound of music changed drastically after that first album – everywhere.' So intrigued was Clapton by the mysterious quintet who'd played behind Dylan that he even went up to Woodstock to meet them. 'They turned out to be great people – very intelligent, very tight,' he said. 'And I've been in awe of them ever since.'

Closer to home, less God-like individuals than Eric Clapton were turning on to *Big Pink* in the same way. Artie Traum remembers running into Albert Grossman at the Tin Angel café in New York when 'The Bear' had just received a copy of the *Big Pink* cover. 'I'd heard little rumblings about the group, of course,' says Artie, 'but Albert turned to me and with his very pretentious way of speaking said, "I have here the greatest group of all time!" When I finally got hold of the album, the overall sound was something I'd never heard before. It was the way they approached the notes. There was a kind of cohesion to it. It was Americana, but it was also contemporary and fresh. I always thought that the person who really shaped the sound was Garth – what he brought to the keyboards and the accordion was very unique.' Another East Village acolyte, one who like Traum would soon wend his way up to Woodstock, was fiddle player Larry Packer. 'I was in awe of them,' he says. 'The intensity, the originality, the musicality. There was no bullshit in this music. For me, it was a kind of carry-over from the Dylan sound and to a certain extent from the sound they'd got on John Hammond's Vanguard records. In my band, we'd get up in the morning and the first thing we'd do was put on *Big Pink*.'

In the late summer, Bill Graham came up to Woodstock to discuss the possibility of the band playing some shows at his two Fillmore theatres. 'I'd had a long relationship, and a good one, with Albert

Grossman and Danny Weiner,' Graham said shortly before his death in a helicopter crash in October 1991. 'They of course had told me about the band, that mythical group of guys who lived up in the country and woodshedded. Everyone had told me about them, but *Big Pink* itself was the first chance to eat the meat. Now, I enjoy sensual music, and The Band to me had a sensuality and a flow. There was a funky, groovy, swirly character to the sound – I mean, for white guys they moved good – and I loved the odd sorta non-voices of Rick and Richard and Levon. They also didn't *sell* anything, in the "Hey, clap your hands!" sense of the phrase. So the music held up to the myth for once.'

Bill Graham hadn't counted on the band's reticence and apparent indifference to fame. 'They told me they weren't thinking about performing live, so I said: "But there are so many people who wanna hear you". What I hadn't yet realized was that they weren't entertainers, they were players.' As people, the group struck Bill as 'reserved but very cordial': 'They were conservative and laid-back, whereas I was a big city boy and not too conservative in my approach. They pretty much set the terms of the relationship, and I didn't probe too much. It was a bit like Dylan – you could ask them what time it was, but that was about it!'

Content to sit back and wait, the band yet again put their feet up. Although 'The Weight' climbed all the way to #21 in Britain, where *New Musical Express* reported that *Big Pink* 'is said to carry on the current Dylan preoccupation with mystical country and western folk tales', the single never climbed any higher than #63 in America, making it unnecessary to hit the road or make TV appearances. Besides, Dominique was now pregnant, so there was at least one good reason for taking it easy. 'We never did want to take that full-throttle sort of commercial gear,' says Levon. 'I never wanted to be recognized on the street and mobbed. I like going to places without all of that star stuff. As for write-ups in the press, we tried to keep it on a review basis as much as we could.

We hoped they'd review the record and leave our personalities out of it.'

In this shying-away from the limelight, the band continued to follow the example of their old boss Bob Dylan, for whom 1968 – at least in terms of music – was virtually a lost year. Just as they were adopting a consciously low-key approach with *Big Pink*, so Bob had asked Columbia to release *John Wesley Harding* 'with no publicity or hype, because this was the season of hype'. 'Dylan was going through a transformation,' recalls Elliott Landy, who shot him for an Al Aronowitz *Saturday Evening Post* feature and would in due course shoot the cover of *Nashville Skyline*. 'He was learning to feel love and express it and experience it in the family way. That's what *Nashville Skyline* was about: very introspective, very country-like, very haven-like music.' With two more children on board – Anna and Seth – Bob seemed to be in a state of semi-retirement, one which bordered on depression. When George Harrison visited him in Woodstock in November, he felt Dylan had lost all confidence in himself.

Ironically, just as the band began to reconsider the idea of performing live, Rick Danko had a very bad car accident that scuppered all possibility of touring. 'He had a big Lincoln Confidential, as he used to call it,' Jonathan Taplin recalled, 'and he just ran off the road, I'm sure drunk or stoned. He still had a very stiff neck the following spring.' The first of several such accidents in Rick's career, the smash-up put him in traction right through the fall and early winter. 'Rick was the real good ol' boy of the band,' says John Simon. 'A real hail-fellow-well-met kinda guy and always up for a good time. Hence the occasional accident.' Because there was no announcement of the accident, the band's silence was seen as an almost mystical statement of disengagement from the rock scene. 'For the outside world, we were this bunch of guys who dressed in black and lived up in the mountains,' says Robbie. 'It was like some kind of cult.' Little did people know that the black-clad hermits of Woodstock were constantly getting into near-fatal car accidents. Shortly after Rick's crash, Levon turned over a gold Corvette on the Ulster County backroads. Only Garth's stately black Mercedes seemed to stay on the road for any length of time.

Robbie put the extra time to good use, beginning work on some of the songs which would end up on the band's second album. One of them was 'King Harvest (Will Surely Come)'. 'It was the harvest time of year, when Woodstock was very impressive,' he says. 'Everything turned red and orange and it just made you realize that this was the culmination of the year for so many people. And there was all the history in the background – that's when it all came down, whether the year worked out or not.' When they came to record *The Band*, 'King Harvest' fittingly proved to be its 'culmination'.

Another of the songs was the sombre, piano-based tune that became 'The Night They Drove Old Dixie Down'. 'It took me about eight months in all to write that song,' says Robbie. 'I only had the music for it, and I didn't know what it was about at all. I'd sit down at the piano and play these chords over and over again. And then one day, the rest of it came to me. Sometimes you have to wait a song out, and I'm glad I waited for that one.'

By the time Rick was fit to entertain the notion of live performance again, the band was bubbling with enough musical ideas to fill three new albums. In January 1969, Robbie told *Rolling Stone*'s Paul Nelson that this was precisely what they were planning. Already assuming the role of spokesman for the group, he outlined the concepts for the records. The first would be put together from 'a whole lot of songs, including possibly some of Dylan's new ones, which I describe as some of the best stuff he's ever done'. The album would be more complex than *Big Pink*, with more instruments used but with all of them played by the band members.

'We aren't going in with any concept idea, but it may seem like it when we're through.' The second album would be made up of songs written by band members for 'friends who've asked for them'. The third, finally, would be 'an old-fashioned sing-song, like beer parties your aunt and uncle used to have': 'We're very much into sitting around the fire and drinking brew and playing songs, and it seems like the people who visit us dig it, too, but they never really get the opportunity to do it.'

Asked about the band's apparent reluctance to perform live, Robbie told Nelson that, despite lots of offers, 'too many of them are the turn-on-the-lights-and-freak-out kind of scene, fads and businessmen with their timetables'. 'We hope to be able to go out and play for people in certain selective dates in the spring,' he added. 'But we don't want to make the arena circuit where people don't hear nothing or know nothing and all that matters is taking three bucks off the kids.'

That winter, the band were stuck in Woodstock, up to their eyeballs in snow. By the time they'd shovelled their cars out of the white stuff each day, there wasn't a lot of time left to work on music. 'Some people like it around Woodstock in winter,' says Jonathan Taplin, who was working part-time for the band before resuming studies at Princeton, 'but this bunch of Canadians had had enough snow for one lifetime.' When the band went to Albert and told him they wanted to record an album in a private house in Los Angeles – 'we've got some groovy things planned', Robbie had told Paul Nelson, 'but they won't work in a studio situation' – Taplin was assigned the task of finding a suitable place and transporting the group's equipment coast-to-coast. 'We didn't wanna go back into studios and use engineers and union people,' says Rick. 'We'd get engineers who'd had hits for people so they'd wanna take you on *their* trip. We'd be thinking Harveyburgers and they'd be thinking caviar.'

In early February, Taplin arranged to rent a house on Sunset

Plaza Drive, just off Sunset Boulevard near the legendary Chateau Marmont hotel.[3] The large house had once belonged to Sammy Davis Jr and boasted not only 'a slew of bedrooms' but a poolhouse that was ideal for temporary conversion into the band's DIY recording studio. With the help of his Princeton room-mate Lindsay Holland, Taplin packed the band's equipment into a Dodge mini-van – Garth's organ included – and headed west. Once they'd arrived, John Simon flew in to supervise the transformation of the poolhouse, baffling the walls securely and setting up the recording console hired for the band by Capitol. 'They set the board up right there in the room, which was fairly radical for the time,' says Taplin.

With the 'studio' ready, Simon flew on to Hawaii, where he and Robbie spent a brainstorming week working on arrangements and planning sessions. 'Robbie is the kind of person who writes voraciously for a couple of weeks and comes up with a whole bunch of tunes really fast,' says Artie Traum. 'He just kind of says, "All right, we've got to do an album, let's go write".' According to Simon, the idea of 'a sort of concept album' about the American South was there from the very beginning. Seated at an upright piano in his hotel room, Robbie completed the songs that would make *The Band* a staple of 'classic album' lists in years to come: songs like 'Across The Great Divide', 'The Night They Drove Old Dixie Down', and 'King Harvest (Will Surely Come)'. 'It was mostly a matter of, "Are these pictures getting this thing across?", and knowing I only had so much time to tell this story in,' Robbie says. 'Sometimes it was condensing, sometimes it was searching, sometimes it was beating my head against the wall. And I never developed a method or a particular technique. It was all just wrenching it out of your gut.' The remaining songs came so fast, in such a surge of creativity, that Robbie even had time to work on tracks for John Simon's own album for Warner Brothers: their co-written 'Davey's On The Road Again' was later a minor hit for Manfred Mann.

After the band had arrived and settled in at the Sammy Davis house, the makeshift and decidedly lo-tech setup quickly became reminiscent of the clubhouse atmosphere at Big Pink. 'It was very cosy recording on our own with nobody there looking over your shoulder and making you stick to schedules,' Robbie told *NME*'s Nick Logan. 'It was also a miracle that it worked, because we'd gone out there with this hair-brained idea and actually pulled it off.' The cosiness notwithstanding, the band had to pull all the stops out to get the work done: Capitol had been late delivering the recording equipment as it was, and now it was down to a combination of super-creativity and 'fat girls' pills' to finish as many tracks as possible in one month. 'It was really a lot of work,' said Robbie, 'especially since I was already wasted before we began.' The fact that critics and fellow musicians had built up *Big Pink* to such a degree only put more pressure on Robbie: 'I really felt my ass was on the line,' he said.

In the end, eight of *The Band*'s twelve tracks were credited to Robbie alone, with three shared by Richard and one by Levon. On the other hand, in contrast to *Big Pink*, Robbie did not sing on the album. 'The biggest reason why I chose not to sing was that it would have unbalanced the whole thing,' he says. 'I didn't want to be the writer *and* the guitar player *and* the singer, because it wouldn't have been a *band* any more. But it was also that I loved being the director. I enjoyed saying, "You know, why don't you try singing this in here? When we get to this section, you go up. Then we'll sing the melody, and the characters will change, and you over here come in on the second line . . ."' Director Robbie may have been; leader he never was. 'I was never the leader and never wanted to be,' he says. 'Everybody did his part, and that's what made us a true band. John Fogerty and Creedence were not a true band, but we were a real unit. Because I wrote the songs, it helped me get a better picture of what I was trying to do by having an ensemble, like a committee kind of thing where we could experiment with it. Rather than being in the midst of it, doing it, I could have an overview of it that I thought would be more helpful in a lot of cases.'

For all these disclaimers, Robbie's songwriting credits remain a matter of some contention, and it is hard to believe that a similar 'unit' working today would divide up the publishing royalties quite so unevenly. Even Robbie has openly admitted that he was often obliged to turn to Garth for help in finding chords: 'If I was trying to do a song that was on the verge of being a little more sophisticated than what we normally did, Garth would help me with the chord structures. I'd say, "I'm playing this, Garth, but there's something missing, something wrong." And I'd have my hands on the piano and he'd just come over and hit a note between my fingers that would complete the chord I was really imagining against the melody I was singing. Or if I heard a horn line in my head, Garth would always know where to take it.' Nor was it just Garth's talents Robbie drew on. 'If there was something about the feeling in a song, an angle I couldn't get, Levon would always find ways to get the feel I hadn't been able to express. And Rick would come up with some great harmony ideas. He'd know exactly where to come in and where to drop out.'

Much has been made of the gradual 'drying-up' of Richard Manuel the songwriter – Richard who'd had three songs all to himself on *Big Pink*. It has been argued that he was intimidated by Robbie's prodigious output and that as time went on, in John Simon's words, 'he just sorta clammed up'. 'Robbie certainly didn't consciously intimidate him,' says Simon, 'but when you met Robbie he was so smooth and urbane and witty, whereas Richard was such a gee-golly-gosh kind of guy.' Richard was also, of course, a heavy drinker and occasionally a heavy drug user – in Simon's wearily tactful phrase, 'the kind of person who was sad enough to be ... susceptible to the influence of external substances'. The periodic bouts of experimentation with substances as dangerous as heroin certainly weren't helping to nurture his singular melodic gifts.

Whatever the rumours and squabbles that ensued in later years, the band's unique chemistry was unaffected during the poolhouse recordings. 'We have five people to bounce things off of,' Rick told *Time* magazine later that year. 'Everybody has their spiritual side, which is nice. One week the spiritual side might come up a little heavier on Garth than on Robbie – you know, the holding-it-together.' In the 'little workshop', each worker knew his role, though some were more equal, or more self-deprecating, than others. 'Robbie was our spokesman,' said Richard. 'He took care of that end because he had the best mind for business. Levon acted as the musical leader for the most part, although we traded. And I was always a side man.'

Having written most of the songs, Robbie's main task was now, as he put it, 'to discover the sound of the band': 'I wanted all the instruments to have their own sound – the drums to have their own character, the piano not to sound like a big Yamaha grand.' *Big Pink* had come close to doing the music justice, but it was too studio-crafted – caviar rather than Harveyburgers. 'Everything in rock was kind of going in that high end direction,' he says, 'and we wanted something different, a kind of woody, thuddy sound.' As the sessions progressed, Robbie took a much more active role in both the production and the engineering of the record. John Simon, who was by now virtually a 'sixth member' of the group, had no problem with this, teaching Robbie most of what he knew and becoming less the producer *per se* than 'the outside ear and opinion you could trust'. 'John wasn't the producer,' says Jonathan Taplin. 'At least in the sense that no one could really tell Levon how to play a drum part or Rick how to play bass. He certainly wasn't a George Martin, but he was a very patient guy and he kept the momentum going.'

'Woody' and 'thuddy' perfectly capture the sound that developed as the sessions pushed into March. In pronounced contrast to the reverb-laden excesses of most of their rock contemporaries, *The Band* was dry, primitive, home-cooked: it sounded like it had been cut in an old shack on the rustiest console Capitol could find. A key ingredient was the deadened snare drum, inspired by the sound of James Van Eaton on Jerry Lee Lewis' great Sun sides. 'That's usually the way I try to fix it,' Levon later told *Modern Drummer*. 'I like that sort of a dull "thud" sound, with lots of wood. I like the bass drum kind of toned down, and I usually muffle the toms down quite a bit more than is usual.' In tandem with this was Rick's bass sound, deep and muted as a heartbeat. 'I don't play bass, I just cover space,' Danko told *Guitar Player*. 'You know, Levon's bass drum and the bass really work well together, because we listen to each other. It's not really what you play but what you leave out that counts. And when you leave space, it's easier to hear everybody. If everyone is just up there churnin', it's going to sound like buttermilk.'

Over this watertight but never oppressive rhythmic base, the guitars, keyboards, and vocals were recorded in a similarly downhome, old-timey style. Garth worked discreet miracles, filling every available space with spine-tingling swirls of counter-melody. One moment he'd be an avant-garde fairground organist, the next he'd sound like he was playing in a country church. 'Through Garth's great open organ chords,' wrote Peter Goddard, 'modern rock met with the sound and spirit of Sunday morning fundamentalist prayer meetings in that part of western Ontario he came from.' Garth himself was fully aware of the church influences in his playing. 'The Anglican church has the best musical traditions of any church I know,' he told *Time*. 'It's the old voice-leading that gives it the countermelodies and adds all those classical devices which are not right out there but which add a little texture.' In contrast to *Big Pink*, there were far fewer electronic embellishments to *The Band*. Even the piano, played by both Richard and Garth, sounded like an old parlour upright. As for Robbie, if he was taking more solos than on *Big Pink*, his playing remained for the most part careful and delicate. 'Where the average group uses flamboyance as a virtual tool of its trade,' observed Mick Farren, 'The Band have been almost Calvinistically self-effacing.' When Robbie did let fly, his playing was spellbinding without ever being slick: the acoustic solo on 'Unfaithful Servant'; the quivering Telecaster solo at the end of 'King Harvest', played through an amp set at the lowest possible volume.

Without vocals from Robbie, the band's three main voices came to the fore as distinct characters that none the less merged as one in ragged country harmony. Indeed, Robbie seemed to use the three singers almost as a ventriloquist uses a dummy, telling his mini-stories vicariously through them. 'I wanted the different characters that Levon's Southern indomitability, Richard's soulful melancholy, and Rick's stoic eloquence represented to intermingle,' he later said. 'It had to be multi-dimensional, one voice telling the story, another contrasting the experience with an ironic counterpoint, and the third playing the role of a kind of Greek chorus.' The effect was brilliant and unique, with the three voices being similar enough in tone and timbre to sound organically connected, and yet different enough for each to stand on its own as a narrative protagonist. 'It was like casting parts,' Robbie later admitted. 'If you got it right you could really pull off something special. If I wanted this tremendous character in the vocal, that drummed up all kinds of timeless pictures, I'd want Levon. If I wanted to make you cry, I'd go to Richard. And when you put these voices together, when they would soar to the heights to-gether, it really made a magical sound that came from years of seasoning. It was never like one guy sang, with the others trying to fit in. They *listened* to one another.'

This time, moreover, Levon's 'Southern indomitability' not only bolstered the overall vocal sound but took the lead on four tracks. Even within those four songs his performances created very different personalities: coming directly after his juke-joint swagger on 'Rag Mama Rag', the wounded but boyishly proud voice of 'The Night They Drove Old Dixie Down' was pretty sobering. Jonathan Taplin once claimed that Robbie had told him he'd written 'The Night They Drove Old Dixie Down', 'right *at* Levon', to let the drummer know how much the tragedies of the American Civil War meant to him. Worried with hindsight that this sounded patronizing, Robbie later denied that he'd written anything 'at', or even for, Levon. But the fact remains that the song, like 'Rag Mama Rag' and 'Up On Cripple Creek', was partly an expression of everything Robbie had experienced in the South with Levon, just as 'The Unfaithful Servant' reflected Rick's personality and 'Rockin' Chair' Richard's.

One of the crucial factors in establishing 'the sound of the band' was what they called 'musical chairs' – the instrument-switching that became such a staple feature of The Band's *modus operandi*. 'They were wonderfully selfless and wonderfully pragmatic,' recalled John Simon, who himself played both horns and occasional keyboard parts on *The Band*. 'It was always a question of whatever worked best for each song, not who was going to sing the lead vocal or who was going to shine instrumentally.' Levon later claimed that it was to accommodate 'the master musician' Garth Hudson that the band started playing 'musical chairs' – Garth who is credited on the album cover with 'Organ, clavinet, piano, accordion, soprano, tenor and baritone saxes, and slide trumpet' – but the versatility extended as much to his own mandolin playing, and to Rick's fiddling skills, as to Garth's virtuosity.

Most radically of all, a couple of the tracks on *The Band* ended up featuring Richard Manuel on drums. 'It was so commendable for Levon, one of the most interesting and soulful drummers ever, to say, "I think Richard can play drums on this one better than me,"'" says Robbie. 'A whole lot of times he was right, and Richard would do something so bizarre it was priceless. He wasn't a drummer at all, but his playing gave the sound a loose, floppy feeling.' It was Ralph J. Gleason who observed that where Richard was rhythmic on the piano, he was melodic on the drums. Untrained as he was, Manuel had an engagingly quirky grasp of rhythm, and it perfectly suited songs like 'Rag Mama Rag' and 'Jemima Surrender.' 'You could always tell Richard's drumming,' says Woodstock musician Andy Robinson. 'There was always the sense that he might not make it back to the beat on time after a roll or a fill, but he always did. I always remember watching his shoulders when he drummed – they said everything about what he was putting into it. Often his hi-hats would break because he hit them so hard. There was nothing tentative about his drumming.'

Of all the tracks on *The Band*, 'Rag Mama Rag' best exemplified the loose, improvisatory nature of the poolhouse sessions. Tackled initially in a more orthodox rock fashion, with Levon on drums, the song wasn't quite taking the shape Robbie had envisaged as he wrote it. 'It didn't feel like what I was hearing in my head,' he remembered. 'So Richard went to drums and Levon switched to mandolin, John huffed and puffed his way through a tuba bass line, and Rick took over my guitar riff on the fiddle, which gave the song its "rag" quality. Finally, because this was meant in some sense to be in the tradition of ragtime music, Garth played an upright, ragtime kind of piano. Somehow all the elements gelled, and you started to hear a real character to the music.' The resulting concoction came straight out of turn-of-the-century New Orleans, with Garth's inspired doodling conjuring up the ghost of 'Cripple' Clarence Lofton and Robbie's lusty tomcat lyrics perfectly bearing out his idea of Storyville 'brothel music'.

Like 'The Weight', 'Rag Mama Rag' was recorded almost as an afterthought, only to become one of The Band's most treasured songs – not to mention a Top 20 British hit in April, 1970. '"Rag" was, like, "Well, this is an extra one and if we don't have anything better to do we might as well cut it,"' says Robbie. 'It didn't have very much importance until after we recorded it, but it showed something else we could do, in a style that didn't exist. It was like, "Name this music"!' The same might have been said of the whole album: as *Time* asked when they put The Band on their cover in January, 1970, 'Can this be rock?'

Rough-hewn as it still sounds, an enormous amount of thought and care went into the making of *The Band*. 'People don't understand how complicated The Band's music is until they sit down and try to play it,' says Rick; 'it's like rare jazz.' With each track, a basic procedure was followed. First, with John Simon's guidance, the group would work out which instruments and sounds best suited the song. 'We took great care with every instrument to make it sound different and appropriate,' Simon recalls. Second, the song would be rehearsed until the arrangement felt absolutely right to all six men. Finally, it would be recorded, usually the morning after the arrangement had been finalized to ensure that they were all as fresh as possible. As with *Big Pink*, the horns – on 'Across The Great Divide', for example – were generally recorded on a separate track from the main instruments and vocals.

'Across The Great Divide' was the album's opening track, and it immediately established a mood very different from the one 'Tears Of Rage' had set for *Big Pink*. As Robert Christgau noted, '"Great Divide" is to the dirgelike "Tears Of Rage" what a little storefront church on East 7th Street is to Riverside Baptist.' Although the song started with a no-good Richard Manuel begging his Molly – perhaps the same Molly that Dylan had sung about in 'Lo And Behold!' – to stop waving her gun at him, it quickly took off on a blithely good-humoured groove, with the unrepentant heel bragging tipsily over some Fats Domino-style piano triplets. Robbie's lyric immediately painted a picture of a one-horse town reminiscent of Hollywood westerns, except that this town, with its riverside and its harvest moon, was clearly located in the South – and not too long after the Civil War, either. *The Band* reminded more than one reviewer of Faulkner's mythical Yoknapatawpha County in Mississippi, and 'Great Divide' certainly provided the perfect overture to Robbie's 'concept' album. What was he if not a Yankee with his nose pressed up against the window of the South? 'There'd be a little shack out in the middle of a field at night,' he recalled of his first visits to Arkansas, 'and I'd wonder who was in there. Not that I wanted to knock on the door, because I preferred to use my own imagination, but that's what kinda led me to this songwriting style. I didn't even know this style was unusual, it was simply that I couldn't find my way into the norm.' Part of Robbie's motivation as a songwriter was to capture the things Southerners themselves took for granted: like the documentarist André Carbiat Desant, whose film about Mississippi preachers he'd seen, Robbie wanted 'to look directly at things which were so obvious that people never looked at them.' One of the many Southerners who found it hard to believe that Robbie was Canadian was Mac Rebennack, by then performing as Dr John, the Night Tripper. 'Me and a bunch of guys from New Orleans would listen to that second album all the time,' says the Doctor, 'and it would just tickle us that Robbie was from Canada. The music sounded to me like a cross between Memphis and New Orleans, it was really in the pockets of those places without ever, like, *copying* the original stuff. The way they presented it was so *innocent*, there was nothing slick about it.'

Richard Manuel played some other wonderful Southern characters on *The Band*. On the exquisite 'Rockin' Chair', he was a septuagenarian seadog finally come home to 'old Virginny' to spend his last days with his crony, Ragtime Willie. It was rare enough to hear a 'rock' song about old people that wasn't just sentimentally patronizing; this one was so tenderly sad it made you want to cry. 'In my time I've run up against some old people who were able to explain things to me and make me see things in a way that nobody else could,' said Robbie not long after *The Band* was released. 'Their experience made me feel like not saying a word. I learned to listen. And it not only had to do with the tone in their voices, it was also to do with the colour of their skin, the lines in their faces and the years in their eyes. And at this time, in this country, there's a whole thing that old people are almost put away. I can't buy that.' Set to an old-time string-band arrangement – Robbie on acoustic, Levon on mandolin, Garth on accordion, Rick on bass, with some of the loveliest close harmony singing the band ever recorded – the song re-established the sense of generational continuity that had informed *Music From Big Pink*.

On 'Jawbone', Richard created a variant on his 'Great Divide' persona, a gleeful roustabout 'boostin' and goin' out on the lam'. For Robbie, who co-wrote the song with Richard, Jawbone was exactly the kind of miscreant who'd come to see the Hawks play in their roadhouse days: 'These people would live this life with other choices and say, "No, this is what I choose, I like the action".' Recorded with the poolhouse bathroom as a vocal echo chamber— which was about as slick as the sessions got—'Jawbone' was full of trademark time-signatures and tempo changes, building to a funky, bass-driven chorus and boasting an open-throttle electric solo from Robbie.

The most haunting of the poolhouse tracks featuring lead vocals by Richard was 'King Harvest (Will Surely Come)', which closed *The Band* and brought the album full circle from the 'harvest moon' of 'Across The Great Divide'. 'The harvest was part of the theme of the album, so I kept coming back to that,' says Robbie. '"King Harvest" was obviously the most focused of any of the material in terms of coming right out and saying it.' In the song, Richard was a dirt-poor sharecropper praying for a good harvest and banking on the union if the crop failed. Something vaguely ominous communicated itself before he'd even begun to tell his story:

Corn in the fields,
Listen to the rice when the wind blows 'cross the water.
King Harvest has surely come.

It was the first of three marvellous images that Levon intoned as prefaces to Richard's verses – just part of the song's intricate structure, which involved several time changes and suspensions. 'The chord progression was a little bit complex,' says Robbie. 'There's a sifty feeling we were trying to get, which was like subtle and bold at the same time.' Just as 'sifty' were the sounds the band attained for each instrument. With John Simon playing an electric piano through the same black box Robbie had used on 'Tears Of Rage', Garth's Lowrey shimmered away in the background and Robbie made tiny Telecaster incisions off to one side. 'This was the new way of dealing with the guitar,' Robbie says. 'Leaving out a lot of stuff and just waiting till the last second and then playing the thing in just the nick of time. It was an approach to playing where it's so delicate, the opposite of the "in your face" playing that I used to do.' After the final verse, Robbie played a solo so intense it was frightening. 'It's like you have to hold your breath while playing these kinds of solos,' he says. 'You can't breathe or you'll throw yourself off.'

If Robbie's guitar sounded as though it was being played through a tiny box, Levon sounded like he was playing *in* a box. 'King Harvest' was one of his greatest, most intuitive performances as a drummer, and the sound of his kit did it more than justice. '"King Harvest" was one track where I got my drums sounding the way I always wanted them,' he says. 'There's enough wood in the sound, and you could hear the stick and the bell of the cymbal.' With Rick sticking to the bass drum like a limpet, the rhythm section sounded like the records Willie Mitchell was starting to make with Howard Grimes and Leroy Hodges in Memphis – which makes perfect sense to Levon Helm. 'For me, that late, leave-a-pocket-for-the-backbeat style is the Memphis way of playing,' he says. 'There's a real soft spot right in there, and when I can lay the beat in that place I like it the best.'

Jon Carroll wrote that Levon was 'the only drummer who can make you cry,' and listening to him on 'King Harvest' – the anguished fills and rolls, the perfect ride cymbal figure accompanying the line 'Scarecrow and a yellow moon, pretty soon a carnival on the edge of town' – it's hard to disagree. One of the handful of West Coast musos who was permitted to enter the inner sanctum of the poolhouse was drummer Jim Keltner, who claimed that watching Levon at work changed his life. 'I watched him play, I talked with him a lot, and I was never the same again,' he says. 'One thing that changed for me was that I started lifting my right hand off the hi-hat when the backbeat came down. I did it because I saw him doing it and thought, "Maybe if I do that I'll get that incredible Levon Helm feel!"'

Lifted by what Levon called its 'musical architecture', Richard supplied a harrowing vocal for 'King Harvest' that fully conveyed the sharecropper's desperation: Ralph Gleason was not alone in hearing it (and most of the album) as a kind of soundtrack to James Agee's epic account of Depression-era tenant farmers *Let Us Now Praise Famous Men*.

> Last year this time, it wasn't no joke,
> My whole barn went up in smoke.
> Our horse Jethro, well, he went mad,
> And I can't ever remember things being that bad.
> Then here comes a man with a paper and a pen,
> Tellin' us our hard times are about to end.
> And then, if they don't give us what we like,
> He says, 'Men, that's when you gotta go on strike.'

Lying behind the mood of the song, too, was the contrast between what the unions had once been and what they had become by the 1960s. 'It's a kind of character study on a time period,' Robbie told an interviewer after the album's release. 'I wanted to leave the listener in a very rootsy kind of place, but to be able to talk about something which had turned into the world of Jimmy Hoffa and the teamsters. You know, at the beginning when the unions came in, they were a saving grace, whereas now so much of it is like gangsters, assassinations, power, greed, insanity.' That Robbie had been able to do this, and to do it in a way that expressed so much more of the human reality of poverty than, say, Dylan's 'Dear Landlord', was no mean feat. 'Robertson's songs went further than Dylan's by going beyond metaphor and actually embodying the experiences they were about,' noted British writer Mick Gold in a thoughtful 1974 piece about The Band. 'Where Dylan used the form and language of country music to mark out some firm ground after the amoral fragmentation of the electric albums, The Band actually *enshrined* the people and places they'd travelled through.'

Of the three songs which the 'stoically eloquent' Rick Danko sang on *The Band*, by far the most interesting was 'The Unfaithful Servant', a piece of music so far removed from what people had hitherto known as rock'n'roll that Ralph Gleason was prompted to remark that it might have been written by jazz pianist Bill Evans. Echoing the mournful note of reproach in 'Tears Of Rage' – with which it shared an intriguing ideological unsoundness – the song concerned the fate of a servant who had in some unspecified way transgressed against his mistress and thus been sent packing from her house. 'To write a song about this kind of thing is not really a very righteous [sic] thing to do, because we're at the point now where there should be no differences between people,' Robbie said in 1971. 'Everybody is now interested in being *the same*, so I was kinda playing a game in writing this song.' If *The Band* as a 'concept album' can be said to take place in or around some imaginary country town, then 'The Unfaithful Servant' is definitely set in 'the mansion on the hill', a Southern household of the kind Robbie had read about in the plays of Tennessee Williams. Backed by Robbie on acoustic guitar and Richard on piano, Rick sang the song with his characteristic mixture of bashfulness and regret. On the second verse, Garth and John Simon came wheezing in with some delightfully doleful horns, enshrouding Rick in a cloud of lonely melancholy. 'Rick is actually a very studied singer,' says John Simon. 'He expresses it in a very unique way, but he really is conscious of working with a microphone in an Appalachian tradition. I mean, he *hears* those old singers and knows *how* they do it.' The overall effect was pure American Gothic.

On 'When You Awake', meanwhile, Rick created a kind of counterpart to Richard's performance on 'Rockin' Chair'. Played in semi-skank time, this enchanting Manuel–Robertson song concerned a young boy picking up sage advice from his grandpa and from Ollie, who may or may not be the same person. 'It's a story about someone who passes something on to you, and you pass it on to someone else,' says Robbie. 'But it's something you take to heart and carry with you your whole life.' With Garth creating an old pump-organ effect behind him, and Levon and Richard harmonizing on the chorus, Rick's folksy vocal almost made the song as special as 'Rockin' Chair'.

'Look Out Cleveland' was about as hard-rocking as *The Band* got; nor was it entirely coincidental that it came the closest of all the album's songs to making a statement about contemporary America. On the surface a warning about an impending and explicitly apocalyptic hurricane, on another level the lyric could only too easily be interpreted allegorically as a warning about less meteorological storms. The fact that the storm in question was threatening major cities as far apart as Cleveland and Houston – both North and South, in other words – made it clear that the horizon had suddenly become a lot wider than the rural concerns of the rest of the album. 'When we were doing this album,' says Robbie, 'there were all these riots and outbursts around the country, and it was kind of like living on the fault-line of revolution.' Coming out of the twilight serenity of 'Rockin' Chair', and presaging the darker moments of *Stage Fright* and *Cahoots*, the song was a sudden blast of urban menace in the sequence of rural story-songs. Levon battered his drums, Richard hammered out some prime rock'n'roll piano, and Robbie – dare one say it – approached ferocity.

When Jonathan Taplin came back to L.A. from Princeton in late March, the group had completed six songs. The first track they played him was 'The Night They Drove Old Dixie Down', and Taplin instantly knew the album was going to be a masterpiece. 'It was just the most moving experience I'd had for, God, I don't know how long,' he says. 'Because for me, being a northern liberal kid who'd been involved in the civil rights movement and had a whole attitude towards the South, it was a very cathartic experience. It was like having it all wrapped up in three and a half minutes, the whole sense of dignity and place and tradition. It brought tears to my eyes.'

'The Night They Drove Old Dixie Down' was sung by Levon, who announced with his first words that he was Virgil Caine, a young survivor of the attacks made on the Danville and Richmond railroad by General George Stoneman's Union cavalry in the winter after Appomattox. It was a vocal that drew from the great well of grief and defiance that still lingered on in the South after a hundred years, and to many young Americans it was simultaneously shocking and refreshing to hear. 'The performance leaves behind a feeling that for all our old oppositions, every American still shares this old event,' wrote Greil Marcus, adding that 'the song is not so much about the Civil War as it is about the way each American carried a version of that event within himself'.

What made 'Dixie' especially vivid was the lyrical detail – the conjuring of place and of family. The instrumentation was sparse and simple – just piano, drums, bass, and acoustic guitar – but the sombre piano chords, descending and then ascending back up to the wailing chorus, almost carried the song on their own. Levon filled the song with military drum rolls, while discreet overdubs – Garth's Hohner melodica, Rick's fiddle – added a pining edge as the song progressed. Two years later, Joan Baez recorded a terrible version of 'Dixie' that seemed to turn Robert E. Lee into a steamboat, but it made Robbie good money when it reached #3 on the *Billboard* chart.

'The Night They Drove Old Dixie Down' became a kind of Exhibit A in the vast amount of critical musing *The Band* inspired on its release in the fall of 1969. Most of this musing was prompted by the album's timeliness as a portrait of a bygone America – an antidote, if you like, to the violence and despair of the '60s comedown. 'If my experience is anything like typical,' wrote Ed Ward, 'I would say that *The Band* helped a lot of people dizzy from the confusion and disorientation of the '60s feel that the nation was big enough to include them, too.' Twenty years after the release of *Music From Big Pink*, Dan Heilman could justifiably claim that the band's first two albums had set them on a pedestal as 'a shining beacon of rock's post-Altamont future . . . with Robbie conceived as their intellectually astute mouthpiece'.

For Greil Marcus, who was eventually to devote one of the chapters of his seminal *Mystery Train* to the group, *The Band* seemed to come to America's rescue, to vindicate its history and its mystery at a time when everything about the country seemed unremittingly bleak and ugly. Indeed, Robbie had thought seriously of calling the album *America*, since 'we felt we knew America, that we'd been around every bend and every block and could talk truthfully about it.' It was as if these four Canadians – with Levon Helm as their guide and interpreter – had penetrated the heart of the country and redeemed it, had shown the unkempt legions of disaffected hippies that there was real poetry and beauty to be found in America's history. 'The Band found a way to understand and present [America's possibilities] in a context that *was* American,' wrote Marcus, 'and to the degree that their presentation was effective they brought us in touch with the place where we all had to live.'

In their pastoralism and their fascination with Americana, The Band showed interesting parallels with the American regionalist painters of the post-Depression era. Turning away from avant-garde European trends, men like Thomas Hart Benton, Grant Wood, and John Steuart Curry had celebrated an America of Midwestern farmers and revival meetings, almost to the point of xenophobia. 'A windmill, a junkheap, and a Rotarian have more meaning to me than Notre Dame or the Parthenon,' wrote the jingoistic Benton. If Grant Wood's famous 'American Gothic' looks satirical to our eyes, there is little evidence that Wood himself thought of his Iowan couple as anything other than 'basically good and solid people'. In rather the same way, The Band were turning away from the legacy of psychedelia, and from the *sturm und drang* of bands like the Doors, to connect with America's musical and cultural heritage.

At the same time, Robbie was sensitive to charges of nostalgia, strongly rebuffing the lurking suspicion that *The Band* were in some sense afraid to confront the present. 'It's not because I want to live there or anything, it's just storytelling,' he told one interviewer. 'I could relate to farmers in the Depression getting together in unions better than I could relate to going to San Francisco and putting flowers in your hair. People hear about the present every day, they see it on TV all day long. To write songs about that seems to me a waste of time. So the way I get the most effect out of something is to come in from another door. And you see, I feel it's been achieved or else the idea of us being "out of touch" wouldn't even come up.' To *Rolling Stone*'s Howard Gladstone, Robbie said that 'we certainly didn't want everybody to go out and get a banjo or a fiddle player, we were just trying to calm things down a little', adding that they were planning to go down to Muscle Shoals, Alabama to record 'four total freak-me songs, just to show we have no hard feelings'. Yet if they weren't nostalgic, The Band were unquestionably elegiac: it was impossible to play through both sides of *The Band* and not hear the recurrent notes of loss amidst the good-time grooves and revelry. When Dave Emblidge compared the group to Andrew Wyeth, a painter who showed certain affinities with the 'regionalists', he was not being entirely unfair.

For European listeners to *The Band* – and *The Band* is where many of us tuned in – questions of nostalgia seemed immaterial. The album opened up America for us in precisely the way that WLAC Nashville had opened it up for Rick and Robbie and Richard. 'It was like receiving a letter from the other side of the world, a world you couldn't possibly understand, let alone visit,' says Elvis Costello, an early fan. 'It was only later when you knew a bit more about Hank Williams and Bessie Smith that you started to fill in the blanks.' For young Declan MacManus and so many others, it was The Band's very anonymity that made them so alluring, as if their lack of 'charisma' allowed a lost or hidden America to speak through them. Who else was singing songs like 'Rag Mama Rag' or 'The Unfaithful Servant' in 1969?

Of course, there *were* other American performers who seemed to stand outside the prevailing musical trends of the day – anomalous characters like John Fogerty and Ry Cooder, obsessed in their different ways with the roots of rock'n'roll and R&B. Fogerty's Creedence Clearwater Revival (who'd begun life as a Hawks-style bar band called the Blue Velvets) kicked off with a raucous reading of Dale Hawkins' 'Susie-Q' in the late summer of 1968, then hit big with a succession of very Southern-sounding classics. Just as The Band were starting work in the poolhouse, indeed, 'Proud Mary' climbed all the way to #2 on the singles chart, first of several Top Ten smashes that would make Creedence virtually the biggest band in America for two years. 'With the Huck-and-Jim-on-the-Mississippi echoes that lent its lyrics about dropping out an historical dimension,' wrote Ellen Willis, '"Proud Mary" was an implicit critique of the idea that radicals had nothing to learn from American tradition.' A nice concept, but one Dylan and The Band had thought of first.[4]

Ry Cooder was more musicological in his approach, but his voice (as well as his occasional mandolin-playing) bore traces of The Band's influence. By 1972, with the *Into The Purple Valley* album, Cooder showed that he was the ultimate blender of traditions, a man who could make the Drifters' 'Money Honey' work alongside Woody Guthrie's 'Vigilante Man', mixing blues, gospel, and Tex-Mex into a swampy if overly painstaking brew. All Cooder lacked was Robbie's ability to create a new version of the past with original songs.

America was not the only alternative title considered for *The Band*. Another was a title later used by their compatriot Neil Young – *Harvest* – which would not only have encapsulated the record's themes but would have said something about the band itself. As Robert Palmer wrote, 'to the world at large, *Big Pink* and *The Band* were the remarkable beginnings of a remarkable new group . . . in reality, they were the crowning fruition of a career that had spanned almost a decade.' For Robbie, the image of fruition was an appropriate one. 'It was like we'd planted our seed,' he said, 'and this was the fruit that we were finally getting from all the work we'd done.'

In the end, it was decided after consultation with Albert and

Capitol that the album should simply be called *The Band*, thus eliminating any remaining confusion about the group's name. The band were finally, officially, The Band.

Part Three

SPOTLIGHT
(1969–74)

1

Taking Fright

As I say, it is perhaps easier to love America passionately, when you look at it through the wrong end of a telescope . . . than when you are right there. When you are actually *in* America, America hurts.

D. H. Lawrence, *Studies in Classic American Literature*

It was time for the band to come out of hiding, to emerge from the protective blanket Albert Grossman had thrown over them in Woodstock. If Rick Danko's neck was still a little stiff from his accident, it was no longer a good reason for the group to defer the inevitable moment of connection with their audience − or with America itself. Determined to stage their debut appearances as The Band, Bill Graham − that loved and loathed godfather of the Bay Area rock scene − had come down to L.A. to offer them two nights at San Francisco's Winterland ballroom in April. Eventually Albert struck a deal giving them $20,000 for the shows, with two more dates to follow at Graham's recently-opened Fillmore East theatre in New York.

It had been almost four years since the band's last performances as Levon and the Hawks, and over a year since they'd been onstage for all of thirteen minutes at the Woody Guthrie concert. Each of them knew what these debut appearances meant, and how much was hanging on them. They were coming out of the shadows to play in the city which had produced so many of the leading lights in the rock'n'roll revolution, and they were coming out without a frontman, something which hadn't mattered in the roadhouses of Texas and Oklahoma but suddenly seemed more than a little relevant here. 'We were scared to death,' admits Levon. 'You knew you were going to make a mistake, you just didn't know when. And none of us was the kind of performer who could stand up and tell jokes and entertain a crowd that way.'

The moment he got off the plane at San Francisco International on Tuesday 15 April, Robbie Robertson felt deathly ill. At first he thought it must just have been airsickness, but soon after the band had checked into the city's famous Seal Rock Inn he developed a high temperature and a fever. At a reception Bill Graham had organized for the group, Robbie did his best just to stay on his feet. 'They were shy and friendly,' recalled Greil Marcus. 'If someone had told them they were supposed to be big stars, they'd most likely have been embarrassed.' The *New York Times*' Susan Lydon reported that Albert Grossman had flown in 'bringing news from Woodstock of spring planting and which dogs had had puppies', which only added to the shy, backwoodsy ambience. 'They were all so *soft*,' remembered Bill Graham. 'I never had to raise my voice with any of them, and I have been known to raise my voice on occasion.'

By Wednesday night, Robbie was too ill to make the soundcheck-cum-rehearsal, which John Simon directed in his absence. After spending hours getting the sound right in the old Ice Capades skating rink, the band adjourned to a nearby Chinese restaurant, where the talk was alternately of Robbie and of the earthquake that had been predicted for the weekend. 'They didn't cancel, because everyone thought Robbie would just get over it,' says Jonathan Taplin. 'This was the long-awaited debut, Bill had sold out both nights, and there was too much pressure and expectation not to go through with it.'

Robbie was still lying in bed when the Winterland doors opened the following evening. 'Albert still thought he might get better, so we were giving him all the shots and vitamins we could,' said Graham. 'By the late afternoon, Albert started wondering if hypnosis might work, so I got the yellow pages and found a 24-hour hypnotist.' At seven o'clock, by which time the first support band was already onstage, a man in a black suit with a shock of white hair showed up at the hotel and proceeded to hypnotize Robbie into believing that he was well enough to do the show. 'We were all allowed to come into Robbie's room as he was put in a trance,' recalls Jonathan Taplin. 'The guy said, "Your stomach will feel as calm as a lake, your head will feel as cool as an arctic breeze. Whenever you hear the word 'Grow', those feelings will come over you." So Robbie came out of his trance and he felt a little better. He nearly fell out of bed, though, so the guy put him back in his trance and said "Your legs will feel like iron springs." At the end of all that, Robbie said he thought he could do it.'

Ignorant of the bizarre scene taking place in Robbie's hotel room, Winterland was buzzing with anticipation throughout the support set by the all-girl Ace of Cups. 'The tribal rock hounds and stone guerilla hippies of the Bay Area had turned out in force for the occasion,' wrote Grover Lewis, a *Rolling Stone* scribe who cared little for rock'n'roll. 'Flapping along the sidewalks, preening and shrilling, they soared into the cavernous recesses of the rock ballroom like flocks of bright, demented birds.' A heavy smell of marijuana hung in the air as the Sons of Champlin, a local band about to sign with Capitol, played the second support set. 'It wasn't hot, and people were hip and friendly,' noted Greil Marcus in his piece for the Bay Area paper *Good Times*.

The friendliness began to fade with the long delay that ensued after the Sons of Champlin had concluded their set. When Bill Graham walked up to a microphone to beg the audience's patience, he was greeted by a volley of jeers and whistles. While Jonathan Taplin and his roadies set up The Band's equipment, the hypnotist sat himself down at the side of the stage, reminding

Robbie that if he felt weak he should turn to him. Next to him stood Jack Casady of the Jefferson Airplane, one of many local luminaries keen to see what all the fuss was about. Finally, after almost half an hour of tuning up in semi-darkness, The Band were ready to play.

It was immediately obvious to everyone that Robbie was in no fit state to do the show. Leaning against Garth's organ, which was mounted at the centre of the stage, he kept glancing over towards the white-haired hypnotist, who was screaming 'Grow! Grow!' at him across Rick and Richard. Nor were any of the others able to relax and enjoy the performance, since it looked as though Robbie might collapse at any moment. Playing minimal rhythm guitar, with one shambolic solo thrown in, he lasted just seven songs before making it clear that he couldn't go on.

As the band left the stage, Greil Marcus witnessed 'an outpouring of anger and rage unlike anything I have ever seen at a rock'n'roll show'. One girl screamed 'I hope you get sicker, Robbie!'; another irate punter shouted 'Take the money and run!' when Bill Graham reappeared at the microphone. 'Well, there must be a lot of tourists here tonight,' retorted Bill, 'because San Francisco people just don't act this way.' Not even the promise of an extra show on the Saturday 'for anyone who didn't feel they got their money's worth' was enough to placate the 'hounds and guerillas' filing out into the night.

The show had been a worst-case-scenario nightmare come true, and the band's relationship with the stage – with its audience, indeed – was never the same again. Whether Robbie's fever was a psychosomatic symptom of the 'Stage Fright' he would describe so vividly in the song of that name, or a genuine illness that just happened to strike at the worst possible moment, it would set a precedent for a group that – for all the panache and professionalism they'd developed during their years on the road – never felt entirely comfortable onstage. 'We like to play music, but we have never had and never will really have it in the palm of our hand,' Robbie admitted five years later, at the beginning of their 1974 reunion tour with Dylan. 'We don't want to. We enjoy that rush of being scared. A lot of people I've gone to see, it just seems to roll off their tongues. You see no pain in them whatsoever, it's just a wonderful evening of entertainment. It's not for us. It's turmoil, it's pulled out like a tooth.'

But turmoil it wasn't when The Band took the stage for their second Winterland show on Friday night. It helped that the backstage area was less cluttered with music industry liggers and groupies – all the 'under-assistant West Coast promo men' who'd crowded the place out the previous night. This time, Robbie lasted a whole hour, and The Band barnstormed their way through a set that included 'Chest Fever', 'Tears Of Rage', and a trio of songs featuring Levon on vocals and mandolin: 'Don't Ya Tell Henry', 'Little Birdies', and 'Ain't No More Cane'. It was during the latter song that Ralph Gleason, co-founder of San Francisco's influential *Rolling Stone* magazine, suddenly clicked that it was really the drummer's Southern roots which gave the band its authority: as he noted in his *Rolling Stone* piece about the show the following month, 'it was instantly obvious that this was no Hollywood studio group in buckskin and beads playing what they'd learned off Carter Family records'. To crown the evening, the band encored with a version of 'Slippin' And Slidin'' that Greil Marcus called 'one of the great moments in the history of rock'n'roll'. The choice of cover was significant, instantly transforming them into the wild party band they'd been in their Hawks days. At a time when rock'n'roll oldies were still somewhat frowned upon by the longhair rock community, a Little Richard song was like a sudden, Dionysiac explosion of raw power.

It was just three weeks later that The Band followed the Winterland dates with their East Coast debut in New York. On a 'Woodstock' night at the Fillmore East, supported by Larry

Packer's band Cat Mother and the All-Night Newsboys, they played roughly the same show San Francisco had seen, but without any of the headaches which had accompanied that nightmarish first performance. 'This is a song Levon's dad taught us,' Robbie introduced 'Little Birdies'; 'hope you like country music here in New York City.' By way of contrast, they ended with a version of the Four Tops' 'Loving You Is Sweeter Than Ever', thereby demonstrating an appreciation for Tamla Motown as unfashionable in rock circles as their predilection for country or vintage rock'n'roll. (As Levon put it, 'if you can take a country tune and play it with a suburban flavour, or take a Motown tune and play it on country instruments . . . that's the kind of thing we do'.) As in San Francisco, they refrained from playing any of the songs they'd recorded for their as-yet unfinished second album, concentrating on the faithful and unsensational replication of material from *Music From Big Pink*. 'The Band have no act, put on no show,' wrote Joanna Schier in the *Village Voice*. 'What they intend to do with their enormous potential as a superduper group is doubtful, because they just seem too sensible and settled and satisfied to be bothered with anything but honest lives and honest music.'

The lack of theatricality may have been refreshing, but it brought its own problems. Just as the wild youth of Yonge Street had been bemused by the change in the Hawks when they returned to Toronto without Ronnie for the first time, so some of their admirers at the Fillmore East questioned whether The Band cared much about communicating their music to anyone besides each other. Even on a good night, thought Susan Lydon, 'their art is a very private thing, and it shows up in the strange distance they keep between themselves and their audience.' There were even mutterings about the very fidelity to the recorded versions of the songs. 'We tried very hard to make the live performances like the records,' Robbie told Joshua Baer in 1982. 'I've heard so many people's records that are great, and then I've heard them in person and it's a big letdown. We thought it was a cop-out to do the songs and then do a big long solo in the middle. If you're going to do a different version of the song, do a different version, but we tried very much to show that we could do it as good as we could on the record. A lot of people said, "Well, shit, you might as well listen to the albums as go and hear them," but we were *trying* not to be disappointing in comparison to the albums. And when we wanted to do another flavour, that's when we did *Rock Of Ages*.'

After the Fillmore East shows, The Band booked into Jerry Ragovoy's Hit Factory studios to cut three more songs for their second album: 'Up On Cripple Creek', 'Whispering Pines', and 'Jemima Surrender', later sequenced in that order at the very heart of the record. 'Cripple Creek' was yet another 'throwaway' number that started to take on a more defined and important identity in the process of recording. 'It took "Cripple Creek" a long time to seep into us,' recalled Levon. 'It was like it just had to simmer with everybody a while. We cut it two or three times, but nobody really liked it. It wasn't quite enough fun. But we fooled around with it, and finally one night we just got hold of it, doubled up a couple of chorus parts and harmony parts, and that was it.' What emerged after the 'simmering' was a genuine good-ol'-boy classic, an irresistible reprise of the 'Across The Great Divide' scenario starring Levon as a devil-may-care drunkard with a mistress called Bessie down in Lake Charles, Lu-zee-ana. Kicking off with a drums/bass/guitar figure so darn funky that rap group Gang Starr sampled it for their hypnotic 1991 track 'Beyond Comprehension', the track was made by a sound – somewhere between a Jews' harp and a frog's croak – that Garth obtained when he played his clavinet through a wah-wah. Levon, whooping and yodelling through the song, was clearly having the time of his life, even when the moment came for the song's picaresque hero to call up the 'big mama' to whom he was actually married.

The next track, closing out Side One of *The Band*, couldn't have been more of a contrast. With its heartrending Richard Manuel melody, 'Whispering Pines' was a cry of exquisite desolation that no one but he could have sung. 'Richard had briefly lived in a house in Woodstock that once belonged to the painter George Bellows,' says Joe Forno, The Band's manager in the '80s. 'There was an old piano in the house which had been left behind, and Richard wrote "Whispering Pines" on it. It had one key that was out of tune, and when he came to record the song he had the studio piano tuned the same way, so that that one key was still out. That's what's responsible for the vamp figure at the beginning and end of the song.' Finding it increasingly difficult to come up with lyrics, Richard took the chords to Robbie. 'Richard always had this very plaintive attitude in his voice, and sometimes just in his sensitivity as a person,' says Robbie. 'I tried to follow that, to go with it and find it musically. We both felt very good about this song.'

The lyric that Robbie worked around Richard's vocal lines was one of the most beautiful he ever wrote, a song of intense loneliness set beside an ocean that seemed to symbolize the singer's endless sense of loss. As sung by Richard in a haunting blend of his falsetto and full voices, the words could once again have been directly about him:

> If you find me in a gloom, or catch me in a dream,
> Inside my lonely room there is no in-between.

Once again, too, his colleagues played behind him with the tenderest touch, Robbie picking out delicate acoustic notes, Garth showering the track with magical sounds from the Lowrey. On the last verse, Levon joined Richard in a call-and-response duet that must rate as one of the saddest and loveliest passages of music in the history of rock:

> Standing by the well, wishing for the rain,
> Reaching to the clouds, for nothing else remains.
> Drifting in a daze, when evening will be done,
> Try looking through a haze
> At an empty house in the cold, cold sun.

If the image was one of almost all-engulfing aloneness, the music none the less spoke of profound peace, producing a remarkable kind of resolution. The last words the two voices sang were simply: 'The lost are found.'

Opening Side Two of *The Band*, the Helm/Robertson-penned 'Jemima Surrender' instantly returned us to the boisterous mood of 'Cripple Creek'. With Levon singing and playing guitar alongside Robbie, it was Richard who supplied the engagingly clumsy drumming and Garth who resumed the barrelhouse piano style of 'Rag Mama Rag'. The lyric was wildly lascivious, as Levon growled and cajoled his way into young Jemima's affections. He even offered to bring his Fender over and 'play all night for you', though one suspects the instrument in question may not have been the six-stringed variety. Crunching little rocker that it was, the song said a lot about the group's occasionally rather Neanderthal attitude towards women.

Once the three extra songs had been mixed, *The Band* was all but complete. It only remained for the group to agree on the right sequence for the songs, and for Elliott Landy to shoot some pictures for the cover. Most Band fans would agree that *The Band*'s running order was one of the most perfect of any rock album ever made; Robbie himself has said that changing the order would be like 'shuffling chapters in a novel'. Both sides of the record began on a humorously upbeat note and ended on a downbeat one of sadness or despair. Both ran the gamut of moods and emotions before finding their resolution in 'Whispering Pines' and 'King Harvest'. Above all, both struck just the right balance between elation and despondency: Robbie may have told P. W. Salvo that '*Big Pink* was Sunday morning and *The Band* Saturday night', but it was never as simple as that – just as it was not enough to say that *The Band* was superior to *Big Pink*.

The album cover was one of the first things to which the band turned their attention on returning to Woodstock at the beginning of the summer. Elliott Landy had flown out to L.A. during the poolhouse recordings and shot umpteen rolls of film there, but the group wanted a muddier, more autumnal image than anything Landy could have captured in California. When the day came for the session, the weather turned nasty. 'It was raining out, but we felt that because of the nature of the music it would have been wrong to have a picture done in a studio,' says Robbie. 'It needed to be out in a dirty road, so we went out on a dirty road in the rain, and it seemed to carry on a look from *Big Pink*, where we looked more like Mormons or rabbis or Amish people than rock stars.' With the gatefold sleeve made up of pictures Landy had taken in the poolhouse and at Winterland, the cover image did almost as much to fix The Band in people's minds as the famous portrait from *Big Pink* had done. Hair matted by the rain and collars pulled up against it, the five unsmiling men bore little resemblance to any of their rock contemporaries.

'I liked The Band because they had *beards*,' says Elvis Costello. 'They didn't look pretty, and they weren't *boys*. I mean, I really hated Led Zeppelin, and found those kinds of bands deeply embarrassing, probably because I was just too young to want to identify with Robert Plant. Whereas with The Band, the sexuality was taken for granted. They were *men*, and yet they weren't dressing up as cowboys or anything. It wasn't phoney.' When

Time magazine questioned Amherst College seniors about the group after the release of *The Band*, many registered the same kind of reaction as Costello's. 'You listen,' said one, 'and you just know that's no group of johnny-come-latelys from the suburbs who've gone off to a commune while Daddy foots the bill.'

For most of June, the band took time out to rest. The good vibes in Woodstock that summer were summed up in a song by visiting Scottish folkie John Martyn, whose *Stormbringer* album, recorded with his American wife Beverley, featured 'Woodstock', a serene portrait of the town in which everyone and his friendly neighbour could sing or strum a guitar. While Robbie and Dominique remained on Albert's estate with their new baby Alexandra, Richard, Garth, and Bill Avis all moved into a new house overlooking the huge Ashokan Reservoir, and it was here that the group now assembled to work and rehearse. 'The living room became a rehearsal space,' recalls Jane Manuel, who'd come back to Richard after a brief engagement to another man. 'Everybody would come by the house – Van Morrison and Janet Planet, Tim Hardin, Paul Butterfield.' Avis, the old Hawks road manager, retains fond memories of that summer. 'Richard was at one end of the house, I was in the middle, and Garth was at the other end,' he says. 'Those were *good* times. We were havin' a barbecue one day. Richard got over there about half in the bag, got on that barbecue, and it fell over on top of his foot. He couldn't work properly for two months coz he couldn't work the damn pedals on the piano, but he just laughed it off and kep' on going.' While Richard spent most of his time soused or stoned, Garth holed himself up in the shed at the back of the house. Here he would either play his Lowrey or work on the miniature pipe organ he was building with a local technician named Bill Putnam. 'Watching Garth sit at that organ with his big beard made me think of Brahms,' says Larry

Packer. 'He was a born tinkerer,' adds Jonathan Taplin. 'He was elliptical, the mountain man in his cabin high above the reservoir, driving around in his Mercedes diesel.'

Morrison, Hardin, and Butterfield were not the only fellow musicians The Band ran into that summer. The whole town was teeming with superstars, as if gearing up for the huge festival which would take place in August. 'You'd see them at the Café Espresso or at the Sound Out field down near the Peter Pan Farm,' says guitarist Jim Weider, a Woodstock native who later filled Robbie's shoes in the reunited Band of the '80s. 'Everybody from Janis Joplin to all the great musicians who backed them lived around town and they'd go and jam locally. You never knew who was gonna come in, whether it was Rick Danko or Jimi Hendrix.' Artie Traum, who'd been caretaking Bob Dylan's Byrdcliffe house ever since Bob had moved his family to a new place off Ohayo Mountain Road, was equally astonished by the rapid transformation of the sleepy Catskills town. 'Back then, any *schlub* musician could live here and make $50 to $75 a night playing backup in a club or doing a recording session,' he says. 'It was a true renaissance. You'd see Joplin, Hendrix, Morrison in the street, playing in the clubs. The combination of old-school Republican farmers and drug-crazed hippies certainly produced an interesting atmosphere.' When the boom was over, Artie was one of the few who stayed behind. Now the clubs – the Sled Hill Café, the White Water Depot, Rose's Cantina – are all gone, and musicians struggle to make $75 a *week*.

Over in Bearsville, both Rick and Levon had shacked up with women who proved to be long-term partners. Somehow it was inevitable that Elizabeth Grafton should have first met Rick when he crashed into her car; all the more amazing, perhaps, that they are still married to this day. The relationship between Levon and Libby Titus was fated to be a rather stormier affair. Libby was a glamorous and intelligent girl who already had a child from her first marriage. Signed as a singer to Albert Grossman's stable of artists, she'd first met The Band in the company of 'an old wizened beatnik' named Mason Hoffenberg, co-author of the notorious bestseller *Candy*. 'I can't tell you how unusual and handsome they were,' she laughs today. 'They were like brothers from another century, incredibly close, loyal, in a way incredibly competitive . . . and the most seductive young men I'd ever met.' After the idyllic summer of 1968, which Libby had spent sitting on various Woodstock porches with Albert and Sally and Robbie and Dominique, it became clear that Levon Helm was seriously smitten with her.

What Levon didn't know about Libby, and what Libby didn't know about Levon, could have filled a hefty volume or two. Put an intelligent but troubled personality like Libby's together with the manic-depressive inferno that was Levon at his angriest and you had the very meaning of 'mismatched'. After the band had returned to Woodstock, Libby moved in with the drummer and began to understand what kind of man he really was. 'I was obsessed with him, and I became very isolated,' she says. 'He felt very competitive around other men, so he wouldn't take his beautiful girlfriend to parties. All the signs were there in front of me, but I ignored them.' The differences in temperament were obvious to other people: Levon's life consisted of guns and turnip greens, Libby lived for books and parties. In time, she would go on to develop severe problems with drink and drugs, at least some of which had to do with the sense of emotional suffocation in the relationship.

Despite these problems, The Band were generally perceived by the Woodstock rock community to be warm and friendly, if fundamentally private. 'It actually took me about ten years before I got comfortable with any of them,' says Artie Traum. 'I was so in awe of them that I really never knew what to say, but they were always very gracious. Rick and Richard and Levon were *extremely* warm, *extremely* open, and there was a camaraderie there that was really precious. When Rick and Levon were living out on Wittenberg Road, I'd drop by and Levon would take out his mandolin and Rick would play guitar, and I always felt that they were incredibly tight and connected.' When Artie and his brother Happy were gathering songs for their Capitol album that summer, they ran into Rick and Robbie in Woodstock's main grocery store and told them they still needed a song or two. 'They took us back to Wittenberg Road and taught us "Bessie Smith", which appeared on our album as "Going Down The Road To See Bessie",' Artie recalls. 'When the record came out, the *Rolling Stone* review said that "Happy and Artie are to The Band what The Band are to Dylan", and that was just the greatest thrill of my life, just being in the same sentence as them.'

On another occasion, Artie was jamming with Rick and Paul Butterfield when Butterfield suddenly rounded on him and belittled his playing. Gently, affirmingly, Rick came to Artie's rescue, asking him to take a solo. 'It was very indicative of the way he looks after his friends,' said Artie. 'I mean, maybe I only saw the gracious side of the guys because of *my* personality, because I'm outgoing and fairly friendly. You see, to me Levon's the guy who calls up and says, "Hey Artie, I got something you're really gonna want," and I'll run over and he'll take out a gallon of barbecue sauce that some old guy in Arkansas made and say, "This is more precious than gold, but I'm gonna give you a little bit . . ." That's the Levon Helm *I* know.'

Not even Artie Traum, one of God's original nice guys, could quite fathom Jaime Robbie Robertson. Robbie hadn't been 'one of the guys' for some years, but he seemed to be distancing himself more all the time. 'He struck me as remote, focused, quietly powerful,' says Artie. 'He'd sort of peer at you from behind his little glasses and you *always* wondered what he was thinking.' In contrast to the others, Robbie was rarely seen around town or in clubs, preferring to stay home with Dominique and continue his rigorous programme of self-education. 'He was the most impressively self-educated man I've ever met,' says Jonathan Taplin. 'He'd dropped out of school, but he'd read all of Cocteau. Dominique helped him a lot, of course, but it was still incredibly impressive.' Others were more irritated by his Grossman-influenced standoffishness and intellectual snobbery. 'I remember somebody calling him "The Wooden Man",' says Jane Manuel with a faintly guilty smile. 'He always kept his distance from people.' As for his fellow Band members, there was the occasional 'bit of joshing' – Jonathan Taplin's phrase – but always tempered by their respect for him. And yet there was almost a sense in which the four other members of The Band had become mere characters in Robbie's fantasy of rural America: the more he dominated the songwriting – as inspired by these 'characters' – the more distant he became. They were country innocents, he was the detached urban observer. It made for an intricate balancing act.

By the end of June, with the release of *The Band* deferred till the autumn, the group were once again turning their attention to thoughts of live performance. Not only was there much talk of the upcoming Woodstock Arts and Crafts Festival, scheduled for late August, but Dylan had been in touch to ask about the possibility of touring with him in the fall. Typically, Bob had been the one superstar *not* in evidence in Woodstock that summer. Tired of people lurking around the house in hopes of seeing him, he had decamped to a house on Fire Island. 'It was like a wave of insanity breakin' loose around the house day and night,' he said in 1984. 'You'd come in the house and find people there, people comin' through the woods, knockin' on your door. We *had* to get out of there.' *Nashville Skyline*, released in April, signalled even more clearly than *John Wesley Harding* that Dylan wanted nothing to do with what he called the 'freaky psychedelic crap' being churned out by most American rock bands. Indeed, sung in a completely new, plummy country voice, the album seemed to suggest that Bob had actually changed his identity.

It was never too clear what The Band thought of 'the new Dylan', though Al Aronowitz claimed Robbie often made fun of the singing on *Nashville Skyline*. Whatever their feelings, they were certainly not averse to the idea of playing with him again, especially after hearing about the planned Isle of Wight Festival in England at the end of August. When they accepted an offer to play the Mississippi River Festival in Edwardsville, Illinois on 14 July, Dylan suggested making a surprise appearance at the end of their set. Introduced as 'Elmer Johnson', he came on to wild applause to sing an old hill tune, '(Black Girl) In The Pines', following it with 'Ain't Got No Home', the Woody Guthrie song he'd performed with the band at Carnegie Hall. He then returned with the group for a rabble-rousing encore of 'Slippin' And Slidin''. The next day, the *St Louis Post Dispatch* hailed The Band as 'the most interesting rock group in America'.

The Isle of Wight Festival had been planned in response to the Woodstock Arts and Crafts Festival, a three-day event at which Dylan, with typical bloody-mindedness, had declined to appear. The Band could ill afford to be so perverse, as Dylan's erstwhile manager Albert Grossman pointed out, and accepted an offer to play the Woodstock Festival on Sunday 17 August. Rehearsals of their own material and of Dylan's followed in Woodstock in early August, with Bob reluctantly returning to the town he now so abhorred. Rick recalls Dylan dismissing the Woodstock Festival as 'just an excuse to sell tie-dye'. He must have been amused when the organizers of the festival were obliged to move it sixty miles away to Max Yasgur's farm near Bethel; it turned out that the good burghers of Woodstock itself were not keen to have upwards of a quarter of a million hippies running amok through their quaint old streets.

1969 seemed to be turning into the Year of Festivals. Another one that served as a useful warm-up for The Band's appearance at Woodstock was the Toronto Pop Festival in early August. Their first appearance as The Band in the town where it had all started for them, it proved to be an unmitigated disaster. Not only was the p.a. abominable, causing an apoplectic Albert to demand an apology, but an amp blew early in the set to add to their woes. Reviewing the festival for *Rolling Stone*, Ritchie Yorke noted that 'the challenge of communicating their soft, tight sound in the wide open spaces threw them,' and it was a problem that dogged the group at almost every open-air festival they were to play. Despite the premiere performance of 'Up On Cripple Creek' and a screaming encore of 'Slippin' And Slidin'' that must have triggered happy memories for any veteran Hawks fans in the audience, they never quite got off the ground at the festival. 'It was awful back there,' recalled Robbie. 'There was a crackling noise and nothing coming out of the monitors. If we'd been smart, we'd just have stopped and come back when they got it fixed. I don't even understand why we did that show. I suppose it was just because it was Toronto.'

Coincidentally, the very issue of *Rolling Stone* in which Ritchie Yorke reviewed the Toronto Festival carried an interview by Yorke with none other than Ronnie Hawkins, who was suddenly in the rock'n'roll limelight again as the man who'd first put 'the band that became The Band' together. All well and good, one might suppose; certainly no reason for The Band to begrudge their old boss the opportunity to capitalize on the success of his protégés. There was a problem, however. In the interview, Ronnie talked very uninhibitedly of the good old bad old days of life on the road, including the regular visits he and Levon had made to 'Odessa' down in West Helena. 'Levon was always the best fucker,' he told Yorke. 'I remember with Odessa that Levon would go first, and when I went in she would say, "Mr Ronnie, you can go ahead, but I think Mr Levon has gone and taken it all. That Mr Levon has a strip of meat on him like a horse." Yes sir, he was a big boy, that one. He had more meat than the Toronto abattoirs.' Among the other smutty titbits the Hawk divulged for the delectation of *Rolling Stone*'s readers was that Richard Manuel was nicknamed 'The Gobbler', adding that 'if you're a hip guy, you'll understand why we called him that'.

When The Band and their manager saw the interview, they were rather less amused by Ronnie's memories than he seemed to be. As Ritchie Yorke himself put it, 'the Band members were exceedingly distressed to read Ronnie's comments on their rip-roaring days gone past, as they conflicted with the purer-than-holy image which Albert felt essential to accompany the first two albums'. Learning of the Band's annoyance, Hawkins promptly got on the phone to Rick, who'd always kept him abreast of how much money the group was making, 'adding another coupla zeros every time he took another pill'. 'Ricky was very cool,' Ronnie told Yorke after his conversation. 'It was like we'd lost all contact with one another, like we were on two different levels all of a sudden. Rick was sure hot about the article, he said all kinds of things about how it was bad for them, how Albert was upset, and how I shouldn't have done that to them. Hell, man, if someone had said I had the biggest dick in America I'd be happier than a dog on heat. And I only talked about Levon, 'cause I know Rick and Robbie are married now and it might upset their wives if I recalled the wild times we had together. Rick told me not to mention their names about anything again. I was real upset about it for a couple of days, drank a lot of booze to try to sort it out.'

The Falstaff of Yonge Street had finally been spurned, only in this case there were five Prince Hals doing the spurning. Ironically, the article in question prompted much renewed interest in the Hawk, and led swiftly to his signing a contract with the very company he'd dreamed about ten years before – Atlantic. It was clear from the outset that Jerry Wexler and Tom Dowd, who took him down to the new Muscle Shoals Sound studio in Alabama to cut the *Ronnie Hawkins* album, saw the Hawk as a kind of unofficial godfather to the new breed of Southern rockers Atlantic was so assiduously cultivating – 'a roughshod cowboy Marshall Tucker kind of guy', in Dowd's words. They loved the mythical outlaw persona of the 'Who Do You Love' protagonist, and figured that putting him together with the Muscle Shoals band was a marriage made in heaven. Unfortunately, the album was very rushed, and only a version of the Clovers' 1953 hit 'Down In The Alley' – championed by John Lennon as 'the single of the year' – stood out as something special. For Ronnie, the session was salvaged by the last-minute appearance of Duane Allman, who came up from his hometown Macon, Georgia in the back of a milk truck. Allman, whose inimitable slide guitar had graced Aretha Franklin's improbable version of 'The Weight' back in January, was exactly the kind of 'longhaired redneck' who so fascinated Wexler and Dowd.

Jerry Wexler's patronage of the Hawk made little difference to the Band camp. When Ronnie wound up supporting Joe Cocker's Mad Dogs and Englishmen troupe at the Fillmore East the following March, he compounded his crimes by confronting Albert Grossman backstage, pulling on his pigtail and accusing him of stealing not only The Band but two members of Janis Joplin's group, Ricky Bell and ex-Rockin' Revol John Till. 'I'll whip enough piss out of you to scald a hog,' Ronnie drawled rather drunkenly, doing himself few favours in the process. 'They told me I wouldn't get out of New York City alive,' he laughs. 'I said that if you're close enough to shoot me, then you're close enough to get shot.' Ronnie's life may not have been in danger, but he had to ask himself whether it was more than just a coincidence when American gigs quickly dried up for him.

Of all the acts featured at Woodstock, that most famous of rock festivals, the quintet who hailed from Woodstock itself were perhaps the most out-of-place. When Bill Graham realized that The Band 'did not *sell* anything, in the "Hey, clap your hands!" sense of the phrase', he could not have foreseen how true that would be in front of the massed tribes at Max Yasgur's farm. 'The Band thought the whole idea of the festival was exciting because of what it stood for,' Robbie told *Rolling Stone* for their twentieth anniversary Woodstock tribute. 'But when we flew in and saw the mass of people sitting on the side of the hill, it was a frightful sight. It was like an army, a ripped army of mud people.' It did not help that the band flew in with their preconceptions shaped by a *New York Times* feature entitled 'Nightmare In The Catskills', which inaccurately reported a severe shortage of food and toilet facilities at the festival. (Levon had even gone to the lengths of forbidding Libby to come, telling her that it was 'no place for a woman'; she came up to the festival with Janis Joplin instead.) 'We'd read on the Saturday in the *Times* that it was a disaster and that there wasn't any food,' said Jonathan Taplin. 'But when we touched down and made our way over to Bill Graham's Winnebago, Barry Imhoff said "Don't worry" and opened up a huge fridge full of steaks!'

Not long after they arrived on Sunday afternoon, the heavens opened. While Taplin ran around trying to ensure that none of their unloaded equipment was damaged, the band huddled inside a truck with Grossman and Al Aronowitz, who was covering the festival for the *New York Post*. 'People were saying "Isn't this beautiful?",' recalls Robbie. 'And it *was* beautiful. But it was also very swampy.' Backstage, everybody seemed stoned or dazed, and The Band felt sober to the point of alienation. 'Backstage was like it usually is for us,' says Levon. 'We'd go in, shake hands, eat, play our gig, and split. There was never anything social.' Only Rick really entered into the spirit of the event, playing 'soothing songs' for acid casualties in the company of John Sebastian. 'You've got to remember that life was *phenomenal* for Rick,' says Taplin. 'Here he was, the son of a woodcutter, playing at the biggest rock festival that had ever taken place.'

With the programming at the festival being contingent on which acts happened to turn up at which time, it should have been no surprise that The Band found themselves sandwiched inappropriately between Ten Years After and Johnny Winter. When they finally took the stage in the early evening, they felt like 'a bunch of preacher boys'. 'After three days of people being hammered by weather and music,' Robbie told *Rolling Stone*, 'it was hard to get a take on the mood.' Despite opening with an all-cylinders-firing 'Chest Fever', the set quickly settled down into what Robbie called 'slow, haunting mountain music'. Songs like 'Tears Of Rage' and 'Long Black Veil' were played beautifully but were hardly guaranteed to rouse a rabble used to reacting in Pavlovian style to the demagogical proddings of what Jonathan Taplin calls 'the attack bands': The Who, Sly and the Family Stone *et al*. 'I thought, "God, I don't know if this is the right place for us",' said Robbie, for whom looking into the audience was 'like looking into purgatory'. 'It seemed as though the kids were looking at us kind of funny. We were playing the way we played in our living room, and that might have given the impression that we weren't up for it. But it could have been that we just couldn't get that same intimate feeling with a few hundred thousand people. As a musical experience for The Band, we were like orphans in the storm.'

It was arguably one of Albert Grossman's bigger mistakes as a manager to have refused permission for any of his acts (The Band, Janis Joplin, Blood, Sweat and Tears) to be included in either the film or the album soundtrack of the festival. 'I always thought it was madness to keep their stuff out of the movie,' says Jonathan Taplin. 'But Albert had a kind of Dr No thing about him – he really liked to say no a lot more than he liked to say yes. He liked to keep things controlled and low-key and inaccessible.' According to Robbie, the band was approached with the proposition that if they wanted to be featured in Michael Wadleigh's film they would have to return half the money that they'd received for the concert itself (a mere $7,500, in any case) in return for a percentage of the movie profits. When John Roberts complained of the festival's rising costs, Albert offered him $1 million for the film and album rights. Roberts refused, which may explain why Albert declined permission for any of his artists to be included in the film. In the event, The Band were filmed anyway, but didn't care for what was produced. 'There were no shots showing all of us onstage, just two or three of us at a time,' said Richard. 'So we let it go.' The same went for the three-album set which Atlantic put together. 'Our tapes were the best of any of the groups,' said Robbie, 'but we didn't like the set-up, and the album seemed pretty shoddy. Crosby, Stills, Nash and Young had to go back into the studio to dub over their voices.'

Exactly what difference it might have made to The Band's subsequent career had they appeared in *Woodstock* is hard to say. Perhaps it was ultimately more appropriate that they were not forever tied to the event in people's imaginations in the way that, say, Richie Havens (with 'Freedom') or Joe Cocker (with 'With A Little Help From My Friends') were. In any case, The Band had other things to think about in the week following their appearance: in particular, the Isle of Wight Festival off the south coast of England. The festival, dubbed 'Woodstock East' by some, had assumed added significance once it was clear that Bob Dylan was definitely not going to appear at Woodstock.

Dylan, who had been made an offer he couldn't refuse by the promoters Ray and Ron Foulks, had intended to sail to England on the QE2 on 13 August. Barely had he boarded the liner with his family, however, when young Jesse Dylan fell ill and had to be rushed to a New York hospital. Twelve days later, once it was clear that Jesse was not seriously ill, the Dylans flew to London, The Band following close behind. As an additional lure to Dylan, the Foulks brothers had rented the lovely sixteenth-century Forelands Farm near Bembridge, and it was here that Bob and the band lived and rehearsed for the next five days. 'The Isle of Wight was kind of fun,' says Jonathan Taplin. 'You've got to remember that we hadn't been playing as a live band with Bob for a long time.'

For Taplin if not for Dylan, the highlight of the stay was the morning of Friday 29 August, when two Beatles employees arrived at the farm in a Daimler and set down a helicopter marker in the backyard: 'Twenty-five minutes later, down comes this chopper, and out get John Lennon, George Harrison, and Ringo Starr!' Harrison had brought with him an acetate of *Abbey Road*, and proceeded to play it through an amp in the barn that served as a rehearsal studio. Al Aronowitz, who had flown over in the capacity of Dylan's road manager, thought he could detect not just awe but envy in Bob and the band; if so, it was well and truly buried by the time the two factions came to jam together. Doubtless it was leaked rumours of this jam session that fuelled talk of the festival climaxing in a huge all-superstar ensemble comprising Dylan, the Beatles, the Stones, and Blind Faith.

After one last marathon rehearsal on 30 August, Dylan and the band repaired to the nearby Hector's Crab and Lobster Inn, where, according to *Disc* magazine, they played an impromptu acoustic set. By this time, almost two hundred thousand people had congregated at the festival site near Ryde, only to be greeted by conditions as bad as those the *New York Times* had inaccurately reported at Woodstock. The Foulks brothers had screwed up just about everything, above all the toilet facilities, of which – even backstage – there were far too few. This time the *New York Times* had assigned the story to Nik Cohn, and the author of the just-published *Awopbopaloobop Alopbamboom* was pretty depressed by what he saw. For him, there were too few 'diversions' to hold people's interest for three days, so that by the second day 'the festival was already sunk deep in apathy': one particularly congested encampment had dubbed itself 'Desolation Row'. Even The Who, wrote Cohn in his 7 September story, 'caused not a ripple' with their headline performance on Saturday night. Other acts – the Nice, the Pretty Things, Blodwyn Pig, and a host of other dodgy British bands – fared no better. Only Joe Cocker and Richie Havens, fresh from their Woodstock triumphs, raised the late summer temperature a little.

The Band were due to play their own set at 8.30 p.m., directly after Havens. Unfortunately, technical problems kept Jonathan Taplin onstage for a further hour and a half, to the exasperation of everyone including Bob Dylan. Bob might have conned a lot of people into believing that he was now a serene seer – a man who could claim that his 1966 stage act had been 'all for publicity' – but he wasn't fooling Al Aronowitz, who became his chief scapegoat backstage. Furious at the delays, Dylan kept sending Aronowitz out to the stage to tell Taplin to get on with it, only to shoot the messenger every time he came back to report that nothing could be done. 'What the fuck's wrong with the fuckin' sound system?!' he shouted at the hapless journalist. 'What's takin' so fuckin' long?!?' After Al had come back a third time, feeling rather like the man sent to hurl Excalibur into the lake, Dylan screamed: 'I want The Band on NOW! RIGHT NOW!'

The delay had the effect of increasing the audience's impatience tenfold: by the time The Band took the stage a little after 10 p.m. the crowd had awaited their messiah long enough. Yet so infectious was the humour and the dignified passion of the group's set that the calls for Dylan only began to sound with any vehemence during 'I Shall Be Released', their seventh number. Starting with a jubilant 'We Can Talk', they worked their way through much of *Big Pink* – including a rare live version of 'To Kingdom Come', with Robbie yelling hoarsely alongside the others – before finishing with a frantic 'Loving You Is Sweeter Than Ever'. 'Hope country music goes down alright in the Isle o'Wight,' Robbie said as Levon strapped on his 1930 mandolin for 'Ain't No More Cane' and 'Don't Ya Tell Henry', numbers which prompted the *Guardian*'s Geoffrey Cannon to note that 'the voice of The Band, dextrously intimate, became an amplified version of old stories told round a fire.' Nik Cohn was even more impressed. 'They were terrific,' he wrote. 'Their harmonies half-country, half-gospel and the beat good hard rock, they made the endless succession of English bands that had gone before seem like so much Mickey Mouse.'

The Band had barely played three-quarters of an hour when the white-suited Dylan joined them onstage. Transformed from the demonic speed-freak Britain had seen three years earlier, he launched into a loose-swinging 'She Belongs To Me' in the limpid new voice of *Nashville Skyline*. More than warmed up by their own set, the group rolled along behind him with the same rangy humour they'd brought to his Woody Guthrie songs at Carnegie Hall, the set giving them the chance to try their collective hand at some of the songs he'd cut without them on *John Wesley Harding* and *Nashville Skyline*: the hit 'Lay Lady Lay', the beautiful 'I Threw It All Away' (a perfect vehicle for Garth's churchier interpolations), together with two of the songs – 'I Dreamed I Saw St Augustine' and 'I Pity The Poor Immigrant' – which Robbie had felt worked better without organ and lead guitar overdubs. The arrangement of 'Immigrant', with Garth on accordion, was especially haunting.

On the fierier numbers, particularly 'Maggie's Farm' and 'Highway 61', the band roared beside Bob like wild dogs, Levon's locomotive drums driving them on as Mickey Jones had never been able to do. Robbie played corruscating runs throughout and contributed one of his greatest solos to 'The Mighty Quinn', the basement song which had provided a hit for Manfred Mann the previous year. If 'Like A Rolling Stone' was hardly the volcanic outpouring it had been on the '66 tour – betraying Dylan's obvious ambivalence about the song – it was still thrilling, the band propelling it along on a groove that was halfway between Stax and Phil Spector. 'The sound at the Isle of Wight was terrific,' says Jonathan Taplin. 'I remember we liked the WEM system so much that we got one ourselves. The sound just punched through out of these huge stacks, and my sound guy Ed Anderson was blown away.'

After encores of 'Minstrel Boy' and 'Rainy Day Women', Dylan said 'Thank you' and left the stage. He had been onstage just over an hour, making his set not just one of the great anti-climaxes of rock history but one of its great 'rip-offs'. The crowd was incensed as it trudged back to Ryde to wait for early morning ferries back to the mainland, and the *Daily Mirror* reported that fans had been on the point of rioting. 'He gave a reasonable, albeit slightly flat performance,' said John Lennon. who accompanied Dylan back to Forelands Farm, 'but everyone was expecting Godot, a Jesus, to appear.' In a radio interview the next day, Levon claimed that both Dylan and The Band had had other songs lined up to play, but had felt so little feedback from the audience that it hadn't seemed worthwhile continuing. 'The fans didn't seem to be music fans,' he said, 'or maybe they were just so dragged by all the hassles that nothing would have worked at that point. I would like to have gotten carried away. I was ready, but I don't think everybody else was. We were prepared to play for another fifteen minutes or so, and Bob had an extra list of songs with question marks by them that we'd have done had it seemed like the thing to do. But it seemed like everybody was a little bit tired, and the festival was three days old by then.' Even

Rick, who'd enjoyed the set, told one interviewer that the crowd had been so 'orderly' that it was like playing 'a giant high-school gymnasium'. Levon was also infuriated by the British press 'clicking their cameras and talking and making a hell of a big deal out of it': for him, the whole Dylan hype had once again been blown way out of proportion, bearing no relation to the music that was being made onstage. In some respects, with hindsight, the anticlimax of the Isle of Wight 'Second Coming' presaged the death of the '60s dream. Coming just three weeks after the Manson killings – and only two months after the death of Brian Jones—it pointed forward to the 'Big Comedown' of Altamont and Kent State.

After the festival, the band spent a couple of days in London with Dylan and the Beatles. While Bob hung out with Lennon, playing piano on the session that produced the harrowing 'Cold Turkey', Robbie and Jonathan ran around town with George Harrison. 'No one really knew they'd broken up,' says Jonathan, 'so George had the run of the city in a way I'd never seen before. It was like being with royalty.' On the morning of Tuesday 2 September, Harrison took Dylan to Heathrow Airport in his Mercedes, The Band following in their tracks.

Reflecting on these first traumatic months of live performance at a later point in their career, Robbie conceded that The Band was never really a festival act. 'Our sound is subtle and slippery, and it's difficult to communicate that at a festival where there are so many variables,' he said the following year. 'When you're playing in the open air, it's very hard to hear what the other people in the band are playing. The sound comes and goes, and what's worse is that we're usually sandwiched between groups like Ten Years After and Led Zeppelin.' As late as 1976, after the Watkins Glen Festival and the 1974 Dylan/Band tour, Robbie could still say that 'anytime we've done those things we've never felt really natural about doing it – we're a puppet show in the distance, and the music is an excuse for something else.' After the long period of rural hibernation, it had been a rude reawakening to find themselves thrust back into the limelight in front of such vast crowds.

For Robbie, there was little time for rest before the release of *The Band* and the inevitable live dates that Albert had lined up for the group, given that he had agreed to produce the debut album by a promising singer called Jesse Winchester. The strain on him was evident in a *Rolling Stone* interview conducted during the Toronto recording sessions by Howard Gladstone, a conversation constantly interrupted by phone calls from Woodstock and New York concerning *The Band*. 'I'm just one of those people who insists on doing more than he can,' Robbie told Gladstone, adding that he'd been 'wasted for a year'. Asked if the success that was threatening to destroy Creedence Clearwater Revival posed the same danger to The Band, Robbie replied: 'To a certain extent. We've got a pretty down-pat thing, but it's still hard. It's harder for us now than it's ever been. We're not breaking up, but just keeping it together.' His general frame of mind could have been gauged by the degree of scorn he showed towards other rock acts. Dismissing not only Jim Morrison and Procul Harum but fellow Grossman client Janis Joplin and the Beatles' *Get Back* album, he had good words only for *Gris-Gris*, the first Atlantic album by Dr John.

Jesse Winchester was just one of many Americans who'd dodged the draft by moving up to Canada in the mid-'60s. He had played in a French-Canadian band in Montreal and written a handful of impressive songs but had never considered taking things any further until Robbie heard him practising in the basement of an Ottawa church and proposed cutting some demos with him. 'I'd say Robbie influenced me a lot in terms of ambition,' he told an interviewer. 'It never occurred to me to do a record until he told me to *think big*.' With Albert offering to release an album on his own recently-formed Ampex label, Robbie flew up to Toronto with engineer Todd Rundgren, a Grossman protégé and all-round whiz-kid whose Philadelphian garage-pop band the Nazz had enjoyed a very minor hit with 'Hello It's Me' at the beginning of the year.

The resulting, eponymously titled album has not dated well. Where The Band's records stand so timelessly outside the quagmire of quaint '60s 'folk rock', Winchester's songs and artless voice were so transparently a product of their time that they make hard going in the 1990s. The fact is, there were a lot of bearded young troubadours warbling in this vein in the late '60s, and exactly what Robbie saw in Winchester that was different remains as elusive as whatever it was he liked about Neil Diamond when he came to produce the latter's *Beautiful Noise* album in 1975. The best moments on the record were those most redolent of The Band: the rocking opener 'Payday' and the lovely country song 'The Brand New Tennessee Waltz', featuring one Al Cherney on fiddle. Besides co-writing 'Snow' with Jesse, Robbie supplied intermittent guitar on the album's other eight tracks, but it wasn't enough to save the record from sounding like a poor man's version of Tim Buckley, or from justified obscurity.

By the time Robbie returned to Woodstock in late September, Bob Dylan had moved back to New York City. Tired of all the blissed-out flower children wandering around outside his house, he decided it was time to lose himself once more in the anonymity of the streets. He wasn't the only star for whom the town had lost its charm. 'Woodstock was getting to be such a heavy number,' Van Morrison told Richard Williams in 1973. 'When I first went, people were moving there to get away from the scene – and then Woodstock itself started being the scene. They made a movie called *Woodstock* and it wasn't even *in* Woodstock, it was sixty miles away. Everybody and his uncle started showing up at the bus station, and that was the complete opposite of what it was supposed to be.' Eventually, Robbie himself – an urban kid at heart – would start to feel the same way.

Rick Danko put it very simply: '*The Band* changed everybody's lives.' Released to almost unanimous approval in the music press, by Christmas the album was in the Top 10 and on its way to selling a million copies. Even Robert Christgau, a 'nervous dissenter' when it came to 'the lugubrious *Big Pink*', had to take his hat off to the group. Having planned a heretical outburst in his *Village Voice* column, he found he loved *The Band* and was obliged to admit that Robbie was 'the only American songwriter to write good fictional/dramatic songs . . . and the only one to master the semi-literate tone, in which grammatical barbarisms and colloquial ellipses transcend affectation to enrich and qualify a song's meaning.'

Nor was it just the music press which rushed to celebrate the group. When *Time* magazine approached Albert for a *cover story* on The Band, he knew the album – lifted by the Top 30 success of the first single 'Up On Cripple Creek' – had touched something deep in the collective unconscious of those Americans who'd heard it. 'The Band appeals to an intelligent segment of this generation,' *Time*'s William Bender was quoted in the opening 'Letter from the Publisher' in the issue of 12 January 1970. 'Many of them have tried the freaked-out life, found it wanting, and are now looking for something gentler and more profound.' The insidious conservatism notwithstanding, the point was a valid one, and the piece that followed in the issue was an admirably thorough account of The Band's journey from Yonge Street to New York's Felt Forum, where they'd sold out four nights in December.

Perhaps the most significant thing about the widespread adulation heaped on the group through the winter was that, despite it all, they remained fundamentally anonymous. 'We were on the cover of *Time* and nobody knew us,' says Rick. 'Maybe that was the mystical side of it. It left something to the imagination.' Part of the reason for this was the ongoing distrust of the press bred by Albert. Levon, wary of The Band's status as 'press darlings', didn't even trust writers who *liked* the group. 'I always thought people treated us almost *too* nice,' he said in July 1982. 'At that point, I guess, The Band offered people an extra alternative to what was going on, which is why we got that kind of response. But I don't want to have to live in its shadow forever.' Only Robbie ever really enjoyed the attention, though he affected to pretend otherwise. 'People treat us so much more intellectually and so much heavier than we ever believe for a minute that we are,' he said rather disingenuously (not to say clumsily). 'We feel kind of foolish.' Jonathan Taplin knew only too well that this was a pose, and that Robbie hungered for intellectual credibility. 'When they wanted to be seductive,' he says with a smile, 'Robbie certainly could be.'[1]

Whatever their individual feelings about the explosion of media attention, the sudden taste of success had a cataclysmic effect on the group, and one from which they never fully recovered. 'Ever make a million dollars fast?' says Rick. 'Well, I have, and it's a goddamn crying shame what success can do.' For the first time in almost a decade of playing together, the band was being lauded in its own right, and none of the five men was quite prepared for it. 'We had become very accustomed to a reality in our lives,' says Robbie, 'and when success came along, part of that reality went out the window. All of a sudden we were on the cover of *Time*, and all of these things were happening, and none of it was for free. All of it took a toll. We thought that because we'd been around and seen what it had done to other people we would be a little wiser. But it's not the same when it happens to you. Suddenly, somebody is running in with a glass of water before you're even thirsty. Next thing, they're dusting off your jacket and it's not even dirty. It does something to your mind. As we went out into the world – left our mountain hideaway – the unit that we had been for all those years started to break apart.'

The most obvious symptom of what Robbie was to call 'the disease of fame' was the pronounced increase in the band's drinking and drugging habits – notably those of Richard Manuel. 'Richard was the sweetest guy in the world, but he was the worst alcoholic I've ever met in my life,' says Libby Titus. 'We're talking *quarts* of Grand-Marnier every day.' Add to the boozing his periodic bouts of drug abuse and it was clearer than ever that The Band had a major casualty on their hands. Rick wasn't a lot better, a grinning garbage-head who was usually stoned on *something*. As for Levon, good Southern boy that he was, he generally stuck to pills, especially downers. 'Levon liked to sleep,' says Jonathan Taplin tactfully.

The trouble was, it was difficult to get any perspective on your drug use when everyone around you was out of his head too. The Band only had to look at Janis Joplin, who by this time had become a kind of surrogate daughter to Albert Grossman, to reassure themselves that they weren't *that* bad. 'It was the drug age,' says Robbie. 'There were a lot of crazy people around, and a lot of them were druggies. Everybody wanted to turn me on to something new. And for the guys in The Band, it wasn't like all of a sudden they got successful and immediately people were running into the bathroom. It wasn't dramatic at all.' But as the drugs got more dangerous, it became harder for Robbie to shrug off his worries. 'Heroin was a problem,' he admits. 'I never liked it, never understood it, and I was scared to death of it. But it came through, you know, like everything else came through.'

Playing intermittently through the late winter and spring of 1969/70, mainly on the East Coast, The Band sustained themselves with what Robbie called 'the veneer of comradeship' and Libby Titus thought of as 'a thread of humour and music'. 'Richard could make you laugh so hard your sides would split,' says Jonathan

Taplin. 'But when the drinking got too much he would become very morose.' The shows were often superb, even when the group were at their most distant and aloof. By early 1970, it was clear which of the songs from *The Band* worked best onstage. 'The Night They Drove Old Dixie Down' segued nicely into 'Across The Great Divide', for instance, and Richard could turn 'King Harvest' into something truly gut-wrenching. 'Jemima Surrender' made a great two-guitar rocker, and 'Unfaithful Servant' was not only a perfect showcase for Rick as a ballad singer but featured a spine-tingling Robertson solo utilizing his remarkable 'trilling' technique and harmonics. 'Taking our music out and performing it, there was something very private about it,' says Robbie. 'The way we performed it was not very flashy or showy. We just came for the business so we could go on and play our hearts out. There was some kind of yin-and-yang between our nature and what concerts were really about. It was almost more like classical music in performance than coming out and wearing cut-off leotards and buckskins. Not being very showy, it all added up to this kind of "stage fright" theme in our lives. It became so vulnerable and sensitive somehow, presenting this music in public.'

The vulnerability The Band felt onstage – the sense, as Robbie was to write in 'Stage Fright' itself, of being 'caught in the spotlight' – led to their developing a kind of protective shell no less alienating for being invisible. *Rolling Stone* critic Jim Miller, who could write that a Band show in Cambridge, Massachusetts was 'the last time I felt part of a tranquil community of rock listeners,' could also observe that there was something cold about them. 'They displayed an awesome slickness that evening,' he recalled. 'Even the raw edges seemed planned. These bar-band *auteurs* were only too ready to embalm their own work beneath a veneer of professionalism, as if to exhibit it behind a glass case in some museum.'

*

Not long after the show that Miller attended in early May, The Band returned to Woodstock to mull over the idea of recording soundtrack music for a couple of movies. Ironically, given Robbie's soundtrack work for Martin Scorsese in the '80s, Albert had a year earlier turned down one offer from Hollywood. 'Somebody called up Albert and asked if we'd like to do the score for a movie about a couple of guys who ride across the country, meet some people, end up with a couple of prostitutes and then get killed,' remembers Robbie. 'He said we weren't interested.' The film, of course, was Dennis Hopper's *Easy Rider*, and The Band were lucky in the end to have 'The Weight' used as the song to which Hopper and Peter Fonda ride out across the California desert. Now there were two other directors who'd been sufficiently impressed by *The Band* to want soundtracks for forthcoming films: Tony Richardson, who was shooting *Ned Kelly* with Mick Jagger, and Michelangelo Antonioni, who came up to Woodstock, swept into Albert's house in a flowing cape and silk scarf, and begged Robbie to write some songs for *Zabriskie Point*. Both were in due course turned down.

The more important item on the agenda was the group's third album. The challenge of following up *The Band* provoked several different 'concepts' for the record, the most attractive being an album cut live in front of a local audience at the Woodstock Playhouse. Robbie, moreover, wanted the record to be more of a light-hearted, good-humoured rock'n'roll affair. 'After *The Band*, I thought this thing was being taken way too seriously,' he says. 'I thought: "Let's have a little bit of a goof here. Let's do some touching things, some funny things. Let's do more of just a good-time kind of record."'

It being out-of-season, before the Playhouse began its run of summer stock plays, the band figured the show would attract only a small audience. The town council, however, did not agree, and feared a huge influx of fans such as they had imagined in their nightmares about the Woodstock Festival. In the end, the group compromised, agreeing simply to use the Playhouse as another of their makeshift studios. It would be the first time they'd recorded in Woodstock since vacating Big Pink. 'It was the same sort of arrangement we'd had before,' says John Simon. 'Capitol provided the equipment. The control room was down in the prop room, with a tent erected around the console to keep it warm, and the recording room was on the stage. Things always go slow in recording studios, and instead of having to hang around and smoke cigarettes by the phone booth the way you had to do in a city studio, we had this big parking lot field out front where we could play touch football. A couple of us even learned how to ride motorcycles during the sessions.'

For John Simon, the sessions were a good deal more relaxed than those at the Sammy Davis Jr house: 'we just whipped through it,' he told *Rolling Stone*'s Phil Levy. When work began at the end of May, Robbie had already completed some of the songs for the album, with Richard taking even more of a backseat than he had on *The Band*. 'I did everything to get him to write,' said Robbie almost defensively. 'I wrote with him, I begged him, I pleaded with him, I offered to become his partner in songwriting. I'd pull him into a song *I* was working on just to get him in the mood or give him a taste for it, thinking he would go on to follow it up. But he didn't. There is no answer. My theory is that some people have one song in them, some have five, some have a hundred.' When the sessions were finished, there were just two co-credits for Richard and one for Levon.

Despite the intention to make a 'lighter', more good-time record than *The Band*, many of the songs that Robbie found himself writing for the album took on an altogether darker hue. It was as if the traumas of The Band's success and live performance were coming out in his writing regardless of his desire to defuse them. 'Without even understanding where it was coming from,' he later said, 'this album *Stage Fright* started to seep through the floor. I found myself writing songs that I couldn't help *but* write. After the fact, I think we could sense what the album was saying, but by then we had already been blinded by the light.' Having always detested the kind of semi-autobiographical/confessional songs favoured by the many angst-ridden 'singer-songwriters' of the age, Robbie surprised even himself by writing several songs which, in veiled ways, spoke of personal concerns and problems within the group.

The album's opening track was deceptive. 'Strawberry Wine', co-written and sung by Levon in a voice that sounded halfway between Lee Dorsey and an Arkansas farmhand, could easily have set the scene for the kind of 'good-time' album Robbie had originally envisaged. It may have been this song (and 'Time To Kill') which persuaded Patti Smith, interviewing the band for *Circus* magazine during the sessions, that the 'feel' of *Stage Fright* would be 'pretty positive, looking at things with a friendly, ironic eye'. The album, she wrote, was 'designed to make you feel good' and 'recorded in friendship'. This was very much an image of The Band already held dear by the music press – even a future punk priestess like Patti Smith who purred in her feature about 'the admiration they have for each other's gifts' and the way 'they tease and cheer each other's smallest successes behind the glass recording booth.'

By the end of Side One, one had to feel less sure of The Band's 'friendly, ironic eye'. Even 'Time To Kill', ostensibly a happy-sounding celebration of the 'mountain hideaway' to which they'd at last returned, could have been seen as an expression of their fears about the world that had so encroached on them over the preceding year. As for 'Just Another Whistle Stop', a Manuel/Robertson song about 'the road' and the violent America that The Band could no longer avoid, here was the reality of the Kent State killings that 'Look Out Cleveland' had presaged a year before:

I've seen a young boy on the run,
And I've seen other children having fun.
Police siren, flashing light,
And I wonder who went down tonight.
People, people, where do you go
Before you believe in what you know?

But it was Side Two which really confirmed that The Band was a decidedly more troubled unit than it had been during the recording of the second album. Blasting off with 'The Shape I'm In', a Robertson song written with explicit reference to Richard's problems, it climaxed with the anguished title track and with 'The Rumor', a darkly haunting portrait of the incestuous, claustrophobic community of Woodstock itself. By the end of the record, with its three ominous tom thuds, one was left in no doubt as to the feelings that had 'seeped through the floor' of the Woodstock Playhouse as the late spring turned into summer. Significantly, the album cover – designed by Bob Cato, photographed by Norman Seeff – suggested a far more autumnal and downbeat ambience than was conveyed by the jolly 'June and July' of 'Time To Kill'. The combination of Cato's semi-abstract sunset landscape and Seeff's shadowy portrait of the group on the porch of a Woodstock ranchhouse gave the distinct impression of a band that had lost the nerve of their second album and gone into hiding. As Greil Marcus was to observe in *Mystery Train*, *Stage Fright* was 'an album of doubt, guilt, disenchantment, and false optimism': 'The past no longer served them – the songs seemed trapped in the present, a jumble of desperation that was at once personal and social.'

In a 1971 piece that touched on the group, Marcus noted one of the symptoms of the album's 'disenchantment': the far greater predominance of solo vocals, without 'the strange out-of-time ensemble shouts that had made *Big Pink* and *The Band* so marvellous, so hard to take for granted, and so rich'. On *Stage Fright*, the five members of The Band actually sounded more distant from each other, less of a gang or 'micro-community' than they had on the first two albums. This obviously made sense on a song like 'Stage Fright', where Rick's trembling voice was at its most vulnerable, but it often left Levon and Richard sounding just as poignantly alone. Only on 'The Rumor' did the three singers work together in the same interweaving, neo-gospel manner which had characterized so many of the tracks on their earlier records. Even so, *Stage Fright* has suffered unfairly from the curse of the 'third album syndrome', especially since it followed on the heels of the almost instantly classic *The Band*. The fact that the record failed to create a kind of parallel world in the way *The Band* had done should not devalue the considerable strength of the songs and their performances. Engineered and part-mixed by Todd Rundgren – himself about to start work on the first of several brilliant albums for Albert Grossman's labels[2] – all ten tracks sounded wonderfully crisp and punchy.

'Strawberry Wine' was an infectiously funky opener, riding on a Rick Danko bass line which bore out his claim that he thought of the instrument more as a tuba than as a guitar. 'I don't think I play bass lines,' he told one interviewer. 'I just try to play where there's no one else hitting it. There's always a thousand spaces in our group, so it's not difficult.' As distinctive on his instrument as Garth, Robbie, and Levon were on theirs, Rick was sounding more distinctive still as a result of acquiring a new Ampeg fretless, which enabled him to 'swallow' notes in a way that was indeed very tuba-esque. 'With The Band, the fretless just melted into what we were doing,' he told a guitar magazine. 'You kind of slide around, playing a little softer with more half-shades.' Coupled with Richard's boxed-in drums and Garth's combination organ-and-accordion textures, he did a great deal more than merely underpin the rhythm of 'Strawberry Wine'. 'The song was just one take,' recalled John Simon, who was once again serving as the band's unofficial sixth member. 'We went in and did it and Levon sang it live. It was terrific on take one and we didn't go any further.'

Richard's greatest moment on *Stage Fright* was 'Sleeping', a kind of follow-up to 'In A Station' by way of 'Whispering Pines'. Written with Robbie, and arranged in waltz time, it was another typical Manuel piece that hovered somewhere between the bluest melancholy and the most blissful escapism. It remains not just one of Richard's liveliest performances, but one of The Band's most intricate arrangements. Based around some inimitably dreamy piano chords, the song builds to a chorus section dominated by Rick's climbing-and-descending bass line and Levon's loose, almost jazzy snare rolls. In the second of these sections, the vocal drops out and Robbie plays a breathless solo in synch with Garth's pitch-bending Lowrey that must rate as one of the most ecstatic passages on any Band record. It was the last time a Richard Manuel classic would be heard on a Band album.

As the first single from *Stage Fright*, 'Time To Kill' played things very safe. Based around a simple strummed guitar riff, and sung by Rick in tandem with Richard, the song was arguably the most harmless piece of music the group had yet recorded as The Band. Only Garth's tinkling electric piano and the interplay between Robbie's piercing solo and Levon's funky rhythm guitar work made it remotely special. The most that could be said for 'Time To Kill' was that it set up a striking contrast with the powerful 'Just Another Whistle Stop', a song that hadn't even been finished when John Simon spoke to *Rolling Stone* at the end of June. Written in the mode of 'Jawbone' and 'Look Out Cleveland', 'Whistle Stop' boasted characteristic time changes and an urgent, panicky vocal from Richard. 'From beside a train,' wrote Jay Cocks in *Time*, 'a man like a carnival pitchman looks out at a street where a boy is pursued by screaming police sirens and flashing lights. The pitchman offers a trip away from all this, and the song becomes a rhythmic invitation to salvation aboard a train to glory.' Coincidentally, while they were working on the song, The Band were asked if they wanted to appear on the 'Festival Express' tour of Canada that summer, joining Janis Joplin, the Grateful Dead, and others on a specially-chartered Canadian National train ride from Toronto to Calgary.

The last track on Side One, 'All La Glory', showed that Levon Helm was far from limited to the redneck holler of 'Strawberry Wine', and could handle a dreamy ballad in a surprisingly soft voice if he wanted to. The song was a kind of lullaby, with Garth's sleepy accordion offsetting Robbie's delicate electric guitar. After a middle-eight section worthy of Hoagy Carmichael, Garth played one of his most enchanting solos, a freeform organ fantasia that conjured images of old cinema Wurlitzers. The overall effect of the song was almost spooky in its pining nostalgia. 'It's a song to a young person,' said John Simon. 'I can't be sure, Robbie may have written it for his little girl, or it may be more universal than that.' It seems fitting that so many children were born to The Band in 1970: by early December, daughters had been born to Robbie and Dominique (their second), to Richard and Jane, and to Levon and Libby.

Kicking off Side Two, 'The Shape I'm In' provided yet another pointed contrast in mood. The fact that rumours were starting to leak out about the shape Richard Manuel was in only made his vocal sound the more frantic. Set to an insistent, crudely funky bass pulse, the song could almost have been the inevitable sequel to 'Jawbone', except that 'The Shape I'm In' was a first-person account of winding up on Skid Row, positing the sanctuary of rural life against the aggravation of hustling on the street. Nothing on *Big Pink* or *The Band* had approached the degree of desperation in Richard's voice: this was like being accosted in the street by a Bowery bum in a rare moment of sobriety. It may have been pure coincidence that in the final bars Garth Hudson quoted the main vocal line from Dylan's 'I Pity The Poor Immigrant', or it may have been a discreet indication that this song, like 'Just Another Whistle Stop', had a clear political context. Greil Marcus, for one, felt that 'The Shape' 'set the stage for the apocryphal political drama that is woven into the fabric of *Stage Fright*', though for him the 'drama' was one that The Band never satisfactorily managed to stage.

'The Shape I'm In' had barely finished when Robbie cranked out the funky intro to 'The W. S. Walcott Medicine Show'. As tailor-made for Levon as 'The Night They Drove Old Dixie Down' had been, this song was the most obvious throwback to the mood of *The Band*. Indeed, based on Levon's memories of the travelling shows he'd seen as a boy in Arkansas, it was almost too contrived as tintype portraiture, and lacked the quirky freshness of Robbie's earlier songs. Instead of creating a compelling vignette from the material, the lyric merely pointed to some of the 'colourful characters' who made up the medicine show and asked us to be enchanted. Musically, the nicest touch was the Garth Hudson/ John Simon horn section, with Garth contributing a tenor sax solo worthy of that great New Orleans sideman Lee Allen.

Equally stilted, if truth be told, was 'Daniel And The Sacred Harp', Robbie's quasi-Appalachian version of the Robert Johnson myth which had so entranced him as a neophyte bluesman. 'I guess it's about greed in the context of Christian mythology,' Robbie has said. 'At the time, I was very into Sacred Harp shape-note singing, so I had that in the back of my mind.' In the song, a man comes into the possession of a famous harp that gives him divine power but robs him of his soul in the process. As with 'Long Black Veil', the song was too studiedly spooky to be truly affecting. Not even the incorporation of Rick's fiddle and Garth's old-time pump organ, or the different vocal roles of Levon and Richard, could lend it half the inspiration that had gone into 'Rockin' Chair'.

Ralph J. Gleason called 'Stage Fright' the best song ever written about performing. Written at the piano by Robbie, it was intended originally for Richard until it became obvious that it was far better suited to the nervous, tremulous voice of Rick Danko. For all the conjecture that the song might have been about Bob Dylan, to those in the know it clearly came out of Robbie's terrifying ordeal at The Band's debut show a year before. Like 'The Shape I'm In', it had an anguished present-tense quality about it that sounded new to aficionados of the first two albums. For all those who treasured a cosy image of The Band in the evergreen sanctuary of Woodstock, it was a disconcerting confession of the pain and stress the five men had suffered since 'going public'.

The final song offered a resolution of sorts, but also betrayed a certain paranoia. Again there were those who assumed 'The Rumor' was about Dylan without appreciating that, as Mick Gold put it, 'the rumour' was 'a metaphor for every insidious, malevolent force that cannot be combatted directly.' '"The Rumor" was about Woodstock,' says John Simon, for whom this was the finest song on *Stage Fright*. 'I had a line in one of my own songs that went, "Rumours fly around this town/Like echoes around a canyon". In Woodstock, you could tell from where someone's car was parked who they were fucking.' Building up a picture of a small town in which a man, any man, could be ostracized and condemned on the strength of idle gossip, the three voices of Rick, Levon, and Richard pleaded for tolerance and compassion, merging finally in soaring harmony to urge the victim to believe there was light at the end of the tunnel. From the song's intro, built around Rick's mournfully sliding bass riff, the atmosphere was one of muted tragedy, with the healing release of Richard's section recalling 'Whispering Pines'.

Greil Marcus thought 'The Rumor' sounded like 'A Sunday school lesson', which couldn't have been wider of the mark.

Interestingly, in a retrospective piece on the group written shortly before 'The Last Waltz', John Swenson speculated that the 'vigilantes' to which the song referred were 'critics like Marcus himself, who are less interested in finding out what The Band is trying to say than in fitting them into preconceived modes.' Swenson was probably taking the group's own paranoia too far, but he had a point. Perhaps it was not so easy to trust the judgement of a man who could write – as Marcus did in a long 1971 piece entitled 'Rock-A-Hula, Clarified' – that the lead singer on 'The Shape I'm In' was Levon Helm.[3]

The mixing of *Stage Fright* had its own peculiar history, and one that said more than a little about the frictions that were brewing within the group. While Robbie wanted Todd Rundgren to mix the album, Levon thought they should send the tapes to Glyn Johns, whom they'd met at the Isle of Wight Festival. 'I don't think Robbie wanted me to do it at all,' Johns told writer Michael Wale. 'And in fact it turned into a game. Todd brought the tapes over to England with him, and we both did separate mixes. It was like a competition, which I thought was howlfully amusing.' John Simon was more diplomatic. 'In the past, we've mixed ourselves,' he said shortly after Rundgren had left for London. 'There's been six of us on the mixes and it's been hard on us all, you know. So this time we decided to go two paths. We've let Glyn Johns mix it with completely fresh ears, though we did send him a sort of rough mix of what we thought it should sound like. Neither he nor Todd cares which mix we use, it's not any kind of competition thing at all. When it comes back from London, the two of them will have decided what's best.'

Johns was not overly enthusiastic about the material, nor the way it had been recorded. With only a week to mix, he hired one of Island's studios in Basing Street and did the best he could.

Most bizarrely of all, given that the album cover credited him with the 'Mix Down', was the fact that the group ended up using only three of his mixes. 'The only reason I know that,' he said, 'is because when I sent my bill in, their manager phoned me up and said, "Well, listen, man, we only used three mixes". I said. "Tough, you're going to have to pay the whole bill. I don't care if you didn't use *any* of it."'

As mixed by Glyn Johns – or so the story went – *Stage Fright* was in the record stores by the end of August. Ironically, after the muted cry for help in the title track, The Band were to spend most of the subsequent year on the road.

'Where Do We Go from Here?'

Life isn't as easy now as it has been in the past, I know that. I don't know if that means you're a star.

Robbie Robertson

The Canadian 'Festival Express' tour at the end of June 1970 was the brainchild of publicist Frank Duckworth, who had actually worked on the Winnipeg section of the railroad that stretched almost four thousand miles from Nova Scotia to British Columbia. 'The idea of the tour,' said Duckworth, 'was to remind people of the romance of travelling by train in the old days when trains were still a vital form of communication, and to combine that with rock'n'roll, which is the most vital form of communication today.'

Put in those terms the tour could hardly have failed to appeal to The Band, who may have left their country far behind but who still understood the romance of the railroad pushing through the empty wilderness to the Rockies. If Robbie slightly winced at the idea of being part of a stoned rock'n'roll caravanserai – 140 musicians and their pals crammed into twelve train coaches – there were probably worse ways of spending five days in the music business.

The tour, comprising three mini-festivals in Toronto, Winnipeg, and Calgary, came at a time when the profile of Canadian rock had never been higher. Not only were exiles like The Band, Neil Young, and Joni Mitchell establishing themselves in America, but groups such as the Guess Who had persevered long enough in Canada itself to earn the breaks that had been denied Levon and the Hawks in the '60s. 'You can't shove Canadianism down people's throats,' the director of one Toronto radio station had argued, but he and other programmers looked pretty silly after the Guess Who's 'These Eyes', ignored by Canadian stations, became a U.S. million-seller in late 1968. Determined to succeed without forsaking their Canadian identity, the Winnipeg band had gone on to enjoy even bigger success with 'No Time' and the #1 'American Woman', paving the way for a string of Canadian hits like Original Caste's 'One Tin Soldier', the Poppy Family's 'Which Way You Goin', Billy?' and Mashmakhan's 'As The Years Go By'. Inevitably there was talk of a 'Canadian sound', and New York A&R men were dispatched to Toronto to root out the local talent. By the end of 1970, Canada's largest retailer Sam 'The Record Man' Sniderman reported that sales of Canadian recordings had increased by 25% over those of 1969. In America, Andy Kim, Steppenwolf and R. Dean Taylor (with the #5 hit 'Indiana Wants Me') all fared well. In an interview, the Guess Who's Burton Cummings said that 'the guy who'd made it all possible' was none other than Ronnie Hawkins.[1]

There was a disappointing turnout of 37,000 at Toronto's CNE Stadium on 28 and 29 June, about 13,000 fewer than expected. This was partly due to a militant group calling itself the May 4th Movement (after the date of the Kent State killings), who persuaded people to boycott the festival because it wasn't free. 'Bashed Heads and Bad Trips', headlined one Toronto paper the next morning. The tense atmosphere affected the show, although in their *Rolling Stone* account of the tour David Dalton and Jonathan Cott noted that 'you could almost forget the hassles of the day during Garth Hudson's intro to "Chest Fever" – suggesting notes, picking them up and transforming them into wondrous and unheard-of structures . . .'

For Cott and Dalton, the 'presiding spirit' of the train was Janis Joplin, a 'Bacchanalian Little Red Riding Hood with her bag full of tequila and lemons, lurching from car to car like some tropical bird with streaming feathers'. To the fastidious Robbie Robertson she was loud and obnoxious, but to Rick and Richard, as to so many others, she was just one of the guys. As the train rattled through the forests of northern Ontario en route to Winnipeg, Rick and Janis got drunk and duetted together on everything from Lee Dorsey's 'Holy Cow' to George Jones' 'I Threw Away The Rose'. Country songs seemed to provide the main soundtrack to the journey: one of Janis' favourites was Kris Kristofferson's 'Me And Bobby McGee', which would be a # 1 hit for her after her death. 'Only Janis,' noted Cott and Dalton, 'could have turned the Dead and other assorted heads into a bunch of "Goodnight, Irene"-singing drunkards.'

The Winnipeg show managed to draw a mere 4,000 fans to the Manisphere Stadium, 17,000 less than promoters Thor Eaton and Ken Walker had needed to break even.[2] 'I think we are in a period where the art of personal performance is declining,' said Robbie after The Band's cursory set, adding that this was probably the last festival the group would ever play. The next morning, only Rick and Jonathan Taplin rose in time to make the train's 8 a.m. departure. Robbie in any case had decided to return to New York to check the *Stage Fright* mixes that Todd Rundgren had brought back from London. On the train, Rick entertained Janis with a solo rendition of 'Ain't No More Cane', prefacing the song with a hokey intro about his old lady visiting him in jail.

At Calgary, the final stop, there was an open jam session featuring Delaney and Bonnie, Jerry Garcia, Ian and Sylvia, and Rick. 'We thought you were just Californian freaks,' Danko told Garcia, 'but you're just like us.' By this time it was clear that 'Festival Express' had been a financial disaster. As Albert Grossman employee Bob Shuster put it, 'Woodstock was a feast for the audience; the train was a feast for the performers'. When it was all totted up, the 'million dollar bash' had lost $350,000.

A week after the Calgary show, The Band topped a bill at the Hollywood Bowl with a line-up of acts that included Miles Davis. 'They read off a list of the support groups,' recalled Robbie, 'and once they got to Miles we couldn't even hear any of the other names.' Unfortunately, despite the fact that his *Bitches' Brew* album had entered the *Billboard* album chart two weeks earlier, the Hollywood Bowl audience was unprepared for the visceral assault of Miles' explosive jazz-rock fusion. 'It was like a horror experience in the audience,' said Robbie, 'and our job for the rest of the evening was just to kind of cool everybody out again.'

The group's set on that balmy night of 10 July caught them at their very best. Opening with a pounding 'Shape I'm In', yet to be released on the B-side of the first single from *Stage Fright*, they worked their way through much of *The Band* and a smattering of the new material. Particularly affecting were 'King Harvest' and 'Unfaithful Servant', while 'Rockin' Chair' provided a lovely interlude between the rowdy renditions of 'Jemima Surrender' and 'Time To Kill'. Garth's intro to 'Chest Fever' had already become a vehicle for all manner of exploratory improvisations, and at the Bowl he moved seamlessly from passages of baroque solemnity to inspired gothic tomfoolery, never once losing the audience's attention as he built up to the familiar riff that opened the song. Two further highlights were a wild 'Strawberry Wine' and a version of another Motown song, Marvin Gaye's 1964 side 'Baby, Don't You Do It'. Gaye's original had been a beat-heavy floor-filler, with the singer for the most part intoning the lyric in his customarily cool tenor. The Band turned the song into something altogether more raucous, with Levon screaming out the verses and the others following suit as they joined him on the chorus. Winding up in a torrent of wailing vocals, cascading organ, and ear-splitting guitar, 'Don't Do It' made a formidable encore that night. By the *Rock Of Ages* shows eighteen months later – beefed up by Allen

Toussaint's wild horn arrangement – it was an equally stunning opener.

The touring began in earnest after *Stage Fright* was released in September. Although it was never as popular as *The Band*, and was received much more coolly than its predecessor, the album reached # 5 on the *Billboard* chart, making The Band one of the major rock acts of the day. The continued success made it possible to hit the road in style. 'We had it set up pretty well,' remembers Jonathan Taplin. 'We had a little turbo-prop airplane that would land near Woodstock in Kingston, so it would literally take twenty minutes to get to the plane and go to any college or venue where we were playing.' That fall, moreover, The Band were in reasonably good shape, staying away from the more dangerous drugs and working hard to present good shows. Even when it came to post-gig liaisons, they seemed to behave themselves. 'The rock star stuff didn't come up for us,' Levon later claimed. 'The Band was never attacked by groupies before, during, or after any show we played.' Certain cities always seemed to inspire powerful performances; others invariably proved tougher nuts to crack. 'Some of the shows were real good,' says Robbie. 'There were periods when we were playing really well. But like anything, it goes in phases and different stages. Sometimes it got real accurate and sometimes we were just crazy rock'n'roll musicians. But when it was really good, when we all played well, it made us feel just tremendous.'

By the end of October, the group was playing in the South for the first time in years. 'We're going to play just a handful of shows there,' Robbie had told Roelof Kiers earlier in the month, 'but this time it'll be under totally different circumstances. Back then we were playing joints and honky tonks for barely enough money to eat on. Now to go back and play the concert halls in those cities is a thrilling experience for us. It's also the only place where everybody can clap on the offbeat!' After shows at the University of Alabama and Memphis' Ellis Auditorium (where the

Hawks had played with Dylan in 1965) the itinerary took a Midwest detour before commencing a string of further Southern dates in December. Starting at Dallas' Texas Memorial Auditorium on 4 December, the band played Houston, New Orleans, Atlanta, Jacksonville, and finally Miami, where Jim Morrison's indecent exposure eighteen months earlier had made it difficult for rock bands to enjoy a relaxed atmosphere. 'We felt the effects, the tension left by The Doors,' Richard told an English interviewer the following spring. 'Some of the police turned a blind eye if there were no injuries, but others didn't hesitate to throw people out of the show.'

After Miami, the group went into hibernation for the winter, prompting Rick Danko to admit that they performed live 'as little as we can'. 'We can't do it all the time,' he told Nick Logan in the spring. 'Living on vitamin pills and strange foods, you can't stay healthy. If you overplay, it's like anything else, you begin to feel like you're going to work.' If this seems to jar somewhat with Robbie Robertson's subsequent accounts of life on rock's 'endless highway', it is worth bearing in mind the man's own admission to *Musician* editor Bill Flanagan that 'it seems like we played everywhere, but we weren't out there like maybe the imagination implies'. Indeed, so reclusive did The Band seem to the rock community as a whole that rumours continued to abound that they were all drug casualties, or at least that Albert Grossman was still encouraging them to keep their distance from the world at large.

As it happened, Albert was taking more and more of a backseat in the running of his empire. 'Albert's situation changed radically after three awful incidents,' recalls Jonathan Taplin. 'Dylan left him, Peter Yarrow was busted, and Janis died. After that, he spent less and less time in New York and more and more time in Woodstock. He lost his aggression, and it was clear that he'd been hurt.' Even Janis had felt neglected by Albert: 'I know I'm not

The Band or Dylan,' she'd cabled him a few months before her death in October, 'but care about me too.' With Janis dead, and The Band more or less self-sufficient as an entity, Albert instead busied himself with the construction of a huge studio complex near his Bearsville estate.

A barnlike wooden structure in the middle of the forest off Speare Road, the Bearsville studio quickly became a second home to The Band, who had never before had such facilities on their doorstep. 'Instead of sitting around home and turning on a 2-track, we can go down to the studio and turn on a 16-track,' said Levon early in 1971. 'And instead of some asshole coming in and bootlegging the music we can have the record company do it for us nice and legit.' Later in the year, Richard admitted that The Band were now considerably more at home in the studio than they'd been when they made *Big Pink*. But, he added, 'we want musicians doing the production, not studio men trained in electronics, who tend to cut out or turn down the foot-tapping and natural noises that go on . . .' Rick rather grandiosely called Bearsville 'our own studio – the first one we don't have to tear down after we're through'. The studio was still having its bugs worked out when the group began working on the tracks that would make up their fourth album for Capitol.

Clive James, the Australian-born writer and latterday TV star, once conjectured that the somewhat 'self-congratulatory' tone of *Cahoots* was the result of 'insufficient critical appreciation' of Robbie Robertson's achievements on the first three Band albums. But there seems to have been a more general malaise within the group as they worked on a collection of songs again written principally by Robbie. It was as if they all secretly knew that the hunger and freshness of their first recordings had gone, and that they could never again be the 'gang' they'd been before the success of *The Band*. 'Everybody had been so easily satisfied before, and then it got harder to do what we did at ease,' Robbie told Joshua Baer in 1982. 'The inspirational factor had been dampened, tampered with, and the curiosity wasn't as strong. We didn't compensate for it, we didn't try. We just did what we did and . . . it was not the centre any more. It was spread out and watered down in a kind of way where we were then thinking about tours and posters and things like that instead.' The feeling that the group had 'become what we'd rebelled against' haunted the sessions that produced the album. 'The only thing left to rebel against was ourselves,' says Robbie. 'That's what a lot of the music after *The Band* was about.'

From the very outset, in February, Robbie felt a complete dearth of inspiration in his writing. 'It was frustrating, a horrible feeling,' he said. 'I was getting a little disillusioned by personal things and it was affecting me. I just didn't have the spirit to write. A lot of the songs were half-finished ideas.' The 'personal things' consisted mainly of Robbie's sense that the others had lost any real motivation to make special music. With the pressure of touring taken off them, they were sinking back into their old ways. Richard, in particular, was hitting the bottle hard; not one of the eleven songs on *Cahoots* was even co-written by him. 'He had the disease of alcoholism, even though none of us realized that it was anything more than that he liked to drink too many beers,' says Robbie. 'We started to think, jeez, how do you survive this situation? If it's a little bent, how do you make it work? You think, "I can't run somebody else's life, I cannot tell somebody that they have to take care of themselves".'

For those around The Band, Robbie became not only the group's leader but virtually its caretaker. 'As I got to know them better,' remembered Bill Graham, 'I saw that Robbie became the leader because nobody *else* wanted to be the leader. Levon had been the leader, but he wasn't enough of a decision-maker.'

Jonathan Taplin thought of Robbie as 'Mr Responsible': 'He effectively took control. They'd all have a vote, but he could propose forcefully enough that people would go along with it. Once Richard had dried up, Robbie had to write everything, and he was up for it, but it put a lot more pressure on him.' Even Ronnie Hawkins could tell that something fundamental had changed within the group's chemistry. 'At the very start, Levon was the boss the way John Lennon was the boss of the Beatles,' he says. 'But after a while he started having too much fun, so it was left to Robbie to take care of business. It's tough when everybody's not pulling their weight, when people aren't able to go onstage because they're falling down and puking in pianos.' For Robbie himself, the group had gone into a 'tailspin': 'Every once in a while we could come to the surface and be who we really were, just because there was a bunch of talent there, but we were fighting the demons the whole time. Today, if I ever hear the old records, they remind me of old dreams, and I think, "Oh, that was a *bad* dream," or "With this dream, we kind of forgot about everything for a moment . . ." With The Band, it was always a bit like throwing the dice.'

One can guess the kind of dreams that Robbie remembers when he hears *Cahoots*. The very album cover, a painting of the group standing behind a mausoleum against a menacing sky, suggested a nightmare. Side One may have blasted off with the rousing, propulsive 'Life Is A Carnival', but the ferris wheel on the horizon in Gilbert Stone's painting was abandoned, and the Preservation Hall jazz band standing inside the summer house looked like ghosts. The painting, which replaced the original cover – an Irving Penn photograph of two Peruvian urchins vetoed because some big cheese at Capitol thought one of them looked pregnant – expressed the mood of loss of nostalgia that dominated the record. The broken toy soldier on top of the mausoleum was symbolic of the way America had neglected its heritage, something which clearly obsessed Robbie on songs like 'Last Of The Blacksmiths' and 'Where Do We Go From Here?' 'The record posed the question, "What are things coming to?"' says Robbie. 'It dealt with extinction, with the fact that things like carnivals and blacksmiths were vanishing from the American scene.'

The trouble was, Robbie seemed so desperate to force his point through that most of the songs sounded lifelessly didactic; as Greil Marcus noted in *Mystery Train*, 'all of the humour and drive' of the first two albums had gone. Instead of growing organically from some musical seed, the songs were constructed like miniature soapboxes; instead of being peopled by flesh-and-blood characters, they were dominated by phantasmic abstractions. The 'pastoralism' that had informed but never cloyed songs like 'King Harvest' was finally veering – particularly on the closing 'River Hymn' – towards sentimentality. More fundamentally, the songs were just so melodically undistinguished: even today, it is hard to recall anything about a song like 'Thinkin' Out Loud'. Garth Hudson, who admitted that it was 'harder for me to find something different for each song', was not alone in feeling that Robbie's songs had become unnecessarily over-complicated.

Naturally, there were exceptions to this, not least the dazzling, antiphonal funk of 'Life Is A Carnival'. The Band had been huge fans of New Orleans R&B ever since their Hawks days – 'we figured we could play Lee Dorsey better than anyone except Lee Dorsey,' boasted Levon – and the release of Dorsey's brilliant 1970 album *Yes We Can* only increased their admiration for producer Allen Toussaint. Boasting songs like 'Tears, Tears, And More Tears' and the original 'Sneakin' Sally Thru' The Alley', *Yes We Can* was a radical reworking of the Crescent City grooves and horn arrangements Toussaint had patented on mid-'60s hits like 'Ride Your Pony' and 'Working In The Coalmine'. Robbie and Levon loved the explosive combination of second-line rhythm, brass, organ, and acoustic guitar that Toussaint used on the album's title track, and wondered whether they might be able to persuade the producer to arrange the horns on 'Life Is A Carnival'. 'I just had Toussaint's name in the back of my head, so I called him up,' says Robbie. 'I really didn't know if he was some old man who was gonna say "*What* band?"'

As it happened, Toussaint *hadn't* heard of The Band – 'I didn't realize what I was missing,' he told Barbara Charone in July 1973 – but that didn't stop him discussing ideas with Robbie. 'They'd heard of Lee's album and they were, I guess, impressed a little,' he recalled. 'They're such good guys and communications were very, very good. Like, they immediately know where you're coming from. The instrumentation was different from what I'd previously used, but I talked it over with Robbie. In fact, it would have been a completely different arrangement if I *hadn't* talked it over with him, 'cause I can remember I wrote the arrangements first, and as we talked I started tearing them up!' What emerged from this brainstorming session was the most complex piece of music The Band had ever committed to tape, a song that seemed to be pulling in ten different directions simultaneously. 'It was great, because the horns didn't all play together,' says Robbie. 'When other people wrote horns, everybody would come in and everybody would go out. With Allen's thing, everybody would play separately. It's kind of like a Dixieland approach.'

A song about 'the hustle and freakiness of the street', in Robbie's words, 'Life Is A Carnival' was about as close as The Band ever came to jazz. Co-written by Robbie, Rick, and Levon, it was sung by Rick and Levon in their best carny voices. Apart from the thrilling horn arrangement, there was further interplay between the acoustic rhythm guitar and an electric lead treated by one of Garth's numerous gizmos. On top of these two, Robbie had further overdubbed a solo. Nobody could have accused him of not using the new studio to his full advantage.

In immediate contrast to 'Carnival', but almost as good, was the album's second track and first single 'When I Paint My Masterpiece'. Written by Bob Dylan, the song was about a struggling American artist in Rome, weighed down by European culture and secretly longing to be back in his native land. Drawing on Scott Fitzgerald's *Tender Is The Night*, it also provided an inadvertent comment on the experiences Dylan and the Hawks had had in Europe in 1966. With Richard switching to drums, Levon played mandolin and sang in a voice at once plaintive and defiantly American. Likewise, the song seemed to hover somewhere between a Parisian *chanson*, thanks to Garth's wistful accordion, and a country hoedown. With Rick's clever bass line pushing the band irresistibly forwards, the song may not have been a masterpiece, but it was an engaging diversion.

The album's other highlight, for its sheer spirit of bravado, was '4% Pantomime', co-written with fellow Woodstock resident Van Morrison. Van had just finished *Moondance* and was in the process of moving to northern California when he dropped in on Robbie one afternoon and helped him finish a song about two musicians stranded in Hollywood with nothing but a bottle of whiskey to console them. Fittingly enough, the song became a drunken duet between the Irishman – the 'Belfast Cowboy', as The Band dubbed him – and Richard Manuel. 'Richard and Van were close pals,' says Mary Martin, the Canadian who'd hooked the Hawks up with Dylan six years earlier and was now working as Morrison's manager; 'for Van, Richard was the real *soul* of The Band.' The song wasn't anything special, but it was thoroughly redeemed by the sound of the two voices trading verses and shouting across each other in the loosest call-and-response style imaginable. The title referred to alcohol – the difference in percentage between Johnnie Walker Red and Johnnie Walker Black – and to the 'pantomime' that Van and Richard staged as they were recording their vocals. 'They were acting this whole thing out,' recalled

Robbie. 'For a second while I was watching it, it became soundless – all hands and veins and necks. It was almost like this whole movement thing was going on and the music was carrying itself.' Rumours of the Band/Morrison session were quickly blown up out of all proportion by the rock press, since nothing else was cut at the Bearsville studio that spring evening.

The rest of *Cahoots* bore out everybody's misgivings. The songs were limp and laboured, with new depths plumbed on 'Thinkin' Out Loud' and the banal 'Where Do We Go From Here?'. The latter was easily the worst offender in the didactic stakes, a desperately forced eco-lament for the American eagle, the railroads, and the buffalo. 'It's a shit-headed version,' admitted Robbie. 'We got into this thing, we got like hammer-headed. It was a terrible time working with these guys, to be really frank about it. It was just impossible to get anything better than what we got on it. I don't like my choices. I don't like what I did then under the circumstances. There's a very moving thing in there wanting to come out, and it ain't there in this version.'

Robbie might have blamed 'Where Do We Go From Here?' on the others, but neither 'Smoke Signal' nor the awkwardly strained 'Last Of The Blacksmiths' were much better. Even 'The River Hymn', which at least featured some heavenly chord changes and one of Levon's loveliest vocal performances, had a flabbily nostalgic air about it. The song was not helped by the over-the-top choral effects, with Libby Titus singing alongside Rick and Richard, but the real problem lay in Robbie's need to reflect on 'the old days' – when 'the family was family-oriented and the building of this country was going on' – in the first place. 'There's so much season to it, so much more character,' he said. 'I mean, what are you going to write about now? OK: "Then they came back home and watched TV." It's not quite the same as: "The whole congregation gathered on the banks of the river."' Nor, one is tempted to add, quite as pretentious.

For Greil Marcus, *Cahoots* was all the evidence needed to show that The Band had retreated from the challenge of meeting the reality of present-day America. 'The group was its own joint-stock world,' he wrote in *Mystery Train*, 'but it could not survive the honest demands of the greater joint-stock world that was the country itself.' Yet it's possible that Robbie's pining for bygone days and lost Americana was in part a sublimation of his feelings about The Band itself. It was as if his very frustration with the group was coming out in songs which expressed a longing to bring the past back to life. His personal sense of distance from the group seemed to have produced a more widespread mistrust and insecurity.

Robbie was hardly the only one who sensed the rifts that were forming within the band. The very drinking that was causing them so many problems was partly Richard's way of coping with the changes. 'We were drifting further apart, we weren't putting our hearts into it,' Manuel later said. 'What was missing was what they used to call soul music. And I know about it, because it's the only kind of music I can play.' For Rick, it was more a case of familiarity breeding contempt: as he put it five years later, 'it was like eating around the table every day with my family', and it had gotten 'pretty old'. No wonder Greil Marcus thought that 'you could feel the friendship go out of their sound' on *Cahoots*.

Of the remaining tracks on the album, 'Shoot Out In Chinatown' and the ballad 'The Moon Struck One' had moments of innocuous prettiness but were marred by a self-conscious wordiness that betrayed their real lack of inspiration. Had Gil Evans orchestrated 'The Moon Struck One', as originally planned, it might have been less drab; certainly it was the closest Richard came on *Cahoots* to the heights of 'Sleeping' or 'In A Station'. Rick did his usual feckless hayseed number on 'Thinkin' Out Loud', but again the lyric seemed pointlessly convoluted. He had more to get his teeth into with the penultimate track 'Volcano', on which he was a lusty

258

teenager exploding with desire. In the absence of John Simon, whose services had not been required for the sessions, Garth not only put together a splendid horn arrangement but played a wonderfully greasy tenor solo into the bargain.

Part of the problem with *Cahoots* was its sound, which was a long way from the 'woody, thuddy' sound Robbie had established as one of The Band's signatures on their second album. 'We had more clarity, more highs, more punch,' said Robbie after it had been mixed. 'The softer sound that made the earlier material a period piece didn't fit in with the overall dynamics on this record.' Later, however, he claimed that the sound of *Cahoots* 'nauseated' him. 'I don't like it, it's bright and cold to me,' he said. 'At the time, there was a kind of race going on to make loud records. At Capitol, they were saying we should master the record with this guy and we did it. They just EQ'd it and limited it to make it sound a lot louder on the disc. In retrospect, I think it was a mistake. I'd like to hear the album pre-mastered. There is work in there that I still enjoy, but it doesn't play comfortably for me.'

The Band had the *Cahoots* tapes with them when they flew to Europe with Albert and Jonathan on 16 May. Stopping over in London before the first German date of a short European tour, they gave an impromptu press conference at the Inn on the Park on Monday 17 May. To the British press they looked out-of-place but self-contained – 'like ill-at-ease woodsmen', noted *Disc And Music Echo*. 'They were country boys, downhome boys,' wrote *NME*'s Nick Logan, 'pinioned in corners by clusters of journalists but linked by an intangible thread of common spirit, eyes and fleeting smiles crossing the room as they set about their separate tasks.' While Richard guffawed nervously, Levon sat next to Albert talking of soul food and Canadian football. Garth Hudson had always claimed to be too inarticulate to do interviews, but when Nick Logan pressed him a little, the keyboard player launched into a riveting 50-minute monologue on the history of jazz piano.

Among the many things Garth divulged to Logan was the fact that he'd wanted Ben Webster, another of his tenor sax heroes, to open The Band's Hamburg show the following night. The 61-year-old jazz legend had lived in Europe since 1964, settling in Hamburg itself at the end of the decade. Unfortunately, the consensus was that a German rock audience would not have been too sympathetic to an ageing jazz saxophonist, so the idea was dropped. Despite this, the group was pleasantly surprised by their reception at Hamburg's Musikhalle, where they played a variation on the sets they'd been performing the previous year. 'We'd heard from friends that Germans were a little stiff, but that doesn't seem to be the case at all,' Rick told an interviewer in Munich. 'Hamburg felt like Pittsburgh to me!'

Hitting the road again seemed to discharge some of the tension and frustration which had built up during the *Cahoots* sessions. By all accounts they were in superb live form as they continued on through Munich, Frankfurt, and Vienna. Starting the sets with 'The Shape I'm In', which had been issued as a European single to tie-in with the tour, they played (in varying order) 'Time to Kill', 'The Weight', 'King Harvest', 'Strawberry Wine', 'Rockin' Chair', 'Look Out Cleveland', 'I Shall Be Released', 'Stage Fright', and 'Cripple Creek'. After a short interval, they then returned with 'W. S. Walcott Medicine Show', 'We Can Talk', 'The Night They Drove Old Dixie Down', 'Across The Great Divide', 'Unfaithful Servant', 'Chest Fever', 'Rag Mama Rag', and the two Motown covers, 'Loving You Is Sweeter Than Ever' and 'Don't Do It'. The encores were usually 'Slippin' And Slidin'' and 'This Wheel's On Fire'.

By the time The Band hit Paris on Sunday 23 May, they were in peak form. Since the show was on Tuesday night, the group had more than enough time to live it up in the city, with an avuncular Albert Grossman keen to show them around. Fortunately, the partying didn't affect the performance at the Olympia Theatre, scene of Dylan's debacle in 1966. If Richard and Levon were constant 'battles' for Jonathan Taplin, they at least delivered the goods once they were onstage. 'Levon and Rick weren't in the same league as Richard,' says Taplin, 'but they both got out there. Levon had some *serious* problems with downers, and he was *very* hard to wake up in the morning. Rick was like a hoover, he'd take whatever was around. Garth would have a little toke once in a while, but nothing more than that. He could go to sleep sitting up, just zone out, but he was always ready on time. Only if a piece of equipment got damaged would he flip out and sulk.'

Although it was only two-thirds full, the Olympia show was an unqualified triumph for The Band. Geoffrey Cannon, who'd been so impressed by the group at the Isle of Wight eighteen months before, thought it one of the greatest rock performances he'd ever witnessed. 'Robbie gives a little abstracted nod of his head, taps his foot, and starts a new song,' Cannon wrote in *Melody Maker*. 'Garth is massive behind an accordion, Richard plays drums in a precise, almost pedantic style, pulling his elbow right out behind him. It's "Strawberry Wine", and the sound comes out chuckling, but with a mystery in it, too, like a story heard in childhood.' For Cannon, in contrast to many American critics, the group really came alive onstage, their records working best as reminders of live performances. Creedence and Chicago might duplicate their albums onstage, but not The Band. As someone muttered during the interval, 'it's kept its punch from cheap bars – they don't get spaced out too much'. One of the ways The Band kept things tight was to play at a volume significantly lower than that favoured by most of their rock contemporaries. A fan who caught some of the European shows remembers that the sound was 'crystal clear but not too loud, like listening to a giant stereo'. 'We still use small equipment,' Rick said later. 'It's important, because when I'm onstage I stand in the middle of everything, and I really get to hear. When you're playing with five people onstage, everyone should find their own space inside the song. That way you can hear everything, and you complement each other in a way that goes beyond harmony. When people covet space, it sinks them. But when the puzzle becomes unanimous – boom!'

It was ironic that The Band should be playing the theatre in which Dylan had once spurned French 'Vietniks' by draping the American flag behind the stage, since the Vietnam peace negotiations were being conducted in Paris that very week. By the time the group reached Stockholm on 28 May, journalists were asking exactly the same kind of questions they'd put to Dylan five years before. 'It was tricky,' remembered Levon, 'because there were all these American servicemen who'd left the army over moral obligations and gone to Sweden. At the press conference, they wanted to talk about all that stuff, and we just couldn't get into it very much. I said to them that we came over there to play music, and that if any of them had any money and wanted to buy a ticket they were welcome to come to the show.' To cover for the others, Levon told the assembled reporters that the rest of the band was from Canada and 'didn't even know what the hell we're talking about'.

After the show at Stockholm's Konserthuset, another venue the Hawks had played with Dylan, The Band returned to London and spent the Whitsun weekend finishing the mix of *Cahoots* at George Martin's AIR Studios. Later in the week, they played two shows at the Royal Albert Hall that people still talk about with awe in their voices. Richard Williams, reviewing the first of them on Wednesday 2 June, called it simply 'the best rock'n'roll concert I ever saw in my life'. 'They've been criticized for playing nothing over two or three minutes,' he wrote, 'but what a gas it was to hear those short numbers, to be able to applaud them so often, and not to have to put up with self-indulgence in the name of "progress." The Band, he concluded, made most other groups look like beginners. For Mick Gold, the first half was 'slightly too crisp and clear', making it hard to believe there was 'a heart inside the machine'. But they loosened up after the interval, and when they returned for an encore they 'tore into an infectious, body-shaking song that had the whole audience leaping around with pleasure'. It was, of course, 'Slippin' And Slidin''.

Mick Gold was one of the few writers who understood the predicament The Band were in after *The Band*. 'Since they descended from the mountain with their second album,' he was to write, 'they've faltered in their progress, and perhaps we should be grateful that they have. They could only have continued in that direction by becoming more and more insulated inside the peculiarly hermetic historical bubble they constructed on that record.' Others would not be so generous when *Cahoots* finally saw the light of day in the autumn, and the received wisdom on The Band's 'decline' has been summed up in a slightly pat dismissal by Simon Reynolds, one of the best rock writers of the '90s. 'From *Stage Fright* onwards,' Reynolds wrote in the very paper which had carried those glowing reviews by Cannon and Williams nearly twenty years before, 'The Band's music grew progressively more slick and studio-bound, seldom reinvoking the ramshackle, rollicking grooviness of their early music. The vignettes of the itinerant adventurers, migrant workers, peddlers and hobos, once so vivid, came to seem somewhat threadbare and *déjà vu*.' The fact that the group still had in them a superb live album, one of the greatest 'covers' albums ever recorded, and another outstanding album of original songs, was overlooked in a reiteration of the consensus view.

The remainder of the summer of 1971 was spent playing intermittent American dates in preparation for the release of *Cahoots*. Included among these were some of the dreaded festivals The

Band had all but sworn never to play again: the Schaefer Festival in Central Park, and an 'Open Air Celebration' at Minneapolis' Midway Stadium, where they shared the bill not only with pals like Paul Butterfield and John Sebastian but with their old hero Muddy Waters. In early September, the group even joined Kris Kristofferson, Happy and Artie Traum, and others for a 'Woodstock Anniversary' show at Monticello Raceway, seven miles from the original festival site.

A string of fall dates was lined up to promote *Cahoots*, including the band's first San Francisco show since their Winterland debut two and a half years earlier. With Taj Mahal in support, they drew 5,000 faithful to the Civic Auditorium in late November, following up the show with East Coast appearances in early December. With the tour due to climax at New York's Academy of Music, where they'd decided to do some live recording, Robbie felt a sudden hankering to do something different in the four shows they were scheduled to play there. The memory of working with Allen Toussaint was still etched into Robbie's mind, and he asked the others how they felt about the idea of getting Toussaint to write horn charts for the shows. None of them needed much persuading; as Levon put it, having Toussaint on board was 'first-class accommodations'.

When Toussaint came up to Woodstock in mid-December, it was the first time he'd seen snow in his life: as Robbie recalls it, 'he felt ill just *looking* at the weather!' The freezing temperatures notwithstanding, the New Orleans native buckled down to the work at hand. 'We put him in one of our cabins and asked him what he wanted,' recalled Rick. 'He said, "Just a tape recorder and some music sheets." We gave him a tape recorder with earphones and he just wrote the arrangements off the top of his head. It was genius.' What concerned Toussaint most was adding something to The Band's music without subtracting anything in the process; Robbie himself was worried that a horn section would sound like 'a cocktail lounge big band' or, worse still, one of those Blood, Sweat and Tears-type jazz-rock bands. 'I was determined to maintain their original sound,' Toussaint said in 1973. 'If I didn't spoil anything they'd already achieved, then it was a good job. I worked mostly with Robbie, and he focuses so well on how a tune will sound when it's finished. The arrangements were quite easy, because he'd already painted such beautiful pictures.'

With Toussaint working on the charts, the next job was to find the right hornmen to play them. In the event, the choices were inspired: five New York jazzmen 'on a busman's holiday', as Greil Marcus put it. Trumpeter Snooky Young had played with Basie and Jimmie Lunceford; Howard Johnson was a veteran of Ray Charles' band; and tenor man Joe Farrell had paid his dues with Mingus and Elvin Jones. Finally, the section was made up by 17-year-old trombonist Earl McIntyre and St Louis alto man J. D. Parron – not forgetting Garth, of course, who somewhat shyly lined up beside these giants to take his solo on 'The W. S. Walcott Medicine Show'.

Inevitably, the rehearsals for the Academy of Music shows were rushed; as Robbie joked to writer Jim Brodey, the group was thinking of calling its production company 'Last Minute Productions'. Ralph J. Gleason, who reviewed the eventual *Rock Of Ages* album for *Rolling Stone*, claimed the horn section only had one proper run-through before the first night. 'We didn't give it as much time as we should have,' Robbie told Gleason. 'We should have rehearsed with these guys a whole bunch, but we didn't because we didn't have time.' If they didn't have time on their side, they at least had an interesting team of 'consultants' helping out. In addition to John Simon, who'd been brought back into the fold to do the live sound from the house, there were two legends of New Orleans R&B assisting Allen Toussaint: Mac Rebennack, a.k.a. Dr John, and Bobby Charles, author of such Crescent City classics as 'See You Later, Alligator', 'But I Do', and 'Walking To

New Orleans'. 'Mac was there all the time,' said Robbie. 'It was something to do with New Orleans and some of the horn men, because of the music we were going to try with Toussaint and because he was a great inspiration at the time.' Rebennack himself would shortly return to the fundamentals of New Orleans R&B: having taken his 'Night Tripper' voodoo act to its logical extreme, he cut the great *Dr John's Gumbo* in the spring of 1972 and then hooked up with Toussaint for *In The Right Place*. Bobby Charles, due to start work on an album at Bearsville in the New Year, was present in the same capacity. 'Because there was all this last-minute craziness, Bobby looked at the charts and kind of figured out how to handle some things,' said Robbie. 'He's a very critical person, and some objective criticism was helpful.'

There was another legend who came down to the Academy on 14th Street. Doc Pomus was one of the great songwriters Robbie had met in New York with Ronnie Hawkins over a decade before, and the band had kept in touch with him throughout the '60s. Somewhat anomalous in the rock climate of 1971, with the Brill Building 'song factory' days long gone, he none the less commanded the respect of The Band, who didn't need to do any homework to know how seminal Pomus and his partner Mort Shuman had been to the sound of New York R&B and pop in the '50s and '60s. 'He's just an incredible guy to have around,' Robbie told Ralph Gleason. 'He's very far out, and his comments and expressions cleared a couple of things up in our heads. He's very simple and acute, and I'm sure he didn't even know he did it.' For Pomus, then churning out songs for Twentieth Century Fox in Hollywood, hearing The Band and the horns tearing up 'Baby, Don't You Do It' or the Chuck Willis anthem 'Hang Up My Rock And Roll Shoes' was a blast of pure joy. Nor was he alone in his enthusiasm. 'There was so much to learn from the relationship between the musicians in The Band,' says Phil Ramone, the chief engineer on the live recordings. 'It was all about how Levon would sing with Richard, and how Danko's voice would come in in the middle and give it that earthy grind. And Robbie would be the centre, without people ever knowing it. He and Garth would create this empire of sound. It was one of the best experiences of my life overall.'

The good news was that The Band felt exactly the same way when they finally took the stage on Tuesday 28 December. 'It was an experiment,' said Robbie, 'and we didn't know if we were going to walk out with these hornmen to find that the purists were insulted. But as soon as we kicked off the first song, it was over. We weren't even touching the ground. You could see the sound covering the people. It was the greatest experience of our lives.' From the moment the horns came in on 'Don't Do It', it was clear that Toussaint had done everything he'd set out to do and more: this was the funkiest, most exciting sound The Band had ever made. On 'Rag Mama Rag', Howard Johnson played an unhinged tuba solo while the other hornmen simulated a drunken Dixieland combo. 'Across The Great Divide' and 'The W. S. Walcott Medicine Show' swung like big-band jazz, and 'Life Is A Carnival' was as thrillingly intricate as it had been on *Cahoots*. On the slower songs, too, the horns worked their magic: Joe Farrell's soprano sax fills on 'Unfaithful Servant', the wavering bugle call with which Snooky Young opened 'The Night They Drove Old Dixie Down'. 'Everything just seemed to go right,' said Levon. 'Nobody's concentration was affected by anything. I love horns, and the bigger the band the better it sounds to my ear. It was great hearing Snooky Young over there hitting that top trumpet note.'

By the final show, on New Year's Eve, The Band themselves were in electrifying form. One listen to the opening bars of the 'Don't Do It' on *Rock Of Ages* – 80 per cent of which came from that final night – was enough to show that Rick and Levon were now the tightest, most soulful white rhythm section outside Muscle Shoals, Alabama. With his bizarre-looking fretless Ampeg, Rick managed to outdo even the original Motown bassman James Jamerson on this Holland-Dozier-Holland classic.[3] Robbie, looking like a movie star in a red velvet suit, played with an unerring touch all night, crowning his performance with a guitar solo on 'Unfaithful Servant' that must count among the ten greatest ever recorded. Never has the brittle, needling quality of the Fender Telecaster sound been used to such devastating effect, or harmonics deployed to send such shivers down the spine.

Garth, of course, was in his element, thrilled to be playing with the horn section and inspired by the occasion to turn his 'Chest Fever' intro into a one-man fantasia that combined nursery rhymes, Scottish reels, Anglican hymns, Charles Ives and Thelonious Monk in one riveting piece of improvisation. Using three keyboards, he created the most remarkable textural and harmonic interplay any rock organist had ever attempted – and he had time to kill. 'We had it planned out that I was going to look at my watch at midnight and signal to Garth, at which point we'd do "Auld Lang Syne",' said Robbie. 'But because we were anxious about this show, we started a little too soon, so he had to play and play and play, killing time waiting for midnight! It became a musical piece in itself. So I asked Garth afterwards, "What are you going to call this thing? You can't call it the intro to 'Chest Fever', it's longer than the song!" It later became a chance for the rest of us to take a breather. Garth would just go out there and fuck up everybody's heads for a few minutes.' The 'thing' of course became 'The Genetic Method', a title that wittily reflected Garth's fascination with nineteenth-century music primers, and on *Rock Of Ages* it eventually led into the greatest 'Chest Fever' they had ever played, an all-stops-out blast of guitar, organ, and brass that finished the set with an almighty bang.

When the band returned to the stage a little after 12.10 a.m., they were accompanied by a familiar-looking figure in shades. Unannounced, Bob Dylan picked up a guitar and launched into a shambling, rambunctious version of 'Crash On The Levee (Down In The Flood)', the horn section ad-libbing along in the background. After three more numbers – 'When I Paint My Masterpiece', 'Like A Rolling Stone', and 'Don't Ya Tell Henry' – Bob left his old 'scrounge band' to reaffirm their bar-band roots with a defiant '(I Don't Want To) Hang Up My Rock And Roll Shoes', a choice of song that said as much about the desire to prove to each other that they still cared as it did about their continued faith in salvation through rock'n'roll. 'The song roars and swings, punches and rocks, jumps and slides,' wrote Charlie Gillett, 'sounding for every second like a sure radio hit – or rather, how we wish radio hits sounded.' (Indeed, when 'Rock And Roll Shoes' was issued as a single the following November, it didn't even chart.)

The Chuck Willis classic brought The Band's music full circle, emphasizing the sense that *Rock Of Ages*, in Robbie's words, was 'a kind of culmination of our stuff'. When the double album appeared in the late summer of 1972 – one of a succession of great 'live doubles' that included *Grateful Dead, The Allman Brothers At Fillmore East*, and Van Morrison's *It's Too Late To Stop Now* – reviewers were clearly torn between their desire to celebrate the group's body of work and their disappointment at the lack of fresh material. Like most live albums, noted Karl Dallas, *Rock Of Ages* was 'something of a holding operation'. Refreshing though it was to hear live versions of 'Caledonia Mission' and 'Unfaithful Servant', the album's sole original song ('Get Up Jake') was little more than a bit of good-humoured fun. If Ralph J. Gleason was right to compare *Rock Of Ages* to the live peaks of Mingus at Monterey or Miles at the Blackhawk, Greil Marcus' fears were not unfounded. Listening to the records, 'so full of playfulness and bite, blazing with soul and love', he said he could not help being struck by 'how long it had been since The Band had put out a single new song that mattered'.

The Band may have been struck by a similar realization when they left the Academy of Music stage in the early hours of New Year's Day 1972. As they made their way back to the dressing room, Robbie recalled years later, the five men felt 'a common sense of depression'. Where could they go from here?

Before and After the Flood

Playing every night kept the boys in my band out of trouble. Not playing enough, I think, got The Band *into* trouble.

Ronnie Hawkins

1972 was The Band's lost year. Hiding away in Woodstock, they neither performed nor recorded anything together as a group. It was as if Robbie Robertson's loss of confidence as a writer had led to an overall loss of confidence as a band — a loss masked by complacency, apathy, and varying degrees of inebriation. 'Everyone's got them a house, got them a car,' Levon Helm had drawled to Nick Logan in London. 'The money don't worry me that much, but after you get a coupla hit records and you come across that geetar you've always wanted ... it matters a little more.' Interviewed by a fawning disc jockey later in the fall of 1971, Levon had sounded positively jaded. 'It's jest our job,' he sighed. 'We're not self-made geniuses.' A job was something The Band's music was never supposed to become.

Ten years later, in a 1981 interview, Levon claimed to be at a loss to explain the long silence. 'Highs and lows, hills and valleys,' he shrugged in his stoical Southern way. 'Some of us felt stronger about touring, others about recording. I preferred playing to just about anything.' But there wasn't much of either during the eighteen months between the Academy of Music shows and the Watkins Glen festival in July 1973. 'I was rebelling against the album/tour/album cycle and questioning whether that was the way to work,' says Robbie. 'I didn't think you could necessarily just set the alarm, wake up, and work. For the benefit of the music, I decided I would rather wait until tomorrow.' Asked in September 1972 what a member of The Band did on an average day in the Catskills, Robbie did his best to avoid the word 'nothing'. 'What anyone else does, what you would do,' he said. 'He goes to the drugstore to get toothpaste, he watches the birds fly over for a while, he visits with somebody – you know, regular things.'

To those 'regular things', Robbie might have added 'drinking yourself senseless from sunup to sundown', which was mainly how Richard Manuel, whose liver had swollen to the point where it was pushing into his stomach, passed the time. 'He scared us to death,' says Robbie. 'We didn't know what the next day might bring, what would come out of this monster that had seeped out of the woodwork.' For Jane Manuel, Richard's alcoholism expressed crushing feelings of inadequacy. 'I remember a lot of anger and frustration from him,' she says. 'A lot of times he felt he wasn't taken seriously by the others.' Jane herself was angered by the way the Woodstock rock community seemed to regard her husband as a drunken clown. 'Richard didn't have the coping skills to survive,' she says. 'People thought it was amusing to watch this guy drowning.'

But it wasn't just Richard who scared Robbie and Albert and others to death. There was a general vibe of self-destruction around the group, and the smalltown calm of Woodstock gave them no immunity from danger. 'It went through cycles of danger,' Robbie recalls. 'And one element of danger surpassed the others until it was just frightening. One thing equals another, whether it's drinking or drugging or driving as fast as you can or staying up for as long as you can.' Levon and Rick were both still prone to car accidents, and both continued to mess with chemicals. 'Levon had his problems, but he seemed to be able to pull himself out of them,' says Jane Manuel. 'Rick definitely couldn't.'

There were, of course, occasional sessions to keep 'the boys' out of trouble. Aside from the mixing of *Rock Of Ages* at Bearsville, the studio played host to Bobby Charles and British singer Jackie Lomax, both of whom recorded albums for Albert's Bearsville label. Co-produced by Rick and Bobby with John Simon, *Bobby Charles* was a perfect marriage between the good-time Danko side of The Band and Bobby Charles Guidry's own swampy cajun roots. On the opening 'Street People', Bobby sounded like a Bowery version of Randy Newman; on 'Long Face', he was a bayou Lee Dorsey. Behind him Rick put together a wonderfully loose sound somewhere between the Muscle Shoals Swampers and the bands Allen Toussaint had used for his great Minit productions in the '60s. With guest appearances by Garth, Levon, and Richard, as well as Mac Rebennack and Woodstock guitar maestro Amos Garrett, it was certainly a far more enjoyable record than *Cahoots*. 'Small Town Talk' was the flipside to 'The Rumor', a good-humoured poke at the incestuously gossipy world of Woodstock, while 'Before I Grow Too Old' took Bobby back to one of his evergreen New Orleans classics, and the country ballad 'Tennessee Blues' featured an immaculate accordion performance from Garth.

Besides the Bobby Charles album, there were sessions for Dylan's old chum Eric von Schmidt and for Peter Yarrow, whose version of Paul Simon's 'Groundhog' brought together Levon, Garth, and Simon himself at New York's A&R studios. When Robbie stopped by at the session, he ended up co-producing the song for Yarrow's *That's Enough For Me* album. There was also talk in the early summer of The Band putting together a book, in Robbie's words 'a mixture of stories and biographies'. Writer Jim Brodey spent some months in Woodstock gathering material for such a book, but nothing came of it. Yet another film project came up, a Canadian production called *Eliza's Horoscope*, which would not only have starred Richard as a member of a secret religious sect but been scored by The Band. By the autumn, with *Rock Of Ages* in the Top 10 and an edited version of 'Don't Do It' making the Top 40 singles chart, the group had told producer Gordon Sheperd they did not want to be involved.

One of the reasons Robbie dropped out of the unpromising *Eliza's Horoscope* was that he had started work on a project of his own, an album far more ambitious in scope than anything The Band had attempted. Known simply as *Works*, the project had been inspired by the music of avant-garde Polish composer Krzysztof Penderecki. 'He was one of my favourite new composers,' Robbie said of Penderecki, whose works included *The Entombment, Victims of Hiroshima*, and a *St Luke Passion*. 'It's very passionate music and depressing and weird. I can't remember what piece it was that influenced me, but it made me think of an idea that I started to work on at the time. It was a mood that I found. I worked out this melody and then I found counter-melodies for it, but I couldn't find any words for it, so I just kept working on it that way.' What *Works* became over the course of the following months was a kind of symphony about the experience of American Indians, a theme that obviously meant a great deal more to Robbie than to the rest of The Band. More than anything, it seemed to indicate Robbie's continuing desire for artistic credibility.

Right up until the end of 1973, Robbie kept returning to *Works*, only to be overcome each time by the scale of the task he had set himself. 'I'd get fifteen minutes into it and I'd be exhausted,' he said. 'I realized it was much more involved and advanced, that it took a whole other kind of writing and attention.' Briefly spurred on by the prospect of his music being used for a film of *Bury My Heart At Wounded Knee*, Robbie tried again to complete his 'unfinished symphony'. But the movie was never made, and *Works* was once more put on the back-burner. 'I didn't finish it because there was nothing for The Band to do on it,' he said. 'It didn't have anything to do with them and there was no demand for it. It wasn't something the record company was interested in.'

By the end of 1972, Levon was so frustrated by the lack of Band activity that he enrolled for the winter semester at the prestigious Berklee College of Music in Massachusetts. 'I wanted to be able to do something about what I heard in my mind,' he later told an interviewer. 'I wanted to play what I was thinking. Timing is what it's all about, split-second timing. You get that down, you're set.' The break from The Band did him good, making for an improvement in his relations with Libby. 'That winter was great,' she remembers. 'Levon was the greatest father, couldn't wait for Amy to wake up in the morning. He even got to read some books!'

Back in Woodstock, the others were almost as restless. Robbie and Dominique had fallen out of love with the idyllic promise of the town and were planning a move to Montreal, Dominique's birthplace. When Greil Marcus came up to talk to Robbie in November, he understood why they wanted to get out. 'I had never seen that part of the country before, and I realized how one could read its signs as a promise of peace of mind,' he wrote. But in fact Woodstock 'seemed more like a private club, inhabited by musicians, dope dealers, artists, hangers-on'; it struck Marcus as 'a closed, smug, selfish place' – what Robbie called 'a little hippie drug town'. Dominique confirmed this feeling, telling Marcus that 'no one in Woodstock has any idea there is really a world different from their own'. 'There's nothing here but dope, music, and beauty,' she said. 'So if you're a woman, and you don't use dope and you don't make music, there's really nothing at all.' The country life was killing her, she laughed: 'Gotta find my way back to the city, get some corruption in my lungs!'

Richard, meanwhile, had separated from Jane and was holed up in a house with Libby Titus' old crony Mason Hoffenberg. Albert Grossman had offered to help Hoffenberg kick his heroin habit, and arranged for him to join a methadone programme in nearby Kingston. With the somewhat naïve idea of using Mason to keep *Richard* off 'the hard stuff', Albert suggested they co-habit to their mutual benefit. All that happened was that the two of them were permanently smashed on booze. When *Playboy* writer Sam Merrill came to Woodstock to interview Hoffenberg in the spring of 1973, he found Richard semi-incarcerated in the house, forbidden to answer the phone in case it was, in Mason's words, 'one of the juvenile dope dealers up here who hang around rock stars'. 'We just sit around,' Hoffenberg told Merrill, 'watching *The Dating Game*, slurping down the juice, laughing our asses off, then having insomnia, waking up at dawn with every weird terror and anxiety you can imagine. The four other guys in The Band are serious about working and he's really hanging them up. They can't work without him and there's no way to get him off his ass. He feels bad about it, but he's just strung out.' Making his way to the kitchen, avoiding the canine excrement that littered the floor, Richard opened a tin of pineapple chunks. He told Merrill it was the first solid food he'd had in three days.

The Band's decision to go into the Bearsville studio that summer and cut a bunch of their favourite R&B and rock'n'roll songs may have saved Richard Manuel's life. It certainly rescued the group's morale. Although he hadn't abandoned the *Works* project, Robbie knew they had to get back to the basics of the music they had always played – to do something 'just to say hello to everybody again'. 'We were really looking to achieve what we said we'd achieve with *Works*,' he said, 'so we agreed that the best thing to do was write it over a period of a year. But in the meantime we needed to do something just to stay in there.' As Rick put it, '*Moondog Matinee* was a nice way for all of us to get back together after a long sabbatical and play a little music'.

The idea of recording some 'golden oldies' – more to the point, songs the band had originally covered back in their days as the Hawks – reflected the general tendency towards nostalgia and revival in 1973. It was as though rock had finally completed its first cycle, and could afford to take stock of itself. 'The way things were going, you could feel a very definite movement towards this music,' says Robbie. 'With *American Graffiti* coming out, and radio stations playing a lot of those old records, it was just becoming valid music all over again. People were feeling nostalgic because what was happening was kind of watery, and they were picking the past apart again.'

More to the point, The Band needed to lighten up, have some fun; Krzysztof Penderecki was fine and dandy, but he wasn't Clarence 'Frogman' Henry. 'By the time of *Moondog Matinee*, there was a need to come off the seriousness a little bit and not necessarily be dealing with interior feelings all the time,' says Robbie. 'It was also an interesting experiment in translation, translating things that usually got lost in translation.' The *Moondog* of the title came from Alan Freed's legendary radio show of the early '50s, the *Matinee* from the frequent afternoon performances the band had been playing as Levon and the Hawks.

'Translating' songs as different as Junior Parker's 'Mystery Train' and Sam Cooke's 'A Change Is Gonna Come' proved rather harder than The Band had anticipated. Even the selection of the ten songs was no easy matter. 'We didn't realize we were competing with already classic material,' says Robbie. 'As we got into it, it became interesting and we decided we'd spend a little bit of time on it. To us, it was more than just a bunch of cover tunes. There was something of a strength-building factor involved in going after these songs.' In the course of working on the songs, and figuring out who was going to sing them, the group realized there was little point in 'competing' with the originals; what *Moondog Matinee* was going to be about was 'complementing' them.

After two or three weeks of sorting through a pool of contenders for the album, junking songs like Larry Williams' 'Bony Moronie' and deciding against such obvious choices as 'Slippin'

And Slidin'' and 'Loving You Is Sweeter Than Ever', the band had a good idea of the tracks that would make up *Moondog Matinee*. Levon would tackle the raucous Southern stuff – 'Mystery Train', 'Frogman' Henry's 'Ain't Got No Home', Fats Domino's 'I'm Ready', and Chuck Berry's 'Promised Land' – while Richard would sing two ultra-melancholy ballads, the Platters' 'The Great Pretender' and Bobby Bland's 'Share Your Love With Me', plus the very apt 'Saved', a Leiber/Stoller Pentecostal pastiche which had provided a minor hit for LaVern Baker in 1961. Rick was assigned 'A Change Is Gonna Come' and the Lee Dorsey classic 'Holy Cow'. As an instrumental vehicle for Garth, Anton Karas' famous theme from *The Third Man* was chosen to round off Side One.

When the smoke had cleared, there wasn't a dud on the whole album. From Garth's opening piano rumblings on 'Ain't Got No Home' to Rick's last falsetto cries on 'A Change Is Gonna Come', *Moondog Matinee* was like a magical jukebox, the sum of whose parts was the music The Band had gone on to write for themselves. This was how *the Hawks* had heard Bobby 'Blue' Bland and Fats Domino, how *they* had absorbed the explosive precision of those three-minute marvels heard in the wee wee hours on WLAC Nashville. It was tradition filtered through love and laughter, and it was raw and downhome: the Phil Spector overkill of John Lennon's similarly conceived *Rock'n'Roll* would have made no sense here. Levon's drums had the same no-frills cardboard-box sound they'd had when he first hooked up with Ronnie Hawkins, while the barrelhouse piano had none of the artificial tinniness it had had on *Cahoots*. Only in the higher registers, those of the guitar and the organ, were the trademark gimmicks and distortions in evidence; but then that was the essence of The Band's 'translation'. Behind Richard's immaculate vocal on 'Share Your Love With Me', Garth carpeted the song in luscious folds and Robbie played sliding soul chords on his Telecaster.

The quietly despairing 'Share Your Love With Me' was the best thing Richard had done since 'Sleeping'. 'I know he was really proud of "Share Your Love",' says Joe Forno. 'It meant a lot to him when Greil Marcus wrote in *Mystery Train* that he'd improved on the original, because Bobby Bland was one of his early idols.' (His pleasure may have been spoilt by the fact that Marcus also thought it was him singing 'A Change Is Gonna Come'.) If they were less subtle performances, both 'Saved' and 'The Great Pretender' benefited from their autobiographical resonance. 'Saved' was a bit of tongue-in-cheek testifying, but the man who sang it knew he was lucky to be alive. As for 'The Great Pretender', Buck Ram's doo-wop lyric about a clowning character who hides his loneliness was almost too close to the bone.

The most audacious 'translation' on *Moondog Matinee* was the reworking of 'Mystery Train', to which Robbie – after obtaining permission from none other than Sam Phillips – had added two extra verses. Recorded at Capitol's Hollywood studio a few weeks after the Bearsville sessions, 'Mystery Train' beefed up the locomotive drive of Presley's version by bringing in ex-Mother of Invention Billy Mundi on a second drum kit. To this propulsively chugging rhythm Robbie added a neo-rockabilly guitar riff and Garth a variety of trainlike organ and clavinet effects. The song had a fascinating history. With its train imagery dating back to the '20s – the Carter Family had sung of the same 'sixteen coaches' on 'Worried Man Blues' (1930) – it had been written by Junior Parker and Sam Phillips and given Sun one of its first R&B hits in 1953. In Presley's playfully spooky reading, it became an archetypal song of American distance and loss, with the train as a sexual robber bearing people away into the night. The resonance of the imagery may be a little lost in our age of commuter planes, but it wasn't lost on a Canadian like Robbie, whose country had been opened up by the railroad in the first place. Nor was it lost on Greil Marcus, whose book *Mystery Train* was subtitled 'Images of America in Rock'n'Roll Music', or on John Fogerty, who wrote a song called 'Big Train (From Memphis)' in which the locomotive in question was virtually a metaphor for Elvis. (Taking his cue from both of these, Peter Guralnick's long-awaited book on Presley's early years is entitled *Last Train From Memphis*.)

The sheer enormity of America also informed Levon's rendition of Chuck Berry's 'Promised Land', whose protagonist travelled all the way from Virginia to California via some of the drummer's favourite Southern pit-stops: Atlanta, Birmingham, New Orleans. Although it was cajun legend Johnnie Allan who would cut the definitive version the following year – the same year Elvis Presley had a Top 20 hit with it – The Band had a good stab at the song, with Richard drumming, Levon playing his best Chuck Berry rhythm riffs, and Robbie simulating a train-whistle by feeding his guitar through a voicebox. In the same good-time rock'n'roll vein, 'I'm Ready' and 'Ain't Got No Home' were better still, Levon hollering alongside Garth's greasy sax licks and tinkling piano runs. Robbie called them 'total jukebox music'.

The *Third Man* theme might have seemed a little anachronistic in the context of the other tracks, but tucked away at the end of the first side it had a dreamy charm and warmth that was pure Garth Hudson. 'I just loved it, because it made pictures in my head,' said Robbie. 'When I listen to it, I can imagine Marlene Dietrich. And I always loved the film. We didn't do it totally seriously, as you can tell. It's only half-serious. I love the way it closes that side.' Almost as dreamy in its way was 'A Change Is Gonna Come', the last track on Side Two. Sung by Rick in his softest, sweetest voice, it was again made by Garth, whose keyboards expressed every ounce of the hurt and yearning Sam Cooke had packed into the song.

When *Moondog Matinee* was released in October, it came with a poster of a wonderful painting by Canadian artist Edward Kasper. The painting was Robbie's idea, depicting the five members of

Above: Onstage with Dylan during the mega-grossing 'Tour '74'. After it was all over, Dylan claimed there had been 'nothing but force' behind the songs played on the tour.
(Neal Preston/LFI)

Below: A smiling Dylan with hatstand, just one of the many 'props' used on 'Tour '74'.
(Jim Douthitt)

Above: The Band on Zuma Beach, at the time of *Northern Lights – Southern Cross* (1975).
Libby Titus described their new California lifestyle as 'a floating gold iceberg'.
(Capitol Records)

Below: The old Shangri-La studio, Zuma.

Above: In sunshine paradise, the Santa Barbara County Bowl, July 1976 – the first date of the tour that climaxed with The Last Waltz. *(LFI)*

Below: Garth Hudson at the controls, Santa Barbara County Bowl. *(Robert Ellis/Repfoto)*

Above: Dylan and Robbie at The Last Waltz. Dylan took The Band back to 1965 with savage versions of 'Baby, Let Me Follow You Down' and 'I Don't Believe You'. *(LFI)*

Below: The all-star finale to The Last Waltz: Dylan takes the lead on 'I Shall Be Released' with (left to right) Neil Diamond, Joni Mitchell, Neil Young, Rick, Van Morrison and Robbie. *(British Film Institute)*

Above: Robbie and Martin Scorsese during the wild spree that was the promotional tour for *The Last Waltz* (1978). *(Ritchie Aaron/ Redferns)*

Below: Levon as Loretta Lynn's father in the acclaimed *Coal Miner's Daughter* (1980), with Sissy Spacek. *(British Film Institute)*

Above: Bob Dylan drops in backstage at a Lone Star show by Rick and Levon, February 1983. *(Lynn Goldsmih/Rex)*

Below: Levon, Garth and Rick on The Band's 'reunion' tour, 1983. *(LFI)*

Above: Richard onstage in October 1985, six months before he hanged himself in a Florida motel room. *(Courtesy Chris and Gail Bell)*

Below: Robbie soundchecking at the Guitar Legends festival in Seville, October 1991. *(Fin Costello/ Redferns)*

Above: 'My whole barn went up in smoke. . .': the remains of Levon's RCO Studio, Woodstock, 1991.

Below: Shangri-La, 1991.

The Band hanging out at a streetcorner eaterie called the Cabbagetown Café. Here was the group's whole world captured in a moment, with a glorious sunset in the sky behind them. After lengthy discussions with Robbie, Kasper had taken hundreds of photos of Toronto bars, later incorporating several key iconographic details into his painting: a juke-box, a dingy-looking poolhall, a pawnshop filled with musical instruments. Parked around the corner was a pink-and-black trailer with the tell-tale hawk insignia, while the maroon automobile outside the pawn shop was modelled on a '56 Thunderbird once owned by Richard Manuel. On the walls of the café, outside which Levon and Garth lounged and Rick scanned a copy of 'C&W Hits', were scratched the names 'Big Albert' and 'Sonny Boy'. Above them – and above the sign that promised a potent juke-joint mixture of 'Rock and Roll, R&B, and C&W' – the alluring silhouette of a woman could be made out in a bedroom. A bottle and two glasses stood on the window ledge.

Robbie was as pleased with the album as he was with the painting, which only made his disappointment at its comparative failure the greater. 'It's the only album I've ever heard of old rock'n'roll songs where I thought the interpretations came anywhere near complementing the originals,' he told Harvey Kubernik in 1976. 'Unfortunately, people compared it to everything else we'd done, which I thought was ridiculous.' Not everyone was dismissive, even if the album did only reach #28. 'The lack of new material might seem predictable after the anxiety and unanswered questions of *Cahoots*,' wrote Mick Gold, 'but I don't feel their performances can be dismissed as a cop-out or a lack of nerve. Just as their early work contradicted widely held views about rock being the music of radical dissent and continual innovation, so their last two albums have subverted the idea that rock depends on the constant production of "significant" responses to the present. What The Band expressed in *Rock Of*

281

Ages and *Moondog* was a faith in rock'n'roll as a living tradition which could be invoked as well as added to.' Gold was one of only a handful of writers who appreciated the degree of *re-invention* that had gone into *Moondog Matinee*. As much as they had done on *The Band*, they were making the past new.

Although the group had decided they would not tour behind *Moondog Matinee*, they found it hard to turn down an offer to play a huge summer festival in north-west New York state with the Grateful Dead and the Allman Brothers Band. 'We didn't really want to play Watkins Glen,' recalls Robbie. 'We were in a mood, and we felt the only reason to do things like that was the money. But we were talked into it – you know. "Oh come on, it's only just up the road".' Little did they know that their return to the stage after eighteen months would be in front of the largest crowd ever assembled for a rock festival. When Bill Graham circled the area around the southern tip of Seneca Lake on 26 July, two days before the festival, he began to suspect that his original figure of 150,000 might have been a serious case of underestimation. 'There seemed to be droves of people coming up on the road, a whole migration,' he said. 'So I suggested to the sheriff that we open up a day before the show, in order to let people trickle in more slowly. That afternoon we must have had 100,000 on the premises already.' By Saturday, the number had increased by half a million. 'The people were on close to eighty or ninety acres,' recalled Levon. 'It looked like little towns out there.'

The thousands who had arrived early at the Watkins.Glen race-track were treated to mini-sets by the three bands. 'Because they all had to do soundchecks and rehearse, the people who'd arrived the day before virtually got an entire extra show as a bonus,' Bill Graham recalled. 'The Allmans started it rolling by saying, "Well, can we play a little?" and the others followed suit.' The next day, the Dead opened the festival proper with a long afternoon set along the lines of their brilliant triple album *Europe '72*. At 6 p.m., Bill Graham came to the front of the stage to announce The Band. 'It's like waiting for fine wine,' he said. 'And it's been worth the wait.'

Opening with a cracking version of Chuck Berry's 'Back To Memphis', all raging guitar, punchy drum rolls, and Levon's Southern feistiness, they followed up with 'Loving You Is Sweeter Than Ever', 'The Shape I'm In', 'The Weight', 'Stage Fright', 'I Shall Be Released', 'Don't Do It', and a new song – 'Endless Highway' – that expressed all of Robbie's personal frustration with the rigours of touring. 'Well, I sing by night and wander by day', Rick cried, 'I'm on the road and it looks like I'm here to stay.' Just as they were finishing the number, the heavy humidity that had built up through the afternoon broke and the heavens opened, forcing the band to flee the stage. 'Rick and Robbie took their hands off their instruments and ran to the side of the stage,' said Levon. 'About this time, a friend of mine shows up and pulls out a bottle of Glenfiddich. So we have a couple of social pulls on it, and Garth has a couple of pulls. All of a sudden, Garth wants to play, and he goes back out and it's great. He starts playing just beautiful stuff.' As Garth worked his way through an extended and increasingly demented 'Genetic Method', the rain at last thinned out, as though responding to the miraculous improvisation. The others quickly piled on and piled into a thunderous 'Chest Fever', following it up with 'The Night They Drove Old Dixie Down', 'Across The Great Divide', a pounding instrumental jam, and a truly sanctified version of 'Saved'. The rest of the set comprised 'Up On Cripple Creek', 'This Wheel's On Fire', 'The W. S. Walcott Medicine Show', and – after a long break sorting out some technical difficulties – a thrilling 'Slippin' And Slidin''. 'You're the most fantastic thing we've ever seen!' shouted Robbie as he left the stage. 'Rag Mama Rag' served as the encore.

Despite the fact that they'd been playing in front of half a million stoned Deadheads and would-be Confederates, The Band had had a ball. 'There was an alertness to the audience I could not believe,' Robbie told a reporter. Later he would claim that the festival, which was followed immediately by two dates at the Roosevelt Stadium in New Jersey, had a significant effect on the group's decision to tour with Dylan in the New Year. Certainly, Bob was curious to know about Watkins Glen, and grilled Robbie on every aspect of the festival as he weighed up the prospect of going back on the road for the first time in eight years.

Dylan had by this time moved to the West Coast, where he was leasing a large property on Pacific Coast Highway in Malibu. When he suggested that Robbie come out to L.A. to discuss the possibility of a Dylan/Band tour, he planted a seed in the guitarist's mind. 'I'd always fantasized about living on the ocean,' says Robbie. 'I'd visited friends by the water and it had always moved me. So I thought I'd try it for a while.' In the autumn, all five members of The Band relocated to California with their families: just as Dylan had lured them up to Woodstock, so they joined him in the laid-back paradise of freeway rock'n'roll, with Robbie moving into Carole King's old Malibu house and the others into properties around nearby Zuma Beach. That fall, Robbie played on sessions for Joni Mitchell ('Raised On Robbery') and for Carly Simon and James Taylor (the Top 10 hit 'Mockingbird').

The main bait for the group was the talk of touring with Dylan. This was no ordinary tour that Bob and Robbie – with the aid of Bill Graham and Asylum's David Geffen – were cooking up. It would be rock'n'roll's first mega-tour, after which the scale of live entertainment would never be the same again. 'All of a sudden, it started to become clear,' Robbie told Ben Fong-Torres of *Rolling Stone*. 'There was a space, an opening, a necessity almost, that just pulled you into it. It was no clever manoeuvre on anybody's behalf to put the thing together, to expand our audience or get a few extra albums. Everybody just felt the same way at the same time.' Dylan himself claimed that he'd been freed up after 'the big, heavy obstacle' of Saturn had gone from his astrological chart – hence the title *Planet Waves* – and surprised Bill Graham by agreeing to most of the proposals for the tour. 'Initially, the idea was that Bob was gonna do ten or twelve dates,' said Graham. 'We met at his home in Malibu and he didn't wanna do that many shows. But everyone else urged him to do more, because no one had really seen him in so long. Well, I came back to San Francisco and made a list of all the important areas, the markets we knew he'd do well in. We ended up with forty, so I brought a map back down to L.A. with me and put dots where I thought he *should* go. And God bless him, he said yes to every one.'

Leaving Geffen and Graham to iron out the details of the tour, but emphasizing that they wanted things kept as low-key as possible, Dylan and The Band assembled to work on building up a repertoire for the shows. Basing themselves at a Jewish boys' camp in the Malibu mountains, they would report for duty each day and work for three or four hours. 'We sat down and ran through an incredible number of tunes,' recalled Robbie. 'It was just instant. We would request tunes, and then Bob would ask us to play certain tunes of ours.' Over the course of a fortnight, something like eighty songs were worked up to an acceptable standard of live performance, giving the six of them a pretty good idea of what was going to work best in front of large crowds. At the same time, they talked about going into the studio to cut an album for Asylum, with whom Dylan had agreed to sign when his Columbia option came up.

According to Robert Shelton, David Geffen had 'long hankered to manage Dylan, and had been trying to lure Robbie as well'. (It may even have been Geffen who urged Robbie to move to Malibu in the first place.) With Geffen and Graham on the scene, there was no longer much demand for the services of Albert Grossman. Not only were Albert's relations with Dylan still sour, but The Band were now three thousand miles away from Woodstock. 'We still have managerial ties to him,' Robbie told *Melody Maker*'s Loraine Alterman, though he sounded oddly vague about it. 'I don't know about Dylan,' he said. 'They may have something going, but I don't exactly know what it is.' Like Ronnie Hawkins before him, 'Big Albert' felt more than a little abandoned by his favourite sons.

Dylan had already written three songs for the Asylum album ('Forever Young', 'Never Say Goodbye', and 'Nobody 'Cept You') when he flew to New York in October to write the remainder of the tracks that would make up *Planet Waves*. By the time he'd returned to L.A. in early November, 'Tour '74' had been announced. 'I took out a full-page in the *New York Times* and put the whole country on sale in one day,' recalled Bill Graham. The response was stupendous, bigger than that for any event in entertainment history: no less than five million postal applications were received for a total of 650,000 seats. When the sums were done, Dylan and The Band netted $2 million between them, with Bill Graham's FM Productions taking a cut of half a million dollars. 'Flood' was an understatement. 'No way do we feel we deserve the money,' Robbie confessed guiltily. 'The whole thing is so out of proportion that it doesn't make any sense at all.'

The contrast between the scale of the tour and the low-key nature of the sessions which produced *Planet Waves* couldn't have been more pronounced. For The Band, now a good deal more studio-acclimatized than they'd been when they last recorded with Bob, recording *Planet Waves* was 'like cutting a blues album'. 'It wasn't the best circumstance to be making an album under,' remembered Robbie. 'We were rehearsing songs for the tour, and preparing and figuring out how we were going to do the tour, so it was like we were making an album in our spare time. Some of it we got pretty good, but with all due respect to the songs I don't think we had the opportunity to concentrate as much as we could have. There was nothing but the distraction of preparing for the first tour he'd done in eight years.' So distracted were they, indeed, that none of them seemed to register a rather surprising fact: this was the first time that they'd actually recorded an album together.

Booking into West L.A.'s Village Recorders studio under the name 'Judge Magney', Dylan and The Band began working on the album – initially entitled *Ceremonies Of The Horseman*, then briefly known as *Love Songs* – on Friday 2 November. As Levon hadn't returned from a trip to see his family in Arkansas, Richard manned the drumstool while they warmed up with 'House Of The Rising Sun' and then cut 'Never Say Goodbye' and 'Nobody 'Cept You'. (The latter failed to make *Planet Waves* but merited inclusion on the Dylan *Bootleg Series* box-set released in 1991.) Both tracks sounded like better-recorded variants on some of the old basement songs cut six years earlier, and much of the album seemed to pick up from the loose approach of the Big Pink tapes. With The Band providing what Robert Christgau described as 'rangy, stray-cat music', Dylan was coasting comfortably on a selection of 'Cast-Iron Songs and Torch Ballads', as he labelled them in the album's sub-title. There was nothing too demanding here, but what there was sounded crisply earthy. 'Precision accompaniment,' Bob Spitz called it, 'wrapped in a roughhewn gunnysack of a sound.'

The sessions resumed on Monday 5 November, by which time Levon had returned to the fold. Most of the fifteen or so songs cut on the 5th, 6th and the 9th were new to The Band, and some were first-take recordings. Only 'On A Night Like This' and 'Going, Going, Gone' required overdubs, though both sounded better for them. 'On A Night' was a cantering, good-humoured affair, replete with some cajun-style accordion from Garth, and made a natural choice for the album's first single. 'Going, Going,

Gone', in contrast, was superbly spare, a bleak ballad featuring some of Robbie's finest playing since *Rock Of Ages*. Combining bubbling single-note trills with clusters of harmonics and sudden tremolo-arm bending, the performance provided a toe-curling counterpoint to Dylan's unsentimental vocal.

Of the album's other songs, 'Forever Young' appeared on *Planet Waves* in two radically different forms. The first, truer to the track's origins as a song written for one of Bob's children back in 1972, was Dylan at his tenderest, with Richard on drums and Levon on mandolin; the second, taken much faster, was pure country rock. (At least two other versions were recorded, one with Garth on accordion.) 'Tough Mama' picked up from 'On A Night Like This', but was a lot funkier, with The Band at their very tightest. As 'love songs' go, 'Hazel' and 'Something There Is About You' were fairly innocuous, and 'You Angel You' wasn't much better. More striking was a song Dylan decided to record on his own on the afternoon of Saturday 10 November. 'Around noon, Bob said, "I've got a song I want to record later,"' recalled engineer Rob Fraboni. 'We were doing what we were doing, and all of a sudden he came up and said, "Let's record". So he went out in the studio, and that was "Wedding Song".' The performance of this hauntingly ambiguous song, addressed to the wife from whom he was shortly to separate, was so intense that Fraboni could not bring himself to stop the tape when he heard the buttons on Bob's jacket banging against his guitar.

Another afterthought, a retake of 'Dirge' cut while *Planet Waves* was being mixed the following week, was darker still. 'We'd mixed about two or three songs,' said Fraboni. 'All of a sudden, Bob came in and said, "I'd like to try 'Dirge' on the piano". We'd recorded a version with only acoustic guitar and vocal the week before, but we put up a tape and he said to Robbie, "Maybe you could play guitar on this". They did it once, Bob playing piano and singing, and Robbie playing acoustic guitar. The second time was the take.' The song, the longest on the album at five-and-a-half minutes, was the flipside to 'Wedding Song', a harrowing renunciation of Dylan's life before his marriage. Bob produced one of the greatest vocal performances of his career, and Robbie played exquisitely in the spaces between the very basic piano chords. It gave the album what it needed, a troubling centrepiece around which the more lighthearted songs could revolve. '*Planet Waves* marked Dylan's return as a committed artist,' wrote Paul Williams many years later. 'It was the first time since *John Wesley Harding* that he'd truly allowed an LP-in-progress to be an open canvas for whatever he was seeing.'

Even so, there remained the general feeling of disappointment that Dylan appeared to be taking no risks. 'It wasn't an appropriate Bob Dylan album,' said Robbie, 'and it wasn't superunusual. All those songs were as simple as he's ever done, and people thought it wasn't a real effort.'

Apart from the juggling of recordings and rehearsals with Dylan, The Band had other things to contend with that November. For one, *Moondog Matinee* had just been released, obliging Robbie to give some interviews. Defending the decision to do an 'oldies' album, Robbie none the less enthused about the *Works* project, with which he claimed they were still intermittently busy. 'We are still writing it and still working on it, which is really fun for us,' he told Loraine Alterman. 'It's a total challenge, unlike anything we've ever done or anyone's ever done. It's a work, not a bunch of tunes. The whole album is a piece of music with lyrics, but it's not divided up in three-minute segments of tunes. It's a great exercise for us, and we have it about 90 per cent done.' There was also talk of a live album from the Watkins Glen festival, featuring all three of the bands. 'So far, the tapes sound really good,' Robbie said. 'A lot of that spirit I was hoping for is there.' Stressed and exhausted as he was, Robbie sounded both excited and fulfilled. 'This is probably the greatest time of our lives,' he told Alterman.

'We are all feeling so good and we're thrilled with our new album. We're thrilled about the other stuff we're doing, too.' With that, he hurried off for another rehearsal with Dylan.

The last major rehearsals took place on 26 and 27 December at the L.A. Forum, where the tour would finish on 14 February. After celebrating the New Year in Malibu, Dylan, The Band, and their entourage boarded the Starship One at LAX and headed for a freezing Chicago. The plane was a 40-seat Boeing 720 furnished rock-star-style for the likes of the Stones, Elton John, and Led Zeppelin. Equipped with full living quarters and vegetarian and kosher food, it took off from Los Angeles at 3 p.m. on 2 January. During the flight, the sense of apprehension was palpable: as David Geffen told a reporter in Chicago, 'this particular event has drawn more response from the people than any event in media – bigger than Woodstock, Watkins Glen, any of those'. Geffen had heard that some Japanese Dylan fans were chartering a jet simply to fly over for the show. Even the Kennedys wanted tickets.

On the evening of Thursday 3 January, in front of 18,500 people at the Chicago Stadium, Dylan and The Band took the stage for the first date of Tour '74. Wearing a black suede jacket, with a grey scarf tied round his neck to protect against the cold, Dylan launched into a 1963 song called 'Hero Blues', a sardonic pre-empting of the anti-climax that his 'second coming' was bound to be. Of course, Dylan could have shouted that it wasn't him we were looking for until he was blue in the face and he would still have been worshipped as rock's very own messiah. For so many of the people crammed into the huge hockey arena that night, Dylan's very silence had made him a more potent prophet than ever. Even more important, he represented the shattered dreams of the '60s for a generation that had few ideals left to hold on to.

After singing 'Lay Lady Lay' and 'Tough Mama', Dylan remained onstage as The Band broke into 'The Night They Drove Old Dixie Down'. Unsure of how they were going to be received on the tour, they played only one more song – 'Stage Fright' – before Dylan took over for 'It Ain't Me Babe', 'Leopard Skin Pillbox Hat', 'All Along The Watchtower', 'Ballad Of A Thin Man', and 'I Don't Believe You'. No long-term Dylan fan who was paying attention could have failed to notice the number of songs that dated back to the scandalous electric tour of 1965. For The Band it was a curious experience being cheered for the very music that had brought them nothing but jeers nine years earlier. If anything, the treatment of a song like 'I Don't Believe You' was even more savage than it had been on that first tour, with Dylan, in Dave Marsh's words, 'spitting out the lyrics like they tasted funny'.

Unsurprisingly, the biggest cheers came when The Band left the stage and Dylan donned his acoustic guitar and mouth-harp to sing 'The Times They Are A-Changin'', 'Song To Woody', 'The Lonesome Death Of Hattie Carroll', 'Nobody 'Cept You', and 'It's Alright Ma (I'm Only Bleeding)'. With the Watergate hearings then dominating public life in America, Dylan's line about the President having to 'stand naked' in 'It's Alright Ma' instantly transformed him back into the protest-singer hero he'd refused to be for so long. 'Who came to see The Band?', muttered one Windy Citizen as the group waited for the subsequent ovation to die down. The answer was, anyone who loved the four songs they then proceeded to play on their own: 'Life Is A Carnival', 'The Shape I'm In', an unexpected and delightful 'When You Awake', and the ever-popular 'Rag Mama Rag'. After Dylan had rejoined them for 'Forever Young' and 'Something There Is About You', the set closed with the inevitable rallying-call of 'Like A Rolling Stone'. The Band came back to encore with 'The Weight', and Dylan returned once more for a final encore of 'Most Likely You Go Your Way And I'll Go Mine'.

The consensus as the six men walked off the stage that night was that the set hadn't really worked. Above all, Dylan himself had seemed unduly bashful about his solo spot. 'Dylan was such a team player with The Band that there was some reluctance about coming out and starting the second half on his own,' remembered Bill Graham. 'We had to remind him nicely who he was to people and from then on, when he came out each night for his five or six acoustic songs, it seemed like every person in every single town locked into a time-frame with him. I've seen it happen with Sinatra, but not many other people.' At a post-mortem on the show that lasted till 4 a. m. the next morning, everyone agreed that the pacing of the set was all wrong, and that its momentum had quickly been lost.

The second night in Chicago was different enough to lay most of the fears to rest. The set still opened with 'Hero Blues', but this time it featured 'Tom Thumb's Blues', 'Knockin' On Heaven's Door', and 'Love Minus Zero', together with 'Maggie's Farm' as an encore. Everyone looked more at home on the stage, which was in any case designed to resemble a Martin Mull-style sitting room, complete with sofa, rocking chair, bunk bed, and Tiffany table-lamp. 'We wanted them to be comfortable,' said Bill Graham. 'No matter where he is, Bob makes you feel you're in a coffeehouse or a living room, so that people are visiting even though they're in Madison Square Garden.' With obvious joy in their faces, The Band thundered behind Dylan, turning songs such as 'All Along The Watchtower' and 'Most Likely You Go Your Way' into thrilling exercises in hard rock'n'roll. As Ralph Gleason was to write when the tour reached Oakland a month later, 'The Band has never played better in person or on record . . . within the total sound of the band, a pulsing, cracking, shaking sound, there was an infinity of variety and internal musical activity'. At the heart of that sound, as ever, were Levon, pushing everyone irresistibly forwards, and Garth, rocking back and forth behind the fortress of his keyboards. Around them, Robbie chopped out angry chords or picked out sputtering solos, and Rick hunkered down in the deep ground-swell of his fretless bass grooves. 'With Dylan,' wrote Greil Marcus, 'they were once again the best rock'n'roll band in the world.'

The sheer power of the sound Dylan and The Band produced over the next five weeks had its detractors, not least Dylan himself, who after it was all over felt there had been 'nothing but force' behind the songs played on the tour. 'The only thing people talked about was energy this, energy that,' he said. 'The bigger and louder something was, the more energy it was supposed to have.' But if the full-throttle approach had its limitations, it was also a vindication of what they had dared to do in 1965. 'The most significant thing about the '74 tour to me was proving that we hadn't been crazy, that this music was valid,' said Robbie. 'It was not incredibly different from what we'd done with Bob before. It was just this kind of dynamics – it got loud, and it got soft. We'd come way down when the singing came in, and when the solos started we'd go screaming off into the skies. It was a thing we'd developed when we first started playing together again, and it became like a reflex action.'

For Rick, the tour was 'like Frank and Jesse James getting back together again and hitting a few banks': 'It was like a family reunion. We had, in a sense, grown up together in that pink house in Woodstock, so we were a lot more familiar with each other than we'd been in 1965. I didn't have to watch his fingers so much this time!' Even Levon, whose previous experiences with Dylan had made him distinctly sceptical about this kind of rock'n'roll hype, was enjoying the tour. 'I thought it was a pretty good show,' he said. 'We were trying to play a genuine show. Nobody had any edge to sharpen or axe to grind.' What made it easier for The Band to enjoy themselves, of course, was that they were no longer mere sidemen but established artists in their own right. Bill Graham was especially pleased that they consistently went down well with the tour audiences. 'I wouldn't say they were *popular*,' he said. 'A diamond is a gorgeous thing to look at and have around, but you wouldn't call it popular. I liked people who liked The Band, so I was pleased with their reception. It meant there were people in America who liked good music.'

Dylan had known 'from the word go' just how tough this tour would be, and had asked Bill to turn down almost all requests for interviews. 'It was a very private tour, and there was a lot of work involved,' said Graham. 'Neither he nor The Band wanted to pal around much.' Even if he wasn't staying awake for three consecutive nights as he'd done back in 1966, the tour itinerary was still a punishing one. 'The last tour we did was like a hurricane,' he said. 'This one is more like a hard rain.' What made the shows particularly gruelling was the fact that the songs spanned so many years, making each performance a kind of retrospective 'self-portrait'. The sense of expectation at each show was such that Robbie missed the open, relaxed spirit of Watkins Glen. 'I think the audiences are a little confused, a little nervous,' he said. 'They're waiting so much for something in there that it really detracts from that other thing at Watkins Glen.'

Doubtless it was this pressure on Dylan that later caused him to dismiss the hype and hysteria of Tour '74. 'I think I was just playing a role on that tour,' he said. 'I was playing Bob Dylan and The Band was playing The Band. It was all sort of mindless. The people that came out to see us came mostly to see what they'd missed the first time around, and what they saw you could have compared to early Elvis and later Elvis. Because it wasn't the same, when we needed that acceptance it wasn't there. By this time it didn't matter. Time had proven them all wrong. We were cleaning up but it was an emotionless trip. Rock'n'roll had become a highly extravagant enterprise: T-shirts, concert booklets, lighting shows . . . it was just a big show, a big circus, except there weren't any elephants.' For Dylan, the tours of 1965 and 1966 had been much more demanding and shocking. Then they had really gone 'out on the edge'.

It was at Philadelphia's Spectrum arena on 6 January that Bill Graham decided to show Dylan just what he meant to his fans. On 'Like A Rolling Stone', he asked lighting director Bruce Byall to inch the house lights up a notch with each successive chorus. By the song's blazing climax, the lights were full on and Dylan could see just what 20,000 of his fans looked like *en masse*. 'He came off the stage mesmerized,' said Graham. Poet Michael McClure, who was tagging along with the tour, said the Spectrum shows made the San Francisco Masonic Auditorium show in 1965 'seem like a jam session in a small nightclub'. Stephen Pickering, author of the bizarre *Bob Dylan Approximately: A Portrait of the Jewish Poet in Search of God*, called the shows 'a fusion of Dylan's Jewish passion and The Band's bacchanalian intensity', a description which actually made some sense. Certainly there was always something about Dylan that set him apart from The Band – and from most other musicians – though whether it was his Jewishness is open to question, despite rumours that much of the money he was earning from the tour would be going to help Israel's war effort in the Middle East. By Philadelphia, most importantly, the structure of the set was established. The show would begin with Dylan and The Band together for an hour, followed by a brief interval. Dylan would then come on for his solo acoustic spot, followed by five or six Band numbers, after which the six men would reunite for the show's finale. As a sequence it seemed to work well.

The third stop on the tour, significantly for The Band, was Toronto. Nine years earlier a local critic had dubbed them 'a third-rate Yonge Street rock'n'roll band', but this time the city showed its pride in their achievement. Refraining from calls for Dylan during their set, the Maple Leaf Gardens audience responded to songs like 'I Shall Be Released' and 'Up On Cripple Creek' with effusive cheers. As Dylan made his first exit after singing 'Ballad

Of A Thin Man', The Band broke into 'Stage Fright', for many people a veiled comment on Bob's long seclusion.

After the second Toronto show on 10 January, Dylan and the band wrapped up tight against the Canadian winter and headed off to the Nickelodeon, Ronnie Hawkins' new lair on Yonge Street. 'They've come all the way from L.A. to hear me play "40 Days"!' bawled the Hawk as Bob's entourage entered the club. Ronnie, who was celebrating his 39th birthday that night, had recovered from the failure of 'Down In The Alley' and resigned himself to ruling the little pond he'd dominated for so long. Neither a second Atlantic album nor *Rock'n'Roll Resurrection*, recorded for Fred Foster's Monument label with a bunch of crack Nashville session-men, had given him the hit he so badly needed, but reworking old chestnuts like 'Odessa', 'Honey Love', and 'High Blood Pressure' seemed to keep him happy for the time being. 'Now hold on, Bob,' he said as he launched into a version of 'One Too Many Mornings'. 'Ah know you're just itching to get up here and sing, but you can't. This is *mah* show!'

When the Hawk had finished for the night, he accompanied his old protégés back to the Inn on the Park. As they drove through Cabbagetown, all but buried under the snow, Robbie gazed out of the window at the streets on which he'd played as a child. It was hard not to take stock of the distance he'd come in fifteen years. At the hotel, The Band's suite was filled with old friends and relatives who'd come to see the show. Dylan retired to a corner to play chess with his friend Louie Kemp, and Garth sang along to a tape of *Planet Waves*. Ronnie wanted to know why Dylan had been so solicitous towards him. 'You were one of his earliest idols,' Levon told him. But it was more than that: Dylan was impressed by anyone who wasn't overawed by him, and the Hawk seemed to treat him as he would treat any other human being. 'Ol' Bob liked me coz I never kissed his ass,' says Ronnie. 'Ah told him I never did understand what he was singin' about!' Dylan called the Hawk 'the guru of rock'n'roll' and ended up casting him as 'Bob Dylan' in the Rolling Thunder film *Renaldo and Clara*.

The following week took Dylan and The Band down the East Coast, all the way from Boston to Miami via Washington D.C. and Charlotte, North Carolina. By Thursday 17 January, the day *Planet Waves* was released, the shows were revolving around a solid core of songs clearly favoured by Dylan: 'Most Likely', 'Lay Lady Lay', 'Ballad Of A Thin Man', 'All Along The Watchtower', 'It's Alright, Ma', 'Like A Rolling Stone', 'Forever Young', and 'Something There Is About You'. Almost as prevalent in the sets were 'Tom Thumb's Blues', 'It Ain't Me, Babe', 'Knockin' On Heaven's Door', and 'Nobody 'Cept You'. The Band, meanwhile, were choosing their numbers from a pool that included 'Dixie', 'Cripple Creek', 'Endless Highway', 'I Shall Be Released', 'King Harvest', 'Life Is A Carnival', 'The Shape I'm In', 'Stage Fright', 'The Weight', 'This Wheel's On Fire', 'Rag Mama Rag', and 'When You Awake'. In addition, they were occasionally playing 'Holy Cow', 'Long Black Veil', 'Loving You Is Sweeter Than Ever', and 'Share Your Love With Me'. Surprising omissions were 'Chest Fever', 'Across The Great Divide', 'Don't Do It', and 'The W. S. Walcott Medicine Show'. With Bob averaging eighteen songs a night, The Band were generally adding another nine or ten to the set.

After the 19 January show at Miami's curiously-named Hollywood Sportatorium, where Dylan wore an Isle of Wight-style white suit, the circus moved back up to Atlanta for two performances at the OMNI Coliseum. Following the first show on 21 January, when 'The Night They Drove Old Dixie Down' must have had a special Southern resonance, Dylan and the band travelled all the way down to Plains to see Governor Jimmy Carter. Sprawling in the back of a limousine with a three-motorcycle escort to speed up their journey, they passed around joints and howled with laughter at the absurdity of it all. The

Carter party was the brainwave of the governor's son Chip, who'd made a pilgrimage to Woodstock in December, 1968 just to shake Dylan's hand. In attendance was Allman Brothers manager Phil Walden, a keen Carter supporter and one of the influential Southerners who would help to put him in the White House over two years later. Levon, needless to say, was in his element.

The Southern leg took the band through their old haunts of Memphis and Fort Worth before the tour headed north-east once more for two shows at Long Island's Nassau Coliseum. By the evening of 29 January, they were checking into New York's Plaza Hotel in preparation for three shows at Madison Square Gardens. Now all the beautiful people came out to play: in attendance at the opening night – and inevitably at the Plaza party afterwards – were Carly and James, Jack and Angelica, Dick Cavett and Shirley MacLaine, along with Yoko, Bette, Paul Simon, Clive Davis, Lou Adler and a host of others. In amongst the movers and shakers were some of Dylan's old folk crowd, including the Traum brothers and Mike Porco of Gerde's Folk City. 'I found the show powerful in a certain way,' said Happy Traum after he'd paid his respects at the Plaza party and split back to Woodstock. 'Maybe it was anger that I felt, which is very powerful, but maybe it was a lack of gentleness.'

Among the reviewers at the Garden, the *New York Times'* Nat Hentoff found The Band 'far more stimulating than Dylan'. As he wrote colourfully: 'The rural churchlike harmonies thrusting out into space like spears; the hard but loose percussion; the joyously unabashed honky-tonk piano; the careening, interstitching instrumental skills of all these raffish minstrels; and above all The Band's beat, are true phenomena. They stretch time, curve it around corners, lash it and caress it, all the while keeping up a whirlpool-like pulsation that almost had me up and dancing, and I don't dance no steps of any era.' In contrast, the *Village Voice's* Lucian Truscott IV complained that The Band 'took no chances with the crowd', arguing that where Dylan's singing was 'unpredictable, solitary, weird', Richard Manuel's was merely 'precise and coarse'.

If the limousines, private jets, and five-star hotel suites hadn't completely gone to The Band's heads, the Plaza Hotel party certainly did. 'That's when the wretched excess began,' said Larry Samuels, who'd taken over Jonathan Taplin's role as the group's administrative manager in L.A. 'Just because there was too much money floating around. It was jets, limos everywhere, and of course the white powder.' Cocaine was hardly new to rock'n'roll, but only now was it assuming its role as the rock community's preferred chemical. As Tour '74 rolled on, there was more and more of it around. Predictably it was Richard who developed the largest appetite for the drug, but the others didn't lag too far behind him. Where amphetamine had kept them going in the mid-'60s, it was the 'champagne of drugs' which sustained them this time around. 'Tour '74 was *very* lavish,' says Libby Titus, who like all the other wives and girlfriends was left at home. 'It was lots of dope and lots of girls. Occasionally the wives and kids were brought in for shows, but it was all so sad and pathetic.' Stories about roadies snapping Polaroids of groupies to facilitate the band's choice of female companions began to leak out, but none of them were much surprise to Libby or Jane or Elizabeth.

Doubtless it was while he was flying high on coke that Rick managed to break his right hand at the Plaza; it could only have been coke that kept him from feeling any pain until the tour had ended. 'I didn't even know it was broken,' he admitted, 'so I finished out the tour with a "bad sprain"! A few months later I was going for acupuncture and I found out that it was broken.' Pain or no pain, Rick was onstage at the University of Michigan in Ann Arbor on Saturday 2 February. The tour's Midwest stretch also took in Bloomington, Indiana and St Louis, Missouri before veering west for two shows at the Denver Coliseum on 6 February. Bloomington was marred by a ticket controversy after a tout managed to obtain 500 tickets which had been held back for VIPs, but the shows at St Louis' Missouri Arena were distinguished by the presence of Leon Russell.

The second Denver show was particularly memorable. 'The audience was very attentive,' Bill Graham told Ben Fong-Torres. 'It was like the last audience at Fillmore East, people who really came to listen to the music. It didn't feel like 12,000 people, it was like a hootenanny. When The Band finished the first half with "Cripple Creek", there was just this tumultuous ovation. Very seldom was the reaction out of kilter in relation to the quality of the music that night, which says something about the audience Dylan and The Band drew. They drew, I think, a very knowledgable audience. And I think a lot of people who came to revere didn't revere; they listened.' A man who liked to roam around the auditorium gauging a crowd's response, Bill also recalled exceptional shows in Montreal, Boston, and Houston.

In anticipation of live recordings in Seattle, Dylan and The Band fine-tuned their large repertoire at Denver's Playboy Club on Thursday 7 February. Both shows at the Seattle Coliseum on the 9th were duly recorded, as were the two at Oakland's Alameda County Coliseum on the 11th. The latter were played in front of a large contingent of San Francisco musicians – members of The Dead, Santana, and Jefferson Airplane – together with *Rolling Stone* writers like Ralph J. Gleason, who thought The Band were 'hard-driving, rocking, swinging accompanists for Dylan and majestic performers on their own'. Robbie particularly impressed the Bay Area veteran with fills and obligatos that 'compared in emotional intensity and artistic simplicity to Louis Armstrong behind Bessie Smith'. For Greil Marcus, already at work on *Mystery Train*, it was as though The Band had finally found their missing frontman. 'With Dylan there to take the heat,' he wrote, 'that side of The Band that was scared of the crowd, that sought shelter in craftsmanship and careful arrangements, disappeared, replaced by the chaos and intensity of those old Howlin' Wolf records.' By the same token, of course, the group's own set was bound by the old limitations: try as one might to overlook the fact in the face of their evident high spirits, only 'Endless Highway' was less than four years old.

The last three shows of Tour '74 brought Dylan and the The Band back full-circle. At Inglewood's L.A. Forum, in front of an even more glittering array of stars, the circus reached its mega-hyped climax. In New York, Lucian Truscott IV had bemoaned the fact that Dylan's appeal was now to 'the white middle class, people lighting up $40-an-ounce grass, snorting coke, flashing gold rings and fancy boots,' but only Hollywood knew how to do rock'n'roll affluence properly. At the final show on Valentine's Day night, the audience included Carole King, Ringo Starr, Neil Young, David Crosby, Jack Nicholson, Warren Beatty, and Joan Baez.

The two 14 February shows produced the bulk of the tracks on the double album *Before The Flood*:[1] the furious opener 'Most Likely You Go Your Way', a bluesy, mid-tempo 'Ballad Of A Thin Man', and a version of 'All Along The Watchtower' which – at least in the pure excitement stakes – trounced even Jimi Hendrix's moody reading of the song. Only 'Lay Lady Lay', 'Rainy Day Women', 'The Weight', 'Rolling Stone', and 'Knockin' On Heaven's Door' were from earlier shows, though the closing 'Blowin' In The Wind' spliced together versions from the evening of the 13th and the afternoon of the 14th. Opinions of *Before The Flood* varied considerably. Elvis Costello thought it 'horrendous, full of overblown arrangements', bearing out Dylan's own feelings about Tour '74, but Greil Marcus and others relished its 'particularly American spirit'. 'It was an old-fashioned, back-country, big-city attack on all things genteel,' Marcus wrote. 'An up-to-date version of Whitman's YAWP.' Listening to 'Up On Cripple Creek' or 'Highway 61 Revisited', it was hard to disagree. Even 'Like A Rolling Stone' was more like a boozy singalong than the vicious castigation it had been back in 1966. The most disappointing thing about *Before The Flood* was that half the Band songs on the album had already appeared in live form, and would indeed appear yet again on *The Last Waltz*. Nor were the performances particularly special: both Richard on 'The Shape I'm In' and Rick on 'When You Awake' sounded the worse for the wear and tear their voices had suffered through thirty-nine shows. Only a gripping version of 'Stage Fright' stood out as worthy of comparison with the best numbers from *Rock Of Ages*.

By 12.15 a. m. on Tuesday 15 February, Tour '74 was over. At the Forum, Bill Graham hosted a dinner for Dylan, The Band, and the crew members, together with their partners and with entertainment from belly-dancers and accordionists. As the meal began, an enormous Valentine's Day banner dropped behind the main table with the words 'We Love You' emblazoned across a heart. Looking back over the five weeks, Robbie was more than just glad to have got through the tour alive: for him, it had been a huge success. 'With all the time we've spent on the road, there's maybe three times I've actually enjoyed it,' he was later to reflect. 'The '74 tour was one of those times.'

The next morning, there was another party at the Beverly Wilshire hotel, this time for Dylan and The Band and their families. 'Bob has so many kids he could have filled up the room by himself,' said Robbie. 'But we all had some by now, and there were cakes and stuff, and all these little critters, and it was really very nice.' Not everyone took such a rosy view of the proceedings. 'Bill had set aside a room for the offspring of all these lunatics,' says Libby Titus. 'The wives who'd been cheated on, the kids who were destined to be scarred . . .'

The final gathering brought Dylan and The Band together with

Bob's old pals Bobby Neuwirth, Louie Kemp, and David Blue. As it broke up in the late afternoon, the five members of Dylan's old 'scrounge band' thought only of heading back to their new beach houses and beginning a long sleep.

Part Four

TWILIGHT
(1974–92)

1

On the Beach

On the surface it was all so beautiful, and underneath everything
was so rotten.

Libby Titus

Après le déluge, the reality of The Band's uprooting to Southern
California finally hit home. For some of them, it might have been
preferable to have stayed on the road and never faced the turmoil
of their private lives. The sense of displacement, coupled with the
comedown from Tour '74, quickly took its toll on everyone. 'We
were like fish out of water,' says Libby Titus. 'It was a floating
gold iceberg, white beach houses and $3,000-a-month rents, but it
was all completely unreal.'

Libby herself wasn't helping matters with her chronic drug
abuse: when she wasn't stoned, she was fighting with Levon. It
seemed that Tour '74 had strained everybody's relationships. Bob
was leaving Sara, Jane was flipping out over Richard again, and
even Robbie and Dominique were having a hard time. 'Everyone
started splitting up,' says Libby, 'and the ones who stayed together
only did so out of a sort of familial remembrance.' At the root of
it all was the sudden influx of money from the tour, with no one
having the first idea how to invest it.

Richard, of course, had no problem parting with his money, as
Malibu's many coke dealers knew well. On the road there was
something to live for, a reason to keep things together, but once a
tour had ended there was only the pain of living with himself.
What did he care that they were neighbours of Ryan O'Neal's, or

that Steve McQueen and Ali McGraw were having dinner at Robbie's house? *His* idea of fun was getting wrecked and tearing down Pacific Coast Highway in a Mercedes coupé. Jane had kicked Richard out once, but she'd allowed him back when their second child Josh was born. After he'd made 'all the usual promises' and broken them all over again, he explained to Jane that it was 'tough at the top of the pile'. 'Pile of shit', was her terse reply.

Levon, too, knew that this Malibu lifestyle sucked the big one. 'He knew it was all wrong,' says Libby, 'and he wanted to get the fuck away from it.' It was no coincidence that John Lennon had chosen L.A. as the scene of his protracted 'lost weekend' that year. In March, while living in a glorified Malibu bachelor pad with Ringo Starr, Keith Moon, and Klaus Voorman, the ex-Beatle was thrown out of the Troubadour on Santa Monica Boulevard for heckling the Smothers Brothers. (Another British superstar, David Bowie, would also temporarily exile himself in the city, almost destroying himself with cocaine in the process.) By May, Levon and Libby had broken up, with Libby moving on groupie-style to Eric Clapton and Levon planning to return to Woodstock.

Appropriately enough, both Levon and Rick played on Neil Young's *On The Beach* album in the spring, lending their inimitable skills to the angry 'Revolution Blues', with its line about killing the 'famous stars' of Laurel Canyon in their cars. The cover of the album, with Young standing on the beach against an overcast sky and a car buried in the sand, said everything about the *ennui* of the Malibu rock community's life. Young had been in L.A. a lot longer than his fellow Canucks, but felt no less alienated by it. He'd also seen 'the needle and the damage done,' and knew enough to warn The Band away from the insidious evils of the Hollywood drug scene.

There were other sessions to keep the band busy before they began a series of summer dates supporting the reunion tour by Young and his old buddies Crosby, Stills, and Nash. Besides occasional work for the likes of Ringo Starr, there was the mixing of the live album from Tour '74 to be done. Dylan was having second thoughts about giving the record to Asylum, who'd disappointed him by being unable to sell more than 700,000 copies of *Planet Waves*. 'He couldn't reconcile those numbers with the five million requests for tickets,' wrote Clive Davis, who'd been fired from Columbia the year before and now flew to L.A. to advise Bob and Robbie on the marketing of *Before The Flood*. Dylan told Davis that he wanted to sell the album himself through a saturation mail-order campaign on television. This seemed undignified to Davis, who proposed instead that they set up their own distribution system and sell the album directly to rack-jobbers.*

Bob and Robbie liked Davis' idea, but still felt that they somehow 'owed' the album to David Geffen. In the event, Columbia itself came back on the scene, offering Dylan and The Band sixty cents more per album in royalties than Asylum were prepared to pay. Clive Davis quickly saw that Dylan and his wily attorney David Braun were forcing the two companies into a bidding war, and in due course Asylum matched the Columbia offer. 'With a little help from a friend,' wrote Davis in his autobiography, 'Dylan had succeeded in making a lot more money. He had surely come a long way from the days of Folk City hootenannies.' The fact that *Before The Flood*, released in June, did even less well than *Planet Waves*, rising to #3 but spending only ten weeks in the Top 40, confirmed that what the five million ticket applicants had wanted was more the vicarious experience of Dylan's '60s legend than the music itself.

The CSNY reunion tour had itself been prompted by the phenomenal success of Tour '74, with David Geffen and Bill Graham once more raking in a large percentage of the profits.

---

* 'rack-jobbers' are wholesaler middlemen who ensure rack space for records in American department stores.

Although the whiz-kid mogul and the veteran promoter had not quite seen eye to eye during Tour '74, the two had clearly resolved their differences in the name of money. Savvy enough to see that rock was now big business, they were pioneering the kind of comeback tours that cleaned up at the box office in the late '80s. The Band were happy to tag along, filling out their Tour '74 set with less familiar numbers. Beginning on 14 July at Oakland's Alameda Stadium, where they had played with Dylan, the tour progressed through America and Canada for the remainder of the summer. By 2 September they were back in Toronto, playing a tremendous set at the Varsity Stadium. Opening with a lusty rock'n'roll instrumental that served as a perfect platform for Garth's love affair with the tenor saxophone, they flowed straight into the rarely performed 'Just Another Whistle Stop', then worked their way through some old favourites before resurrecting the segue from 'Dixie' into 'Across The Great Divide'. More unexpected were versions of 'Smoke Signal', 'Time To Kill', and 'Mystery Train', the latter scarcely suffering for the lack of a second drummer and sung with all the snarling gusto at Levon's command. Where the voices of Rick Danko and Richard Manuel had begun to deteriorate, the drummer still never missed a note.

Two weeks later, the tour headed for Europe with Joni Mitchell and ex-Youngblood Jesse Colin Young in tow. Rehearsing their set in a studio owned by admirers Brinsley Schwarz, The Band left the English group mesmerized, organist Bob Andrews watching over Garth's shoulder in awe. At Wembley Stadium on Saturday 14 September, playing in front of 70,000 people, they seemed as out of place as they had ever done at a festival. 'They were thrown on in the brilliant sunshine,' recalls Elvis Costello, then a part-time Brinsley Schwarz roadie. 'They were great in their own way, but somehow so inappropriate – not dynamic enough, I guess.'

*

Ever since settling in Malibu, The Band had wanted to build a studio of their own. As Richard said, 'we always got our best effects when we threw together our own places'. Due to begin recording another album for Capitol, the group were keen to avoid using one of the big L.A. studios. When they stumbled on a rambling, run-down old ranch just off Pacific Coast Highway at Zuma Beach, they knew they'd found a West Coast version of Big Pink, another 'clubhouse' where they could take their time and keep a safe distance from the music industry.

The Shangri-La ranch, at 30065 Morning View Drive, had once been a high-class bordello. There were still mirrored walls in the bedrooms, and the corridors were lined with crushed-velvet wallpaper. Down below the house stood a small cottage which had served as a stable for Ed the Talking Horse, and it was here that Richard and his family were to live for the best part of a year. Converting the ranch into a studio, complete with kitchens and recreation rooms, was no overnight job: work was still being done on the building when Neil Diamond came to record his *Beautiful Noise* album there in early 1976. But with Larry Samuels working as studio manager, Shangri-La was functioning by the end of 1974. 'It felt like we were a street gang that had a place to go every day,' said Robbie. 'We were like the Dead End kids. We'd all go down to the studio and shoot pool, play music, talk and figure things out. We didn't begin each day saying, "Oh God, we gotta work, we gotta rehearse". But we *did* work, in a kind of punk way. We were a bunch of punks again.' Long-time Band fan Eric Clapton remembered Shangri-La as 'a very special place'. 'It was great because it was all wood,' he said. 'The room you recorded in was originally a master bedroom or playroom, and it had a couple of sliding doors you could just leave open to the outside, with the sea no more than a hundred yards away.'

The first real work done in the studio was the tidying-up and mixing of the 'historic' *Basement Tapes*, a project The Band had discussed with Dylan after Tour '74 had finished. 'All of a sudden it seemed like a good idea,' said Robbie. 'We thought we'd see what we had, so I started to go through the stuff and sort it out, trying to make it stand up for a record that wasn't recorded professionally. Whether it went Top 10 or not didn't concern me, I just wanted to document a period rather than let them rot away on the shelves somewhere.' It seems possible that one reason for releasing the basement recordings was to pay for Shangri-La itself, since the band had already frittered away so much of the money they'd made. In his Dylan biography *Behind The Shades*, Clinton Heylin takes Robbie to task for including Band tracks that hadn't been recorded in the basement at all. 'Whatever his reasons for conjoining The Band material with the Dylan material,' Heylin wrote, 'they do not mesh comfortably together.' Heylin also accused Robbie of 'poor judgement', not only in omitting songs such as 'Sign On The Cross', 'I'm Not There (1956)', 'I Shall Be Released', 'Quinn The Eskimo', and 'All You Have To Do Is Dream' but in picking inferior takes of 'Tears Of Rage' and 'Too Much Of Nothing'. He might have added duplicity to the list of charges, since Robbie not only cleaned up the tracks by filtering out tape hiss and compressing vocals but actually recorded overdubs like the acoustic guitar on the intro to 'This Wheel's On Fire' and a couple of bars of drums at the end of 'Apple Suckling Tree'.

At the end of the day, though, Heylin's objections were the academic ones of a touchy Dylanologist: *The Basement Tapes* still contained some of the greatest music either Dylan or The Band had recorded. As William C. Woods had written of the original *Great White Wonder* bootleg in 1969, 'this is vexing, troublesome, fascinating, transition Dylan . . . his voice is altogether unique, black and country at once, as though he were on the brink of some improbable fusion that might speak not only of a new music but of a new world'. Coming a year after the hard-rock bravado of

312

Tour '74, *The Basement Tapes* plunged reviewers back into the mystery of Dylan's post-accident retreat, and into an America altogether purer and darker than the country the money-spinning '74 tour had traversed. 'It sounds like a testing and a discovery of memory and roots,' wrote Greil Marcus in his sleeve-note to the album. '*The Basement Tapes* . . . seem to leap out of a kaleidoscope of American music no less immediate for its venerability.' Did 'Yazoo Street Scandal' really sound so odd coming after 'Million Dollar Bash'? Or 'Ain't No More Cane' coming between 'Yea! Heavy' and 'Crash On The Levee'?

The album was released in July 1975, complete with Felliniesque gatefold portraits of Dylan, The Band, and a Rolling Thunder-style troupe of carnival freaks and entertainers. Apart from the standard clown, midget, belly-dancer, and strong-man, there were several other oddballs who all looked as though they'd walked directly out of 'Million Dollar Bash': a grinning man in a strait-jacket, an obese woman in a T-shirt emblazoned with the words 'Mrs Henry', and a curvaceous nun seated tenderly on Bob's knee. The Band themselves looked eccentric enough, with Robbie in a blue Mao suit, Garth clutching an ancient tuba, and Richard – most mystifyingly of all – wearing a U.S. Air Force uniform. Issued with a sticker proclaiming 'The Historic Basement Tapes', the album made #7 in the first week of August – not a patch on the brilliant *Blood On The Tracks* (which had spent two weeks at #1 in February), but not bad for a bunch of songs cut mostly on a portable reel-to-reel eight years before.

Aside from *The Basement Tapes*, Robbie continued intermittently to work on the symphonic concept album he had been mentioning in interviews since 1972. 'We still work on it and keep moving ahead,' he told Harvey Kubernik. 'It's particularly interesting for Garth, who is probably the foremost musicologist in popular music today.' Garth, as it happened, had acquired his own ranch in the Malibu mountains, and spent much of his time tinkering in his workshop with old theatre organs and other keyboards. Among the companies who sought his expertise were Yamaha, whom he helped to develop the new CS-80 polyphonic synthesizer. After a hard day's tinkering, he liked nothing better than to take his Mormon girlfriend Maude to a Hollywood nightspot called Ali Baba's and listen to the oud players who accompanied the club's belly-dancers. In the World Music stakes, Garth was already way ahead of the pack.

In early February 1975, Garth flew east to join Levon in Woodstock. Hating the West Coast as he did, Levon had gone back to the Catskills to – in Libby Titus' words – 'stake out this swampy Ponderosa' off Plochmann Lane, a piece of land where he ultimately wanted to put down roots. But there was another reason to be in Woodstock: to his great delight, Levon had been asked to co-produce a Muddy Waters album with none other than Henry Glover. The Chess budget was minuscule, but in two days they managed to get down eight more-than-adequate tracks, including the great 'Why Are People Like That' and infectious versions of 'Caldonia', 'Kansas City', and 'Let The Good Times Roll'. The band featured Paul Butterfield and Muddy's great pianist 'Pinetop' Perkins, who'd played with Sonny Boy Williamson back in Helena. When Garth arrived, his superb accordion runs added a distinctly cajun flavour to the proceedings. *The Muddy Waters Woodstock Album* was probably Waters' best '70s record besides the superb Johnny Winter-produced *Hard Again* (1977). Nor was Muddy the only artist to benefit from the presence of Levon and Garth in Woodstock: the pair also played on Butterfield's album *Put It In Your Ear*, recorded for Albert Grossman's Bearsville label.

By the time Helm and Hudson returned to L.A., Robbie had begun writing songs for the next Band album. It was clear to him, and to others, that if The Band didn't get their act together and record some new material soon they might well fall apart. Significantly, one of the first songs he finished was 'Forbidden Fruit', which was about as close as The Band ever came to admitting they'd had drug problems. With its ironic use of the phrase 'shoot the whole works away' and its reference to a 'bad connection', the song was Robbie's little homily to the bad boys in the group, complete with the Biblical image of the Golden Calf.

The Band spent most of 1975 working on *Northern Lights – Southern Cross*. 'Of all our albums, *Northern Lights* took the longest,' said Rick. 'Because we had our own studio, everybody would just saunter in when they felt like it. It was hard to arrive in the same place at the same time.' Even when all five members of the group *were* in the studio at the same time, the recording process was more protracted than usual: Shangri-La was a state-of-the-art 24-track studio, fully equipped with the latest synthesizers, and Garth spent many hours on his keyboard parts. Absorbed in the possibilities of the new technology, he saw no problem in incorporating Mini Moogs and ARP string ensembles into The Band's essentially lo-tech sound. One listen to the intricate layers of keyboards on 'Jupiter Hollow' is enough to show that he succeeded.

All the songs were Robbie's this time, though he was disingenuously modest about his creative monopoly. 'It's no different than it's always been,' he claimed. 'It's just a particular time when one of the guys has more songs written than at other times. It just fell that way this time and will probably change again.' Fortunately, the eight songs showed that Robbie's muse had not deserted him, and the others felt none of the misgivings that had characterized the *Cahoots* sessions. For the most part these were extended story-songs that built up musical ideas over several minutes, and four of them – including 'Forbidden Fruit' – had a much more urban feel to them than one was used to hearing from The Band. 'Rags And Bones' drew on Robbie's memories of his Toronto childhood, and

'Ophelia' came straight off the streets of old Storyville. Balancing these out were the two longest tracks on the album, 'Acadian Driftwood' and 'It Makes No Difference'. Both six and a half minutes long, they were the most moving songs Robbie had written in five years, one an epic account of the British driving Acadian farmers out of Nova Scotia in 1759, the other an artlessly simple country-soul ballad sung by Rick Danko.

If the album had a major flaw, it was that the three main uptempo tracks – 'Forbidden Fruit', 'Ophelia', and 'Ring Your Bell' – sounded too similar. But 'Forbidden Fruit' made a rousing opening, with its ominous, tremolo-bent guitar intro and feisty Levon Helm vocal. If the production was considerably slicker than anything The Band had previously recorded, there was still a sassy downhome groove at the heart of the sound, and Robbie released all his pain and frustration in a quivering, enraged solo. It was inevitable that Levon would also be elected to sing the splendidly punchy 'Ophelia', which was musically a first cousin to 'The W.S. Walcott Medicine Show' and even distantly related to 'Life Is A Carnival'. 'It had all those old vamp changes and major chords,' says Robbie. Levon's account of searching for the eponymous heroine – her monicker deriving not from *Hamlet* but from Robbie's discovery of Minnie Pearl's real name – had the same flavour of good-humoured regret with which he'd infused 'Up On Cripple Creek'. For the song, Garth managed single-handedly to re-create the rollicking Dixieland horn section of *Rock Of Ages*, playing all the brass and twirling woodwinds himself.

One of the most welcome aspects of *Northern Lights – Southern Cross* was the return of the tumbling, overlapping vocal lines that had been so crucial to their classic early recordings. If Levon led the way on 'Ring Your Bell' – Robbie's account of the band getting busted by Mounties on the Canadian border – Rick and Richard were both in there grabbing their share of the lines and harmonies. All three played an equal part in the gorgeous 'Jupiter Hollow', a song inspired by Robbie's perusal of an encyclopaedia of Greek mythology, and on 'Acadian Driftwood' they traded lines and sang the most beautiful harmonies of their careers.

The two songs Richard had to himself – 'Hobo Jungle' and 'Rags And Bones' – were tailor-made for him. The first was piano-based, its downbeat chords evoking memories of his own great songs, and featured some of Robbie's loveliest writing. Richard's exquisitely wistful vocal captured all the rootlessness and loneliness of the hobo's life without ever resorting to sentimentality. Like 'Rockin' Chair', the song was about reaching the end of a journey, a tender obituary for an old man who'd spent his life chasing the horizon. 'Rags And Bones' made a curiously low-key finale to the album, but was again distinguished by the careful detail of Robbie's lyric. Based on stories he'd heard about his great-grandfather, the scholarly immigrant forced through lack of work to become a junkman, the song was filled with thumbnail sketches of Depression-era street characters – newsboys, fiddlers, organ-grinders, preachers on orange crates. Richard sang the song beautifully, and Garth danced around the cantering rhythm with a magician's touch.

If Rick had never been as strong a ballad singer as Richard, only he could have caught the true note of desolation on 'It Makes No Difference'. 'I thought about the song in terms of the saying that time heals all wounds,' Robbie told Robert Palmer. 'Except in some cases, and this was one of those cases.' Never before had The Band tackled such a straightforward 'love song', such an achingly naked plaint: always wary of mawkishness, Robbie had invariably pulled back from first-person outpourings of woe. In this case, he knew there was something so elemental about the sense of loss in Danko's performance that it went way beyond self-pity. Bolstered by harmonies on the aching choruses, Rick was a ploughboy soul man in full flight, and his bewildered, hopeless pain found a kind of corollary in the anguished guitar and sax solos by Robbie and Garth.

However great the other songs on *Northern Lights*, the album's centrepiece was still 'Acadian Driftwood'. Comparable in its evocation of defeat and injustice to 'The Night They Drove Old Dixie Down', and inspired by a show he'd seen in Montreal called *Acadie, Acadie*, this epic track turned Robbie's old American dreams on their head. Instead of pining for the South, the Acadians of Louisiana yearn for their cold Canadian homelands:

> Everlasting summer filled with ill-content,
> This government had us walking in chains.
> This isn't my turf, this ain't my season,
> Can't think of one good reason to remain.
> We worked in the sugarfields up from New Orleans,
> It was evergreen up until the flood.
> You could call it an omen, point you where you're going,
> Set my compass north, I got winter in my blood.

It was as if Robbie had finally lived outside Canada for long enough to see it through the same romantic lens he'd used to view the American South a decade before. When Levon sang 'I've got winter in my blood', he was speaking not for himself but for the four Canadians in the group. As Greil Marcus observed, 'the tale must say something about the strangeness The Band still feels, and that they cannot evade or transcend, as Canadians living in America'. What, Marcus wondered, must Levon have felt 'as a Southerner imagining himself an exile in a land he truly knew as home'?

Drawing on Longfellow's epic 'Evangeline', which actually mentioned the 'driftwood' from wrecked Acadian ships in the Gulf of St Lawrence, Robbie centred his saga around one uprooted family forced to sail down the East Coast in search of a new home. From the opening acoustic guitar chords, immediately reinforced by Garth's haunting martial chorus of bagpipes and piccolos, the song carried all the weight of an ancient woe:

The war was over and the spirit was broken.
The hills were smoking as the men withdrew.
We stood on the cliffs and watched the ships
Slowly sinking to their rendezvous.
They signed a treaty and our homes were taken,
Loved ones forsaken, they didn't give a damn.
Try to raise a family, end up the enemy
Over what went down on the plains of Abraham.
Acadian driftwood, gypsy tailwind,
They call my home the land of snow.
Canadian cold front moving in,
What a way to ride, oh what a way to go.

Richard took the first verse and Levon seamlessly picked up the second. Rick joined them in falsetto for the heartbreaking chorus, and Garth came back in with his piccolo motif. On the fourth verse, Country Gazette's Byron Berline introduced the mournful cajun fiddle that threaded its way through the rest of the song, meshing with Garth's accordion and synths to create a soaringly lovely sound. 'We've known Byron from way back when we used to play the circuit in Oklahoma,' Robbie told Harvey Kubernik. 'Rick has played fiddle on a few songs in the past, but we needed a special flavour for "Driftwood". It was difficult to do, and we didn't want to take an incredible amount of time to get it right.' The total effect was so breathtakingly beautiful it made you want to cry. The care that had gone into each vocal phrase, and the love that seemed to burst from the three voices blending in harmony, restored all one's faith in the group.

For Robbie, the pleasant sense of reunion that accompanied the *Northern Lights* sessions had a lot to do with recording 'Acadian Driftwood'. It seemed to bring them closer together, and to reaffirm some of the things that made them so different from American rock'n'roll bands. The album title itself expressed the band's peculiar sense of homelessness, of being caught between two worlds. For Greil Marcus, 'Acadian Driftwood' was 'a tale of people who dream of northern lights as they bear a southern cross', and the same could have been said of The Band's own story. 'The title just came from the air,' says Robbie. 'I was sitting by the water one night, looking up at the sky, and it just popped into my mind. I mentioned it to the others and they all seemed to like it.' For the album cover, the group built a log-fire on Zuma Beach and sat out under the stars. They looked more inscrutably self-contained than ever.

Greil Marcus, reviewing the album in *Creem*, reported a consensus among fellow critics that *Northern Lights – Southern Cross* was 'The Band's best since *Stage Fright* and maybe even since *The Band*'. Initially he himself had found the songs 'flat' and 'obvious', but after repeated exposure to it he'd begun to hear 'music of great confidence'. 'They sound as if they're aiming their music at each other, not at a finished product,' he noted, adding that Garth in particular had 'never played with such imagination, or with deceptive anonymity': 'What Randy Newman got from a string section on his luminous and tragic 'Louisiana 1927', Hudson gets on his own . . . with supreme delicacy, he wraps his sound around The Band, enfolding their performance with a warmth of spirit that may well prove to be what this album is best remembered for.'

Given the relaxed nature of the *Northern Lights* sessions, there were frequent diversions and distractions from the hard work of recording an album. On Sunday 23 March, Rick, Garth, and Levon appeared at a one-day festival in aid of Bill Graham's SNACK (Students Need Athletics, Culture, and Kicks) organization. Staged at Golden Gate Park's Kezar Stadium in San Francisco, the festival drew 60,000 people, who were duly treated to a 'supersession' consisting of Bob Dylan, the Band trio, and Neil Young with his regular sidemen Ben Keith and Tim Drummond. Marlon Brando gave a speech, Dylan sang 'I Want You', and Neil Young did 'Are You Ready For The Country?' From the Band quarter came 'The Weight' and 'Loving You Is Sweeter Than Ever', with an all-star encore of 'Will The Circle Be Unbroken?'. By the end of the day, SNACK was $200,000 wealthier.

In addition, there were occasional sessions for pals old and new. Garth guested on Poco's *Head Over Heels*, and Levon played on the Crosby and Nash album *Wind On The Water*. On the first Asylum album by his Arkansas chums the Cate Brothers – produced by fellow transplanted southerner Steve Cropper – Levon drummed on the very soulful 'Standin' On A Mountain Top', a song he would himself cut for his second solo album. Meanwhile, Robbie had taken more than a passing interest in an oddball singer-songwriter named Hirth Martinez. 'Bob Dylan said this guy was really extraordinary and that I should check him out,' Robbie told Harvey Kubernik. 'When I met him I totally related to him. His music fused melodies with eccentric chord changes and mixed time signatures, and he sang of UFOs as well as loneliness and self-doubt.'

Martinez was a complete unknown, a strange man who lived in a Hollywood bungalow littered with tapes of songs he'd recorded. Barely able to support a wife and child by gigging as a guitarist at the Beverly Hills Hilton, he'd met Robbie with Norman Harrison, owner of a guitar shop in the San Fernando Valley. By early 1975, Robbie had decided he would not only try to get Martinez a record deal but would actually produce an album for him. After Warner Brothers had committed themselves, Robbie began turning up at Hirth's bungalow every morning at 10 a.m. Together they went through almost 300 songs, picking out the best ones for the album. When Martinez rang a friend to say that Robbie was going to produce his album, he heard splutters of disbelief on the other end of the line. 'Do you realize what you've done?' the friend shouted. 'Robbie Robertson must be the most conceited person in the music business!' Martinez was taken aback. 'I was shocked,' he told Timothy White in 1976. 'But since then I've heard other people saying similar things, that Robbie is cold and unfriendly and that he's a snob. "Snobby Robbie", I've heard people call him. I can understand how people might take him that way, since he's quiet and not outgoing or talkative. Their feelings seem to be a mixture of misunderstanding or mistrust of his mysteriousness, and regret that they cannot get close to him.'

On first listening, *Hirth From Earth* seemed a strange project for 'Snobby Robbie' to have undertaken. Where Jesse Winchester's songs at least bore some relation to the music of The Band, Hirth's had nothing to do with it. They were among the loopier products of L.A.'s singer-songwriter underbelly, pitched somewhere between the Van Dyke Parks of *Song Cycle* and the Dr John of *Gris-Gris*. There was Sandpipers-style samba ('Altogether Alone'), some soft California funk ('Djini'), a slice of cosmic Beach Boys dippiness ('Be Everything'), and even the sub-Captain Beefheart 'Comin' Round The Moon'. Notwithstanding some interesting moments ('Silent Movies') and snatches of inspired playing from Robbie and Garth, Hirth's nutty lyrics were at best an acquired taste.

'I thoroughly enjoyed doing the album,' protested Robbie after *Hirth From Earth* received uniformly disparaging reviews. 'The only negative thing I can say about it is that I didn't realize how many people would miss the fucking point and see Hirth in the wrong way, or how few people had the musical background to understand where he was coming from.' Always sensitive to charges of failure, Robbie strongly defended his decision to produce the album. 'He's a great songwriter and people will cover his songs', he said. 'Believe me, I don't go around overrating people.' Martinez himself recalled that 'people around Robbie' were singularly unenthusiastic about the project from the start. 'They didn't mind telling me that what Robbie was doing with me could really hurt his career if it didn't work out.'

What really baffled Martinez was that throughout the time he was working on the album with Robbie he never felt he got to know him. 'I know it sounds strange after spending so much time with him,' he told Timothy White, 'but to me he's still a mystery man.[1] For instance, it seemed to me that if I asked him *anything*, he'd know the answer, just like a wise man. But he's so young it really throws you off.' With his interest in UFO's, Hirth even began to wonder if Robbie was a 'spaceman': that would at least have explained 'how he could guess my thoughts and was intelligent and skilful beyond his years'.

Not long after the release of both *Hirth From Earth* and *Northern Lights – Southern Cross* in November, Robbie was approached by an even more unlikely client for his production skills. Neil Diamond had heard the Martinez album and been intrigued by a side of Robbie Robertson he'd never detected on The Band's records. For his part, Robbie said he was fascinated by the Tin Pan Alley tradition that Diamond represented, and claimed that the concept behind *Beautiful Noise* was to pay tribute to 'that rock'n'roll version of Tin Pan Alley I'd first encountered with Ronnie Hawkins when I was fifteen'. 'It's kind of an interesting project for both of us,' said Diamond. 'We're working around a story, telling a tale musically about a certain period of time, and using the events and music of that period. The time is just about the early '60s – the Beatles, Kennedy, some of the social stuff that was going down then – seen through the eyes of the songwriter.'

The pair started work on *Beautiful Noise* at Shangri-La in January, with Robbie receiving $250,000 upfront for the job. 'I'm not coming in to help him write songs,' Robbie told Harvey Kubernik. 'I play a much bigger part than that. From my aspect, I'm trying to make a much more musical album. I'd like to make a record that matters all the way up and down the line.' With a little help from Garth, who played organ on the gospel-Broadway hybrid 'Surviving The Life' and the sole Diamond/Robertson collaboration 'Dry Your Eyes', Robbie put together a suite of string-saturated MOR songs only tangentially connected by the themes he and Neil had discussed. His own guitar-playing was not much in evidence, though one could make it out on 'Lady-Oh', 'Jungle Time', and 'Dry Your Eyes'. It was all pretty schlocky stuff, failing even to produce a hit single, but Diamond's fans liked it enough to push it up to # 4 when it was released in the summer. Diamond himself was impressed enough by Robbie to hire him for an equally turgid, son-of-*Hot August Night* live album recorded at Hollywood's Greek Theater.

With the disappointing performance of *Northern Lights – Southern Cross*, which only reached # 26 on the *Billboard* album chart, there was speculation that Robbie's extra-curricular activities were presaging some kind of split from the other Band members. Robbie denied this. 'There's never a conflict between my Band role and my projects,' he said. 'It's not that kind of relationship anyway. We've watched each other grow up and go from teenage kids to grown men. There's been obvious changes and responsibilities, but it's *never* in control, and it never will be in control, I hope, because it would make things very boring. That's what enables us to work together, because it's never the same old story.'

But these denials masked a continued exasperation – and not just with Richard, whose umpteenth car accident scuppered plans for a spring tour. The band's drug use was getting way out of hand, as was the whole Malibu scene. 'Rick told me someone came over to their house and killed himself right in front of Elizabeth,' says Al Aronowitz. Libby Titus had already realized that if she didn't get away from the beach she was going to die, but Jane Manuel struggled on as Richard's nurse. 'Things got pretty hellish in Malibu,' she says. 'I looked at myself one morning at the age of

31 and decided I'd had enough.' For Robbie, the turning point seemed to come with just another beautiful morning in paradise. 'I walked out of my house,' he says, 'and the first thing I saw was Keith Moon lying unconscious on the beach with the tide coming in and lapping around his body. I remember thinking, hey, this is taking things a little *too* close to the edge.' Jonathan Taplin, who was now a movie producer, says that Robbie definitely began to pull away from the others. 'That was the first sense I had of Robbie's slight alienation from the whole thing,' says Taplin. 'He'd made a good bit of money, and he had a beautiful house on the beach. He didn't really want to be a babysitter any more.' When Ronnie Hawkins came to stay in Malibu, he sensed a major shift in his ex-protégé's priorities. 'It certainly looked like Robbie was takin' care of business,' the Hawk laughs. 'He was doin' movie scores, the phone was ringin', and Warren Beatty was comin' over for dinner! He'd become a white collar worker, a big boss . . . what we used to call a tah-coon.'

The 'bad boys' of the group had in turn begun to resent the money Robbie was making and the limelight he was hogging. 'The chemistry in a band has got to be right,' says Levon. 'As we got down towards the end of our contract with Capitol, it had grown from a privilege and a pleasure into an obligation.' Things weren't helped by the fact that Capitol themselves appeared to have lost all interest in The Band. 'There've been times when I've felt Capitol could have sold more records for us than they did,' admitted Levon at the time of *The Last Waltz*, though he added that 'they probably felt *we* weren't active enough.' One Capitol employee who deplored the label's neglect of the group was A & R man Gary Gersh, who would later bring Robbie Robertson to the Geffen label. 'In those days it was all Bob Seger and Steve Miller,' says Gersh. 'I was telling them, "You guys are missing the boat".' A case in point was 'Christmas Must Be Tonight', an out-take from *Northern Lights* subsequently included on *Islands*. The song, written by Robbie after the birth of his son Sebastian, was originally intended to have been a Christmas single in December 1975, but when no one in the A & R department got behind the idea it was dropped from the label's schedule.

In March, Eric Clapton booked into Shangri-La to record the *No Reason To Cry* album. Atlantic had refused to allow Tom Dowd to work with an RSO act, thanks to Robert Stigwood's severing of ties with the label, so Clapton took a shot in the dark and elected to co-produce the album himself – with help from engineer Rob Fraboni and ex-Domino Carl Radle – in a new and unfamiliar studio. The sessions were fun for everyone, and had the incidental effect of reuniting The Band for the first time since *Northern Lights – Southern Cross*. 'It was the first time they'd played together for about a year,' recalled Clapton. 'It took us coming in there to get them all in the studio with one another, because there was a lot of bitching.' Although Eric had his own band with him, the Band members popped up all over the album. Rick was constantly pushing songs and ended up persuading Eric to use his brooding ballad 'All Our Past Times'. In addition, he and Richard pulled a lovely old basement song called 'Beautiful Thing' out of the vaults and exhumed it for the album. Finally, on Bob Dylan's 'Sign Language', Robbie played a blistering solo and Dylan himself dropped in to duet with Eric.

Dylan wasn't the only superstar to 'drop in' at the Clapton sessions. When Eric held an all-night birthday party in the studio on 30 March, he ended up hosting a drunken jam session with Billy Preston, Ron Wood, and Jesse Ed Davis. By the time Dylan showed up at 8 a.m. the booze had run out and the tapes were rolling. One of the album's reviewers accused Clapton of 'cronying', but it was hard to stem the flow of visitors at Shangri-La – or the flow of alcohol. 'Richard and I would always end up being the last people at the session,' Eric remembered. 'We'd have pissed everybody else off, and we'd be out of our brains playing a Little Walter song called "Last Night I Lost The Best Friend I Ever Had".' Despite the chaotic nature of the recordings, twenty-five tracks had been cut after three weeks. Unfortunately, Fraboni decided to mix the album at Village Recorders, which Clapton felt cost them the 'original feel' of the record. Released in August, in the impasse between *461 Ocean Boulevard* and *Slowhand*, it only made # 15 on the *Billboard* chart.

By the early summer, when Richard had recovered from his accident, there was renewed talk of touring. Capitol were about to issue the eleven-track *Best Of The Band* – complete with 'Twilight', another *Northern Lights* out-take – and wanted the group to promote it with some live shows. None of them was terribly keen, not even Levon. 'I like to tour, but there's a real danger of burning yourself out,' he told John Swenson. 'A lot of people have criticized us for not touring enough and taking too much time between albums, but that's the way we are. I don't feel like we're all that hot anyway. I mean, it's great to play in just about the best band around, but it's no life-and-death struggle like so many people wanna make it out to be.' Levon's disenchantment as a member of The Band was implicit in the excitement with which he talked about the $250,000 studio he was building back in Woodstock, and in his ideas for the 'dream production' that would become his *RCO All-Stars* album the following year.

Despite the cold feet, The Band finally agreed to hit the road again. After a warm-up date at Stanford University in Palo Alto on Sunday 27 June, they played their first proper southern California show in over five years at the Santa Barbara County Bowl, where Mac Rebennack, Carole King, Carl Radle, and Leon Russell came to see them and where Garth – by way of a nod to the Bicentennial celebrations – incorporated snatches of Bernstein and Sondheim's 'America' into 'The Genetic Method'. 'There was still a sense of mystery in the concert,' wrote Harvey Kubernik, 'but there was a fear that the group was a step closer to boredom.' As the tour progressed through Kentucky, Missouri, Illinois, Milwaukee, and New York state, the balance between mystery and boredom seemed to grow more precarious with each show. 'I watched The Band coming apart through substance abuse and musical stagnation,' recalls Gary Gersh. 'On that last tour you could see the most brilliant concert or the biggest piece of shit. The chemistry began to unravel, and as with most of these situations it wasn't a pretty sight. Having been in the business a while I'd become a little more hardened, but it was still very painful.'

When the chemistry was right, and Richard had laid off the sauce, the band were still sublime. 'Whatever was happening to them, the fellas had a way of pulling together that was real special,' says Mac Rebennack. 'Doc Pomus said to me, "Even if bad things are going on, you'd never know it from their hearts."' At Washington's Carter Baron Amphitheater on 16 August, they stormed their way through a set that included superb versions of *Northern Lights* songs like 'Ophelia', 'Forbidden Fruit', and 'It Makes No Difference', as well as such vintage material as 'The Shape I'm In' and 'Up On Cripple Creek'. Yet when it came time for Richard to tackle numbers as vocally demanding as 'King Harvest' and 'Tears Of Rage', he clearly wasn't up to the job. 'The Shape I'm In' was one thing, but listening to the once-great baritone straining and cracking through 'Tears Of Rage' was excruciating. 'The touring got harder and harder by the day,' says Robbie. 'It was particularly hard on Richard, whose health was not great. We felt we were kinda dragging him along on this thing. We weren't able to go out and give it our best shot, working without our full force.'

Perhaps it was an unconscious attempt to close ranks around Richard's fragility that made The Band seem more insular than ever. At one of the three shows they played at Hollywood's open-air Greek Theater in early September, Mick Farren observed that for all the sense of 'family reunion' in the audience, there was 'a strange kind of distance between the performers and the crowd.' 'There has always been an aloofness about The Band,' Farren wrote. 'Part of it is the extreme expertise of their music, but that's hardly the whole explanation. Whatever creates the barrier between us and them, there's little attempt to bridge the gap across the footlights. Scarcely a word is directed to the audience between songs and you start to get the impression that they are happier playing in a basement than on a public stage.' During the interval, one member of the audience told Farren that ten years hence The Band would be like Fats Domino, playing the same old tunes to the same old audience. Farren wasn't sure this was 'altogether a bad thing', but it was precisely why The Band themselves were feeling so stale. At the party after the show, Farren noted that many of the coke-snorting liggers and freeloaders present were people who hadn't returned to the auditorium after the interval. Even at the party they didn't seem too interested in The Band, 'steering around them as if they were surrounded by an impenetrable barrier'. Perhaps the separation was essential, thought Farren. 'If people got too close to them, the unique communication they have between them might somehow be impaired.'

Richard managed to throw everything into complete disarray again after a couple of dates down in Texas. In Austin, home to Willie Nelson and a burgeoning country rock music scene, he almost broke his neck when a powerboat in which he was riding on Lake Austin took a big wave at full throttle. Doctors recommended six weeks in traction, which would have meant cancelling nearly thirty shows. In a scenario reminiscent of Robbie's hypnosis in San Francisco, Larry Samuels instead contacted a team of Tibetan-trained healers in Dallas, who charged the group $2,500 to work on massaging Richard's neck while he lay in bed for three days. In the end only ten dates were lost, but the accident made the others think seriously about their future. 'Richard needed proper recuperation and he didn't get it,' says Robbie. 'It started to make me aware of how long we'd been doing this, and I began to wonder if we were really learning or growing from this experience. The sparkle was slipping away, and it was all becoming very *business*-oriented. It felt like we were spinning our wheels. We'd play a concert, pick up the money, and go on to the next town. There was not a tremendous amount of enthusiasm doing it, and I thought "Why are we here?" Gradually the idea grew that we should somehow bring the whole thing to a head.' For Robbie, dragging themselves around the same old venues and hotels, and being hit on by 'the same goofy, pushy people', had rather lost its appeal.

The first date after the accident was a sell-out show at New York's 3,500-capacity Palladium Theater on Saturday 18 September. It was opening night for the theatre on East 14th Street, where The Band had played in the days when it was still called the Academy of Music. To add to the sense of occasion and the pressure, Robbie had hit on the brainwave of doing what they'd done on their last appearance here: using a horn section, supplemented this time by Woodstock fiddler Larry Packer. Predictably, of course, the rehearsals with Packer and the hornmen were a classic 'last minute production', leaving Robbie severely overworked and stressed. 'Smile, Robbie,' someone teased as he walked into the revamped theatre. 'I'm saving my smiles tonight,' he replied.

By the second number, 'The Shape I'm In', all fears were banished and Robbie was grinning from ear to ear. It was the *Rock Of Ages* experience all over again. With every song filled out and reinforced by the hornmen – once again featuring tuba wizard Howard Johnson – The Band sailed exultantly through 'It Makes No Difference', 'The Weight', and 'Twilight', a song which had just been released as a single but which live performance had honed into something far more powerful and desperate than the insipid studio original. Only 'Acadian Driftwood', with Larry Packer standing in for the irreplaceable Byron Berline, proved too much of a challenge for live translation that night. 'They just surrounded me and sang four-part harmony,' says Packer. 'It was quadrophonic heaven!' It must have sounded better onstage than it did in the auditorium, for once again Richard was gruff and uncertain of his lines. Fortunately, they were able to go out in the blaze of glory that was Allen Toussaint's horn arrangements for 'Don't Do It'. 'Life Is A Carnival', and 'The W. S. Walcott Medicine Show', the last two numbers being encores on which they were joined by their harp-blasting pal Paul Butterfield.

Exiting the Palladium stage, the five Band members all knew this was one of the best shows they would ever play. That it was also one of the last was something only Robbie Robertson knew for sure.

2

End of 'the Road'

We wanted one last statement, and it was more than I expected it to be.

Robbie Robertson

It took a little while before everyone realized just how serious Robbie Robertson was about 'bringing this whole thing to a head'. For Rick and Levon in particular, the decision to stop touring suddenly seemed less appealing, threatening something altogether more terminal. 'I was probably the least in favour of doing it that way, without being in any kind of intractable position,' Levon admitted. 'I could certainly see people not wanting to travel any more, but I'm the one that don't mind travelling. The hotel manager don't bring me down, I'll sit there and jaw with him all day.'

The truth was, Robbie had finally had enough of caretaking The Band. Ever since moving to the West Coast he had virtually been managing the group, and he couldn't cope with them any longer. Throughout the summer tour, he'd felt a constant sense of impending disaster, one centred not just around Richard Manuel but around 'The Band as a train itself'. More prosaically, the sales of *Moondog Matinee* and *Northern Lights–Southern Cross* – both albums of which he was justifiably proud – had disillusioned him profoundly. He didn't want to be 'out there' when people started telling the group to 'go home'.

Deep down, Robbie knew it was time to cut his losses – to quit while he was still (just) ahead. The concept of a farewell concert along the festive lines of a New Orleans funeral gradually crystallized in his mind as the nicest way to say goodbye. 'I came up with the idea of the The Last Waltz,' he says. 'I thought it would be a very soulful move. I said to the guys, listen, we don't want to travel town to town any more, we should evolve to the next stage. I think we should do this and do it in a very musical fashion. Gather together people who represent different spokes of the wheel that makes up rock'n'roll. And everybody said, "yeah!"'

The obvious man to turn to at this point was Bill Graham, who immediately flew down to L.A. to discuss the concept with Robbie. Given that The Band were already booked into Winterland on Thanksgiving Day, Thursday 25 November, it made sense to turn the show into 'The Last Waltz', bringing everything full circle from their San Francisco debut seven and a half years earlier. But Bill had further, grander ideas. 'I wanted to make it an all-in-one concert and Thanksgiving dinner, one price, and I didn't wanna announce who the guests were,' he said. 'I told Robbie, trust me that our reputation in San Francisco is good enough that when we say "The Band and Friends" and a seven-course meal for $25 they know they'll get something.' In addition, Bill wanted to bring in an orchestra and some professional waltzers, and to dress up Winterland as the most sumptuous ballroom imaginable.

The fact that 2,500 Band fans had already bought $5.50 and $7.50 tickets for the scheduled show and had to be refunded or charged extra was conveniently overlooked. As Greil Marcus pointed out, many of the band's truest fans were now unable to share in the farewell. 'For a guy and his old lady, fifty smackers is two lids of good dope,' admitted Graham in his best 'I-may-be-stinking-rich-but-I'm-still-hip' argot. 'But this isn't some dust bowl somewhere. They know they are going to eat caviar.' Pointing out that caviar might not have been the highest priority for Band fans cut little ice with Bill.

While Graham returned to San Francisco and busied himself

with turkeys and chandeliers, Robbie began making telephone calls. To his surprise, none of the stellar guests he had in mind for the show was otherwise engaged on Thanksgiving Day. 'It was almost automatic, the chips just fell into place,' Robbie recalled. 'We didn't work out the names from a big list, it just happened naturally. Some were people we'd been involved with, some were friends, and some were just musical influences.' Most, he might have added, were people who just happened to be extremely famous: not since George Harrison's Concert For Bangladesh would so many superstars be gathered together for one show. One name, of course, stuck out above all others, and that was Bob Dylan. Had Dylan been unable – or unwilling – to do the show, The Last Waltz could only have been an anti-climax.

Once the rough list of guests had been drafted, The Band certainly had their work cut out for them. Not only would there have to be many hours of rehearsals for the show, but the group also owed Capitol one last album before they could consider a very lucrative offer from Warner Bros. For two months, Shangri-La became a 24-hour-a-day music factory, in Ronnie Hawkins' words 'a reverse Shangri-La where you came in aged 19 and left aged 300!' Half the time the band would be struggling to finish the collection of half-hearted tracks that made up *Islands*, the other half they would be learning and arranging the songs for The Last Waltz, twenty-one of which they'd never played before in their lives. 'The whole experience was long and gruelling,' says Robbie. 'I was wearing too many hats on both business and artistic levels, and it wore me out.' Towards the end of the rehearsals in November, Robbie was playing so much guitar that his fingers started going. If sixteen years on the road hadn't killed him, it looked like The Last Waltz would finish the job.

To complicate matters even more, Robbie had the further brainwave of documenting The Last Waltz on film. Here was a once-in-a-lifetime event, a gathering of superstars on a unique occasion: surely there was a film here, even if it was just a glorified 'home movie'. Perhaps remembering the error they had made in not being part of the *Woodstock* film, Robbie went to see Jonathan Taplin to discuss the idea of shooting the concert. Most concert films and 'rockumentaries' left him cold, he told Taplin: 'I watch music on TV and in movies and I ask myself, "Is this the line of work I'm in?" Because if it is, I find it embarrassing, obnoxious, and very poorly done – so much less than listening to it in my imagination.' Taplin agreed, and suggested that if they were going to do something different with The Last Waltz they should approach Martin Scorsese, whose *Mean Streets* he had produced not long after leaving The Band's employ back in 1971. 'I said I thought Marty would be the perfect guy, so I just introduced them,' says Taplin. 'We went over to Marty's office on the MGM lot late one night and put it to him.'

Scorsese, who coincidentally had worked as the supervising editor on Michael Wadleigh's *Woodstock*,[1] was even more exhausted than Robbie. Not only was he in the process of finishing *New York, New York*, he was due to start work directing a play with Liza Minnelli. 'We hit on him at the worst possible time,' says Robbie. 'But after I'd told him what we were going to do, he said "Holy Jesus!" and then "I can't afford to pass it by". There was no "Let me think it over", it was just "When do we start?"' The only problem was that Scorsese was under exclusive contract to United Artists, and under enormous pressure to finish *New York, New York*. Had producer Irwin Winkler learned that Scorsese was working on anything else there would have been hell to pay. Thus meetings to discuss the film were invariably clandestine nocturnal affairs. 'The whole thing was planned at night,' says Taplin. 'Which was kind of an omen of things to come.'

Scorsese's initial instinct was simply to document the concert in 16mm., but the more he thought about it the bigger it became in his mind. 'In the end I came up with the idea of shooting it in

35mm., with full synch sound and seven cameras,' he said. 'The Band were paying for the raw stock ($150,000), while the camera-men and I would get a percentage if the picture was ever made, and in the meantime we'd enjoy the show.' Once Robbie had worked out a set list for the show, Scorsese began work on a 200-page script giving cues for all seven cameras. Every line in every song was scripted so that he could focus closely on the person who was singing it. Robbie was blown away by the director's knowledge of The Band's music. 'He knew the music as well as I did,' he said. 'Obscure songs on *Cahoots*, fifth song on the second side . . . he knew all the words to the third verse!'

When Robbie asked the others how they felt about filming The Last Waltz, the reaction was lukewarm. 'They felt there were so many complications already that nobody really wanted to be bothered with it,' he said. 'Everybody was like, "Well, fine, as long as it doesn't get in the way too much . . ." Levon, especially, was concerned about our other responsibilities and thought we might be short-changing some other things by having to concentrate on the film.' What none of them appeared to dispute was Robbie's assumption of the mantle of producer on the film, with Jonathan Taplin serving as executive producer. Later this would cause as much bad blood between Robbie and the others as the extra hundreds of thousands of dollars he'd made from songwriting royalties. Looking at The Last Waltz with hindsight, Robbie could be said to have turned the band's death throes to his own profit and glory.

While Jonathan Taplin applied himself to the task of putting together a film crew – bringing in art director Boris Leven and cinematographers Laszlo Kovacs, Vilmos Sgismond, and Michael Chapman – The Band holed up at Shangri-La, frantically trying to keep several balls in the air at the same time. Fuelled by copious quantities of stimulants, they worked on *Islands* in between rehears-als for The Last Waltz. 'It was a piecemeal kind of work situation,' admitted Levon, and Robbie went even further: 'It wasn't an album, because we weren't in album mode.' So desperate were they to get the record out of the way that even Rick and Garth got a look-in when it came to songwriting credits. With a little help from Robbie, Rick's 'Street Walker' – an unbelievably crass song about 'ladies of the night' – was deemed to have made the grade as 'filler' material. The less said about the Danko/Hudson/Robertson title track, a hideous piece of elevator muzak which remained at the instrumental stage simply because Robbie hadn't written any lyrics for it, the better for all concerned.

The band even turned to Richard's old standby 'Georgia On My Mind' after Phil Walden had pestered them to do something for the Carter campaign, and to the Homer Banks soul classic 'Ain't That A Lot Of Love' in hopes of dredging up some of that 'Don't Do It' magic. Neither cover helped to rescue the album: even 'Georgia', which they performed on *Saturday Night Live* on the eve of the election, carried little of the soulful power it had had in the days when Richard sang it in the Rockin' Revols. It seemed a cruel thing to have to admit, but even Richard knew he had 'oversung' this song he loved so well. 'Ain't That A Lot Of Love', which the Flying Burrito Brothers had done much better on *Last Of The Red Hot Burritos*, was simply a shambles. Levon did his best to inject some fire into the track, but it sounded as though it had been put together in a couple of hours, which it probably had.

Of the other songs on *Islands*, two more were sung by Richard: the opening 'Right As Rain', a balmily inoffensive love song set in 'old Paree', and 'Let The Night Fall', which boasted a chorus as numbingly unimaginative as 'Where Do We Go From Here?' Garth did his best to lift these monotonous constructions off the ground, overdubbing keyboard tracks right up to the week of The Last Waltz, but he worked in vain. The only redeeming moments of musical magic came in the saccharine 'Christmas Must Be

Tonight', in the cryptic 'Saga Of Pepote Rouge' – faintly reminiscent of earlier Rick Danko vehicles like 'Caledonia Mission' and 'Ferdinand The Impostor' – and in the two tracks which concluded Side Two, 'Knockin' Lost John' and 'Living In A Dream'. The first track Robbie had sung since 'To Kingdom Come', 'Knockin' Lost John' was set in the Depression and had all the daft energy of the basement tapes, complete with some deranged sparring between Robbie's guitar and Garth's accordion. 'It was one of the weirdest things I've ever done,' he says. 'I have no idea what's going on in this thing. It was just an expression, some kind of off-beat idea.' 'Living In A Dream' was more straightforward – was even a little trite – but under its whimsical, upbeat surface lurked the album's only real expression of valediction. Listening to Levon whistle out the last bars, it was hard not to sense an air of false optimism, as though he were blinding himself to what Robbie was saying in the song.

The Band were still putting the finishing touches to 'Living In A Dream' on the weekend of 20 and 21 November, by which time they were on the point of collapse. Having rehearsed the show all day Sunday, they called in engineer Ed Anderson at midnight to help them put down harmonies on the song. Emmett Grogan, former Haight-Ashbury hustler and Digger, watched them 'fighting exhaustion' in the studio. 'With Rick Danko at a microphone trying to punch in his harmony around Levon's vocal, and with Robbie at the board in the control room, they were the only ones left standing,' Grogan wrote in his Last Waltz story for *Oui*. 'The others had completed their parts and staggered off to bed.' It was 6 a.m. before Rick got his harmonies right. 'If I don't go home right now, I'm going to cry,' groaned Robbie. Nobody laughed.

Rehearsals for the Last Waltz guests had begun two weeks earlier. Ronnie Hawkins, playing the deferential Good Ol' Boy to the hilt, watched the stars arrive at the studio, 'all these heroes of the world pulling up in their limousines, coked out of their heads, smacked out of their brains, bumpin' into walls'. When Quincy Jones produced USA For Africa's 'We Are The World' in 1985, he put up a sign saying 'Check Your Egos At The Door'; The Band's version at Shangri-La simply read '*Cows May Come; Cows May Go*'. What a motley collection they were, these friends and colleagues and 'influences'. 'That was a *wide* spread there, from Muddy Waters to Neil Diamond,' the Hawk laughs. 'I told old Neil, "I know you've made a billion dollars, but you're not my type"! A hillbilly like me up against one o'them upper-class Jewish cats, now that's a big contrast!' In fact, wide though it was, the spread was almost too narrow to include Hawkins himself. 'I heard that Robbie didn't really want me and Muddy at the Last Waltz, 'cause of the budget,' he says. 'It was Levon who insisted.' If that was true it was shameful, but then Robbie himself was always more 'upper-class Jewish cat' than 'hillbilly'. Certainly Ronnie, chortling good-naturedly along in the background, never got the chance to rehearse that Neil and Joni and Eric and Van and Bob did.[2]

During the rehearsals, that faithful old retainer John Simon sat in the corner of the studio and transcribed each song, later adding horn parts and anything else that was needed to bridge gaps. When Joni Mitchell expressed doubts that The Band were up to backing her on 'Coyote', 'Darkness And Light', and 'Furry Sings The Blues', Simon's arrangements for the songs convinced her that she had nothing to fear. The same procedure applied to the solo spots by Mac Rebennack and Van Morrison, who had just finished working together on the unjustly maligned *Period Of Transition* album, and to the numbers by Dylan, Neil Young, Eric Clapton, and Neil Diamond. In addition, the group held several rehearsals for the horn section, which comprised Howard Johnson on tuba, Tom Malone on trombone, and Jim Gordon on tenor sax, together with L.A. stalwarts Jerry Hey, Rich Cooper, and Charlie Keagle.

By the time The Band had arrived in San Francisco on the evening of Monday 22 November, there were several other old friends on hand besides John Simon. Allen Toussaint had flown in to help with the horn section, and Henry Glover was there to proffer any advice he saw fit. Ed Anderson was serving as chief technical engineer, and co-ordinating the whole spectacle for Bill Graham was Barry Imhoff. What a spectacle it already was. Graham had hired the San Francisco Opera set for Verdi's *La Traviata*, which included kitsch classical statues from the prop department of 20th Century Fox and the chandeliers that had been used in *Gone With The Wind*. 'Without the dinner and the ambience it would just be a musical event,' one of Bill's stooges told Greil Marcus. 'When Bill gets excited about a challenge, money just doesn't matter to him.' As Scorsese gazed at the dark-red hallway entrances and velvet curtains, he smiled. 'It's a strange Visconti kind of setting,' he said. 'I love it.' *Rolling Stone* weren't quite so sure. 'For a while there,' the magazine noted, 'it looked like The Last Waltz might be overtaken by Bill Graham's cornball express.'

There were two nights of rehearsals at Winterland before the show. On the Tuesday, The Band ran through their own opening set, which only departed from their summer tour repertoire with its inclusion of their new single 'Georgia On My Mind'. As Robert Palmer watched them warm up with some makeshift blues shuffles, he was astonished by how 'raw and powerful' they could still sound: it was almost as if he was watching the Hawks he remembered from the Arkansas roadhouse circuit in 1964. On the Wednesday, with most of the guests already encamped at the nearby Mikayo Hotel, the group rehearsed numbers with Eric Clapton, Van Morrison, Joni Mitchell, and Dr John. A late addition to the roster of artists was Bobby Charles, who'd flown in from New Orleans to add more weight to the Crescent City contingent. As the rehearsals continued, an impromptu party began on the floor below. Along with various friends and journalists, there were people like David Bromberg, Michael McClure, and local rock attorney Brian Rohan. Walking around almost unnoticed was none other than Albert Grossman, who'd flown in from New York to watch his adopted sons call it a day. All the while, Scorsese and his cameramen worked at the foot of the stage. In an effort to be less obtrusive, one of the seven cameras was being sunk into a subfloor, with a gazebo constructed around the base. 'We're taking a lot of risks,' Jonathan Taplin told one of the journalists present. 'No one has ever tried to shoot a rock'n'roll film with 35mm. before.'

There were just as many administrative headaches when it came to the food, all $42,000 worth of it. In all, Bill Graham had ordered 220 turkeys, 2,000 lb. of candied yams, 800 lb. of mincemeat and pumpkin pies, 6,000 rolls, 400 gallons of apple juice, 90 gallons of gravy, and yet more hundreds of pounds of stuffing and cranberry sauce. In addition, courtesy of His non-turkey-eating Bobness, 400 lb. of fresh salmon was arriving from the fishery owned by his pal Louie Kemp's family up in Bethel, Alaska. This was going to be some Thanksgiving pig-out.

Dylan himself was busy rehearsing for his Last Waltz spot in the Mikayo Hotel's Osaka Room, running through the songs behind locked doors while a bodyguard stood watch. For all his generosity in donating the salmon, he was proving somewhat obstinate over the terms on which he would allow himself to be filmed. Worried that the film of The Last Waltz – if it ever came out – might clash with his own *Renaldo And Clara*, he had stipulated that Martin Scorsese could only shoot him singing two songs, 'Forever Young' and 'Baby, Let Me Follow You Down'. According to Howard Alk, who'd worked with him on *Renaldo And Clara*, Dylan seemed to feel there was too much footage of him around. Scorsese had little choice but to agree.

*

At 5 p.m. on Thursday 25 November, the doors of Winterland opened and the first of 5,000 ticket holders entered what *Rolling Stone*'s Chris Hodenfield called the 'antebellum ballroom' of The Last Waltz. By 7 p.m. the first Thanksgiving Day dinners were being served, to the accompaniment of the 38-piece Berkeley Promenade Orchestra and three pairs of professional waltzers. To Bill Graham's great chagrin, Martin Scorsese and his crew chose not to film any of the dining or dancing. 'The music was there, but not the whole event,' he complained after watching *The Last Waltz* two years later. Among the diners were Jimmy Cliff, Patti Labelle, actors Brad Dourif and Michael J. Pollard, and Marty Balin of Jefferson Starship.

As each table finished, it was folded up and the chairs were removed. By 9 p.m., the ballroom had resumed its function as a dance-floor, albeit one brimful of people. All of a sudden, a curtain of shimmering confetti was let down in front of the stage, followed immediately by the lowering of the chandeliers. As the confetti cleared, a spotlight picked out Levon behind his drum kit and The Band launched headfirst into one of the rowdiest versions of 'Up On Cripple Creek' they had ever played. Never had Garth's Jew's-harp clavinet gurgled quite so lewdly, or Levon and Rick yodelled with such abandon. As it came crashing to its climax, everyone knew the evening was going to go fine – everyone, that is, except Martin Scorsese and his crew, who couldn't get any of their cues because the applause was so deafening.

After an obligatory 'Shape I'm In' and an impassioned 'It Makes No Difference', the horn section came on for a *Rock Of Ages*-style sequence of Band classics kicking off with 'Life Is A Carnival' and taking in 'This Wheel's On Fire', 'The W. S. Walcott Medicine Show', 'Georgia On My Mind', 'Ophelia', 'King Harvest', 'The Night They Drove Old Dixie Down', 'Stage Fright', and 'Rag Mama Rag'. The best of these were included on the three-album

Last Waltz released in April 1978 – and the very best in Scorsese's film – but there were other highlights for which no room could be found. On 'Georgia', Richard left the piano to John Simon and sang standing at the microphone, for once a proper Soul Man. (His voice, however, gave out on the more demanding 'King Harvest', obliging Rick and Levon to come to his rescue and Robbie to mask the gaps with an extended solo.)

The horns were especially welcome on the full Preservation Hall-style arrangement of 'Ophelia', and on the almost tearful version of 'The Night They Drove Old Dixie Down'. Listening to Levon as he assumed the role of Virgil Caine for the thousandth time, it was unbearable to think that The Band would never perform this song live again. 'There was a lot of love in the performance,' noted Greil Marcus, 'and a certain desperation as well.' The desperation was felt, too, as the lights faded and Rick picked up the thread for 'Stage Fright', the stage illuminated only by the stark spotlight trained on his face. Garth's solo seemed full of terror as the Tom Malone-arranged horns blasted behind him, and when Robbie came in screaming on the final choruses there was a frenzy to his playing that hadn't been heard since Tour '74.

A little after 10 p.m., The Band finished their set on the cheerfully rambunctious note of 'Rag Mama Rag', with Howard Johnson repeating the huff'n'puff tuba marathon he'd endured at the *Rock Of Ages* shows. 'As you mighta heard,' announced Robbie while the applause died down, 'we got a coupla friends joining in with us tonight.' In the wings stood rompin' Ronnie Hawkins, his grizzly visage obscured beneath a giant Stetson and a pair of sunglasses. 'Sixteen years ago when we started,' he heard Robbie saying, 'we started with a guy, and we'd like to start with him – the Hawk!' It said a lot about Robbie's lack of respect for his Falstaffian mentor that he'd momentarily forgotten the intro to the mighty 'Who Do You Love'. Not that Ronnie let it get to him: he was just tickled to death to be here at all. 'Big time, Bill, big time!' he whooped as Robbie finally chopped out those savage Bo Diddley chords. Prowling around the stage and addressing the members of his old band – 'take it easy, Garth, doncha gimme no lip!' – the Hawk was momentarily transported back to those innocently hellraising days on Yonge Street, momentarily able to act like he was the boss all over again. Defusing the potential solemnity of the occasion, he fanned Robbie's Stratocaster with his Stetson as the boy tore into his solo.

It was another bearded hulk who took the stage as Hawkins made his way off it. Wearing his usual beret and shades, together with a huge pink bow-tie, Dr John made his way over to Richard's Steinway and rolled out the irresistible opening chords to 'Such A Night'. The original 'White Negro' from New Orleans, the Doctor sounded blacker with every record he made. This was one of his most endearing and enduring songs, and he milked it for every last drop of lubricious sensuality. When he'd wound up the song with some dazzling piano runs, he switched to guitar to accompany his fellow Louisianan Bobby Charles on the classic 'Down South In New Orleans', replete with fiddle and accordion courtesy of Larry Packer and Garth Hudson. According to Emmett Grogan, it was Charles' first time on a stage in twenty years.

Travelling up the Mississippi from New Orleans to Memphis, the set now took in 'Mystery Train', with Paul Butterfield coming on to blow a storm through his harp. 'I have never heard Butterfield play with such strength,' wrote Greil Marcus. 'His harp was a hoodoo night call hovering over the crowd, cutting through the "event" of The Band's last performance to show why such a performance could have become an "event" in the first place.' For his own part, Levon sang and drummed like a man possessed, wailing for the woman he'd lost to that phantom locomotive. It took a lot to laugh, but it took a train to cry . . .

It was Levon's delta roots that showed through, too, when the august, grey-suited figure of Muddy Waters took the stage to sing the old Louis Jordan chestnut 'Caldonia'. Altogether more thrilling was the version of his anthem 'Mannish Boy', with Robbie punctuating Muddy's every guttural growl and Butterfield adding to the song's relentlessly lurching beat. 'We'd tried three or four songs with Muddy in the Osaka Room,' recalled Robbie. 'I'd really wanted to do "40 Days", but Butterfield said there's nothing in the world like Muddy doing "Mannish Boy" – or at least, nothing like it if you don't drive the poor man until he has a heart attack.' Which was what Muddy sounded in grave danger of giving himself as he howled and stamped his way through the last minute of the song.

The look of nervous bliss on Robbie's face during 'Mannish Boy' said everything about his emotional state onstage. On the one hand he was watching an extraordinary dream come true, and on the other there was still an eternity to go before they were out of the woods. 'It was "so far, so good" as we were going along,' he said later. 'I mean, we'd had to learn some twenty-odd songs we'd never played before in our lives, so every time out of the chute it was like throwing the dice. It seemed hard enough to remember our own stuff, let alone everyone from Muddy Waters to Joni Mitchell.' Down below the stage, meanwhile, Martin Scorsese was feeling the same mixture of dread and euphoria as Robbie. Despite having to abandon all his meticulously scripted cues, he knew he was getting some marvellous footage. What really fascinated him was the very reality of performing onstage: the mistakes, the nervous glances between the players, Robbie's moments of panic. When Eric Clapton followed Muddy Waters on to the stage and broke his strap midway through a solo on 'Further Up The Road', Scorsese was delighted. Later an editor suggested cutting it out, to which Scorsese responded: 'Are you kidding? When have I ever seen Eric Clapton's guitar fall off?!'

Starting with 'All Our Past Times', the song he'd written with Rick at Shangri-La, Clapton launched into 'Further Up The Road' with a searingly fluid solo. 'Kick the fucking shit out of it, Eric,' shouted Robbie, who then suddenly had to take over as Clapton's strap gave way. Watching the pair of them sparring together made for a telling study in contrast, Clapton all detached poise and control, Robbie all hectic spirit and attack. As Alastair Dougall once observed, there had always been something of the enthusiastic amateur in Robbie Robertson's playing, and nowhere was that better illustrated than here.

For Greil Marcus, The Last Waltz degenerated into mere West Coast stargazing with the performances of Neil Young, Joni Mitchell, and Neil Diamond. Singing the CSNY song 'Helpless', Young established a Canadian connection, but otherwise seemed faintly irrelevant as he joined the two Band guitarists at Rick's mic to sob the song's monotonous chorus in his high, fragile voice. After he'd followed through with the Ian Tyson song 'Four Strong Winds', Joni Mitchell came on with her central parting and her severe cheekbones and kicked into 'Coyote', a song which – with its allusions to drugs and all-night studio sessions – could almost have been read as a veiled comment on The Last Waltz itself. As Mitchell was to observe some years later, nothing killed the spirit of West Coast rock in the '70s more effectively than cocaine. She loved The Band for what they were, but felt as intolerant as Robbie himself did of their sloppy approach to rehearsing. All her doubts about the group's ability to do justice to the complex nuances of her music were borne out when they came to 'Darkness And Light' and 'Furry Sings The Blues', songs which in any case had only the most tenuous connection with The Band. Still, at least she looked like a rock'n'roll hippie maiden: when Neil Diamond came on to declaim 'Dry Your Eyes' he looked more like a movie producer than a musician.

Van Morrison, who was due on next, almost didn't make The Last Waltz. 'Twenty minutes before he was supposed to go on he just disappeared,' recalled Harvey Goldsmith, who at the time had the thankless task of managing the man. 'He ran back to the hotel, decided he didn't look right, and changed. Then he wasn't going to do it. I literally went to the hotel, got him back and virtually pushed him on to the stage.' As Van was thrust on, John Simon was at the piano and Richard was finishing the second verse of a soulful Irish lullaby called 'Too Ra Loo Ra Loo Ral' – for Mac Rebennack the 'high spot' of the whole evening. It was no wonder that he'd been concerned about his appearance, squeezed as his stumpy figure was into a hideous maroon suit; as for so many of its other participants, The Last Waltz marked for Van a high watermark of sartorial bad taste in the '70s. But once he opened his mouth and let out his first roar, all the fears were dispelled and he instantly became as integral a part of the proceedings as anyone else. 'It was one of the most magical performances I've ever seen him do,' said Goldsmith. 'He went out there and really stormed the place. All the artists like Clapton, Dylan, and Joni were standing in a little area on the side and everybody came out to watch him. To a person, they all stood up and roared with the audience.'

There were even more roars from the audience when Rick and Robbie cranked out the intro to 'Caravan'. With John Simon virtually conducting the band and the horns from the side, Van gave it his all, climaxing the song by kicking his little legs in the air like a would-be Rockette. In ten minutes he managed not only to push The Last Waltz to the brink of emotional uproar but to restore all the standing he'd ever had with the American rock press. 'I don't usually come out in situations like that,' he said later. 'I didn't want the promotion, but it was the right situation because of something karmic. One of the basic principles is that it wasn't a hype. Robbie didn't want to hype it and it wasn't hyped, it was a pure situation. That show couldn't be *done* – it was something that *happened*.' As Van left the stage to further cheers, Robbie announced that they were going to do 'another Canadian song, with two fellow Canadians'. Neil and Joni dutifully wandered back on to supply added harmonies for 'Acadian Driftwood', a song that once again proved too delicate and intricate for successful translation to live performance – hence its non-inclusion either in the film or on the album.

'Driftwood' was followed by a forty-minute intermission, during which various veterans of the North Beach beat scene read poems. Introduced by Emmett Grogan, who in his own words 'drew a kind of frame around them, explaining who they were and what they meant to our generation', the poets represented San Francisco's only real contribution to The Last Waltz, since none of the great Bay Area bands were invited or were available to pay their tributes. First up was Hell's Angel Sweet William, who'd seen the Hawks with Dylan in 1965 and whose offering was carved in wood. After a poem about 'JOY!' from Lenore Kandel, Michael McClure read from the Prologue to *The Canterbury Tales*, drawing a loose parallel between Chaucer's motley band of pilgrims and the gathering of celebrities at Winterland. Finally, following on the heels of Diane DiPrima, the grand old man of the beat scene Lawrence Ferlinghetti came on to recite his toothlessly subversive reworking of the Lord's Prayer. What Levon made of these woolly-headed old pseuds was never too clear, but they presumably fulfilled some need in Robbie to bring all the arts under the all-embracing umbrella of The Last Waltz.

As ever, it was Garth Hudson who picked up the slack. Swaying from side to side, with long strands of hair unpeeling themselves from his domelike forehead, he magicked up a 'Genetic Method' the crowd would never forget. As Robert Palmer remarked in his notes to the double *Anthology* album compiled to tie in with the release of *The Last Waltz*, 'by this time Garth had begun mixing organ, synths, and pre-recorded tapes of Tibetan monks and a cow mooing for effects that were truly otherworldly'. After the umpteenth version of 'Chest Fever', the band felt confident enough to play three sections of the sequence that would form 'The Last Waltz Suite' on the studio side of the album: 'Evangeline', a country story-song Robbie had just completed; the 'Last Waltz' itself, an Anton Karas-style instrumental more than a little reminiscent of the *Third Man* theme; and a 'refrain' which had only been finished that morning. After 'The Weight', which would itself be incorporated into 'The Last Waltz Suite' in a magnificent new version featuring the Staple Singers, Robbie announced that they had one more special guest they wanted to bring on. To howls of hysterical delight, a very longhaired Bob Dylan ambled on to the stage in a white pimp's hat and the kind of polka-dot shirt he'd worn so often on the tours of '65 and '66.

Dylan's appearance immediately threw the film crew into confusion. Not wanting to jeopardize the film, Martin Scorsese had asked whether he would receive any signals to indicate when he could start shooting Dylan. 'Well, yeah, kind of,' was the none-too-helpful reply from the Dylan camp. 'When he came on, it was so loud on the stage I didn't know *what* to do,' Scorsese recalled. 'Bill Graham was next to me shouting "Shoot him! He comes from the same streets as you, don't let him push you around". But as I said to the guys later, we had a seven-hour concert and I didn't want to press it.' Fortunately, Scorsese got his cues right and shot the two songs Dylan had specified.

The first was Dylan's opener, 'Baby, Let Me Follow You Down', as rough and acerbic as it had ever sounded in '65 and '66. His guitar was so loud in the mix that it drowned everybody else out, but it didn't seem to matter. Next up was 'Hazel' – perhaps the least interesting song from *Planet Waves* – quickly redeemed by 'I Don't Believe You', a second throwback to the glorious sonic assault of 1965. To hear the band on this song – to hear Garth's organ and Levon's locomotive triplets and Robbie's staccato guitar fills – was to be instantly transported back to those first electric shows eleven years earlier. When the audience had recovered, it was time to simmer down again, this time with the tentative opening chords of the anthemic, arm-wave-inspiring 'Forever Young'. In Scorsese's film, the camera pans down dramatically on to Dylan's head as though consecrating him, and the passion of the performance almost justified such veneration. Dylan almost sang the roof off Winterland, and Robbie responded with two choked solos before the band piled back into a reprise of 'Baby, Let Me Follow You Down'.

Dylan had been onstage almost twenty minutes when Robbie asked him to stay and lead the all-star finale of 'I Shall Be Released'. Slowly, the stage filled up with the other guests, who gathered around The Band and Dylan to make up what now looks like a missing link between The Concert For Bangladesh and Live Aid. Looking at them all huddled round microphones in their scarves and flared trousers was like witnessing the Last Supper of '70s rock'n'roll. Already punk was beginning to overthrow the old dinosaurs of West Coast rock, but here they all were taking a final heroic stand against the blank generation, one of them coming on with a lump of coke so big sticking out of his nose that Scorsese had to doctor the film when he came to edit it. 'No future for you,' the punks railed, yet with hindsight The Last Waltz was a harbinger of survival, an ancestor of all the superstar jam sessions that came to dominate the post-Live Aid music scene in the '80s.

With Ringo Starr and Ronnie Wood joining the throng of famous faces, Dylan took the first verse of 'Released', joined on the chorus by the cacophonous supporting cast. Completely obscured by Neil Diamond, Joni Mitchell, and Neil Young, Richard sang the second verse in his croakiest baritone, then switched to falsetto to share the third with Dylan. Somewhere at the back of the crowd one could make out the Stetson of Ronnie Hawkins, who did not presume to add his voice to those of the rock immortals. Looking a little harder you could even see

Governor Jerry Brown, waving discreetly at the side of Rolling Thunder veteran Ronee Blakely. When it was all over, The Band bid their adieus. 'Thank you . . . goodnight . . . goodbye,' said Robbie.

But it wasn't quite goodbye. Barely had the stage been cleared when Levon and Ringo fired up a jam session. 'Ringo started laying into the drums, lickety-splitting a funky rock beat with Levon,' wrote Emmett Grogan. 'Ronnie Wood popped up from nowhere, Clapton came back. On came Mac, Butterfield, Carl Radle, Neil Young, Steve Stills, and various other Band members.' After half an hour of meandering solos by the very people who would prove so ubiquitous at charity rock gatherings a decade later, The Band brought The Last Waltz to a close with a version of 'Don't Do It' that testified to both their exhaustion and their relief that it was finally all over. By 2.20 a.m., Bill Graham had wrapped it all up and The Band were en route back to the Mikayo for a party that lasted most of the night. Dylan, affably drunk, waxed nostalgic about his chums and talked excitedly of his Rolling Thunder film. He was still dancing – by himself – when breakfast was being served the next morning.

That night, Ted Nugent played Winterland. It was back to rock'n'roll business as usual.

After the Waltz

You must, after the age of 33, continue to do a certain type of work, or else go into the shoe business; forget music or it'll turn into hatred, or else reiteration, redundancy, and in many cases death.

Garth Hudson, 1984

The Last Waltz was over, but the long gestation of *The Last Waltz* was only just beginning. Not only did The Band have to wait till the New Year for Martin Scorsese to finish editing *New York, New York*, but Robbie was bubbling with new ideas for both the film and album of the show that would add further time and expense. For starters, it seemed to him that two key musical ingredients in The Band's music – country and gospel – had not been properly represented in the film. Everything else was there, from blues to rockabilly to Tin Pan Alley, but there was nothing to explain the gospel flavour of 'The Weight' or 'We Can Talk', nothing that had any bearing on the country harmonies of 'Rockin' Chair' or 'Ain't No More Cane (On The Brazos)'.

Secondly, Robbie had various musical ideas and sketches for songs that he wanted to use for a 'Last Waltz Suite' on the final side of the album. These included the 'Last Waltz Theme' and 'Refrain' that The Band had performed in makeshift versions in the second half of the show, as well as two completely new Band songs, 'The Well' and 'Out Of The Blue'. Gradually, it dawned on him that he could kill two birds with one stone by incorporating country and gospel numbers into this 'suite'. Everyone in the group was agreed that there could be no more fitting guest artists for a 'gospel' track than the Staple Singers, whose overlapping, gut-instinct vocal arrangements had made such an impact on them when they were still the Hawks. As for the country song – 'Evangeline', also performed at The Last Waltz – Emmylou Harris seemed an obvious contender to sing it with Rick and Levon.

By the time Scorsese was finished with *New York, New York*, Robbie had talked the Staples into singing on a new version of 'The Weight', and Emmylou into duetting on 'Evangeline'. The version of 'The Weight' was pure Baptist church, with Mavis and Pops each taking a verse and all four of the Staples whooping and hollering interjections as the song built to its climax. 'Beautiful,' Mavis whispered after the voices had finally died away. The singing was just as lovely on 'Evangeline', which Rick commenced in his best 'Long Black Veil' manner and Emmylou picked up for the second verse. With Richard on drums, Garth on accordion, Levon on mandolin, and Rick overdubbing fiddle, The Band updated the string-band bluegrass sound of 'Ain't No More Cane' to sublime effect.

With the *Last Waltz* project sold to United Artists, Robbie was able to raise enough money for Scorsese to shoot new footage at MGM. 'Marty had always said, "Let's see if we can do something really different",' says Jonathan Taplin. 'So we wound up with Emmylou and the Staples on a sound stage in front of 250 people.' Robbie had envisioned the setting for 'Evangeline' as 'this area in the Everglades, a bayou that you visualize in a misty way', and Scorsese shot Emmylou and The Band accordingly, draping them in dry ice and pale blue light. Levon was in seventh heaven during the filming. 'I just sat around waiting to sing harmonies with Mavis Staples and Emmylou Harris,' he said; 'what more could you ask for?' Between them, the two women seemed to symbolize the twin poles of his musical experience as a Southerner. For Greil Marcus, moreover, the revisited 'Weight' symbolized the 'pluralism and community' at the heart of The Band's greatest music: when the group took the stage with the Staple Singers, they brought together men and women, whites and blacks, young and old, North and South, creating 'a parable of their career, and an elegy for it'. Elegiac or not, it made a magnificent spectacle, with Mavis completely losing herself in the song. It certainly made a lot more sense than Aretha Franklin's version.

Robbie wasn't finished yet. Having worked the crucial country and gospel influences into the film, he now wanted to include some interviews with The Band as well: rather than just being a concert film, he wanted *The Last Waltz* to tell the group's story. Scorsese liked the idea, but was less taken with the suggestion that he interview the band himself. 'They were very quiet, very formidable,' he said. 'Especially Levon, who didn't want to talk about *anything* to *anybody*, no how!' When Robbie begged him to do it, United Artists came up with more money and a small film crew was duly dispatched to Shangri-La.

Getting The Band to co-operate with the filming was no easy matter. 'I had two 35mm. cameras all the time on the guys, and I just didn't know what they were going to do next,' Scorsese recalled. 'Robbie was all right and got into it. Rick was fun, but he'd suddenly get up and walk down the hall, and I had to walk with him.' The other three played much harder-to-get, Richard because he was soused, Levon because he didn't talk to nobody no how, and Garth because he didn't talk. 'I was there and knew I had to be there,' says Garth, 'but I hated it and tried to avoid it. Finally they caught me and sat me down at six in the morning. I didn't want to say anything, and I hated what I did say. I should have sat down and written it out.'

The most revealing scenes Scorsese caught were the ones where all five members sat together and traded tales of old times: the first impressions of big bad New York City, the shoplifting excursions in food marts. Significantly, Robbie either stood at the back or walked around, playing up shamelessly to the camera and emphasizing his distance from the others. Richard looked like a twinkly-eyed tramp stroking his beard, the others treating him with the fond indulgence accorded a backward child. When Rick talked about having 'too much fun', Richard and Levon burst into naughty-schoolboy guffaws; Robbie and Garth barely smiled. 'Ah thought we were supposed to pan away from that sorta stuff,' grinned Levon when Scorsese asked them about women. Watching the interactions between the five of them, one could see the little allegiances and divisions that had undermined their unity and fraternity.

Gradually, Scorsese built up the wide assortment of interviews he would use to punctuate the songs from The Last Waltz: conversations with individual members, or with two or three of them at a time; an impromptu Appalachian-style jam by Rick, Robbie, and Richard. When the time came to insert these segments into the film, he was able to link each interview or anecdote with a particular song or performer. Reminiscences of Sonny Boy Williamson in Helena prefaced 'Mystery Train', while Garth's ruminations on jazz led perfectly into 'Ophelia'. Immediately after The Band had been chortling about women on the road, on came Joni Mitchell, that least groupie-like of female performers. As Robbie and Marty worked on the film through 1977, all the pieces began to fall into place.

One of the individual interviews in *The Last Waltz* was with Rick, who was seen playing pool and leading Scorsese down Shangri-La's corridors to the studio itself. Asked what he'd been doing since The Last Waltz, he replied: 'Oh, makin' music . . . just tryin' to stay busy.' He then proceeded to play Scorsese a few bars from 'Sip The Wine', a song he was cutting for his first solo album. Rick had been the first of the Band members to sign a solo deal –

with Clive Davis' new Arista label – and he was already putting together the tracks for the eponymous debut. As far back as 1972, when he was co-producing Bobby Charles' album at Bearsville, he'd known that he wanted to make his own record. 'I've been likely working on this album all my life' he was to tell Mikal Gilmore. 'For me to sing three or four songs a year, do some background vocals, and not go on tour, just isn't enough to keep my mind occupied.' Rick told Gilmore that it was hard to 'grab anybody's attention' in The Band, and that he'd ended up turning to friends like Bobby Charles and Emmett Grogan for help with his songs. 'I mean, I *love* playing with The Band,' he added hastily. 'I'm sure they would never abandon me, and I would never want to abandon them, but it's a very collective thing and I'm only one-fifth of it.'

Using a motley crew of musicians – everyone from his brother Terry to Doug Sahm and the other members of The Band – Rick cut a collection of rather nondescript songs with lyrics by Bobby Charles and Emmett Grogan. The Bobby Charles songs, which included the old favourite 'Small Town Talk', were the most soulfully downhome and Band-like. On the laid-back 'New Mexicoe' [sic], Garth contributed a delicate accordion part and Eric Clapton added a discreet guitar solo. Robbie's harmonics were unmistakable on the funky 'Java Blues', ex-junkie Grogan's hymn to the 'volcanic rush' of caffeine. On the opening 'What A Town', it was Ronnie Wood who did the six-string honours. Better as songs, and as vocal performances, were the wistful ballad 'Sweet Romance' and the slightly Steely Dan-esque 'Tired Of Waiting'. 'Shake It', featuring Richard on Fender Rhodes piano and America's Gerry Beckley on guitar and backing vocals, was archetypal West Coast soft-rock, but the closing 'Once Upon A Time', with Levon supplying harmony, was Danko at his 'Unfaithful Servant'-style best. All in all, a pretty muted affair, and one that managed to climb no higher than # 119 on the *Billboard* chart.

Levon Helm had followed Rick's example and signed to the

ABC label, for whom he now began work on his RCO All-Stars album. The All-Stars were a dream aggregation of his favourite musicians, American legends who also happened to be pals. Some of them were veterans of the all-star Last Waltz itself – Mac Rebennack and Paul Butterfield, natch – but a real coup was the involvement of all three surviving members of Booker T. and the MGs: Duck Dunn, Steve Cropper, and Booker T. Jones himself. Finally, in addition to hornmen Howard Johnson, Tom Malone, Lou Marini, and Alan Rubin, there were two men who went back a long way with Levon: Henry Glover, who came in on the project as Levon's 'Band Master', and Fred Carter Jr, Robbie's predecessor in the Hawks and now a successful sessionman-producer in Nashville. The band had first assembled for *Saturday Night Live* on 19 March, but in the early summer of 1977 they came together in twos and threes to record their parts for cover versions of 'Milk Cow Boogie' and 'Havana Moon', and for such originals as Booker T.'s 'You Got Me' and the Mac Rebennack/ Bobby Charles song 'The Tie That Binds'. Given the obvious difficulties of bringing together such busy musicians, only half of *Levon Helm and The RCO All-Stars* was actually cut at Levon's spanking-new RCO studio in Woodstock. The other half was recorded back at Shangri-La, thus making it possible for Robbie and Garth to guest on the stomping version of Earl King's 'Sing, Sing, Sing (Let's Make A Better World)'.

Despite being a kind of missing link between The Last Waltz and *The Blues Brothers*, the All-Stars album only confirmed what one had always suspected, which was that Levon's musical ambitions did not extend much beyond good-time bar-band rhythm and blues. The music was fun at best, lazy at worst. 'With the All-Stars, I felt strength in numbers,' he said. 'It's just a hell of a lot more fun to cut up anything with your friends, no matter how good or bad you do it by yourself. The better it is by yourself, the more lonesome it is.' What Levon might also have admitted was that he found it difficult to write songs on his own: out of the album's ten tracks only the very primitive 'Blues So Bad' so much as boasted a co-credit for him.

Lazy or not, Levon was determined to launch the All-Stars with a bang at the RCO Studio. The barnlike edifice, built with the finest lumber the Catskills could offer, was the pride and joy of his life, and he was damned if he wasn't going to show it off. On Saturday, 27 August, with the music industry still reeling from the shock of Elvis Presley's death, a posse of rock journalists was bussed up to Woodstock from New York for a 'million-dollar bash' on Levon's Plochmann Lane estate. In typical Helm style there was an enormous barbecue, with burgers, hot dogs, and buttered corn provided for all. After lunch, while his kids Amy and Ezra bashed out 'Wild Thing' with Ronnie Hawkins Jr on drums, Levon tooled around the grounds in his jeep, at one point emerging from the woods with none other than Robbie Robertson in the passenger seat. At dusk, the All-Stars – or at least Reben-nack, Butterfield, Cropper, Dunn, and Carter – finally plugged in and cooked up some prime country funk for the scribes, who sat swilling beer on hay bales. Around 8.30 p.m., Ronnie Hawkins heaved his bulk on to the stage and joined the gang for a few old songs, after which there was a modest fireworks display. At 10 p.m., T-shirts were distributed commemorating 'The First Annual RCO/ABC Picnic & Rodeo', and by 11 p.m. the last press-junket bus was pulling out on to Plochmann Lane.

Unfortunately, none of this transplanted Southern hospitality helped push *Levon Helm And The RCO All-Stars* further than #142 on the album chart, although a handful of memorable live dates almost compensated for the disappointing sales. 'We were able to match everyone's schedules there for a while,' said Levon. 'The tour went quite well but in the end there were too many different schedules and plans to keep it together – too many chiefs and not enough injuns!'

*

Although Robbie was still talking about 'the next Band album' when *The Last Waltz* was released in the summer of 1978, the prospect of such a thing ever materializing already seemed remote. 'It's not necessary to break up,' he'd said at the time of the concert itself. 'It would just be a silly emotional outburst . . . we don't have to break up the band to get that sense of relief everyone is striving for.' But now everyone seemed to be pulling apart, not least Robbie himself, whose 'sense of relief' was undoubtedly the greatest out of the five of them. 'Part of the idea behind The Last Waltz was that afterwards everyone would have the chance to grow and educate themselves a little bit more,' he has said. 'The idea was that we wouldn't go on the road any more, but that we would continue to make music together and share it in more modern technology through the video process or through film. At a certain point everybody was supposed to meet back at the corral, but as solo projects came up we kind of dispersed and never got to regroup. Everyone became *more* distant.'

The truth was actually a little more complicated. Finally freed of his responsibility for The Band, Robbie was letting rip in a way he'd never been able to do before: in fact, he was partying – and every night – in the company of Martin Scorsese. It was as though he'd had to wait over sixteen years to begin the rowdy adolescence he'd never had. The two of them made a curious double-act, a tall Jewish-Amerindian and a tiny, hyper-intense Italian, but *The Last Waltz* had brought them closer together than either could have foreseen. If it was a kind of midlife crisis for both men, they certainly made the most of it, running around like two wild bachelors as they worked together on their film. In Marty's unassuming Mulholland Drive house, perched on the side of a canyon, the pair of them indulged in two-man cocaine orgies that lasted most of every night. 'There was a period there where Robbie and Marty saw the sun come up every day for at least six months, maybe longer,' says Jonathan Taplin. 'They were the two craziest guys anybody ever saw. It was major coke binges, waking up editors in the middle of the night, a complete bachelors' paradise.'

Indeed, it wasn't long before both men had separated from their wives and families and Robbie moved into the Mulholland Drive house permanently. 'We saw ourselves as "misunderstood artists", and our wives threw us out,' Robbie recalled. 'We were just kind of lost in the storm. You're a tame house pet and you get thrown out in the woods, pretty soon you're not tame any more.' As costs on *The Last Waltz* mounted to $1.5m, they continued to live it up, sometimes in the company of certain well-known actresses, though more often they simply entertained themselves with all-night screenings of classic movies. 'I had always been a film buff, and he was a music buff,' said Robbie. 'When I moved into the house I brought these huge studio speakers into the living room, and on the other side of the house he turned a bedroom into a screening room. The screen was a whole bedroom wall.' At their disposal, Robbie and Marty had an entire library of films that they'd borrowed from MGM: Buñuel and Jean Renoir, Sam Fuller and cult vampire films. 'Marty had things to do on the film, I had things to do on the soundtrack album,' Robbie remembered. 'We'd get back to the house around midnight and have dinner. Then in the middle of the night we'd screen a movie or two. We'd watch them until it seemed like the sun was going to start coming up. It was like "Uh-oh" and we'd have to scatter.'

The pair of them were like a married couple: if Robbie got home later than expected, Scorsese would be pacing the floor and demanding an explanation. Finally, blackout covers were put on the windows and an interior air system installed, so that neither of them ever had the first idea whether it was day or night. Everywhere you looked in the house there were movie posters on the walls: *Rebel Without A Cause*, *Saraband For Dead Lovers*, Marty's own *Mean Streets*. In the bathroom, Robert Donat leered down at you with the legend, 'Phantom Lover or Evil Genius?' under his face. If a movie wasn't playing, there was invariably music booming out from Robbie's sound system. When Greil Marcus came to interview them shortly before the release of *The Last Waltz*, they played Van Morrison's *Astral Weeks* at deafening volume while Scorsese explained that he'd based the first fifteen minutes of *Taxi Driver* on the album. 'Marty has an extraordinary knowledge of music, from obscure New York punk to street-corner vocal groups,' Robbie told Marcus. 'He's been into new music since the very beginning of the punk thing, and he brings me tapes.' After *Astral Weeks*, Robbie put on Ray Charles' 'What Would I Do Without You', a mournful blues ballad which had appeared on the flipside of his 1956 hit 'Hallelujah, I Love Her So'. As they listened, Robbie told Marcus that there was 'more heroin in it than in anything you'll ever hear'.

Things came to a head when *The Last Waltz* was finally released in the early spring of 1978. Flying all over America and Europe to promote the film, the two men were close to being out of control. 'Seems like there was always a commotion wherever we went,' said Robbie. 'One minute Marty would be laughing, the next he'd be throwing telephones out of the window. Everywhere I looked there were people doing drugs and alcohol.' When they returned to L.A., an article appeared in a Californian magazine blowing the lid on their debaucheries. Scorsese wanted to sue, but Robbie advised him not to. Not long afterwards, the asthmatic director wound up in hospital. 'It was either change your lifestyle or die,' Robbie recalled. 'I remember seeing him in the hospital and thinking, "Boy, this is definitely the end of an era, right here".'

Fortunately for both of them, *The Last Waltz* elicited almost uniformly rave reviews from rock critics and film critics alike, many of whom thought it the finest rock'n'roll movie to date. 'It is not merely the best rock-concert movie ever made,' said the *Village Voice*; 'it is as intensely personal as anything Scorsese has done.' Everyone was agreed that Scorsese had transcended the limitations of the genre and fashioned a spectacle that caught both the sweep of the band's history and the edgy reality of live performance. 'It doesn't *look* like a rock'n'roll movie,' observed Greil Marcus. 'There's no hand-held camerawork, it's all smooth dolly shots, zooms, and framed images. Instead of simply watching people play music, we often get to see how the music is made. We pick up the cues one musician tosses to another, the moments of uncertainty and panicky improvisation.' Film critics were particularly struck by Robbie's smouldering, heavy-lidded presence in the film, marking him out for future movie roles.

There were only a few dissenting voices, though they were authoritative ones. Dave Marsh, writing with the hindsight that punk had given him, lamented Scorsese's neglect of the Last Waltz audience, which only emphasized the degree to which the celebrities seemed to be playing for each other rather than for their fans. As one of the few rock writers who took Robbie's estimation of himself with a large pinch of salt, Marsh was scathing about the 'sycophantish' interview footage and the manner in which Scorsese had filmed the Band guitarist as a kind of 'devotional object'. He also felt that at the heart of *The Last Waltz* lay a profound fraud, which was the assumption that the concert had been 'a momentous event in the history of rock': in fact, he said, the general sense at the time had been that the show was 'a bit boring, far too long, confused, a prime example of The Band taking its stature as an institution far too seriously'. Ending on an even more savage note, Marsh opined that 'as a chronicle of a certain group of once-important musical figures, *The Last Waltz* is a weird sort of triumph: those dark spaces are perfect for a gang of aesthetic bankrupts trying to hide from a world where there's no future for them.' Perhaps Scorsese himself, with his taste for punk rock, had taken to heart the Sex Pistols' chant 'No Future For You'.[1]

In *Rolling Stone* of all places, Jim Miller adopted the same iconoclastic, Sacred Cow-bashing tone in his review of the *Last Waltz* triple album. Writing in the very issue that carried myth-reinforcing pieces on The Band by Robert Palmer and Chris Hodenfield, Miller argued that the whole Last Waltz event was nothing more than a 'self-serving elegy' to the moment The Band had 'seized' back in 1968. Throughout the six sides of the album, he wrote, 'there is an earnest and turgid air about the proceedings – and that air, one fears, may just be The Band's special signature'. For Miller, the group only really came alive on the record with the 'galvanic' Dylan, who alone pushed them to performances that were 'full-blooded, eloquent, and forceful'. Finally, and most damningly of all, Miller compared the *Last Waltz* album to other 'coffee-table' artifacts like *Woodstock* and *The Concert For Bangladesh*: 'Like them, The Band's farewell seems destined merely to quench a momentary craving for nostalgia, only to be stuffed away on a shelf, unlistened to and forgotten.' (Not even the inclusion of 'The Well' and 'Out Of The Blue', new songs which were vastly superior to anything on *Islands*, was enough to redeem the album for Miller. 'The Well' was a funky, intense number sung by Richard, 'Out Of The Blue' a soulful, Lennonesque ballad providing Robbie with his third lead vocal in The Band's oeuvre.)

These were merciless drubbings, to be sure, though both said more about The Band's 'Sacred Cow' status than about a film which, hoax or no hoax, remains riveting after almost twenty years. In any case, Robbie was hardly about to lose sleep over such attacks, since *The Last Waltz* had put him precisely where he wanted to be: in the biz-speak jargon of '90s Hollywood, he was 'a player', a hot property. 'When *The Last Waltz* came out, there were all these articles talking about how I supposedly had all this "charisma",' he remembers. 'Believe me, I took a lot of teasing for this. I'd get in a car, and my buddies would say, "Wait, wait, be careful, you're getting some of that charisma on me – would you move over, please?"' MGM weren't teasing, however. They not only inundated him with movie scripts and offers but gave him Carole Lombard's old dressing-room as an office. 'Marty thought the whole thing was very funny and felt totally responsible for this change in my life,' he said in 1983. 'I'd never even thought about acting before, and suddenly I was being bombarded with all this stuff. Of course, most of the scripts were about screwed-up rock stars overdosing on drugs, and that was the one thing I was determined not to do.' In the end, Robbie spent almost two years reading scripts, talking to agents, flying to meet directors, all to no avail. The biggest problem was his inability to conceive of himself as a 'hired gun'. 'It's not in my nature to show up at seven in the morning and be told what to do,' he told Robin Denselow. 'I'm used to initiating things.'

While Robbie killed time in Tinseltown, the other Band members 'stayed busy'. Rick continued to tour on the back of his solo album, and Levon made sporadic appearances with and without the RCO All-Stars. After a big *Rock Of Ages*-style bash at New York's Palladium on New Year's Eve, 1977, Levon and the All-Stars supported Neil Young on a 23-date tour lasting from February though to April, resurrecting such Band staples as 'Ophelia', 'The Weight', and 'Back To Memphis' alongside 'Milk Cow Boogie' and 'The Mood I Was In'. In the summer, he began work on his second album for ABC, calling it simply *Levon Helm*. Recorded this time at Cherokee Studios in Hollywood and Muscle Shoals Sound in Alabama, the album was produced by Duck Dunn with a little help from fellow Southern luminaries like Steve Cropper, Barry Beckett, David Hood, and Roger Hawkins. 'Muscle Shoals was a great tonic for me,' said Levon. 'They really have the equipment and the know-how down there. There's no distractions. It's a pretty place with a lot of water, mountains, and good food.' Sadly, the surroundings inspired almost as bland a collection of songs as one had heard on the *RCO All-Stars* album: a dash of New Orleans funk on Allen Toussaint's 'Play Something Sweet', some cloying country-soul balladry on Tony Joe White's 'I Came Here To Party'. Even the version of Al Green's immortal 'Take Me To The River' lacked any real grit, while the Gerry Goffin-Barry Goldberg song 'Audience For My Pain' seemed hopelessly unsuited to Levon's vocal style. Only 'Standing On A Mountaintop', the reggae-fied Cate Brothers song he'd drummed on back in 1975, stood out as truly satisfying, with Earl and Ernie Cate howling soulfully along in the background.

If Garth managed to occupy himself with sessions for friends like Van Morrison (*Wavelength*) and Emmylou Harris (*Quarter Moon In A Ten Cent Town*), Richard was sinking fast. Having been abandoned for the last time by Jane, who had taken the children back to Toronto, he'd hooked up with a rock'n'roll groupie named Arlie and was drinking and drugging himself senseless. Ronnie Hawkins caught wind of a rumour that he was dead: 'I called him up and said, "Where do you want the flowers sent?" And Beak said, "If they're poppies, you can send 'em right now!"' At the end of August, Richard finally entered a detox programme and sobered up for the first time in years, emerging to play shows around L. A. with an *ad hoc* combo he christened The Pencils. In October, a fire at Garth's ranch destroyed many of the Hudsons' and Manuels' possessions, prompting Garth and Maude to move to nearby Agoura Hills.

1979 continued in the same vein, with no sign of any official Band product on the horizon. 'I like to think we'll get back together,' said Levon poignantly, 'but I've learned over the years it's best not to push. So I try to stay ready and hope for the best.' Robbie was still talking about the *Works* project – 'a symphony opera of this music I know, done in the traditional sense but dealing with my influences' – but it was still only '80 per cent finished' after all these years. Garth did sessions for Hoyt Axton,

Karla Bonoff, Leonard Cohen, even Ronnie Hawkins. Rick began gigging with his favourite drinking pal Paul Butterfield, and Levon hung out with the Cates, contributed backing vocals to their Tom Dowd-produced Atlantic album *Fire On The Tracks*. By the summer, Levon was gigging regularly with the Cates. 'When I'm working, I feel successful,' he told an interviewer. 'When I'm not, I feel useless as hell.'

Levon's biggest break came when his Woodstock neighbour Brad Dourif introduced him to fellow actor Tommy Lee Jones. The two of them hit it off, and Jones recommended Levon for the role of Loretta Lynn's father in Michael Apted's *Coal Miner's Daughter*. The next thing he knew, Levon was on a plane to Nashville, where he duly read for the part of Ted Webb. (When Loretta Lynn first set eyes on Levon she burst into tears, so strikingly did he resemble her father.) 'I left thinking that was the end of a brief and sweet affair between movies and myself,' he said. 'But a month later I got a call to return to Nashville, and suddenly we were filming. I guess some people thought it was going to be another hokey movie like *The Hank Williams Story*, but once I saw the script and how they were handling it I knew different.' En route to the film's first location in Wise, Virginia, Tommy Lee Jones gave Levon a crash course in acting technique.

Levon took to acting like a duck to water. 'It was purty easy,' he said affably. 'You got someone combing your hair, someone telling you what to wear, and someone telling you what to say.' That was plenty good enough for ol' Levon, who was to make a comfortable living for a few years as a decent, God-fearin' cracker in denim overalls. 'I got lucky with the critics,' he said after the film opened to excellent reviews. 'If another good-ol'-boy role comes up and it doesn't take too much time, I'll jump on it.' Only once during the filming of *Coal Miner's Daughter* did the drummer speak his mind, and that was when he was lying in a coffin listening to his mourners singing 'Amazing Grace'. 'Ah figured that it was my funeral,' he laughed, 'and I wanted the song sung the way I liked it: the traditional, old-fashioned way. I just got up, with my gone-for-good make-up on, and we worked it out, sang it a few times, and then I got back in the coffin.'

Given the natural Appalachian twang in his voice, it only made sense that Levon should contribute a song to the *Coal Miner's Daughter* soundtrack. Thus it was that he found himself in Nashville's legendary Bradley's Barn studios cutting a superb version of Bill Monroe's 'Blue Moon Of Kentucky'. Produced by his old pal Fred Carter Jr, the session went so well that they decided to cut a few more songs while they were at it. 'Once we did "Blue Moon" we figured, why not put a little hay in the barn,' said Levon. 'Two weeks later we'd laid down twenty tracks.' The resulting *American Son*, featuring such seasoned Music City session-men as Buddy Emmons, Steve Gibson, and Hargus 'Pig' Robbins, was perhaps the best of Levon's solo albums. The country-rock flavour of the songs and arrangements seemed to suit him: boasting a couple of Harlan Howard numbers, including the evergreen 'Watermelon Time In Georgia', it was certainly a more satisfying offering than *Levon Helm*. Later in the year, Levon returned to Nashville to 'play' the lead role on songwriter Paul Kennerley's concept album *The Legend Of Jesse James*. Engineered by Glyn Johns, who helped Kennerley put the project together, the album also featured Johnny Cash, Emmylou Harris, Albert Lee, Rodney Crowell, Rosanne Cash, and Charlie Daniels.

Having completed both *Coal Miner's Daughter* and *American Son*, the newly beardless Levon hit the road with the Cate Brothers, playing sets that featured songs from both the new album and the Cates' *Fire On The Tracks*. On the West Coast, meanwhile, Rick, Garth, and Richard had joined forces for occasional performances as a trio. When Garth was too busy doing sessions, Rick and Richard would perform as a duo, periodically flying east for shows in New York and Philadelphia. It was pretty small-scale stuff, but it got them out of the house. As Levon put it with a typically agrarian metaphor, 'I like to think I'm always out there breaking a little ground – a few stumps and a little underbrush don't bother me any.'

Robbie felt none of Levon's urges, either to perform or to record, but his curiosity was piqued by one of the innumerable screenplays which had landed on his desk at MGM. The subject of novelist Thomas Baum's script for *Carny* appealed to him immediately, and for obvious reasons: it was about a present-day carnival show travelling through North Carolina – in Robbie's own words 'one of America's very special, creepy, wonderful things, a conglomeration of freaks and hustlers and illusions and lies.' 'It was the kind of movie I thought should be made,' he said. 'It's all Magic Mountains and Disneylands now, and the travelling circus is a dying breed. The carnival always had a mystique for me, and I just thought somebody should do it.' What Robbie really loved about carnivals was their microcosmic quality: each one was a miniature city moving through the country, with rides for skyscrapers and little stores on the midway. He'd worked on one as a boy, written about them in 'King Harvest', 'The W. S. Walcott Medicine Show', and 'Life Is A Carnival'; now was his chance to translate those themes into images. 'It's not a matter of me shifting from rock'n'roll into movies,' he told Chet Flippo. 'It's all storytelling, whether it's music or movies or books. I never wanted to "be in the movies".'

After meeting with documentary director Robert Kaylor, Robbie agreed to produce the film for Lorimar. Only after talking further with Kaylor and the film's star Gary Busey did he consider the idea of doing any more than that. Both Kaylor and Busey had seen *The Last Waltz*, and thought Robbie a natural for the role of carnival manager 'Patch' Beaudry. (The film was in great part an exploration of the buddy-buddy relationship between Beaudry and Busey's bozo, the clown figure who taunted customers from a cage and had baseballs thrown at him for his troubles.) Not realizing exactly how much it would entail, Robbie undertook the role and soon found himself snowed under with responsibilities as shooting commenced in the summer heat of Savannah, Georgia. The syndrome was a familiar one: wearing too many hats and letting stress build to a point where the only relief came through a kind of rebellion. This time his partner-in-crime was Busey, with whom he'd rented a porticoed antebellum mansion on the outskirts of Savannah. 'We just spent a lot of nights holding on to each other for dear life,' Busey recalled of their afterhours cocaine marathons.

Despite everything it had going for it, including Jodie Foster as a teenage runaway and such genuine carnival 'freaks' as the obese 'Jelly Belly' Harold, *Carny* bombed at the box office. Before it even opened, word had flashed through Hollywood that the film stank, immediately making it a leper.[2] This was a pity, because it wasn't such a terrible piece of work. If Robbie found Robert Kaylor's 'let-it-happen' approach to direction a trifle uninspiring, the overall ambience of the carnival came across well, and Robbie himself gave a commendable performance as the distant, efficient Beaudry – a man not unlike himself. ('He looks kind of dark and ominous, but he's not,' went one of Busey's lines in the film.)

Robbie had more fun working on the music for *Carny*. Collaborating with Hollywood veteran Alex North, who'd scored such classic films as *Spartacus, Viva Zapata*, and *Who's Afraid Of Virginia Woolf?*, he put together a soundtrack that veered between old-fashioned, *noir*-style mood music and funkier pieces recorded with musicians like Mac Rebennack and Randall Bramlett. 'People were expecting "Life Is A Carnival" and they got something very different,' he said. 'The combination of North's stuff and the sleazy stuff I did – kootch music, the burlesque tradition – was a a real counterpoint.' Alongside instrumental pieces like 'Pagan Knight', 'Freak's Lament', and 'The Garden Of Earthly Delights', Robbie cut a version of Fats Domino's 'The Fat Man', only his fourth vocal recording in twenty years. The experience of working with North was critical for Robbie. 'He's the one who got me addicted to vision and sound,' he said when North died in 1991. 'He taught me how powerful this tool can be.' It was the combination of vision and sound that got Robbie off his behind the following year, after he'd been reunited with his family and taken time out to heal some wounds. 'I thought, God, I've always been thinking of things to say, I've always been showing up,' he told Bill Flanagan. 'I thought I would just hang around the house for a while, talk to my kids. But when Marty called to ask me if I'd do something for the soundtrack to *Raging Bull*, I couldn't resist.' It was Robbie who found the Moscani piece – played by a little Bologna orchestra – which accompanied the opening sequence of the film. With the help of Garth and Richard, moreover, he put together various incidental pieces that met with Scorsese's approval. 'I just did a little section where they had a band in the background,' said Garth. 'Martin wanted some music from the mid-40s, so I listened to a bit of Basie's "One O'Clock Jump" and Harry James' "Two O'Clock Jump" and we came up with something from that period.' For Robbie, the experience of working on the film was a revelation, and would lead directly to his involvement with both *The King of Comedy* and *The Color of Money*.

The other Band members, especially Levon, were only too keenly aware of how easy it was for Robbie to 'take time out' with his family. Having made a great deal more money from the Band albums than they had, Robbie was under no pressure to gig or play sessions. On the other hand, the guys only had themselves to blame for their problems: they'd made hundreds of thousands of dollars over the years and frittered most of them away. 'I saw a lot of money wasted,' says Ronnie Hawkins. 'Sometimes now they get mad at Robbie because he's done all right, but they shouldn't. He took care of business.' Levon was in the worst shape of all, thanks to a bitter and protracted custody battle with Libby over his daughter Amy. In 1981, he went up to Hamilton, Ontario to see the Hawks' old agent Harold Kudlets. 'In my mind at this point they were all multi-millionaires,' says Kudlets, 'but Levon poured his heart and soul out to me and I was shocked. Where in hell did all the money go? He asked me if I'd come back with him and get things rolling again, so I started booking Levon and the Cates.'

Levon and the Cates was all very well, but it was hardly big-time. Nor were the others exactly raking it in. Despairing of getting a break as a solo artist on the West Coast, Rick decided to up sticks and follow Levon back to Woodstock. 'Malibu was like a long vacation,' he said later, 'but it's not a good place for teenage children. The Catskill mountains are a much more productive and social environment. They offer a sense of foundation, filled with middle-class and average people.' For Rick, The Band's decision to call it a day had perhaps been hardest of all. 'The aftermath was tough for Rick, who'd been a frontman in a major rock'n'roll band,' says Jonathan Taplin. 'Levon managed to get into acting, but Rick was left with nothing.' Richard wasn't faring much better, despite surfacing on albums by Bonnie Raitt and Willie Nelson.

Only Garth, whose genius was always in demand, kept busy. Aside from one-off sessions for the likes of Don Henley and David Lindley, he became involved with The Call, an unsigned band who'd long been admirers of The Band. 'The Call knew a lot of our songs and had performed them,' recalled Garth. 'They once asked me about the bridge of a song on *Cahoots* that I'd completely forgotten about.' Garth played on five of the songs that made up the band's demo tape, and on their eventual debut album for Mercury. They even persuaded him to join them for some West Coast shows. 'We were playing in the Vets Hall in Santa Cruz for a flood relief fund when they went into this tune I didn't recognize,' he remembered. 'We got into it, and I began learning it as we went along. It turned out to be "Knockin' Lost John"!' When he wasn't playing sessions, Garth maintained his sideline interests in more arcane music. Obsessed with the great accordion players of Norteno music, he even played a couple of shows as an accordionist with Norteno combo Greg Harris and the Bandini Brothers. At home, he practised Bach chorales and played jazz for Maude. Neither of them felt any great temptation to follow in the footsteps of Levon or Rick. 'I miss Woodstock for three weeks in the spring and three weeks in the fall, and for three or four days around Christmastime,' he told Ruth Albert Spencer. 'Otherwise I'm very happy out here.'

The late summer and fall of 1981 found Levon back down at Muscle Shoals Sound, to whose Capitol-affiliated label he had signed after the demise of ABC. With Jimmy Johnson and Barry Beckett at the controls, he cut the dismal *Levon Helm*, another eponymously titled album of covers ('Money', 'Willie And The Hand Jive') and songs by hack Southern writers. The LP stiffed but led sure enough to a tour by yet another 'all-star' aggregation, this time the Muscle Shoals All-Stars, in company with ex-Amazing Rhythm Ace Russell Smith. Drawing from a mixture of Band and Amazing Rhythm Aces evergreens and tracks from solo albums by both Helm and Smith, the All-Stars – comprising Mike Chapman (bass), Milton Sledge (drums), Randall Bramlett (sax), and ex-Ace James Hooker (keys) – embarked on a nationwide club tour through the spring of 1982. 'I never could quite get a solo project to flip over just right in a commercial sort of way,' says Levon. 'There were two or three albums which were OK, but they never sold. So there is the frustration of trying to do as well on your own as you can with your buddies, and you've got to live with that.' Hollywood was rather kinder to Levon than rock'n'roll. After a useful part in Daniel Petrie's TV film *The Dollmaker*, which saw him playing opposite Emmy-winning Jane Fonda as a scrawny bluegrass coal-miner who heads north to the automobile factories of Detroit, he landed a major supporting role as Chuck Yeager's sidekick Jack Ridley in Philip Kaufman's Tom Wolfe adaptation *The Right Stuff.*

By the end of 1982, Levon and Rick had been out in the cold long enough to consider combining forces. Figuring that the most economical way to make a living would be to go out as an acoustic duo, they began putting together what they called their 'living-room set', a mixture of blues and country and Band songs played with guitars, mandolins, fiddles, and harmonicas. In truth, it was the best, most honest music either of them had made since The Last Waltz. On 'Caldonia' and 'Short Fat Fanny', they were lechorous backwoods bluesmen, on 'Evangeline' and 'Fifteen Years Ago' Appalachian farmboys, harmonizing in the mournful Stanley Brothers style they'd learned round the camp-fire when they were kids. 'It's a great feeling, because you're right there in people's laps,' said Rick of the 'living-room' shows. 'You either cut the mustard or go home.' For Levon, the pride-swallowing factor was more than offset by the fun he was having with his old buddy. 'This is completely new to me,' he said. 'Rick's already done shows on his own, but I've never looked at it any way other than as a drummer for a high-power band. I've come all the way back to the basics, but it's really all the same. The main thing that juices me up is to get over there the night of the job, and the man that's runnin' the joint knows I'm comin', and he invites me in and helps me set up, and I play and he pays me. That's the only way I've ever really wanted it.' The two-man tour continued on through the spring of 1983, taking in dates all over America and Canada. At New York's Lone Star café on Wednesday 16 February, they were joined by a very drunk Bob Dylan, who wailed along on versions of 'Your Cheating Heart', 'Blues Stay Away From Me', and 'Ain't No More Cane' before the set collapsed into inebriated chaos.

On one of the duo's trips up to Toronto, where they often played a club called B. B. McGoon's, Levon began talking to Harold Kudlets about a Band reunion tour. 'All the Band guys were talking, but they weren't that friendly,' remembered 'The Colonel'. 'And there was very bad blood, as far as Levon was concerned, between him and Robbie. He was always under the impression that Robbie somehow shafted him.' Implicit in the discussions was Robbie's non-involvement: not only would Levon have nothing to do with him, but all of them knew that Robbie would himself want no part of a Band reunion. For Richard, the idea of a reunion was music to the ears; as Joe Forno put it, 'he often said he was so sure The Band would get back together that he sat around six or eight years and waited for it to happen'. The biggest surprise was Garth, whose commitment to a reunion had seemed doubtful. 'We all thought he'd be reluctant, because he was so busy in the studio with his machines,' said Levon. 'But when he heard about it, hell, he was happy as a pig in the sunshine!'

To Robbie, whose blessing the others needed, the idea of a reunion was indeed anathema. 'I'd made a movie and a three-album set about the fact that The Band was over,' he said in 1987. 'To come out a few years later and say, "Just kidding" . . . I mean, that's my idea of *horrible*.' But he knew the livelihoods of his old cohorts might depend on re-forming, and graciously said he would not stand in their way. 'As far as I was concerned, we'd done it and it was over with,' he says. 'But you forget when you're doing these things that people have in-bred music, in-bred road. It isn't like all of a sudden they can say goodbye. So it turned out after a while that everybody didn't feel the same way I did about it.' In the words of Gary Gersh, the A&R man who'd tried to interest Robbie in a solo career, 'The Last Waltz had been about going out in style – I'm not sure all five guys realized it meant *staying* out.' Chuck Willis had put it best, of course, and it was hardly coincidental that the re-formed Band regularly included his '(I Don't Want To) Hang Up My Rock'n'Roll Shoes' in their sets. 'People say they might blemish what The Band has done as a group, even that it's sacrilegious,' said Robbie. 'I don't think people should write about it that way. I mean, we're not talking about Matthew, Mark, Luke and John here. These are just some guys in a rock'n'roll band who miss it, y'know? I hope they have a real good time and don't stay up too late.'

Rehearsals for the reunion tour began in the late spring, with the group's line-up bolstered by the Cate Brothers: Earl on guitar, Ernie on Keyboards, Ron Eoff on bass, and Levon's nephew Terry Cagle on a second drum kit. It didn't take long to work up a repertoire of old and new, borrowed and blue: from Band staples like 'The Weight', 'Rag Mama Rag', 'The Shape I'm In', and 'Up On Cripple Creek' to such undemanding covers as 'Willie And The Hand Jive' and 'Get Out Your Big Roll, Daddy', it was just the kind of nostalgic, easily digestible assortment one might have expected without Robbie around to make decisions. The only real highlight was Richard's anguished rendition of 'You Don't Know Me', revived after nearly twenty years. On the plus side, the group still boasted the three voices that had sung the classic Band songs in the first place, but on the minus side they lacked not only the inimitable guitar playing of Robbie Robertson but his presence. Not for nothing did critics carp that The Band without Robbie was like *Hamlet* without the prince – even, in Greil Marcus' view, 'the ultimate indignity, the final rock'n'roll self-humiliation.'

After a warm-up show at the Joyous Lake in Woodstock on Saturday 25 June, 'The Band' kicked off the Canadian leg of the tour at Montreal's Place Des Arts a week later. For Richard, the tour 'started out nervously', as far as he was concerned because 'some of us aren't too big on rehearsing'. (It didn't take a genius to figure out that he was referring to Rick and Levon.) Shows followed in Ottawa, Toronto, Hamilton, Kitchener, London, Winnipeg, Regina, Calgary, Edmonton, and finally Vancouver, where a full sub-*Last Waltz* video was shot at the Queen Elizabeth Theatre on Monday 18 July. It was hard to disagree with the critics about the reunion. Even with a youthfully fresh-faced Levon in obvious command as the band's leader, the shows lacked any real authority. Everything was so trite and obvious, from the American and Canadian flags flying together over the stage to the homely intros with which Levon prefaced each song. 'Some purty country you got out here,' he said by way of introducing 'Milk Cow Boogie' to the Vancouver audience. 'Might help ya come out and do a little ploughin' next sprang . . .' Most depressing of all was the beefed-up sound, which sacrificed everything that had been funky and intimate about the five-piece Band. 'Even if we do one of our old tunes,' Levon told an interviewer, 'it sounds better having three keyboards instead of two, five voices instead of three.' But it didn't sound better: had Levon of all people never heard of overkill? However much the expanded line-up freed the four Band members to do things they'd never been able to do before, it diffused most of what had been special in their singing and playing.

After a handful of Californian shows, the band headed west – with their old road manager Bill Avis – for the first Japanese dates of their career. Starting out in Osaka on Saturday 27 August, they played Nagoya, Sapporo, and no less than four shows in Tokyo. Received warmly in all four cities, the group none the less found the trip stressful. Richard loved the electronic muzak version of 'Camptown Races' that was piped through their Sapporo hotel, but before the tour was over he'd freaked out and threatened to fly home. 'That was the time I realized he was on something,' says Harold Kudlets. 'Whatever it was, Garth's wife gave him some and calmed him down and he finished off the tour.' More American dates followed in October, lasting through to a New Year's Eve show at San Francisco's Civic Auditorium. After attending a première of *The Right Stuff* in Washington on 16 October, the band played the city's Wax Museum, then continued up the East Coast with shows in Pennsylvania and New Jersey. On Saturday, 22 October, they supported The Grateful Dead in front of 33,000 people at the Carrier Dome in Syracuse, New York. November took them across America from Pittsburgh to Colorado, and by the 26th, seven years after The Last Waltz, they were playing a Thanksgiving Day show at New York's Beacon Theater. Ironically, Robbie was in the city at the time, but chose not to attend the gig.

Despite the comparative success of the reunion tour, the same old resentments and frustrations seemed to dog the group. 'The band toured for about six months and we did exceptionally well,' recalls Harold Kudlets. 'Then the old things started to crop up: "He's singin' too many songs", "He's standin' too long in the spotlight", just as if they were kids starting over again. But we got over that and kept them going.' The financial problems persisted, however. Levon, who was being taken to court on a paternity suit, was on the point of losing 'the barn', his term for the RCO studio-cum-house on Plochmann Lane. Kudlets, who'd been Levon's best man at the wedding to his second wife Sandy, was unable to raise even $75,000 for mortgage repayments and had to go back to Hamilton to get the money. Through it all, Levon seemed to keep smiling. 'He always said to me, "Colonel, you worry too much",' says Kudlets. 'Even with the IRS breathing down his neck he'd say, "Something'll come up", and I'll be damned if it didn't. He'll live to be 90!'

Back on the West Coast, Robbie had done precisely what he'd

said he would do, which was to put his feet up. 'I just had nothing left to say,' he told one interviewer. 'I would look around and see all these other people who had nothing left to say either, but who insisted on making records. I thought, "I don't want to do that, I just want to clear the air, do something else for a while, and maybe at some point I'll feel inspired to do it again. Or maybe not." Either way it intrigued me.' In the meantime, he kept busy by working as 'musical producer' on *The King Of Comedy*, one of the most overlooked of Scorsese's films. His soundtrack, a blend of already-recorded tracks or out-takes by Ric Ocasek, the Pretenders, the Talking Heads, and Rickie Lee Jones, and specially-produced contributions from Ray Charles, Van Morrison, David Sanborn, Bob James, and B. B. King, worked brilliantly as a kind of subliminal commentary on the film's dialogue. 'It was to be just source music, like in life,' said Robbie. 'Marty got some flak along the lines that he and I were just using music that we liked, but I always thought the diversity would work.'

The most essential figure for the soundtrack was B. B. King, since Robbie felt he was the one artist talk-show host Jerry Langford would definitely have in his record collection. But it took all Robbie's powers of persuasion to convince King that he could sing 'T'Ain't Nobody's Bizness'. 'I sang in his ear, gave him signals, got behind him on it in a way he wasn't used to,' recalled Robbie, who was overawed to be producing a man whose records he'd first bought as a 15-year-old apprentice Hawk on Beale Street. 'When it was over he was astonished, because he flew in here, did it, flew out that night and was playing in Reno or Lake Tahoe.' More difficult still was Van Morrison, whom Robbie went to visit in Mill Valley. 'I showed him the movie, and he was very disturbed about how to relate to the whole thing,' said Robbie. 'He took the job much more seriously than I thought necessary.' Morrison became absurdly indignant about Rupert Pupkin (Robert De Niro), saying the character had no right to demand fame when he hadn't paid his dues, but agreed to try out Robbie's suggestions. It was only when he began singing some lines from an old, half-finished song called 'Wonderful Remark' that Robbie knew he'd got something for his soundtrack. It was a superb song, one that simultaneously embraced and condemned Pupkin, just as the viewer had to. Scorsese loved it and decided to use the track for the closing credit sequence.

Robbie may have felt he had 'nothing to say' as a musician, but when a Scorsese assistant called 'Cowboy' Dan Johnson died suddenly of meningitis while they were in New York, the shock prompted him to write one of the loveliest songs of his career. 'Between Trains' was a tribute to Johnson, an eccentric loner who'd made a big impression on Robbie, and it featured both Garth on synthesizer and Richard on backing vocals. With its heartbreaking chord sequence and vocal lines, the song sat perfectly alongside the soundtrack's other highlights, which included Ray Charles' version of the Johnny Mercer/Harold Arlen classic 'Come Rain Or Come Shine', The Pretenders' then unreleased 'Back On The Chain Gang', and Rickie Lee Jones' divine 'Rainbow Sleeves', a song by her old beau Tom Waits.

Finishing tours invariably propelled the other Band members into varying degrees of depression, and winding up the reunion tour proved no different. By February 1984, Richard and Arlie were living in Woodstock and using whatever chemicals they could get their hands on. Al Aronowitz, himself a major freebase casualty at the time, remembers coming back to his Woodstock house at 3 a.m. one morning to find Richard and Arlie loading up their car with his record collection. 'Rick's wife had told me the week before that I was gonna be robbed,' says Aronowitz, 'so he was in on it, too.'

Realizing that his meal ticket could go up in smoke at any

moment, Levon decided the only answer was to pull the reunited Band together again, and quickly. Once again, it all depended on Garth. 'If Garth says yes, we'll tour again,' he said with admirable candour. 'Garth is the key, the one who will rub off on the rest of us and make us sound real good, too.' The shows Harold Kudlets subsequently lined up for the spring and summer seemed to have the desired effect. Starting out in the Pacific Northwest in early March, there was a series of East Coast dates in April and a mini-tour of Florida in May, followed by shows in Toronto (with the Grateful Dead on 21 June), Banff, and Calgary. The set was the usual assortment of Band material and R&B covers, though for an encore the group often sang a superb *a capella* version of 'By The Rivers Of Babylon'. When they played Fort Lauderdale on 19 May a dissolute Jaco Pastorius joined them for an encore in the club outside which he would be beaten to death three and a half years later. After the Canadian dates, Harold Kudlets stepped out of the ring and handed over managerial responsibilities to Joe Forno, a Woodstocker The Band had known ever since he'd helped his father as a boy in the town drugstore. Forno's first headache was a festival at Nostell Priory in England that came right in the middle of their American tour. Levon was so livid about the festival that he refused to go to England at all, and only a brief guest appearance by Van Morrison saved their first British show in a decade from being a total washout.

Resuming the American dates that had been so rudely inter-rupted, the group hitched their wagon to a Crosby, Stills and Nash tour at the end of August, only to experience the same depressing come-down when it ended in September. Once again it was back to sporadic two-bit shows in or around Woodstock and New York: Levon and Rick, Levon 'and Friends', Rick and Richard with Paul Butterfield. It wasn't even as if the reunion itself had amounted to anything very meaningful. Simply touring on the strength of the past without producing new material was tantamount to admitting that they were lost without Robbie. 'I want to press ahead,' Richard told Ruth Albert Spencer in November. 'I'm tired of dwelling in the past. We're well established in the history books, and I don't want to continue doing what we've been doing for the last year and a half, because we've done it to the point where we're dragging ourselves down, unless we come up with new product.' Richard told Spencer he was tired of watching doors open and The Band not taking advantage of them. 'That why I'm irked to the point of just telling them, "Fellas, this is it, I'm going on with my own career",' he said. 'I've been planning how to catapult this whole thing with myself into a position where I can remain occupied all the time . . . because it's the down time that drives me crazy. I get nuts when I'm not working, when there's nothing to look forward to.'

The first few months of 1985 began in the same inauspicious manner, with what Garth described as 'various and sundry menus in places from small clubs to the Beacon and Capitol Theaters'. Garth himself returned to the West Coast, saying that it was 'time for everybody to work on their own enterprises' and bemoaning the fact that touring – 'a route to deterioration' – had destroyed 'the considerable piano technique I'd built up'. For Levon, who played several shows with his latest motley crew the Woodstock All-Stars, it was a case of 'operating at a minimum, playing around here just enough to stay in shape'. This particular bunch of all-stars had grown out of a loose aggregation known as the Woodstock Mountains Revue, whose sometime members included Happy and Artie Traum, Bill Keith, John Sebastian, Eric Andersen, Maria Muldaur, Larry Packer, and dobro wizard Cyndi Cashdollar. Playing clubs like the Lone Star, My Father's Place on Long Island, and Woodstock's own The Getaway, Levon rounded up Richard, Larry Packer, Artie Traum, Cyndi Cashdollar, and the latter's bassist husband Frank Campbell. Also featured was original Hawk and keyboard legend Stan Szelest, who'd settled in

Woodstock and had his own band The Ravens. The shows were the usual beer-drinking fare, with Levon dominating the proceed ings: among the songs played were 'Don't Ya Tell Henry', 'Milk Cow Boogie', 'Watermelon Time In Georgia', 'Rag Mama Rag', and 'Mystery Train', with the odd version of 'Whole Lotta Shakin' Goin' On' or 'Rockin' Pneumonia And The Boogie-Woogie Flu' thrown in for good measure.

Less exhaustingly cheery were the shows Rick and Richard played, both as a duo and in the company of people like Paul Butterfield. It made a change to hear such forgotten Band classics as 'The Rumor' and 'Caledonia Mission' alongside the more obvious 'greatest hits'. On the other hand, Bill Flanagan was hardly wide of the mark when he dubbed Danko, Manuel, and Butterfield 'The Chemical Roulette Trio', though of the three it was Rick -- 'the hyper-active, fidgety, fast-talking, song-calling, grinning ringleader' – who seemed to Flanagan 'the most in danger of flying off the side of the earth'. Rick and Richard also took part in several shows commemorating the twentieth an- niversary of the formation of The Byrds, of whom the only original members present were Gene Clark and Michael Clarke. By the summer, it was back to touring as The Band again, with a support slot on another Crosby, Stills and Nash tour.

Stephen Stills thought Richard 'on top of the world, delighted to be back on stage and playing superbly' after the tour kicked off in Sacramento on 28 June, but Ron Horning was probably more accurate in his 1988 *Village Voice* piece 'The Moving Shadow Of Richard Manuel'. 'We sing and play songs that were our lifeblood once,' Horning imagined Richard thinking. 'But what we meant back then, to ourselves and everyone else, is as dead as a racoon hit by a semi. Not that the audience minds. There go the guys in flannel shirts, waving their long-neck bottles: hey Richard, hey Garth, hey Levon, hey Rick. No one will ever play our stuff better than we do, but now the music seems as canned as Rick's line about the bar reminding him of my living room.' At least The Band were back to playing as a five-piece again, with Woodstock native Jim Weider stepping into the shoes of Earl Cate and Robbie Robertson. After the tour had finished in Allentown, Pennsylvania on 31 August, the exhausted band flew to Portugal to play a festival and take a week's vacation.

In early November, a benefit show for the Shakespeare festival in Richard's hometown Stratford, Ontario saw him reunited for the first time in over twenty years with his boyhood pals the Rockin' Revols: Ken Kalmusky, John Till, Garth Picot, and Doug Rhodes, all of them still playing for a living except Rhodes, who had a pizza business in nearby London. 'It's a return to my roots,' Richard said, 'and I'm bringing my partners of twenty-five years with me.' That night there was magic and love in the air. 'Coming home after all those years was really exciting for him,' said Richard's brother Don. 'I've never seen him so excited and nervous. So many people had come back to Stratford to see the show, people I hadn't seen for twenty years.' After a Revols set that featured 'Before I Grow Too Old' and a blues number called 'Crazy Momma', the second half of the show featured a set by The Band. His spirits temporarily lifted by the experience of homecoming, Richard went on to play some solo dates at The Getaway, singing such Tin Pan Alley ballads as 'She Knows' and 'Miss Otis Regrets' alongside his favourite Ray Charles numbers.

That winter, The Band not only recorded six tracks for a possible album but appeared in a low-budget thriller called *Hidden Fear* alongside Robert Logan, Kathleen Quinlan, and Bradford Dillman. Shot down in Arkansas, the film featured Levon in a leading role as a sheriff, Rick as the father of a kidnapped boy, and Garth as 'a recluse'. Richard, who must have thought this destined-for-video-only piece of trash the ultimate in self-abasement, was merely one of the vigilantes out to find the kidnapper.

*

Richard knew things couldn't get too much worse. By the time The Band hit the road again in February 1986, he had finally gone back to the bottle. 'That disease comes back like a sledgehammer,' said Robbie, 'It drove him crazy. People were telling him, "Oh, I'm so disappointed in you" and all this stuff, but he was the poor guy left at the end of the pack who's saying, "Wait for me, I can't help myself".' In the first week of March, the group were supporting Crosby, Stills and Nash on a string of dates in Florida. Ironically, the highlight of the Band sets in Hialeah and West Palm Beach was 'The Shape I'm In', sung by Richard in his most raggedly throaty voice.

On Monday 3 March, The Band were booked into the hideously-named Cheek-to-Cheek Lounge in Winter Park, a suburb of Orlando. The Art Deco club was packed to capacity for two shows, and both went well, despite the fact that Rick had complained to Richard about his drinking. 'We'd played a good show for good intelligent people,' Rick said. 'Talk was of the next show, that's what we were all living for.' After leaving the club, Richard headed back to the nearby Quality Inn and stopped by Levon's room en route to his own. To Levon, he did not seem especially depressed. 'Around 2.30 a.m., he went back to his room,' Levon recalled. 'I don't know what got crosswise in his mind between leaving the foot of my bed and going into his bathroom.' Once in the room, Richard finished off a bottle of Grand Marnier and his last scrapings of coke. Sometime between 3 and 3.30 a.m. on Tuesday 4 March, he went into the bathroom and hanged himself.

Arlie told the police that she'd woken at midday and gone straight out to Bojangles' fast-food restaurant for breakfast. She said she'd found Richard's body hanging from the shower rod on her return, and that her screams had brought Levon, Rick, and Elizabeth rushing into the room. It took the three of them five agonizing minutes to cut the body down.

Among the press statements made after the body had been taken away, none showed as much denial of the reality of what had happened as that of Rick Danko, who was clearly in shock. 'I can't believe in a million years that he meant for that to happen,' he said. 'Things had been in a shining bright place for us since we toured with Crosby, Stills and Nash last summer, and Richard really enjoyed being on the road. I have to think this was just a goddamned silly accident. He had such a flair for dramatics that I think he was maybe just checking a new sophisticated knot. That may sound weird, but that's what I believe.'³ Slightly less implausible is the oft-mooted theory of 'autoerotic fatality': every year between 500 and 1,000 asphyxiations occur in America as a result of men cutting off the blood supply to their brains to increase the pleasure of orgasm. Yet it's hard to believe that Richard was in a sexually excited state when he returned to his room. It seems much more likely that loneliness and a profound sense of failure combined to convince him of the futility of his life.

All over America, Richard's friends and fellow musicians heard the news of his suicide with disbelief. 'I was devastated,' recalled Robbie. 'You never prepare for those kinds of things. It knocked me to my knees, I was literally torn apart by it.' Fellow Rockin' Revol Garth Picot was flying from Montreal to Toronto when he saw the news in a Montreal paper. 'It seemed to me that an era had ended,' he said. 'We'd all still be playing music, but things would just not quite be the same.' Jane and the children were hit worst of all. 'Joe Forno called me at work with the news, and I took it very hard,' she says. 'We'd been talking again since his move back to Woodstock. You have no idea how my kids' lives were altered. The last time Paula saw him she was mad at him – there were lots of things she never got to say.' The Band themselves cancelled a string of dates, helping to arrange the funeral in Stratford on Sunday 9 March. Supported by Joe Forno and the kids (Paula was 16 and Josh 10), Jane somehow got through the service. Robbie had agreed to deliver a eulogy to Richard, but a bad flu kept him in L. A. Garth played 'I Shall Be Released' on the organ, but no one could bring themselves to sing along. Only weeks before, Richard himself had sung the song at a memorial service for Albert Grossman in Woodstock.[4]

With ex-Beach Boy Blondie Chaplin taking his place and doubling on guitar and drums, The Band resumed their tour in St Louis. 'Four shows later, it's still a strange feeling,' Rick told an interviewer. Amidst the usual talk of music 'keeping them together', the group soldiered on through the summer. A critic reviewing a show at Passaic's Capitol Theater in New Jersey noted that Richard's death had robbed them not only of their greatest voice but of the keyboard interplay with Garth that had provided 'the mid-range texture on which Robbie Robertson's melodies traditionally rest'. True, Blondie Chaplin could hit the high falsetto notes, but hitting the notes was not what The Band was all about. On the other hand, a reviewer at a Boston Channel show thought their set served as 'wondrous therapy for themselves and their fans'. In late March, the group broke off from touring to attend the memorial service for Richard in Woodstock. Levon stayed home, saying there were 'some things you do in private', and Jane Manuel avoided what she thought would turn out to be merely 'a show'. 'I wish all those people had cared while he was still living,' she said. The most moving tribute came from the normally reticent Garth, who accompanied Rick's rendition of 'I Shall Be Released' on an accordion while tears streamed down his face.

The Band continued to play till the end of the year, just one more bunch of greying relics trotting out old songs, singing for not much more than their supper. 'You can run things into the ground or you can grow old gracefully,' said Rick after a Thanksgiving Day show at the Lone Star. 'I'd rather be around for a while than run things into the ground.' But in this case Neil

Young may have been right: it would have been better to burn out than fade away. Fred Carter Jr livened up that show when he came on to sing 'Susie-Q' and 'Kansas City', but it hardly compensated for Rick's sickly rendition of Lionel Richie's 'My Love', the choice of which alone signalled that it was really all up for 'The Band'.

If Richard's death could hardly be said to have galvanized Robbie into making a comeback as a recording artist, it certainly prompted one of the few good songs on *Robbie Robertson*, 'Fallen Angel'. The idea of a solo album first arose when Robbie was in Rome with *Untouchables* producer Art Linson in 1983. 'Why start at the beginning as an actor?' Linson had said. 'Go back and get to work! Make a record!' After mulling the idea over for a year, Robbie decided he was ready. 'All of a sudden, I had this yearning, this need,' he said. 'I felt angry, possessed. It was all very instinctual, like breeding time.' Signing to EMI, where Gary Gersh had become head of A&R, he began preliminary work on the album in the fall of 1984. At least $50,000 was spent on pre-production, with Robbie flying to New York and Europe to meet with record producers. In England, he even talked to The Smiths' Johnny Marr and the Cocteau Twins' Robin Guthrie about the possibilities of their producing him.

After setting up shop at Village Recorders at a cost of $12,000 a month, songs began to come thick and fast. 'Suddenly the spirit moved me enough to start having the occasional idea for a melody line or a lyric, and everything started building in my mind from there,' Robbie said. 'Gradually the ideas mounted up, I was turning them into songs, and I was on fire with the whole thing. I was *gone*, I was getting into the studio before eight in the morning because I couldn't wait to get my mitts into it.' Still there was the problem of finding the right producer, with various false starts as a consequence. 'I think he wanted to do this very badly, but didn't know how to go about it,' said Gary Gersh. 'We just started getting into a series of very intense discussions of what we wanted to do. I didn't want to do it if he wanted to make another Band record, and he didn't want to make another Band record, so we hit it off immediately.'

It took another eighteen months for recording to get properly under way, by which time Gersh had taken Robbie with him to David Geffen's label and French-Canadian producer Daniel Lanois had finally finished work on Peter Gabriel's *So* album. The choice of Lanois was critical, since he brought with him many of the ideas and most of the musicians he'd used for *So*. Flying in such session superstars as drummer Manu Katché and bassist Tony Levin, Lanois began fashioning a sound that was light years away from *Rick Danko* or *Levon Helm And The RCO All-Stars*. 'I never went in saying, "Let's get a contemporary sound",' said Robbie. 'But a lot of people pretend that nothing has happened, that technology is meaningless, and I don't believe that.' For Robbie, it was 'commendable' that John Fogerty had made his comeback with an album, *Centerfield*, that hardly sounded any different from *Cosmo's Factory*, but it wasn't what *he* wanted to do. Significantly, given his higher artistic aspirations, he talked of 'finding locations' and 'casting characters' for the album. 'The old way of making records, just a-pickin' and a-singin', didn't seem to apply any more,' he said. 'Now I wanted to *score* these songs, I wanted a different kind of emotion to come out of the music.' In many ways, the album was to be a kind of high-watermark of '80s over-production, and the absolute opposite of everything The Band had stood for.

By the midsummer of 1986, the album had grown into a monster. Rumours began circulating that it was costing far more than originally planned, and that David Geffen himself was getting nervous. 'I was uncomfortable about what it was costing,' the whiz-kid mogul later admitted. 'I have complete faith in Robbie as a musician and songwriter. The only question that ever came up in my mind was how much this was going to cost.' Continual rewrites and re-recordings were not only pushing costs up to $1m but eating into other projects. For some time, Martin Scorsese had been hounding Robbie to do the soundtrack for *The Color Of Money*, and Robbie had eventually given way. 'To work with guys like Marty and Gil Evans is a gift from heaven, but the timing was terrible,' he said. 'Daniel wasn't crazy about the idea, but he kind of put up with it. Then *he* had to go over to Ireland to do *The Joshua Tree* with U2.' There was also Taylor Hackford's film about Chuck Berry, *Hail, Hail, Rock'n'Roll*, on which Robbie had agreed to serve as musical director. In the end, Berry proved such a handful that Robbie handed the project over to Keith Richards, content to be credited merely as a 'creative consultant' on a rock film that turned out to be almost as good as *The Last Waltz*.

Suddenly, everything became a frantic rush. David Geffen, annoyed that the album was being interrupted, refused permission for Robbie's voice to be used on the *Color Of Money* soundtrack.[5] Instead, Robbie recorded various instrumentals and did what he'd done on *The King Of Comedy*, which was to blend already-recorded songs with special performances. Scorsese wanted to get away from the prevailing '60s soundtracks of the time and 'actually get the artists we like'. In this he was helped by a special deal inked between Touchstone Pictures and MCA Records, enabling Robbie to approach the likes of Eric Clapton, who'd just recorded 'Holy Mother', his own tribute to Richard Manuel. In the end, the soundtrack boasted contributions from Clapton, Don Henley, B. B. King, Willie Dixon, Mark Knopfler, Warren Zevon, and Robert Palmer, who cut an affecting version of Little Willie John's obscure but brilliant 1963 side 'My Baby's In Love With Another Guy'. (Scorsese tells a charming anecdote about Willie's wife waking him to say they were offering $2,000 for the use of the song. If she did wake him, it was from a very long sleep: he'd been dead since 1968.)

Robbie was still trying to help Eric Clapton with the lyric for 'It's In The Way That You Use It' when he flew to Dublin to record two of the songs for his album with U2. One minute he'd be in the studio sparring with The Edge, the next he'd be singing over the phone to Clapton. As one might imagine, it wasn't the easiest way to work. In any case, there was something a little opportunistic about working with U2 in the first place, for all Robbie's claims that the link-up had nothing to do with their being virtually the biggest rock band on the planet. 'We got together because we both wanted to see what would happen when the two worlds we inhabit were mixed together,' he protested rather feebly. The two tracks which emerged from this little marriage of interests, 'Testimony' and 'Sweet Fire Of Love', were mere blasts of hot air, overblown trumpetings of rock 'spirituality'.

From Dublin it was off to the city of Bath, where Peter Gabriel had built his own studio. 'Peter is an old friend of Robbie's,' said Gabriel's personal engineer David Bottrill, who'd once worked with Daniel Lanois in his hometown Hamilton, Ontario. 'The connection was even stronger when Daniel was producing U2. When Robbie arrived from Dublin, we went straight into "Broken Arrow".' Gabriel made all the difference to *Robbie Robertson*, contributing not only the keyboards and Linn Drum programming on the beautiful 'Broken Arrow' but also the stacked backing vocals on 'Fallen Angel'. 'Peter has exactly the quality I was looking for,' said Robbie. 'There's a ghostly edge to his voice which is very moving.' Gabriel even seemed to lift Robbie to the peak of his limited vocal abilities: on this anguished, rapturous hymn to Richard, Robbie almost managed to simulate the kind of falsetto which had been The Band pianist's trademark. '"Fallen Angel" isn't directly *about* Richard,' Robbie explained. 'It's more written *for* him, like a little prayer. It's just some things I never got to say to him. I thought it's not too late to say them, that I should just say them anyway.' When it came time to remix the album with Bob Clearmountain at Bearsville, memories of Richard in the Band days came flooding back.

Robbie Robertson was least good when it strayed furthest from its Band roots into the territory of hard rock. Listening to Robbie blustering his way through 'American Roulette' or the hamfisted 'Hell's Half-Acre', with their overblown themes and lyrics, was excruciating. As a kind of concept album centred around his own identity as a 'half-breed', the record showed Robbie overreaching himself and getting lost in flights of airy verbosity. All the lyrical details which had anchored The Band's music in tangible Americana were sacrificed to endless images of fires and 'storms raging within'. '(I'm the storyteller of the shadowland,' Robbie announced pompously as he made his press rounds. 'It's all mythology to me, all this stuff I write.') Even the hit single 'Somewhere Down The Crazy River', which went back in time to the fascination the South had exerted on Robbie as a teenager, was more like a storyboard for a Southern Comfort commercial than a real song.

The awful truth was, Robbie appeared to have become a kind of Hollywood ad-man, riding around in a black BMW wearing Comme des Garçons suits and drinking champagne at ultra-chic restaurants in Santa Monica. He was a yuppie rock'n'roller who'd been in L.A. so long that he'd completely lost touch with his rock'n'roll roots, which was why *Robbie Robertson*, released eventually in the fall of 1987, sounded so bloated and grandiose. For all the predictably fawning reviews from the likes of *Rolling Stone*, who seemed to have a vested interest in sustaining the myth of Robbie's 'genius', long-term lovers of The Band could only deplore the yawning gulf between *Music From Big Pink* and, say, 'Showdown At Big Sky'. 'I didn't like it at all, at least not nearly as much as Danko's solo album,' said Elvis Costello. 'It was like he'd decided to make a Peter Gabriel album, whereas his song-writing was much more interesting and enigmatic when he was working on that smaller scale. It's almost like the best songs on the record are the ones that operate on that scale but have then been artificially inflated with steroids to become this widescreen Peter Gabriel music. With Peter Gabriel or Bono, that's fine, because they write like that, they think like that. It almost makes you suspicious as to how *accidental* those Band records were. Maybe it was *much* more of a band than it has always been portrayed.'

Despite the belated success of 'Crazy River', with its unsensational Scorsese video, *Robbie Robertson* never came close to recouping the money which had been spent making it. In May 1988, Robbie attempted to rekindle interest in the album with a planned Cinemax special, *Robbie Robertson And Friends*, to be directed by Scorsese. Tellingly, the film was cancelled when U2 and Peter Gabriel turned out to be unavailable. By the fall, the idea had been expanded into a more ambitious film project, described by Robbie as 'a combination of *The Red Shoes* and *All That Jazz*, only dealing with music instead of dance' and by Scorsese as 'an evolution of rock'n'roll through Robbie's perception of it from when he was fifteen to now'. With *American Roulette* as a projected title, the screenplay was about a reclusive '60s rock legend and the son who is searching for him. After running a kind of rock'n'roll gauntlet, the son tracks down his father's old manager on a large Woodstock estate and eventually manages to find the legend himself. Perhaps it was for the best that this, too, foundered before filming could start.

Levon must have viewed the hyping of *Robbie Robertson* with distaste. (Significantly, where both Garth and Rick had appeared on Robbie's album – Garth playing keyboards on 'Fallen Angel' and 'American Roulette', Rick contributing a backing vocal to the unmemorable 'Sonny Got Caught In The Moonlight' – there was no sign of Levon on it.) Granted, he was still finding occasional work as an actor, but his roles in films like *Smooth Talk* and *The End Of The Line* – a story of railroad folk filmed in and around Little Rock – were hardly testing ones.

The Band gamely set forth on another tour in the spring of 1988, occasionally supported by the great but chronically alcoholic Roy Buchanan. Although the group themselves sobered up in the wake of both Richard's and Paul Butterfield's deaths,[6] tragedy continued to stalk them as the decade drew to a close. Rick's son Eli died of a severe asthma attack, and Levon nearly died in a fire at the barn. Maude Hudson became very ill, making it impossible for Garth to spend long periods away from home. Fortunately, there was just enough work to keep the three men from going crazy. Rick and Garth appeared on Robert Palmer's *Heavy Nova* album, and Garth played with Mac Rebennack as part of Marianne Faithfull's band.[7] (In May 1990, Faithfull's producer Hal Willner staged a concert by 'Garth Hudson and Friends' at St Ann's Church in Brooklyn: with the help of thirty-odd musicians, Garth played a highly eclectic selection of music that ranged from Romanian folk songs to jazz standards to Appalachian hymns. Said Janine Nichols, Willner's co-producer, 'I've never seen someone more able, and less willing, to take the spotlight than Garth'.)[8] Levon and Rick were members of the umpteenth 'all-star' touring group, one put together by Ringo Starr in July 1989. Nicknaming themselves 'The Ringoburys', the other 'All-Stars' included Billy Preston, Mac Rebennack, Nils Lofgren, and Joe Walsh. 1989 also saw Rick and Garth reunited onstage with Robbie when The Band were presented with an honorary Canadian Juno Award by Ronnie Hawkins. (Levon was playing a gig down in Arkansas, or so he said.) At the ceremony, Paula Manuel joined them to say a few words about her father. 'It just tore the place apart,' said Robbie. 'It was so touching and so beautiful.'

Not even an album deal with Columbia seemed to bring The Band much luck. Barely had the great Stan Szelest joined them to form an awesome keyboard combination with Garth when a heart attack killed him in January 1991. Like Richard, ironically, Stan had sworn off the bottle for several years, only to relapse into chronic cocaine abuse in his last weeks. Even more ironically, he had just co-written a tribute to Richard and Paul Butterfield with Levon called 'Too Soon Gone'. No sooner had Billy Preston been drafted in as a replacement, making his debut with the group at a benefit for the Woodstock Youth Center on Saturday 3 August, when the famous keyboard player was arrested and charged with the rape of a 16-year-old boy in California.

The Band's biggest problem without Robbie has always been coming up with songs. This was why they began turning to writers like Jules Shear and to cover versions of Dylan's 'Blind Willie McTell' and Springsteen's 'Atlantic City' when Columbia's Rick Chernoff prodded them into action in 1991. By the end of the year, The Band had departed from the label. More recently the trio have teamed up once again with John Simon, the producer who proved such a sympathetic 'sixth member' back in The Band's golden days. With ex-Hawk and Janis Joplin sideman Ricky Bell taking Billy Preston's place on keyboards, they've been cutting a slew of fresh material, including some Muddy Waters tunes and new songs like 'Move To Japan' and 'The Caves Of Jericho'. 'We've gone back to analogue recording, that warm sound we had in the old days,' says Simon. 'No DAT here!' Other guests include Bruce Hornsby, veteran bluegrass fiddler Vassar Clements, and the legendary Clifford Scott, tenor saxophonist on Bill Doggett's classic 1956 hit 'Honky Tonk'.

Perhaps it is too late for The Band to find their way back into the mainstream of American rock'n'roll as recording artists. Maybe they are actually happier eking out a humble existence on rock's margins, playing the tiny redneck bars of New York state.[9] 'They're all vagabonds,' says D. A. Pennebaker, who spent part of the summer of 1991 filming the irrepressible Rick Danko as he bumbled around the country in the company of Eric Andersen and their Norwegian pal Jonas Fjeld. 'They're a little more mature now, a little softer, but the spirit hasn't changed,' concurs Elliott Landy, another figure from The Band's past who was working with them in the early '90s. When the English singer Graham Parker settled in Woodstock in 1990, he quickly realized that if he was going to do shows with Rick Danko he'd have to forsake the 'tight military discipline' of his usual live performances and simply go with Rick's flow. 'It's always a case of "expect the unexpected" with Rick,' laughs Parker. 'It's "Will he turn up?", "Will the bass strap fit?", "Is the amp working?". But somehow it works, and I learned from that. He's always excitable and enthusiastic, and flowing with ideas.'[10]

The Band are not helped by the fact that Woodstock itself is hardly the bubbling musical mecca it was twenty years ago. In the *Woodstock Times* review of the 1991 Youth Center benefit show, the paper's critic said he suspected the town was 'a pariah in the music industry at this point, having more the reputation of a rock stars' retirement community than a hotbed of fresh, undiscovered genius'. Artie Traum, who played a support slot on the show with his brother Happy, confirms this suspicion. 'There's really not a lot of work here, it's become remote again,' he says. 'See, Albert held the place together. He had the cash resources to do it and he had the vision. When he died, the focus of the place sort of disintegrated.' Albert's widow Sally keeps the Bearsville complex going – with its theatre and restaurants – but most of the famous studio's customers these days come from a long way out of town. If there remains a 'working class' of musicians like the Traums, Amy Fradon, Scott Petito, Cyndi Cashdollar, Larry Packer, Vinnie

Martucci, Betty MacDonald and others, most of the town's great clubs have closed down. In the words of Betty MacDonald, 'the alcohol and bar scene fostered the music and then bottomed out'. By the late '80s the process of 'gentrification' by weekending New Yorkers meant that few struggling musicians could afford any longer to live in the area. 'The weekenders have made things a lot more uptight,' said Nancy Haney, secretary of the Woodstock Historical Society, in 1987. 'It gets very congested in town, but it doesn't have the creative atmosphere it once had. The artists hide in the hills and show in New York. I miss the old bohemians.'

Three thousand miles away, Robbie continues to operate in the very different world of L.A., where the artists in the hills hide inside Spanish colonial fortresses. In 1991, he followed up *Robbie Robertson* with *Storyville*, 'a sort of concept album' built around a story of romantic infatuation that stretched not only across time but halfway across America. Ostensibly the album was centred in Robbie's own love affair with the American South in general and New Orleans in particular: 'Making a record that incorporated the mystery and spice of New Orleans has been a dream of mine ever since I heard Smiley Lewis and Huey 'Piano' Smith as a kid in the '50s,' he said. But when it was finally unveiled, the record seemed as cold and clinical as its predecessor, despite the presence on it of such Crescent City legends as Aaron Neville, The Meters, and Indian chiefs Bo Dollis and Monk Boudreaux. The preoccupation with Southern mythology was so laboured, so overdetermined, that songs like 'Resurrection' and 'Go Back To Your Woods' merely sounded forced and hollow.[11]

It was all very well for Robbie to say that he was still working the South out of his system – 'like in therapy' – but it was hard to take such a smooth Hollywood operator seriously when he attempted to convince the world that his fingers were still dirty with rural Americana. The best moments were the most dreamily rhapsodic ones – the gorgeous chorus of 'Day Of Reckoning', the interweaving of Robbie's voice with The Blue Nile's Paul Buchanan on 'Breakin' The Rules', the 'River Hymn'-style finale of 'Sign Of The Rainbow' – but they weren't enough to save the record from an ignominious commercial death. Once again, Rick and Garth made discreet appearances and Levon was nowhere to be seen. By a curious twist of fate, Levon's barn all but burned to the ground while Robbie was mixing *Storyville* at Bearsville – just one more disaster in the long saga of The Band's life after the Waltz.

Coda

I miss them on a musical level, and I miss them just as people. But we all grow up and have to leave home sooner or later.

Robbie Robertson, 1983

Nik Cohn wrote that the price The Band paid for being 'free of all the pretensions which fouled their more poetical contemporaries' was 'a shortage of drama'. It wasn't clear whether he was talking about their music or their lives as rock stars, but if he meant both he wasn't far from the truth. The Band – onstage, offstage, on record – never reached out and grabbed anyone by the throat. They never demanded attention in the petulant, histrionic way many of their peers did. In fact, they were hardly what Kenneth Tynan called 'show people' at all.

Most of The Band's music was made in the spirit that novelist Toni Morrison attributes to jazz: 'a music not originally made *for* anyone but its players . . . a private art for public consumption'. In the 1983 video *The Band Is Back*, Levon Helm claimed that music 'ain't theatre'. Perhaps that was a naïve claim to make on the eve of the age of Madonna; indeed, it was The Band's very lack of theatricality that made them unfit to function as part of America's rock'n'roll circus. Yet there was something about the group's very reluctance to make themselves a pop spectacle that was both refreshing and admirable, something which set them apart from the madding crowd of rock victims on both sides of the stage.

The other side of the coin was an aloofness that still surfaces in the kind of remarks Robbie Robertson makes about contemporary music. 'I'm not a little pop tart who is trying to think of something cute for people to dance to,' he said scornfully when he was promoting *Storyville*. To which one felt like replying: 'But you *are* an old rock fart who's completely lost his direction and done almost nothing worthwhile in fifteen years.' To many of the people around them in the '60s and the '70s, The Band always thought they were above rock'n'roll. 'They were too precious for their own good, and rock'n'roll's too public for that,' says Mary Martin. It's an attitude that still manages to offend old friends to this day. 'I've tried to get in contact with him several times over the years,' says John Simon, 'and he's never returned my calls. Although he's cordial when I bump into him, he doesn't ever get back to me. I think he's up on another level.'

In a sense, Robbie was always 'up on another level'. If he hadn't been, The Band would never have made the extraordinary music they did. Without Robbie's insatiable need for artistic credibility, they might have been content with exactly the kind of good-time, beer-drinking country rhythm'n'blues they ended up purveying without him. But then without *them*, Robbie Robertson might have been nothing more than a pretentious, frustrated singer-songwriter. It was Levon and Rick who rooted him, Garth and Richard who gave his songs flesh and blood. This is what made The Band a band, the unique kinesis that occurred when they found themselves playing together behind Ronnie Hawkins. Never has there been a rock group in which there was such a balance, such an even distribution of talent. None of them put any less into the sound than any other. None of them was ever 'just' the drummer or bassist or keyboard player.

The trouble was, the balance was so delicate, so fragile: once it had been exposed to the world, it became harder and harder to maintain it. 'After *The Band*, something threw us off the track,' said Robbie. 'We had something we were experimenting with and it was only ours. It had, in one sense, been shared in a way that you feel wonderful about, but then it gets taken and talked about and ... mentally, healthwise, success was not the best thing for The Band.' In the tug-of-war between The Band's privacy and the demands of the American rock machine, the Big Pink spirit of brotherhood was lost irrevocably. Their moment come and gone, they struggled to make sense of what America had done to them. 'To indulge in the sort of hyperbole Robertson likes to abuse,' wrote Dave Marsh, 'they never quite reached the promised land. And because the Top 10, the region that indicated mass acceptance rather than cult success or some species of hype, eluded them, the group's story feels unsettled, unfinished.'

Ultimately, the story of The Band *is* unfinished. The four surviving members of the original group have never been able to call it a day, and at least one of them couldn't give up rock'n'roll if he were paid to do so. 'I don't have to swallow my pride to play the Lone Star Café,' says Levon. 'From my side of it, it's been the same since the early part of my life. I'm still learning and trying to transform musical sounds for people. When people start throwin' beer bottles I'll quit, but not until then.' Yet in another sense The Band died long ago, and no one was there to pick up where they left off, not even the excellent Little Feat, who served up a similar brew of blues, gospel, country, and New Orleans funk. 'It's hard to think of someone who carried on from The Band,' says Elvis Costello. 'It's a unique little cul-de-sac in rock'n'roll history. If they left a legacy, unfortunately it was a kind of muso mentality, people who wanted to be like them but didn't really understand that what was great about them was this mysterious quality the music had, a quality you can't buy off-the-peg. They were more like jazz musicians in that respect, like one of Miles' really great line-ups. Five really incredible players, and *three* great singers. How many other bands can boast that?'

Asked in February 1982 whether he considered himself an 'ex-member' of The Band, Robbie Robertson replied: 'I can't think of anybody or any combination of musicians that I would rather play with. If someone said, "Listen, you can pick out anybody you want," I'd choose them very quickly over anybody else.' Given the Lennon-and-McCartney/Jagger-and-Richard-style friction between the two men, the chances of Robbie ever walking on to a stage with Levon Helm again must seem very slim. (When The Band appeared at the Bob Dylan tribute concert at Madison Square Garden in October 1992, Robbie was nowhere to be seen.) However, that hasn't stopped rumours of a rapprochement between the two men, or of a projected reunion tour by Dylan and The Band. 'Levon is an ornery, stubborn kind of fellow,' says one Band insider, 'but my guess is that when he needs the money badly enough they'll reform.'

For all the painful memories he retains of life as a member of The Band, Robbie Robertson continues to look back over those sixteen years with pride and pleasure. 'I wish we'd been able to put out twenty albums and play twice as much and touch ten times as many people,' he says. 'But I don't have any regrets about it.' Pausing and smiling, he adds: 'For the most part I don't think about the darkest hours. Mostly I remember the wonderful things.'

Notes

PART ONE

Chapter 1

1. 'Acadie' was the name given to an area on the north-east coast of North America by French settlers in the 1680s. It included Nova Scotia, New Brunswick, Prince Edward Island, and parts of Quebec and Maine. Expanding on the historical background to 'Acadian Driftwood' in 1975, Robbie Robertson said the following:

> After the battle between Montcalm and Wolfe on the Plains of Abraham in 1759, it was put to the Acadian people that they had to swear allegiance to the British or give up their land. So some of them went back to France, some went to the French islands in the Caribbean, and some crossed the border and went down to Louisiana. The ones who went to Louisiana became the Cajuns, and the ones who stayed became Canada's outcasts.

2. *RPM* was Canada's first music trade magazine, founded in 1965 by Grealis, a former policeman.

3. Other Canadians who in different ways have 'looked at what makes the American imagination tick' include Louis B. Mayer, Marshall McLuhan, Saul Bellow, J. K. Galbraith, Dan Aykroyd, Lily Tomlin, Michael J. Fox, Donald Sutherland, John Candy, Rick Moranis, Albert Brooks, David Letterman, k. d. lang, and Mike Myers of *Wayne's World* fame. (Notable Canuck musicians, some of whom cross The Band's path in this book, include Neil Young, Joni Mitchell, Gordon Lightfoot, Bryan Adams, and Jeff Healey.) In a piece for the English newspaper the *Guardian* on 25 July 1992, Canadian-born Peter Freedman suggested that his fellow countrymen, after years of suffering dismissal and con-

descension from most other nationalities, were secretly taking over the world.

4. Asked in 1971 about the influence of Canada on The Band, Robbie conceded that 'if nobody in the band had been Canadian, I think it would have been different'. But he added that, excepting the odd jig or reel, 'there is no Canadian music hardly – no music you can say, "Oh, that's Canadian" about.' The fact that even the young Leonard Cohen played in a Country and Western trio in Montreal in the '50s shows the prevalence of the American country influence on Canadians.

5. The deep-rootedness of the bluegrass and string-band influences on Rick (and The Band as a whole) can be felt in the impromptu rendering of 'Old Time Religion' in *The Last Waltz* by Rick (fiddle), Richard (mouth-harp), and Robbie (guitar).

6. The character in *Eraserhead*, Henry, was played by Jack Nance.

7. Boladian would later found the Westbound label, recording everyone from the early Funkadelic and Ohio Players to Southern soul mama Denise LaSalle. The label was still going strong when Boladian's gospel artists the Clark Sisters had a surprise crossover hit with 'You Brought The Sunshine' in 1983. 'Arman always did like gospel,' says Paul Hutchins. 'He said more hits came out of the black church than anywhere.' The author has warm memories of Boladian from a visit to Detroit to interview the Clark Sisters, during which he was taken on a tour of Detroit by the Westbound owner and his old friend George Clinton.

Chapter 2

1. A sometime Texan supergroup comprising Doug Sahm, Freddy Fender, and Flaco Jimenez.

2. Ronnie's sister Winnie claims he took not only her car but her last $35. 'Such bullshit I never heard in my life,' snorts the Hawk.

3. One of the releases on End (E-1043) was a version of 'Kansas City' (b/w 'Cuttin' Out') by Rockin' Ronald & the Rebels in April 1959. Because of the Levy connection, this has frequently been attributed to Ronnie and the Hawks. Hawkins himself disclaims any involvement in the record.

4. Levy's luck was to change in 1985, as Fredric Dannen details in his bestselling *Hit Men: Power Brokers and Fast Money Inside the Music Business* (1990). 'Moishe' was sentenced to ten years' imprisonment in May, 1988, but remained free on bail after an appeal. He died of cancer in 1990.

5. Dale's classic 'Susie-Q', cut at KWKH in Shreveport, Louisiana with James Burton on guitar, reached #7 on the R&B chart in June, 1957. Ronnie later claimed that he only learned his cousin was in the same business when he saw his name in the charts.

Chapter 3

1. Born in Ozark, Arkansas in September 1939, Buchanan grew up in the little town of Pixley, California, raised on revival meetings and R&B radio stations. His first use of harmonics was on the 1962 Bobby Gregg instrumental 'Potato Peeler'. After years of playing sessions – at one point he was even touted as a replacement for Brian Jones in the Rolling Stones – Roy was 'discovered' in the early '70s when PBS aired a documentary called *The Best Unknown Guitarist in the World*. He recorded several albums for Polydor and Atlantic, but drink and drugs destroyed what could have been a great career. See Jeffrey Ressner, 'Roy Buchanan, 1939–1988', *Rolling Stone*, 22 September 1988.

2. According to Greil Marcus in *Mystery Train*, the Hawks listened obsessively to the *Blues Consolidated* album, which featured one side of Bobby 'Blue' Bland and one of Junior Parker.

3. The very month, incidentally, that Bob Dylan first appeared at Gerde's Folk City in Greenwich Village.

4. Kudlets estimates that Ronnie was making $1,000 a week at the Le Coq d'Or, with the Hawks earning little more than $100 a piece. This may not have applied to Levon and Robbie, the 'senior' members of the group: Robbie himself recalls making $225 per week at one stage, not a bad living for a nightclub musician in the early '60s.

5. David Clayton-Thomas recalled playing the Friar's Tavern for $150 a week when 'some crummy group from Boston' (who didn't even have a record deal) were making twice as much up the road at the Le Coq.

6. Born and raised in Tallahatchie County, Mississippi, Sonny Boy

had assumed a role as an ambassador for the blues after touring Europe with Horst Lippmann's American Folk Blues Festival in the early '60s. Richard Manuel called him 'just about the best blues harp player of all time'. See Paul Oliver, 'The Original Sonny Boy', in *Blues Off the Record* (Baton Press, 1984).

7. Robertson and Danko also played on Hammond's *I Can Tell* album, produced by Jerry Leiber and Mike Stoller for their own Red Bird label but released in 1967 on Atlantic. Rick shared bass duties with one Bill Wyman.

PART TWO

Chapter 1

1. Albert Grossman had built his whole reputation on managing folk acts. Among his other artists were the black singers Odetta and Richie Havens, together with the hugely successful pop-folk trio Peter, Paul and Mary. He'd also discovered Joan Baez, staging her debut at the first Newport festival.

2. Fariña was a singer-songwriter whose marriage to Joan Baez's sister Mimi had drawn him into the folk movement in the early '60s. (The couple were one of the major successes at Newport in 1965.) A friend of the legendary Thomas Pynchon, he was about to see his first novel (*Been Down So Long It Looks Like Up To Me*) published when he died in a motorcycle crash – almost three months to the day before Dylan's accident.

3. On 9 November, the night of a famous blackout in New York City, Dylan and Robbie wound up jamming in a hotel room with Brian Jones.

4. Konikoff, like Stan Szelest, was from Buffalo, and had been playing with Hawkins for some time. 'Robbie may deny that he stole Sandy from me,' says Ronnie, 'but I was on the other extension when he did it!'

5. The famous 'Swinging London' cover of *Time* had appeared in April.

Chapter 2

1. The Maverick was founded in 1904 after Hervey White broke away from Byrdcliffe. The first of the famous annual Maverick festivals took place eleven years later.

2. Alk went on to make films about the Black Panthers and other radical organizations. The first was *American Revolution II*, about the notorious Democratic Convention of 1968, while the second, *The Murder of Fred Hampton*, concerned the alleged killing of a Chicago Panther leader by government agents. (It was bankrolled by none other than Albert Grossman, who'd first met Alk when both men were running folk clubs in Chicago in the '50s.) A heroin addict, Alk maintained his association with Dylan through *Renaldo And Clara* and *Real Live* to his suicide in 1982. See Clinton Heylin, 'A Profile of Howard Alk', in *All Across the Telegraph*, ed. Michael Gray and John Bauldie (Sidgwick & Jackson, 1987).

3. The 'basement tape' acetate was not widely circulated in the music industry until the spring of 1968. The most famous subsequent cover versions were by the Byrds ('You Ain't Goin' Nowhere' and 'Nothing Was Delivered'), Julie Driscoll, Brian Auger and the Trinity ('This Wheel's On Fire'), and Manfred Mann ('The Mighty Quinn'), but there were countless other versions of these and other songs. *The Great White Wonder* consisted of nine basement tracks and seventeen solo Dylan tracks from 1961. Another bootleg album (*Troubled Troubadour*, 1970) contained new songs and different takes of *Great White Wonder* tracks. Subsequent basement material, purported to have been sold to a wealthy Dylan collector by a Band insider, emerged in late 1986. There are undoubtedly more tapes in 'The Garth Hudson Archives', kept in Garth's Agoura Hills ranch. For the full background on the bootlegs, see John Morthland and Jerry Hopkins, 'The Rock & Roll Liberation Front?', in *The Penguin Book of Rock 'n' Roll Writing*, ed. Clinton Heylin (Viking, 1992).

4. Among the many other songs heard on recent basement 'supplements' are Presley's 'A Fool Such As I', Ian and Sylvia's 'Four Strong Winds', Johnny Cash's 'Waltzing With Sin', the traditional 'Trail Of The Buffalo', the folk standard 'Bells Of Rhymney', and an early take of

'Spanish Is The Loving Tongue', plus: 'All You Have To Do Is Dream' (not the Everly Brothers song), 'The King Of France', '900 Miles From Home', 'I'm Guilty Of Loving You', 'I Can't Make It Alone', 'Get Your Rocks Off', 'Bonnie Ship The Diamond', 'He's Young But He's Daily Growing', 'Silent Weekend', 'Rock Salt And Nails', 'One Man's Loss', 'The Hills Of Mexico', 'One For The Road', 'Try Me, Little Girl', 'Baby Ain't That Fine', 'A Night Without Sleep', 'Gonna Get You Now', 'Lock Your Door', 'Baby, Won't You Be My Baby', 'Don't You Try Me Now', 'Confidential To Me', 'Babylon', 'Mississippi', 'Big River', 'Goin' Down The Road Feeling Bad', 'Under Control', 'Next Time On The Highway'; various Band oddities like 'Silhouettes' and an instrumental 'Orange Juice Blues'; and alternate takes of songs such as 'Odds And Ends', 'Crash On The Levee', and 'You Ain't Goin' Nowhere'.

5. Back in December 1966, Dylan had spent several days talking with MGM Records president Mort Nasatir, and had looked set to switch labels the following February. Thanks to Allen Klein, an MGM shareholder who didn't believe in Dylan's commercial potential, the deal never went through, prompting Albert Grossman to make renewed overtures to Columbia.

6. There was another live version of the song recorded that year, on The Doors' *Absolutely Live*.

7. A second Guthrie tribute concert was held at the Hollywood Bowl in September 1970, featuring Joan Baez and Country Joe McDonald. Proceeds from the eventual album, which collated the two shows, went to the Guthrie library funds and to help research on Huntingdon's Chorea, the disease which had killed the singer.

8. 1968 was the year Martin Luther King and Bobby Kennedy were assassinated, as well as being a year of invasions and near-revolutions in Europe. King's assassination set off a wave of black rioting throughout America, while protests against the Vietnam War became increasingly violent.

Chapter 3

1. John Simon remarks that 'a lot of Robbie's standoffishness came from Albert, not so much from Dylan, who was really as much a hick as any of them . . . Robbie was overawed by Dylan, but that was the stardom of it, not the intellect'.

2. The 'old timey' effect of Landy's *Big Pink* portrait was taken to a typically Californian extreme on the cover of Crosby, Stills, Nash and Young's aptly titled *Déjà Vu* (1970), complete with the shotguns and cartridge belts that would re-emerge on the cover of the Eagles' 1973 album *Desperado*.

3. Lenny Bruce had died of a heroin overdose on this street in August 1966.

4. Another non-Southern band which absorbed Southern musical tradition was, of course, the Rolling Stones, who abandoned the psychedelia of *Their Satanic Majesties Request* for the rootsy country blues songs of 1968's *Beggar's Banquet*, complete with fiddles and jug-band arrangements. Over the course of their next three studio albums – *Let It Bleed*, *Sticky Fingers*, and *Exile On Main Street* – they demonstrated an understanding of and affinity with American blues, soul, country, gospel, and vintage rock'n'roll unparalleled by any other major rock artists.

PART THREE

Chapter 1

1. Note Robertson at his most disingenuous in 1978: 'It was never in our nature to voice an opinion – what would we do in interviews other than talk about what was private to us?'

2. Rundgren had a Top 20 hit that December with the lovely 'We Gotta Get You A Woman' (Ampex 31001). Levon Helm can be heard on the *Runt* album, drumming on 'Once Burned'. Besides recording some of the most enduring rock albums of the early '70s – particularly the dazzling *A Wizard, A True Star* (1973) and *Todd* (1974) – Rundgren

produced a motley assortment of acts throughout the decade, including Grand Funk Railroad, the New York Dolls, and Meat Loaf.

3. Robertson later claimed that The Band were well-received, 'to the point that I didn't think they knew what they were talking about'. He also maintained at one point that he had 'no idea' what Marcus was talking about in *Mystery Train*. 'It's kind of beautiful, but he's telling me what I mean, and that's dangerous work.'

Chapter 2

1. Subsequently, a body known as the Canadian-Radio-Television-Commission (CRTC) was formed to force station programmers to play at least 30% domestic music, something which was to have consequences as recently as 1991, when it turned out that much of Canadian superstar Bryan Adams' *Waking Up The Neighbours* album had been co-written with transplanted South African producer 'Mutt' Lange.

2. Walker had been involved in the Toronto Rock and Roll Revival Show in early October 1969.

3. 'Don't Do It' had originally been recorded in the studio during the *Cahoots* sessions but never issued in that form. An edited version of the live track on *Rock Of Ages* reached #34 in October 1972 – The Band's only American Top 40 single besides 'Up On Cripple Creek', which got to #25 in November 1969.

Chapter 3

1. The title was a reference to 'Après le Déluge', the first of Rimbaud's *Illuminations*.

Notes

PART FOUR

Chapter 1

1. Another artist who found it hard to get close to Robbie was Peter Gabriel, who in five years of friendship was only once invited to his house.

Chapter 2

1. Scorsese became known as 'The King of the Triple Screen' for his editing work on *Woodstock*. (Robbie remembered Scorsese as 'this little guy with headphones on running around organizing everything . . .') He also worked as Associate Producer on François Reichenbach's 1971 film *Medicine Ball Caravan* (a.k.a. *We Have Come for Your Daughters*) and as montage supervisor on the 1972 documentary *Elvis on Tour*.

2. None of the guest megastars was paid anything more than expenses for appearing at The Last Waltz. Bill Graham charged a 10% administrative fee which was consumed by cost overruns but more than recouped by the eventual box office receipts from the film.

Chapter 3

1. Marsh noted the obvious chronological neatness of punk's rise in America at just this time. Don Letts' *The Punk Rock Movie* was on release by the summer of 1978.

2. *Carny* wasn't helped by the financial problems Lorimar was experiencing at the time. A paltry $146,000 was spent promoting the film in the U.S.

3. Danko also told a reporter that Richard had had 'a few heart attacks', 'but the good Lord threw him back to us many, many times'.

4. Bloated by years of overeating, Albert died of a heart attack while flying to London.

5. Of David Geffen's refusal to compromise with Disney's Jeffrey Katzenberg on this matter, Scorsese said: 'I could never understand this, they're friends and they have dinner together, but during the day they negotiate fiercely. So we lost the chance to have Peter Gabriel, and we could only use Robbie without his voice. I was even told to clear the moaning!' See *Scorsese On Scorsese*, ed. David Thompson and Ian Christie (Faber, 1978).

6. Butterfield, a chronic alcoholic, died in L.A. in early May 1977. 'Paul's death had a big effect on me,' Danko told the *Boston Globe* in February 1988, adding that he'd played six shows with the mouth-harp maestro shortly before his death: 'We made a deal that we'd get up in the morning and there'd be no drinking – and hopefully no drugging – until after the shows. We were getting too old for it. But I remember, after one show, Paul had the bus driver immediately pour him two glasses of tequila. It finally caught up with him. You can only do so much.'

7. Hudson can be heard in superb form alongside the good Doctor on the resulting live album *Blazing Away* (1990).

8. Other projects in which Garth was involved during the '80s included an exhibition at the L.A. Museum of Science and Industry by sculptor Tony Duquette, together with work by the Encino-based Visual Music Alliance.

9. And popping up as ghosts on all kinds of albums: appropriately enough, Levon can be heard on Michelle Shocked's 1992 album *Arkansas Traveller*, singing and playing mandolin on the Bearsville-recorded 'Secret To A Long Life'. The track also features Garth on accordion.

10. In the late spring of 1992, Rick and Elizabeth Danko finally came to terms with their addiction problems and checked themselves into a rehab. When they emerged in the summer, Rick was clean and sober for the first time in almost thirty years.

11. 'Go Back To Your Woods' certainly sounded 'forced and hollow' when Robbie played it live – along with 'What About Now', 'The Weight', and 'Shake This Town' – at the 1991 Guitar Legends Festival in Seville. The appearance also confirmed that he never was, and never will be, a frontman.

Acknowledgements and Sources

I have many people to thank for help with this book. But for the generosity of Gail and Chris Bell of the sometime Band Appreciation Society, I could scarcely have contemplated writing it in the first place. I am also indebted to Martin Colyer, who provided a wealth of ideas and suggestions. In New York, Alastair Bates and Judith Wolff kindly allowed me the use of their apartment; Annene Kaye and Jim Sclavunos offered similar hospitality in Los Angeles. In Ontario, Ronnie Hawkins and Steve Thomson bent over backwards to assist me, and Al Hoffman was most helpful in Woodstock. John Bauldie proved an invaluable guide when it came to researching The Band's association with Dylan. Others who gave generously of their time include Biba Kopf, Mat Snow, Rod Tootell, John Hersov, Peter Doggett, Steve Turner, Richard Wootton, Ian Wallis, Clinton Heylin, Raymond Foye, Willie Jeffrey, Greil Marcus, Robert Christgau, Derek Taylor, Regine Moylett, Russ Smith, Bill Millar, Fred Dellar, Rob Bowman, John Roy, Tony Scherman, Barbara Charone, Nick Logan, Bob Bettendorf, Larry Van Acker, Sally Reeves, Jerry McCarthy, David Cronenberg, Eve MacSweeney, Wanda Hawkins, Rayner Jesson, Ritchie Yorke, Bob Grace, Paul Bursche, Karen Holmes, Lisa Kirk, Bibi Andersson, Queenie Taylor, Jared Levine, Danny Heaps, Muir Mackean, Dan Levy, Chris Gaiser, and staff at the Central Music Library in London and the Library of Performing Arts in New York. Thanks are also due to Jonathan Riley, Miranda McAllister and Josine Meijer at Viking-Penguin, and to my agent Tony Peake. Finally, my wife Victoria was a constant source of support and affirmation throughout the work: all my gratitude and love to her.

Among the interviews I conducted, the following were especially valuable: Ronnie Hawkins, the late Bill Graham, D. A. Pennebaker, Robbie Robertson, John Simon, Al Aronowitz, Jonathan Taplin, Elliott Landy, John Hammond Jr, Colonel Harold Kudlets, Libby Titus, Elvis Costello, Mac Rebennack, Terry Danko, Jane Manuel, Mary Martin, Gordon Josie, Artie Traum, Graham Parker, Gary Gersh, Larry Packer, and Paul Hutchins.

In addition the following books and articles provided invaluable information and quotations:

Alterman, Loraine: 'Band of Gold', *Melody Maker*, 10 November 1973

Aronowitz, Al: 'Country Soul From Bob's Backup Band', *Life*, 26 July 1968

'A Family Album', from *The Age Of Rock*, ed. Jonathan Eisen (Vintage, 1969)

'Gotta Serve Somebody: An Insider Remembers Dylan's Hard Reign', *New York Press*, 7–13 August 1991

Baer, Joshua: 'The Robbie Robertson Interview', *Musician*, May 1982

Bauldie, John: *The Ghost of Electricity* (Privately published, 1989)

'Ceilings, Basements, and Evening Things Up', *The Telegraph 20*, Summer 1985

Bender, William: 'Down To Old Dixie And Back', *Time*, 12 January 1970

Bloomfield, Michael: 'Dylan Goes Electric', in *The Sixties*, ed. Lynda Rosen Obst (Random House/*Rolling Stone*, 1977)

Bowman, Rob: Sleeve-note, *To Kingdom Come* (Capitol, 1989) (expanded version in *Goldmine*, 26 July 1991)

Brook, Stephen: *Maple Leaf Rag: Travels Across Canada* (Picador, 1989)

Cannon, Geoffrey: 'The Band: A Report From Paris', *Melody Maker*, 5 June 1971

Christgau, Robert: *Any Old Way You Choose It* (Penguin, 1973)

Dalton, David, and Jonathan Cott: 'The Million Dollar Bash', in *The Rolling Stone Rock'n'Roll Reader*, ed. Ben Fong-Torres (Bantam, 1974)

Dannen, Fredric: *Hit Men*: *Power Brokers and Fast Money Inside The Music Business* (Times Books, 1990)

Davies, Robertson: *The Papers of Samuel Marchbanks* (Viking, 1987)

Davis, Clive, with James Willwerth: *Clive: Inside the Record Business* (William Morrow, 1975)

Dougherty, Steve: 'A Haunting Suicide Silences the Sweet, Soulful Voice of The Band's Richard Manuel', *People*, 24 March 1986

Draper, Robert: *The Rolling Stone Story* (Mainstream, 1990)

Dylan, Bob: *Writings and Drawings* (Panther, 1973)

Emblidge, David: 'Down Home with The Band', *Ethnomusicology*, 20 September 1976

Farren, Mick: 'Mounties, Maple Syrup, The Band', *NME*, 25 September 1976

'Ten Years of Stage Fright: The Life and Times of Robbie Robertson and The Band', *NME*, 17 June 1978

Flanagan, Bill: 'Time Loves a Hero: Robbie Robertson', *Q*, December 1987

Flans, Robyn: 'Interview with Levon Helm', *Modern Drummer*, August 1984

Flippo, Chet: 'After The Last Waltz: Robbie Robertson Takes a Chance on *Carny*', *Rolling Stone*, 26 June 1980

Ford, Mark: 'Among The Bobcats', *London Review Of Books*, 23 May 1991

Friedman, Myra: *Buried Alive*: *The Biography of Janis Joplin* (William Morrow, 1973)

Gilmore, Mikal: 'Rick Danko's Wink is as Good as a Nod', *Rolling Stone*, 29 December, 1977

Gladstone, Howard: Interview with Robbie Robertson, *Rolling Stone*, 27 December, 1969

Gleason, Ralph J.: 'The Band', *Rolling Stone*, 17 May 1969

Review of *The Band*, *Rolling Stone*, 16 October 1969

'Perspectives: The Excellencies of The Band', *Rolling Stone*, 6 January 1972

'*Rock of Ages*: A Crackling, Mind-blowing Moment Preserved', *Rolling Stone*, 12 October 1972

Glover, Tony: 'A Wonderful New Group', *Eye*, October 1968

Gill, Andy: 'The Big Easy', *Q*, October 1991

Gold, Mick: 'A Tree With Roots: The Band', *Let It Rock*, April 1974

Goldberg, Michael: 'The Second Coming of Robbie Robertson', *Rolling Stone*, 19 November 1987

Goldstein, Richard: *Goldstein's Greatest Hits* (Prentice-Hall, 1970)

Gray, Michael: *The Art of Bob Dylan* (Hamlyn, 1981)
    (ed., with John Bauldie) *All Across the Telegraph* (Sidgwick & Jackson, 1987)

Grogan, Emmett: 'The Band's Perfect Goodbye', *Oui*, May 1977

Harris, Art, with Ben Fong-Torres: 'Notes on The Last Waltz', *Rolling Stone*, 30 December 1976

Hawkins, Ronnie, with Peter Goddard: *Last of the Good Ol' Boys* (Stoddart, 1989)

Heilman, Dan: 'Robbie Rides Again', *Buzz*, March 1988

Heylin, Clinton: *Stolen Moments* (Wanted Man, 1988)
    Dylan: Behind The Shades (Viking, 1991)

Hodenfield, Chris: 'The Last Waltz', *Rolling Stone*, 1 June 1978

Horning, Ron: 'The Moving Shadow of Richard Manuel', *Village Voice* 'Rock & Roll Quarterly', 5 July 1988

Humphries, Patrick: 'Robertson's Jam', *Vox*, October 1991

Jackson, Marni: 'Ronnie Hawkins: Coming Back to Where You Ain't Never Been', *Rolling Stone*, 14 May 1981

Jung, Daryl: 'Helm Comes Home', *Now*, 31 March – 6 April, 1983

Kent, Nick: 'Robbie Robertson: He was that Masked Man', *Arena* Winter 1987/88

Kiers, Roelof: 'Interview met Robbie Robertson', *Aloha* 45/46. (Transcripts of interviews conducted for VPRO-TV in October 1970.)

Kooper, Al: Review of *Music From Big Pink*, *Rolling Stone*, 10 August 1968
    Backstage Passes: Rock'n'Roll Life in the Sixties (Stein & Day, 1977)

Kubernik, Harvey: 'Across the Great Divide with Robbie Robertson: A Portrait of the Artist as a Mystery Man', *Crawdaddy!*, March 1976

Landau, Jon: 'The Band: It's a Restless Age', *It's too Late to Stop Now* (Straight Arrow, 1972)

Landy, Elliott: *Woodstock Vision* (Hamburg: Rowohlt, 1980)

Lane, Dakota: 'Band Stand', *Woodstock Times*, 1 August 1991

Lawrence, D. H.: *Studies in Classical American Literature* (Thomas Seltzer Inc., 1923, Penguin Books 1971)

Lewis, Grover: 'Big Pink in Quake City: Respite for the Restless', *Village Voice*, 1 May 1969

Lydon, Susan Gordon: '"The Band" Shuns the Bandwagon', *New York Times*, 4 May 1969

'The Band: Their Theme is Acceptance of Life', *New York Times*, 12 October 1969

McGregor, Craig (ed.): *Bob Dylan: A Retrospective* (Sydney: Angus & Robertson, 1972)

McKenna, Kristine: 'Robbie Goes Way Out West', *NME*, 11 June 1983

Marcus, Greil: 'We Can Talk About It Now', *Good Times*, 23 April 1969

'Rock-a-Hula, Clarified', *Creem*, June 1971

Mystery Train: Images of America in Rock'n'Roll Music (E. P. Dutton, 1975)

Sleeve-note to *The Basement Tapes* (Columbia, 1975)

'Drifting In and Out of an American Dream: *Northern Lights – Southern Cross*', *Creem*, March 1976

'The Band's Last Waltz: That Train Don't Stop Here Anymore', *Rolling Stone*, 30 December 1976

'Save "The Last Waltz" for Me', *New West*, 22 May 1978

Marsh, Dave: 'Schlock Around The Rock', *Film Comment*, July/August 1978

The Heart of Rock'n'Soul (Penguin, 1989)

Marx, Leo: *The Machine In The Garden: Technology and the Pastoral Ideal in America* (New York: OUP, 1967)

Merrill, Sam: 'Mason Hoffenberg Gets in a Few Licks', *Playboy*, November 1973

Meyer, Musa: *Night Studio: A Memoir of Philip Guston* (Thames & Hudson, 1991)

Miller, Jim: 'The Band's Last Supper', *Rolling Stone*, 1 June 1978

Oliver, Paul: 'The Original Sonny Boy', in *Blues Off the Record* (Baton Press, 1984)

Ondaajte, Michael (ed.): *The Faber Book of Contemporary Canadian Short Stories* (Faber, 1990)

Palmer, Robert: Sleeve-notes to *Anthology* Vols. 1 & 2 (Capitol, 1978)
  'A Portrait of The Band as Young Hawks', *Rolling Stone*, 1 June 1978
  Deep Blues (Viking, 1981)
  'Robbie Robertson: The *Rolling Stone* interview', 14 November 1991
Pickering, Stephen: *Bob Dylan Approximately* (New York: David McKay
    Co., 1975)
Pidgeon, John: *Eric Clapton: A Biography* (rev. edn, Vermillion, 1985)
Rogan, Johnny: *Van Morrison* (Proteus, 1984)
Rolling Stone, authors of: *Knockin' on Dylan's Door* (Straight Arrow, 1974)
Salvo, Patrick William: 'Playing in The Band: A Conversation with
    Robbie Robertson', *Melody Maker*, 7 October 1972
Scherman, Tony: 'Youngblood: The Wild Youth of Robbie Robertson',
    Musician, December 1991
Shelton, Robert: *No Direction Home: The Life and Music of Bob Dylan*
    (Penguin, 1987)
Sloman, Larry: *On the Road with Bob Dylan* (Bantam, 1978)
Smith, Joe: *Off the Record: An Oral History of Popular Music* (Pan, 1990)
Smith, Patti: 'The Band: The Notch #3', *Circus*, September 1970
Snyder, Patrick: 'The Band's Grand Finale', *Rolling Stone*, 16 December
    1976
Spencer, Ruth Albert: 'Conversations with The Band', *Woodstock Times*,
    March–April 1985
Spitz, Bob: *Dylan: A Biography* (McGraw-Hill, 1989)
Swenson, John: 'In No-One's Debt: The Story of The Band', *The Music
    Gig*, September 1976
  'Levon at the Helm', *High Times*, July 1982
Thompson, David, and Ian Christie (eds.): *Scorsese On Scorsese* (Faber,
    1989)
Turner, Steve: 'By The Time I Got Back To Woodstock', *Independent*, 4
    August 1990
Valentine, Penny: 'Contemporary Songwriters: Robbie Robertson',
    Sounds, 27 November 1971
Vallely, Jean: '*Coal Miner's Daughter*: Levon Helm Makes Acting Look
    Easy', *Rolling Stone*, 1 May 1980
Wade, Dorothy, and Justine Picardie: *Music Man: Ahmet Ertegun, Atlantic
    Records, and the Triumph of Rock'n'Roll* (Norton, 1990)

Wale, Michael: *Vox Pop: Profiles of the Pop Process* (Harrap, 1972)

Ward, Ed: 'The Band', in *The Rolling Stone Illustrated Encyclopaedia of Rock'n'Roll*, ed. Jim Miller (Random House, 1976)

Wasilok, Carol: 'Who Do You Love? An Interview With Ronnie Hawkins', *DISCoveries*, August 1991

Watts, Michael: 'Robbie Robertson: In the rural tradition', *Melody Maker*, 13 April 1974

Weinberg, Max, with Robert Santelli: *The Big Beat: Conversations with Rock's Great Drummers* (Contemporary Books, 1984)

Williams, Paul: *Performing Artist: The Music of Bob Dylan, Vol. 1, 1960–73* (Underwood-Miller, 1990)

Williams, Richard: Interviews with Robbie Robertson and Rick Dando, *Melody Maker*, 29 May 1971

Yorke, Ritchie: 'Ronnie Hawkins', *Rolling Stone*, 9 August 1969

   Axes, Chops, and Hot Licks: The Canadian Rock Music Scene (Edmonton: M. G. Hurtig, 1971)

Zimmer, Dave: 'Robbie Robertson Between Trains: From Big Pink to *The King of Comedy*', *Bam*, 6 May 1983

Zollo, Paul: 'Robbie Robertson's Adventures in Songwriting', *Songtalk*, Winter 1991

I have also drawn on various radio interviews, such as Roger Scott's Radio One 'Classic Albums' interview with Robbie about *The Band*, and the two-part Robertson special Radio One aired in 1991.

Every effort has been made to contact all copyright holders. The publishers will be pleased to make good any errors or omissions brought to our attention in future editions.

The Band: A U.S. Discography

RONNIE HAWKINS AND THE HAWKS
(featuring future members of The Band)

Singles

As THE RON HAWKINS QUARTET:
Bo Diddley/Love Me Like You Can (Quality X 8127) 1958

As RONNIE HAWKINS AND THE HAWKS:
Forty Days/One Of These Days (Roulette 4154) 1959
Mary Lou/Need Your Lovin' (Roulette 4177) 1959

As RONNIE HAWKINS:
Southern Love/Love Me Like You Can (Roulette 4209) 1960
Lonely Hours/Clara (Roulette 4228) 1960
Ruby Baby/Hay Ride (Roulette 4249) 1960
Come Love/I Feel Good (Roulette 4400) 1961
Who Do You Love/Bo Diddley (Roulette 4483) 1963
There's A Screw Loose/High Blood Pressure (Roulette 4502) 1963

Albums

As RONNIE HAWKINS AND THE HAWKS:
Ronnie Hawkins (Roulette 25078) 1959
Forty Days; One Of These Days; My Gal Is Red Hot; Odessa; Wild Little Willie; Ruby Baby; Mary Lou; Need Your Lovin'; Whatcha Gonna Do; Dizzy Miss Lizzy; Oh Sugar; Horace
Mr Dynamo (Roulette 25102) 1960
Clara; Hey Boba Lou; Someone Like You; Dreams Do Come True;

Hay Ride; Honey Don't; Lonely Hours; Sick And Tired; Love Me Like You Can; You Cheated, You Lied; Baby Jean; Southern Love

The Best Of Ronnie Hawkins (Roulette 25255) 1964

Bo Diddley; Come Love; Honey Love; High Blood Pressure; Arkansas; Boss Man; I Feel Good; Who Do You Love; Searchin'; Mojo Man; Sexy Ways; You Know I Love You

N.B. The versions of 'Farther Up The Road' and 'She's Nineteen' with Levon on lead vocals appeared on the Canadian Roulette album *Mojo Man* (SR 25390) along with a jumbled assortment of Ronnie Hawkins tracks.

THE BAND

Singles

As THE CANADIAN SQUIRES:
Uh Uh Uh/Leave Me Alone (APEX 76964) 1965

As LEVON AND THE HAWKS:
The Stones That I Throw/He Don't Love You (ATCO 6383) 1965
Go, Go, Liza Jane/He Don't Love You (ATCO 6625) 1965

As THE BAND:
The Weight/I Shall Be Released (Capitol 2269) 1968
Up On Cripple Creek/The Night They Drove Old Dixie Down (Capitol 2635) 1969
Rag Mama Rag/The Unfaithful Servant (Capitol 2705) 1970
Time To Kill/The Shape I'm In (Capitol 2870) 1970
Life Is A Carnival/The Moon Struck One (Capitol 3199) 1971
When I Paint My Masterpiece/Where Do We Go From Here? (Capitol 3249) 1971
Don't Do It/Rag Mama Rag (Capitol 3433) 1972
Hang Up My Rock'n'Roll Shoes/Caledonia Mission (Capitol 3500) 1972
Ain't Got No Home/Get Up Jake (Capitol 3758) 1973

Third Man Theme/W. S. Walcott Medicine Show (Capitol 3828) 1974
Ophelia/Hobo Jungle (Capitol 4230) 1976
Twilight/Acadian Driftwood (Capitol 4316) 1976
Georgia On My Mind/The Night They Drove Old Dixie Down (Capitol 4361) 1976
Out Of The Blue/The Well (Warner Bros. 8592) 1978

Albums

As THE BAND:

Music From Big Pink (Capitol SKAO–2955) 1968
Tears Of Rage; To Kingdom Come; In A Station; Caledonia Mission; The Weight; We Can Talk; Long Black Veil; Chest Fever; Lonesome Suzie; This Wheel's On Fire; I Shall Be Released. (Gatefold sleeve)

The Band (Capitol STAO–132) 1969
The Great Divide; Rag Mama Rag; The Night They Drove Old Dixie Down; When You Awake; Up On Cripple Creek; Whispering Pines; Jemima Surrender; Rockin' Chair; Look Out Cleveland; Jawbone; The Unfaithful Servant; King Harvest (Will Surely Come). (Gatefold sleeve)

Stage Fright (Capitol SW–425) 1970
Strawberry Wine; Sleeping; Time To Kill; Just Another Whistle Stop; All La Glory; The Shape I'm In; The W. S. Walcott Medicine Show; Daniel And The Sacred Harp; Stage Fright; The Rumor. (Single sleeve with Norman Seeff portrait included inside)

Cahoots (Capitol SMAS–651) 1971
Life Is A Carnival; When I Paint My Masterpiece; Last Of The Blacksmiths; Where Do We Go From Here?; 4% Pantomime; Shoot Out In Chinatown; The Moon Struck One; Thinkin' Out Loud; Smoke Signal; Volcano; The River Hymn. (Gatefold sleeve with lyrics inside)

Rock Of Ages (Capitol SABB–11045) 1972
Don't Do It; King Harvest (Will Surely Come); Caledonia Mission; Get Up Jake; The W. S. Walcott Medicine Show; The Genetic Method; Chest Fever; Hang Up My Rock'n'Roll Shoes; Stage Fright; The Night They Drove Old Dixie Down; Across The Great Divide; This Wheel's On Fire; Rag Mama Rag; The Weight; The Shape I'm In; Unfaithful Servant; Life Is A Carnival. (Double album in triple-fold sleeve)

422

Moondog Matinee (Capitol SW–11214) 1973
Ain't Got No Home; Holy Cow; Share Your Love With Me; Mystery Train; Third Man Theme; Promised Land; The Great Pretender; I'm Ready; Saved; A Change Is Gonna Come. (Single sleeve with wraparound poster)

Northern Lights – Southern Cross (Capitol ST–11440) 1975
Forbidden Fruit; Hobo Jungle; Ophelia; Acadian Driftwood; Ring Your Bell; It Makes No Difference; Jupiter Hollow; Rags And Bones. (Single sleeve)

Best Of The Band (Capitol ST–11553) 1976*
Up On Cripple Creek; The Shape I'm In; The Weight; It Makes No Difference; Life Is A Carnival; Twilight; Don't Do It; Tears Of Rage; Stage Fright; Ophelia; The Night They Drove Old Dixie Down. (Single sleeve) *Note that the British release of *Best Of The Band* featured a very different track listing, replacing Tears Of Rage, Don't Do It, and It Makes No Difference with Rag Mama Rag, Time To Kill, Ain't Got No Home, and I Shall Be Released.

Islands (Capitol SO–11602) 1977
Right As Rain; Street Walker; Let The Night Fall; Ain't That A Lot Of Love; Christmas Must Be Tonight; Islands; The Saga Of Pepote Rouge; Georgia On My Mind; Knockin' Lost John; Livin' In A Dream. (Single sleeve)

The Last Waltz (Warner Bros. 3WS–3146) 1978
Theme From The Last Waltz; Up On Cripple Creek; Who Do You Love; Helpless; Stage Fright; Coyote; Dry Your Eyes; It Makes No Difference; Such A Night; The Night They Drove Old Dixie Down; Mystery Train; Mannish Boy; Farther On Up The Road; The Shape I'm In; Down South In New Orleans; Ophelia; Too Ra Loo Ra Loo Ral; Caravan; Life Is A Carnival; Baby, Let Me Follow You Down; I Don't Believe You; Forever Young; Baby Let Me Follow You Down (Reprise); The Last Waltz Suite; The Well; Evangeline; Out Of The Blue; The Weight; The Last Waltz Refrain; Theme From the Last Waltz. (Triple album in single sleeve with booklet enclosed)

Anthology (Capitol SKBO–11856) 1979
The Weight; Chest Fever; I Shall Be Released; Rag Mama Rag; The Night They Drove Old Dixie Down; Up On Cripple Creek; King

Harvest (Will Surely Come); Stage Fright; The Shape I'm In; Daniel And The Sacred Harp; Life Is A Carnival; When I Paint My Masterpiece; This Wheel's On Fire; The Great Pretender; Mystery Train; Ophelia; It Makes No Difference; Acadian Driftwood; Right As Rain; Livin' In A Dream. (Double album in gatefold sleeve with notes by Robert Palmer)

To Kingdom Come (Capitol EN 5010) 1989

Back To Memphis; Tears Of Rage; To Kingdom Come; Long Black Veil; Chest Fever; The Weight; I Shall Be Released; Up On Cripple Creek; Loving You Is Sweeter Than Ever; Rag Mama Rag; The Night They Drove Old Dixie Down; Unfaithful Servant; King Harvest (Will Surely Come); The Shape I'm In; The W. S. Walcott Medicine Show; Daniel And The Sacred Harp; Stage Fright; Don't Do It; Life Is A Carnival; When I Paint My Masterpiece; 4% Pantomime; The River Hymn; Mystery Train; Endless Highway; Get Up Jake; It Makes No Difference; Ophelia; Acadian Driftwood; Christmas Must Be Tonight; The Saga Of Pepote Rouge; Knockin' Lost John. (Triple album in single sleeve with notes by Rob Bowman)

THE BAND with BOB DYLAN

Planet Waves (Asylum 7E-1003) 1074

On A Night Like This; Going, Going, Gone; Tough Mama; Hazel; Something There Is About You; Forever Young; Forever Young; Dirge; You Angel You; You Angel You; Never Say Goodbye; Wedding Song. (Single Sleeve)

Before The Flood (Asylum AB-201) 1975

Most Likely You Go Your Way (And I'll Go Mine); Lay Lady Lay; Rainy Day Women #12 & 35; Knockin' On Heaven's Door; It Ain't Me Babe; Ballad Of A Thin Man; Up On Cripple Creek; I Shall Be Released; Endless Highway; The Night They Drove Old Dixie Down; Stage Fright; Don't Think Twice, It's Alright; Just Like A Woman; It's Alright Ma (I'm Only Bleeding); The Shape I'm In; When You Awake; The Weight; All Along The Watchtower; Highway 61 Revisited; Like A Rolling Stone; Blowin' In The Wind. (Double album in gatefold sleeve)

The Basement Tapes (Columbia 33682) 1975

Odds And Ends; Orange Juice Blues; Million Dollar Bash; Yazoo Street

Scandal; Goin' To Acapulco; Katie's Been Gone; Lo And Behold!; Bessie Smith; Clothes Line Saga; Apple Suckling Tree; Please, Mrs. Henry; Tears Of Rage; Too Much Of Nothing; Yea! Heavy And A Bottle Of Bread; Ain't No More Cane; Crash On The Levee (Down In The Flood); Ruben Remus; Tiny Montgomery; You Ain't Goin' Nowhere; Don't Ya Tell Henry; Nothing Was Delivered; Open The Door, Homer; Long Distance Operator; This Wheel's On Fire. (Double album in gatefold sleeve with notes by Greil Marcus)

RICK DANKO:
Rick Danko (Arista AB-4141) 1977
What A Town; Brainwash; New Mexicoe; Tired Of Waiting; Sip The Wine; Java Blues; Sweet Romance; Small Town Talk; Shake It; Once Upon A Time. (Single sleeve with photo insert)

LEVON HELM:
Levon Helm & The RCO All-Stars (ABC AA-1017) 1977
Washer Woman; The Tie That Binds; You Got Me; Blues So Bad; Sing, Sing, Sing (Let's Make A Better World); Milk Cow Blues; Rain Down Tears; The Mood I Was In; Havana Moon; That's My Home. (Single sleeve with cut-out cover and printed inner sleeve)
Levon Helm (ABC AA-1089) 1978
Ain't No Way To Forget You; Driving At Night; Play Something Sweet; Sweet Johanna; I Came Here To Party; Take Me To The River; Standing On A Mountaintop; Let's Do It In Slow Motion; Audience For My Pain. (Single sleeve)
American Son (MCA 5120) 1980
Watermelon Time In Georgia; Dance Me Down Easy; Violet Eyes; Stay With Me; America's Farm; Hurricane; China Girl; Nashville Wimmin; Blue House Of Broken Hearts; Sweet Peach Georgia Wine. (Single sleeve with inserted lyric sheet)
Levon Helm (Capitol ST-12201) 1982
You Can't Win 'Em All; Lucrecia; Even A Fool Would Let Go; I've Got A Bet With Myself; Money; Get Out Your Big Roll Daddy; Willie And The Hand Jive; The Got Song; Give A Little Bit; God Bless 'Em All. (Single sleeve)

425

The Band: A U.S. Discography

ROBBIE ROBERTSON:

Robbie Robertson (Geffen WX-133) 1987

Fallen Angel; Showdown At Big Sky; Broken Arrow; Sweet Fire Of Love; American Roulette; Somewhere Down The Crazy River; Hell's Half Acre; Sonny Got Caught In The Moonlight; Testimony. (Single sleeve with lyrics on inner sleeve)

Storyville (Geffen GEC 24303) 1991

Night Parade; Hold Back The Dawn; Go Back To Your Woods; Soap Box Preacher; Day Of Reckoning (Burnin' For You); What About Now; Shake This Town; Breakin' The Rules; Resurrection; Sign Of The Rainbow. (Single sleeve with lyrics on inner sleeve)

The following are albums by other artists with major involvement by Band members:

JOHN HAMMOND: *So Many Roads* (Vanguard VSD-79178) 1965
– featuring Robbie Robertson, Levon Helm, and Garth Hudson
JESSE WINCHESTER: *Jesse Winchester* (Ampex A-10104) 1971
– produced by Robbie Robertson, featuring Robbie and Levon
BOBBY CHARLES: *Bobby Charles* (Bearsville BR2104) 1972
– produced by Rick Danko, Bobby Charles, and John Simon
The Muddy Waters Woodstock Album (Chess 60035) 1975
– produced by Levon Helm and Henry Glover, featuring Levon and Garth
HIRTH MARTINEZ: *Hirth From Earth* (Warner Bros. 2867) 1976
– produced by Robbie Robertson, featuring Robbie and Garth
ERIC CLAPTON: *No Reason To Cry* (RSO 1-3004) 1976
– featuring Rick Danko, Richard Manuel, and Robbie Robertson
NEIL DIAMOND: *Beautiful Noise* (Columbia JC33965) 1976
– produced by Robbie Robertson, featuring Robbie and Garth
NEIL DIAMOND: *Love At The Greek* (Columbia KC234404) 1977
– produced by Robbie Robertson
Coal Miner's Daughter: Soundtrack Album (MCA 5107) 1980
– featuring Levon Helm
The Legend of Jesse James (A & M 63718) 1980
– A concept album featuring Levon Helm alongside Johnny Cash, Emmylou Harris, and Charlie Daniels

The Band: A U.S. Discography

Carny: Soundtrack Album (Warner Bros., HS 3455) 1980
– produced by and featuring Robbie Robertson
The King of Comedy: Soundtrack Album (Warner Bros., 92-3765-1) 1983
– produced by and featuring Robbie Robertson
The Color of Money: Soundtrack Album (MCA 6189) 1988
– produced by and featuring Robbie Robertson

The Very Best Of The Band
(A Very Personal Selection)

1 Acadian Driftwood *Northern Lights – Southern Cross*
2 Whispering Pines *The Band*
3 King Harvest (Will Surely Come) *The Band*
4 The Rumor *Stage Fright*
5 Rockin' Chair *The Band*
6 Tears Of Rage *Music From Big Pink*
7 Share Your Love With Me *Moondog Matinee*
8 Don't Do It *Rock Of Ages*
9 In A Station *Music From Big Pink*
10 The Night They Drove Old Dixie Down *The Band*
11 Unfaithful Servant *Rock Of Ages*
12 We Can Talk *Music From Big Pink*
13 Back To Memphis *To Kingdom Come*
14 Jupiter Hollow *Northern Lights – Southern Cross*
15 Rag Mama Rag *The Band*
16 The Genetic Method *Rock Of Ages*
17 Sleeping *Stage Fright*
18 The Weight *The Last Waltz*
19 Life Is A Carnival *Cahoots*
20 Ain't Got No Home *Moondog Matinee*

Index